I0632145

EVICTED FROM ETERNITY

EVICTED FROM ETERNITY

The Restructuring of Modern Rome

MICHAEL HERZFELD

THE UNIVERSITY OF CHICAGO PRESS
CHICAGO AND LONDON

MICHAEL HERZFELD is professor of anthropology at Harvard University. He is the author of ten books, including *Cultural Intimacy*, and with the University of Chicago Press, *Portrait of a Greek Imagination* and *The Body Impolitic*.

The University of Chicago Press, Chicago 60637
The University of Chicago Press, Ltd., London
© 2009 by The University of Chicago
All rights reserved. Published 2009
Printed in the United States of America

18 17 16 15 14 13 12 11 10   2 3 4 5

ISBN-13: 978-0-226-32911-6 (cloth)
ISBN-13: 978-0-226-32912-3 (paper)
ISBN-10: 0-226-32911-9   (cloth)
ISBN-10: 0-226-32912-7   (paper)

Library of Congress Cataloging-in-Publication Data
Herzfeld, M. (Michael).
        Evicted from eternity : the restructuring of modern Rome / Michael Herzfeld.
              p. cm.
        Includes bibliographical references and index.
        ISBN-13: 978-0-226-32911-6 (cloth : alk. paper)
        ISBN-13: 978-0-226-32912-3 (pbk. : alk. paper)
        ISBN-10: 0-226-32911-9 (cloth : alk. paper)
        ISBN-10: 0-226-32912-7 (pbk. : alk. paper)
      1. Gentrification—Italy—Rome.   2. Urban renewal—Italy—Rome.   Title.
      HT178.182R664 2009
      307.1'4160945632—dc22   2008024435

♾ The paper used in this publication meets the minimum requirements of the
American National Standard for Information Sciences—Permanence of Paper for
Printed Library Materials, ANSI Z39.48-1992.

FOR STANLEY J. TAMBIAH

who insisted I did this first,

with gratitude and affection

CONTENTS

This book is the labor of a love deepened by the realization that Rome, despite its magnificence, is also splendidly, sometimes tragically, a place steeped in all the weaknesses of the human condition. My parents first took me there when I was a schoolboy and marked my life with a passion for this extraordinary place that has only grown with the years. I have tried to convey this powerful affect, along with the Romans' salty humor and gorgeous architectural frenzies, their harsh social realities and their warm gregariousness, the appealing fragility of their lives and the towering strength and self-confidence with which they meet its disappointments as well as its excitements. Monti, the sector of Rome about which I write in these pages, welcomed me to a world strongly marked by these human dimensions. No anthropologist, no scholar—indeed, no sentient human being—could ask for more of any place.

In the work that is laid out here, many people played their parts. Lists are invidious and someone is sure to be omitted, simply because there were so many who enthusiastically supported my project; and because so many of the conversations I had with them continue to this day, sometimes briefly interrupted, but always insistently returning to the themes of a shared passion. A few people nonetheless made especially sustained efforts, and I want to record my appreciation of their counsel, insights, and support: Loredana Acca, Paolo Berdini, Carlo Cellamare, Adriana Goni, Luigi Lombardi Satriani, Berardino Palumbo, Andreina Ricci, Paolo Sciarroni, Riccardo Troisi, and the entire Valeri family (Vincenzo, Francesco, Andrea, and Paola). Certain colleagues also offered helpful advice on specific technical questions; these include the economist Ricardo Hausmann and the linguist Paolo Di Giovine. Karen Hendrickson-Santospago converted my confusing instructions into a splendidly legible map. Those generous souls who read the manuscript and offered their extremely perceptive comments on it—Augusto Ferraiuolo, Cornelia (Nea) Mayer Herzfeld, Douglas Holmes, Guy Lanoue, Lilith Abdelwahab Mahmud, Maria Minicuci, Borden Painter, Miriam Shakow, and Claudio Sopranzetti—deserve special gratitude. Carlo Cellamare and Maria Minicuci also arranged for me to hold visiting appointments in their respective parts of the University of Rome–I ("La Sapienza") and engaged me in larger and extraordinarily productive discussions throughout these years of research, while Nea Herzfeld, constant companion in so many places, brought insight and a generously critical eye to this work as it progressed, besides cementing many of our shared friendships with the people of Monti and of Rome in general. At the University of Chicago Press, I am deeply indebted to my old friend T. David Brent, his extraordinarily efficient assistant Laura J. Avey, and my meticulous, understanding, and stylistically sensitive manuscript editor Mary Gehl. To the many other friends whose voices are heard with varying degrees of explicitness in these pages, or who proffered useful advice along the way, my debt is as deeply felt and appreciated as it is wide-ranging.

While the usual provisos about personal responsibility apply, I do genuinely want to thank the foundations that helped me bring this work through the main research phase. These are the National Endowment for the Humanities and the John Simon Guggenheim Memorial Foundation, which sequentially supported my sabbatical year research in 1999–2000. Harvard University's Weatherhead Center for International Affairs generously supported a further leave in 2007 and thereby facilitated much of the writing for this project. My sojourns at the University of Melbourne also provided me with an invaluable retreat.

All unattributed quotations are my translations of remarks made by informants; I have, except in the case of unavoidable exceptions (such as public figures or individuals whose role received significant attention), avoided using their own personal names. Many of them spoke in a mixture of "standard language" and "dialect," and, while these mixed utterances have sometimes occasioned surprise on the part of educated local readers, they do represent habits of speech (notably code-switching) that are themselves useful evidence of subtly but ceaselessly shifting identity politics in social interactions.

When I began to toy with the idea of doing field research in Thailand, my departmental colleague Stanley J. Tambiah, a leading light in Thai studies, at first demurred and then showed some apparent discomfort with the idea—until he was satisfied that I would first pursue my interests in the comparison of Greek and Italian nationalisms. When I told him that I intended to go to Rome before I attempted anything substantive in Thailand and asked him for a letter of support for one of my fellowship applications, he immediately responded with all the extraordinary generosity and care for my scholarly life that had, it became entirely clear, animated his original concern and hesitation. Tambi, whose personal modesty and kindness are as legendary as his intellectual inspiration, has, quite simply, made all the difference. He also shares my enthusiasm for Rome as a city. This book is, in a very real sense, a response to the combination of intellectual stimulation and radical kindness that he has brought to all our encounters, and I dedicate it to him with the deepest and most grateful affection.

Cambridge, Mass.
May 2008

Encountering the Eternal City

The three proud, angry women made their stately way down from the lofty offices of the Rome municipal administration overlooking a square designed by Michelangelo atop the remnants of the ancient Capitol. They crossed the triumphal road that Mussolini had cut through the ancient forums and headed determinedly toward their homes somewhere behind the emperor Trajan's markets—today upheld by the proponents of a remorseless neoliberalism as a precursor of malls. Their fury at the failure of local politicians to protect them from eviction from their homes by those same neoliberal forces seeped into their dignified, measured steps and their fluid gestures of deep affront. The bureaucrats could play a delaying game, but in the Eternal City the local people still determined the *tempi*, the rhythms, of social engagement.[1] Their deliberate pace, in which a knowledgeable observer could easily recognize the imperturbable self-assurance of Roman artisans and shopkeepers, promised long months of caustic confrontation still to come.

I write these lines, conscious of my own anger at the failure of imagination that today makes the ancient capital of empire and church the scene of a potentially explosive housing crisis—one of the worst in Italy's history, but a reflection of processes occurring in many parts of the globe today under the pressures of the new international economy. And I look again at what I have written. Out of context, it probably makes little sense. My words describe the debris of ruined lives—the tip of a rubbish heap, like the ancient landfill of broken pots that became the modern working-class quarter of nearby Testaccio. Fragments of the past are everywhere. An elderly Jewish vendor who survived the Nazi dragnet declaimed in staccato bursts that he had counted every one of these stones, his upthrust lower lip and sharp bristly chin pointing to the very heavens in outraged protest. Traces of multiple pasts are piled up in artful disorder, scattered and shattered among the dying homes. They are a lunatic archaeology's scrambled detritus, now promiscuously straddling a prose that can only hope to do justice to the pained beauty of this place through the recitation of its own failures, its own falterings before the layered magnitude of both disaster and triumph.

We are in the heart of old Rome, in Monti, *er primo rione de Roma*—the first district (*rione*) of Rome, whether historically or in importance is never clear, and is there really a difference? This is the ancient Subura, red-light district then and now, a marginal place in a capital that for many has itself been marginal to its encompassing nation, a city of bureaucrats and workers despised by other Italians for their allegedly uncultured ways. Monti is luscious with the magnificently stained grandeur of baroque architecture, interspersed with reminders of high antiquity as well as the intrusive, heavy-handed trumpetings of nineteenth-century and fascist grandiloquence. It offered a sensuously attractive context in which to conduct fieldwork; but that same beauty had brought the blight of gentrification. Many residents were welcomingly eager to share their thoughts and knowledge.

Monti, like the whole city, was experiencing a focalization of global connections that would have seemed familiar to its ancient forebears. A German physics student stood in the quiet street where I lived recording a solar eclipse; a Peruvian couple living nearby stopped to watch, and they were joined by two Asian women as well as three local artisans, including a printer and an ironworker (who had set up his own makeshift equipment for the same purpose). Such scenes were not unusual. At the end of the street, the owners of a Chinese restaurant—well respected and long established in the neighborhood—exchanged pleasantries with customers in the distinctive cadences of the city. Other immigrants were less popular, and there were some nasty expressions of racism. But those who had mastered the local courtesies won more approval than wealthy Italians who had moved in without showing any interest in their neighbors' lives.

When I first started exploring Monti, a friend who accompanied me on one of my forays, himself a university professor, courteously greeted a familiar-seeming gentleman who turned out to be a former leader of the Italian Communist Party. This man, Giorgio Napolitano, had become the president of the Republic by the time I set to writing this book some years later. Residents would point with pride to the imposing building where he lived; a butcher, also a Communist, was especially proud of supplying such distinguished figures with prepared meats. Romano Prodi, then president of the European Union and twice prime minister of Italy, had lived in temporary quarters in a *Residence* almost directly opposite our house. An ironworker had been evicted from his home in the building where Prodi now resided. Monti, said he, is no longer for the poor! Even those not directly affected by the arrival of famous neighbors display an ambiguous mixture of pride and exasperation. One resident lamented that half the district had been taken over by rank outsiders—actors, politicians, prostitutes! Given Monti's ancient notoriety, his observation perhaps encapsulated a touch of perverse pride.

The process he described is that of gentrification—the upgrading of a run-down residential district. Those who have the wealth to purchase elegance pursue the new fashion for old houses, with disastrous consequences for lower-income inhabitants. Monti, at the core of Rome's historic center, is one of the last major complexes of centuries-old residential buildings to yield to the heritage industry, despite the presence of signature monuments of Western civilization—the Colosseum, the imperial Forums, the churches of San Pietro in Vincoli and Santa Maria Maggiore, and other architectural gems representing every phase of Roman history from the early Republic to the Fascist era. This historic center has become a UNESCO world heritage site. Cosmopolitan fashion now invests owning and inhabiting a piece of an allegedly universal history of civilization with irresistible appeal; the rhythms of daily sociability surrender to the commercialization of eternity. The newcomers may not be as uninterested in the district as these poorer residents imagine, and indeed have constructed their own social lives both within and outside its confines. Deepening class divisions have nevertheless created an unfortunate collective impression of disengagement and hauteur.

Those locals whose lives are now being ravaged by an epidemic of evictions are especially aware of the irony whereby those who displace them can proclaim themselves the guardians of a national heritage. The key term here is *patrimonio*—usually translated into English as "heritage" or "inheritance" and the central theme of official discourse of historic conservation. Like the English term "heritage," but with an added patrilineal emphasis,[2] *patrimonio* evokes notions of a material inheritance given in trust for future generations. Rome is not only a city rich in historical monuments belonging to Europe's civilizational past but is also the capital of a nation-state that has yet to complete the work of consolidating a national identity—a fact that throws into high relief the intense contrast between those who speak of a national heritage and those who instead emphasize their birthrights as Romans and indeed as residents of a particular neighborhood.[3]

Another term, *civiltà*, conveys the lofty evolutionism usually associated with "civilization" in English and socially realized as urbanity. It is impressively cognate with "civility," which certainly forms an important

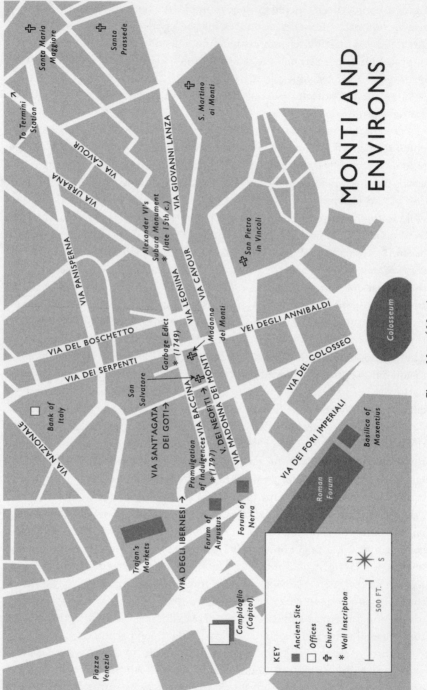

Fig. 1. Map of Monti

component inasmuch as good manners make for easy social relations. But it only represents the *civic* virtues insofar as these also contribute to the maintenance of social calm and order. People sometimes become very uncivil when they think that their civic rights and responsibilities are being usurped.

The idea of *civiltà* is, for many Italians, part of their *patrimonio* as Europeans, as Italians, and as inhabitants of a particular city. Those who purchase a share in the historic center of a city such as Rome are claiming possession of a majestic civilizational status, one they contrast with the rough manners of the Roman working classes. For their part, the artisans, laborers, and small merchants who constitute the majority of the older population reject that claim to superior status and knowledge.

The conflicts that emerge over eviction are primarily over living spaces and economic rights and goals. But they are also, and in parallel fashion, about cultural capital. The new residents are not simply enjoying the benefits of their greater economic power; they are also redefining the significance of the capital, Italian identity, and the future of a past claimed by many groups of people. The global implications of gentrification and the class conflicts that they generate, implications that are certainly replicated in widely differing sites, are filtered through local perceptions and practices in each.[4]

Rome offers a peculiarly effective magnifying lens for examining these issues, because the global significance of its history comes perpetually into conflict with the parochial loyalties of its residents, and because the current process of gentrification has occurred at a time when the city's housing crisis has become a matter for international concern. Rome was a center of globalization long before the term was ever coined. It is the administrative and spiritual center of the Catholic Church, which, having willingly accepted the mantle of the long-defunct secular empire, has perhaps been the longest-lived and most geographically ramified and then locally refracted global project in human history.[5] This study can serve as a counterweight to both the generalizations of the globalization literature and the exclusivist rantings of Fascism disguised as a defense of local cultural rights. I hope to show that neither stereotype adequately describes or explains the sometimes excruciating complexities of life in one of the most tragically beautiful products of human artifice anywhere in the world—a city dubbed "eternal" where not only the buildings but the very people themselves are being "restructured."

CHAPTER ONE

Sin and the City

Nothing here is perfect; everything, even failure, is magnificent; and prose must reflect the gnawing putrescence that strangely enhances the city's aging beauty, veining its robust surfaces with splinters and fractures that intimate the fragility and contingency of its social life. Rome, after all, is the capital city of a country that has fought a long and complicated battle with a corruption of which its citizens are not totally, sometimes not even at all, ashamed. Rome is also the capital of a religion that allows its devotees to appeal to the imperfection of original sin not only as an explanation of their venality but also as a pretext for sustaining it—where even popes and cardinals could order musically gorgeous masses, sung by brilliantly robed choirs, to save their souls from the sordid acts that scattered their seed among the city's underworld.

An entire government office works tirelessly to recapture a small fraction of unpaid fines for building violations by offering absolution on a papal model of confession and repentance; perhaps this is why, as one architect remarked as we scanned the whole city from a high rooftop, in the end most of Rome's gloriously riotous accumulation consists of violations of legal building codes. There is a saying in Rome—"What the barbarians did not do, the Barberini did" (Quello che non fecero i barbari fecero i Barberini)—that recalls Pope Urban VIII's and his nephews' despoiling of the Colosseum for the ornamentation of their family palace in 1623.[1] A city policeman invoked this historical allusion to criticize Mayor Francesco Rutelli's expropriation of a public garden and palazzo and his destruction of hundred-year-old pine trees in order to construct a reinforced concrete Jubilee information booth with money provided by the Volkswagen corporation. Perhaps, too, he intended a sly allusion to the once strongly anticlerical Rutelli's sudden embrace of the Vatican and his cooperation with the papal authorities in the construction of huge new works ostensibly meant to facilitate the celebration of the Jubilee of 2000.[2] His comment exemplifies the Romans' cynical familiarity with the events and personalities of the past and their recognition of its echoes in the present.

Genealogies of Imperfection

Sin, no less than virtue, has its genealogy—a genealogy that links ordinary men and women with popes and politicians, priests and police officers. And it is a genealogy embedded in the torrent of speech through whose self-consciously working-class, dialect-inflected cadences so many Romans celebrate their ironic skepticism about everything represented by the nation-state of which their city is the grudging capital, much as they lampooned the papacy and its temporal powers through the device of the "talking statue," Pasquino, during those earlier times.[3] It is certainly relevant to my story that in recent years Pasquino has again begun making acidulous fun of the municipal and national authorities, most often in a saucy rendition of Roman dialect that recalls his baroque versifications. And it was Pasquino who coined the famous phrase about the Barberini that my police acquaintance found so apposite to current affairs.

Romans must come to terms with a corruption so pervasive that perhaps it could only have emerged in an ancient seat of religion and power.[4] The Spanish libertine pope Alexander VI (1492–1503) even erected a monument marking the place under its ancient name of *Subura;* the humorless bureaucrats of the municipality have carefully juxtaposed a street sign reading *Piazza della Suburra* to show that they, at least, can spell their Latin (and thus have it wrong!), and do not use dialect (which uses the same spelling as the Latin!)—although in another neighborhood some local authority insisted on dialect signage as well. But what these competing monumentalizations conceal is that Subura was the red-light district of ancient Rome, and that it still houses a brothel population, formerly the haunt of military conscripts and even of priests—who, after all, are people of flesh themselves, as one local indulgently remarked, and are thus as corruptible as any.[5]

These are resilient realities. In 1948, the state tried to close down the bordellos, but some were subdivided into tiny units that could be rented to the prostitutes on an individual basis, allowing them to return to the secretive work and ways of their trade.[6] When the police recently charged two madams—one aged 79, the other 83—with sexual exploitation, locals were bemused; these revelations hardly came as a surprise.[7] Today, however, some right-wing localists profess to hate the fact that the familiar old madams and whores of the "houses of convenience" are increasingly displaced by women from Eastern Europe. Those women of earlier times were "our stuff," said one.

Even the more permanent, architectural features of the district bear witness to intimate secrets.[8] Alexander VI's monumental marker of the *Subura* connects a tawdry antiquity (Augustus built a huge wall, still extant, to shield the forum from the district's notorious fires, dirt, and criminals) to more recent imperfections (echoed yet again in the new spray-paint graffiti over the lower half of this monument) in the heart of grandeur and faith. Another good example of spray-paint wisdom, this one in the main square, told the Lazio soccer team to "eat its liver out" with a bitter blend of regret and jealousy when the Roma team triumphed. Graffiti are indeed everywhere, along with neglected garbage dumps; and, while this is not unusual throughout Italy, their presence in Rome often asserts the salty intimacy and lacerating self-criticism associated with the dialect. "*Romani monnazzari,*" (Romans [are] garbage-people) declared one spray-painted dialect inscription, perhaps objecting to the dumping of waste outside the author's house (as a friend of mine speculated), but in a language that made it clear that this generic complaint was for domestic consumption only—a language too coarse, as some Romans insist, for more public use. But Monti has also tried to glorify the same language by linking it to a celebrated folk tradition that is itself a remarkably durable expression of cultural intimacy; a monument to the writer Ettore Petrolini, author of a comedy about a local tough (*Gigi er Bullo*), praises him for reviving the language that "gave Pasquino to the Roman people."

This city of saucy impertinence and robust scandal is a national capital, albeit an eccentric one; a study of Roman life should have something to say about the nature of the state and the relationship between the capital and the nation of which it is the symbolic center. Ethnography offers especially persuasive answers, since it provides grounded access to the lives of the citizenry, including those of bureaucrats, intellectuals, and politicians. Rome's peculiar marginality to its own nation-state—like Monti's notoriety within the city—offers a rich opportunity to delve into the dimly illuminated alleys of cultural debate and to peer behind the public stage of monumentality.

Monti: Paradoxes of Poverty

The tales of madams and prostitutes, of houses built illegally and corruption in high places, and of a scabrous language considered to be especially fit for comedy and satire illustrate the heart of the seeming paradox that is Rome:

the religion that has made its headquarters in this city defines its flock as unavoidably mired in sinful weaknesses and, by accommodating to those weaknesses and organizing various forms of penance through which the penitent can then seek redemption, both exercises enormous power over the population and provides a model of exploitable compromise that the various secular authorities have often been eager to follow—not least in their organization of urban space.[9]

Monti, in particular, is quite literally a sunken district—its streets lying several feet below the nineteenth-century thoroughfare of Via Cavour, its houses reproducing—so it is said—the forms of ancient dwellings or shadowing the final stages of all the roads that have forever led to this city of Rome.[10] Monti is "below the city" (sub urbe), as the name Subura is sometimes taken to imply[11]—today, physically below the busy arteries attesting to Rome's sudden emergence as a busy capital city after 1870, in a stark display of physical as well as moral stratigraphy that has struck professional urbanists and novelists alike. By mid-morning, there is always an air of expectancy in the streets. Even on busy Via Cavour, the nineteenth-century artery that slices through the old quarter, the tingling smell of celery-flavored broth being prepared in one of the many restaurants can still overcome the aggressive fumes emanating from the cars screeching their way down to the Via dei Fori Imperiali. Everywhere there are deep shadows and steep side streets. The noise of traffic racing down Via Cavour and the roar of protest songs and slogans from the huge demonstrations that in the afternoons often snake their way down that broad thoroughfare to the ancient forums and Piazza Venezia seem to work their way in from a chaotic, burning, upper world, seeping into the secretive quiet of Monti's domestic spaces and intimate squares. The traffic that tries to force its way down Via del Boschetto—named for a "little forest" long since displaced by the old palazzi that line the cobblestoned roadway—is a brash intrusion. And when the glowing light of the sunset echoes in the ochers and russets of the facades, their lower reaches are already quite dark, only intermittently illuminated by the gentle light from the studiedly antiquarian electric streetlamps and, on special occasions, from the cupped candles of pilgrims visiting the sacred images that punctuate and accentuate the domestic intimacy of this shy, deep place. Light glows from windows, revealing wooden ceiling beams; briefly glimpsed through street-level doorways, winding, rickety stairs give access to the upper floors.

The depth is historical. It displays, as in a stratified archaeological site, the wild historical and aesthetic profligacy with which Rome has been blessed and cursed. The architect Riccardo d'Aquino invokes a Braudelian sense of the *longue durée* to suggest that the sense of belonging to a particular place, to this remarkable city, is a product of indirect emotional attachments generated by a specific pattern of relationships between elements of the built environment and the local culture.[12] There is a continuous interplay among institutions and individuals, producing continuities as well as ruptures and especially focusing on the play of eternity and evanescence evoked by the pervasive presence of ruins—of fragments of a past made present by their constant incorporation into the living city. The dramatic artificial lighting that is one of the glories of Rome today has precedents in the romantic prints of Piranesi and others, taking advantage of the way light can reveal unsuspected structural features exposed in a suspended state of collapse.[13] Rome exists in a state of perpetual tension between monumentality and the sprawling disarray of untended ruins.

That tension reflects the experienced realities of social life as well, the practical challenge of living an ordinary life in a city that is truly the cynosure of the Western world. Time, the teachings of the church remind us, is the source of the imperfections in all human existence; that life is necessarily, and nowhere more than in Rome, a shifting compromise between the lofty ideals enshrined in monumental architecture and scriptural writ on the one hand and the makeshift adjustments necessitated by social life on the other. What gets preserved may not always follow the dictates of the state. Residents of Monti, despite their leftist sympathies, refused to follow the general destruction of Fascist insignia when their own war memorial was in question, because this would have meant desecrating their own dead— victims of Fascist geopolitics, to be sure, but above all else kinsmen and neighbors in a tightly knit community.

A persistently disobedient streak in the self-representation of Romans allows them to experience continuities in the numerous violations of laws that might otherwise fix the city's architectural fabric in a temporal vacuum. The political scientist Filippo Sabetti has addressed the question of why Italy, long the site of apparently dysfunctional administrations at virtually every level, has nevertheless achieved an enviable reputation in many fields of human endeavor, including the economic.[14] He especially explores a set of laws relating to the planning of Rome, in which, like other scholars, he identifies a persistent pattern of compromise between theoretical legality and practical necessity, built, as often as not, into the legal provisions themselves.[15] Rome is the capital of this paradoxical country; it is also one of those places where the sometimes outrageous deployment of the resulting ambiguities depends on a remarkable mixture of ironic humor, inventive casuistry, and agile adaptation.

That cheeky vitality, as much as the solidity of the Colosseum or of St. Peter's, is the substance of Rome's capacity to remain recognizable through the centuries. It offers an alternative eternity to those of the grand sweep of ancient history or the eschatology of a power-saturated church—or, rather, it offers a set of eternities, fragmentary snatches of social experience, of a way of life embedded, reworked, and recaptured in the interstices of the city's most imposing structures. True, the ruins have been idealized, by locals as much as by the tourist hordes; but the fast-talking modern centurion impersonators who demand fees for being photographed at the Colosseum, and the impudent spray-paint graffiti announcing that "Rome is pagan," are no less integral to the invocation of history than the most solemnly restored and framed of the ancient temples and baroque churches. The continuing battle against a state whose representatives are themselves implicated in a wide range of scams and schemes is a far richer source of temporal profundity than are the pronouncements of formal historiography.

The paradox of a great city glorying in the mire of its corruption—a metonym of that larger paradox of the perverse Italian nation-state—is etched in brilliant, deep lines filled with the grime of a hard life. Romans, with a few exceptions (such as the bourgeois residents of Parioli), like to think of themselves as working-class. Their often deep dislike of the Vatican, intensified rather than muted by a religiosity and a respect for the sacred that they have made very much their own, springs in part from a collective social memory of oppression. It permeates the smallest details. Not least among these is the distinctive Roman diet; a butcher pointed out (and this was a claim I heard several times) that Roman specialties of offal—the famous *pajata* (stewed intestines), *coda vaccinara* (oxtail), *trippa* (tripe), and *coratella* (chopped heart and innards)—reflected the fact that the princes of the church took all the best pieces for themselves. Little regular meat remained for the masses, and the butcher claimed that the unusually thin slices that characterize his craft reflect that paucity.

But note how Romans here snatch self-respect from humiliation: the slices are thin, yes—but the butcher describes them as delicate and fine, reflecting a culture that concedes nothing to deprivation. A Roman expression decrying stinginess and greed—"We don't eat so that we don't have to shit" (*Nun magnamo per nun cagá*[16])—also reflects the conviction that the Vatican deprived the people of their daily bread to build its wealth. I heard this proverb in the context of a complaint that the Vatican inherits the homes of those heirless but wealthy unfortunates in whom the terror of eternal damnation can be made to induce paroxysms of piety in anticipation of their departure from this earthly coil.

It is not, after all, as though Romans are indifferent to the quality or quantity of what they eat; they are not ascetics by cultural choice. To the contrary, food is one of those areas in which Romans revel in their distinctiveness—a space of cultural dialect, no less the object of derision by outsiders than their rough speech. A salad of young chicory shoots in an anchovy-flavored vinaigrette (*puntarelle*)—like the dishes of offal, a poor people's food—is virtually unknown fifty miles from the capital. And food is the anchor of memory; a man facing eviction from the house in which he was born recalled, in a moment of despair, "chicken with peppers and the strange smell of exquisite things"—whereas today, he said, they simply eat a sandwich, a common, ready-made convenience such as one would find anywhere.

The local diet is austere in terms of prestige, and reflects a history of poverty, but it also serves as a proud marker of Roman distinctiveness. Romans insist that its defining richness is not some elaborate set of sauces but the agile, split-second timing of its production; it is, in other words, a living tribute to manual dexterity and quick wits rather than to monumental recipes moldering in leather-bound tomes. It is very much a part of social interaction, which is why festive meals are often recalled; and the precise tempi of its production insinuate a refined artisanal sensibility that is, again, ingrained in bodies and memories and reproduced in a delicate appreciation that the more luxurious cuisines of other regions might drown in rich and creamy sauces.

Many Roman dishes also recall the cultural significance of the Jewish community, itself a monument to past poverty and deprivation and today credited with having conserved ancient recipes that would otherwise have been lost centuries ago. Other dishes, in an unholy but tasty alliance with these culinary emblems of the Ghetto, reflect the products of the pig farmers in the Amatrice hinterland. Both these genealogies are, let us again recall, genealogies of poverty and deprivation. Both have proved extraordinarily resilient. Their intermingling represents the habit of accommodation that Romans stereotypically, and repeatedly, attribute to centuries of evading the cruelties of papal power. There is still a widespread feeling that the Vatican's presence is oppressive, so that it is necessary to hold back from criticism or resistance—"because, if you don't, you can't live."

Despite its history of local poverty, Rome is still, whether its citizens like it or not (and many do not), the national capital. What happens in its intimate side streets reflects and refracts decisions made in its grand administrative palaces and in the halls of international conference centers, not only as part

of the continuing attempt to harmonize local life with national and transnational bureaucratic institutions, but also because, at the end of the day,
many of these influential bureaucrats are either Roman themselves or have
been transplanted to the city and must live with the city's realities.

Sociable Spaces

Much of Rome's public space was built for theatricality and still serves to
frame the national leaders' histrionic style; a friend remarked on what a
theater the city was when we were enjoying the New Year's Eve celebration,
as the late maestro Giuseppe Sinopoli was conducting a full orchestra in
the open near the Quirinale, the presidential palace, and massed crowds
were thronging the steps and byways. Its side streets and smaller squares,
too, are the places of *intermezzi*, full of pulsing intrigue and the bitterness of
stagnating failure. Rome contains and displays the passions that animate the
larger world that it both leads and follows. Like the richest of operatic stages,
it offers a startling panorama of human complexity and of the intimations
of an eternity that forever eludes the grasp, by turns both amiable and
avaricious, of a citizenry schooled in the arts of both patient resignation and
robust cunning.

    Not all the spaces of sociability are equally public. Men (and sometimes
women) visit bars for quick slurps of espresso, enjoying a moment of companionship that is as brief and as intense as the coffee before returning to
shop, taxi, or daily chores, especially during the working day. More serious social encounters take place at lunchtime; in the more relaxed evening
dining hours, friends will sometimes send over a bottle of wine, but each
table is an island of privacy. Larger gatherings in restaurants, usually in
the evenings, signal the regular conviviality of a group of men and women
belonging to a rotating credit association. At the weekend, some families
gather to enjoy the food at a favorite restaurant—usually the same one week
after week, until perhaps some minor disagreement sours the relationship
and the clients' opinion of the cuisine. Restaurateurs greet regular customers
with demonstrative gestures of affection, occasionally taking them aside to
whisper some ribald joke or impart secret news; and the bill will always
be reduced from official prices. But many men as well as women are proud
cooks; close friends dine in each other's houses, especially as the tourist
trade increasingly alienates locals from once-favorite restaurants.

    Tourism certainly has an impact on the forms of social engagement,
although it is also a convenient scapegoat, or metonym, for the effects of

encompassing economic realignments. Romans are heirs to a view of public space as an extension of their homes.[17] Even though they no longer engage in the dramatic brawls that were a feature especially of Monti's streets until the interwar years, and no longer share their food and banter of a warm evening sitting in full view of the street, they still often stop to greet acquaintances.

They also share semi-public spaces for the numerous meetings in which they engage. The Monti Social Network, the latest and most inclusive of the various local associations, is often convened in the soothing but spacious interior of a local bookstore; one of its meetings adjourned, on a hot evening, to the steps of a side street where the looming presence of a magnificent palazzo from which ten families were being evicted gave urgency to the agenda item about the rapid depopulation of the district.

Meeting the People

Other meetings have a provisional air. One left-wing counselor sought to boost his popularity by organizing a street meeting to discuss traffic flow issues. Informally attired, lounging on the seat of a motorbike, and with a deep, resonant, dialect-inflected voice that carried far down the narrow, cobblestoned street, he handed out copies of a relevant edict (*ordinanza*) and chatted easily with local shopkeepers and residents.

At the beginning of the meeting an elderly resident had wanted him to talk about the district market and its failure to generate any business. The politician would have none of this; he had not come to discuss the market, said he, and the market was not generating any business—only three merchants had responded to the city government's initiative with bids. "Now I think they should hold a fourth competition. Well then! But—no one participates. No one participates. On the other hand, it's even understandable that no one participates, because in reality"—and here he made an open-and-closing gesture with the fingers of his left hand and then an up-and-down gesture with the fingers closed together, to show that there was no money to be made in the district market. In any case, he added rather dismissively, the old man was probably seeing things "with the mindset of thirty years ago." Then, waving the index finger of his left hand in the vague direction of the surrounding buildings, he declared, "Today the type of population that lives hereabouts has changed."

The mostly younger women and men gathered around him seemed disposed to agree. The old man again insisted; the politician, visibly irritated, began to respond more brusquely, reiterating that the city authorities had invited bids for stalls on three occasions, all to no avail.

When the old man persisted yet again, the councilor's speech—after an ironic "have patience!"—became slightly agitated. Turning to his sympathetic younger hearers with a pained grin that invited complicity, he pointed out that the failure of the local market "is not my fault, sure, but it's not my job either, right?"

His audience, although not directly interested in the old man's plaint, had still seemed willing to contemplate alternative strategies for utilizing the market space and thus also for regenerating local business—concerns that also animated their interest in dealing with traffic flow, to which they were then happy to return, allowing the politician to expatiate on all the hard work he had done to improve their lives.

The larger economic and demographic processes at work, however, were hurting some residents more directly, over their right to remain in their homes. Here, the frequent public meetings would ultimately prove to be of little avail. A protest meeting on evictions was held in the main square of the district, the Piazzetta (little square, actually the main social gathering place of the *rione*), with a table laid out for people to register their concerns. More formal meetings could be conducted in the halls of a university facility located conveniently next to the parish church, especially when action involving more than one district was involved. But the plague of evictions would not be stayed by mere talk.

A few newcomers and some of the more educated residents of long standing also took part in various public gatherings, both within the district and elsewhere. Political party offices were one important type of venue. Local intellectuals could visit the offices of a free-thinkers' association named for Giordano Bruno, the four hundredth anniversary of whose death was celebrated before his statue on the other side of the historic center, in the Campo de' Fiori, where he was burned at the stake as a heretic; here activists had set up a "pope-free zone"; and here we encountered most of our left-wing friends from Monti, some fresh from a party political meeting in the nearby offices of the *Democratici di Sinistra* (Left Democrats) just off the square. Public protests against the government were also common, although not usually organized only at the district level. We would hear them coming down Via Cavour long before they were visible, with their band music, flags (mostly with the red of the various Communist groups), and sporadic chants and songs, as they pulsed down the street, their leaders sometimes greeting acquaintances who had turned out to wave them by.

Meetings and demonstrations thus span a range of spaces and degrees of formality. The most important moments of communication in all these occasions are often transient and evanescent, conveyed in a sudden gesture or a hint in the voice. Even in some of the more formal meetings, I often thought that the real decisions were taken in those quick exchanges after the formal business was completed. The thicker the dialect, it seemed, the more significant the information conveyed. Formality was not the Romans' preferred order of interaction, although they often mastered its rules and parodied its procedures. For them a quick exchange over coffee in a bar, or while strolling with their children across the Piazzetta with its sixteenth-century marble fountain and its busy newsstand, offered more reliable insights.

The Village in the City

This reflects the frequently repeated perception that Monti was a village (*paese*)—an intimate term of social inclusion that also has implications of territoriality and rusticity.[18] In the way that nostalgia often seems to contradict itself, residents would often remark both that the district retained this village-like character in that one met one's friends in the street all the time, and that it had ceased to do so. Those who emphasized change recalled that even the poorest resident had formerly been able to point to a whole street full of uncles, aunts, and cousins, and that people would swap food items from their market shopping to increase the variety of their frugal fare and where they would greet each other and then burst into cheerful song.

Until the 1960s and the beginning of the present inflation of the real estate market, many Monti artisans lived on the edge of penury. But a warm sociability, they now assert, alleviated this harsh reality; families would gather at small *trattorie*, or wine-and-oil shops—several houses still sport lintel inscriptions advertising *vini* and *olio* as well as the presence of a *forno* (bakery)—and share out the food (especially bread and cheese) that some of the men, known in this role as *fagottari*, would bring wrapped up in a kerchief (*fagotto*) that was folded in a distinctive and immediately recognizable manner. Such establishments, bars, and occasional shops would serve as the gathering places for rotating-credit associations; indeed, a few still do. But the sociality of yesteryear cannot survive in a world in which the drinking taverns have either disappeared or become modishly expensive bars and pubs.

Today, said one, "no one sings any more . . . we're all fakes now" (*Mó non canta più nessuno . . . Siamo tutti finti adesso*). The narrative switch from the Romanesco (Roman dialect) word *mó* to the standard Italian *adesso* (both meaning "now"), with the positioning of the Italian *adesso* at the end of the sentence adding further emphasis, reproduces a sense of shifting through time—the time of the sentence reproducing the historical sequence—from affectionate neighborliness to the bland and perhaps hypocritical politeness of modern national culture.

Such traces achingly recall times past, or what those times are now fondly imagined to have been. Once a barber's client remarked that he had been waiting for two hours; when the barber started to respond a little defensively, the customer explained that he had meant it as a compliment—that here, alone in all of Rome, he could still see people greeting each other warmly as friends. But the barber's initial defensiveness shows how new ideals—here, of punctuality—have already invaded and restructured the idioms of social interaction.

When I began my fieldwork in 1999, one could occasionally still see an elderly person lowering a large basket (*sporta*) from a balcony to the street to receive groceries and other supplies; but this is a rare sight now, and people no longer talk from balcony to balcony as they once did. A woman living on the ground floor of a building in which all the tenants were resisting eviction did serve as an unofficial concierge (the bank that owned the building refused to appoint her officially); she dealt with the daily postal deliveries and alerted other residents whenever there was a visitor or some official business— and was an effective lookout when the threat of violent eviction loomed. And locals often still gathered on the street to shake their heads over a vandalized car or share some bit of scandal. But they also lamented the passing of the old sociability.

A garage attendant recalled the old Monti social idiom as "more neorealist" in the cinematic sense—an invocation of filmmakers like Fellini and Pasolini, with their evocations of a picaresque intimacy, that I was to meet often.[19] As another resident put it, recalling both the frequent conviviality on the street to the accompaniment of guitar and mandolin and the simpler living conditions such as a complete lack of heating in the winter: "We were a peasant culture.... Then, with the wind of the economic boom, we became industrialized."

Much of the regret is about the passing of care for the weak and unprotected. The old neighborhood bosses saw their role as especially that of protecting women from harassment and ensuring that the poor were not mistreated. And sometimes there were adventures. During the grim, food-deprived months of the German occupation of Rome in 1943, two men (one of them a *carabiniere*) broke into the barracks that the German soldiers had sequestered and stole a large box of rationing coupons. Another kinsman gave the coupons out to the poor; but, as the son of one of these men recalled, had anyone tried to steal them, he would have been knifed to death. The sense of communal solidarity also encompassed the possibility of retributive violence; but it was violence in defense of a moral community.

Some traces of this solidarity, too, remain. When an old woman was evicted from her apartment, the sister-in-law of one of the last true underworld bosses to have operated in Monti organized a support fund, so that customers picking up their wash would each time leave 10,000 or 20,000 *lire* as an anonymous contribution. Those who donated were merchants with shops nearby; many of them had lived for decades in the area and saw in the old lady the sad relic of their once vibrant social life.

One plaintive remnant of that old sense of collective identity is an elderly, bearded man, neatly dressed for the most part but muttering and shuffling as he paces the streets, occasionally erupting in drunken anger. Locals give him food, cigarettes, and sometimes money, gently refusing his own plaintive attempts to reciprocate by returning the odd cigarette or banknote, and make sure he has a safe place to sleep at night; indeed, he was eventually given a more permanent berth beside one of the sidewalks. Some say he was once a skilled physician but suffered a catastrophic illness. His erratic perambulations evoke only sympathy and kindness. Everyone knows him and addresses him by name, and people often remark on his highly educated, formal style of speech.

His familiar eccentricities and outbursts evoke more amused affection than contempt. Occasionally someone gives him work; once, when the manageress of a small supermarket for which he was unloading crates of detergent and toothpaste told him not to mix them up, he irritably retorted, "But toothpaste *is* a detergent!" When he ambled into a Japanese restaurant in search of a free cigarette one day, the owner of a neighboring store went in after him and gently persuaded him to leave again; the storekeeper then explained to me that on a previous occasion he had been very drunk and broke a glass panel in the restaurant and the Japanese woman who runs it had been afraid of him ever since—so the storekeeper wished to spare her further terror!

Monticiani attribute the resilience of their compassion for street people to the fact that the new rich who have moved into Monti are predominantly of left-wing political persuasion (and a cynic might add that it gives them some absolution from the guilt of contributing to the torrent of evictions); but the fact is that this man is known to most of the residents who have lived here for a long time, and it is they, in particular, who look after him

and make sure he comes to no harm. A health food storekeeper picked up
the 2,000-*lire* note she had intended as a tip for the waiter in the bar where
we were talking and gave it to the old man; then she explained that the
waiter would certainly understand why, this time, he himself had received
no tip and would not be offended.

∽

But the number of vagrants dropped sharply in the mid-1990s, after a series
of incidents in which some were harmed by Fascist gang fighters (*brigatisti
neri*) who also seem to have been responsible for beating up an activist who
wanted to open a reception center for immigrants, for raiding a jeweler's
shop (in this case evidently aided by a spy they had planted in the police),
and for setting fire to the local offices of *Rifondazione comunista* (the Re-
formist Communist Party). Nonetheless, eccentrics and vagrants still meet
kindness here. A gaunt, elderly man totters from restaurant to restaurant in
the evenings, warbling songs—some of them foreign—in a reedy, out-of-tune
voice that sounds like something emanating from an equally elderly phono-
graph and accompanying himself with vague wavings of the hand that holds
his musical notes; always smiling benignly, he tries to engage customers in
conversation, especially if they are foreigners. On one occasion he was so
overwhelmed with gratitude at getting some money from another customer
and from me that he offered to start singing again, whereupon the exasperated restaurateur, politely but firmly, said that this would certainly not be
necessary and hastily ushered him out of the door.

Such scenes recall the ghostly traces of communal solidarity, now almost more emaciated than the old songster. A very high proportion of those
who gather in the small main square for such special occasions as the October festivities no longer live in Monti but return to relive their memories.
Pushed out of the district either by Mussolini's grandiose urban hygiene and
surveillance in the 1930s or during the current neoliberal rush to gentrify,
they return because, as the tag goes, "in Rome, if you're far from people's
eyes, you're far from their hearts." Some participate in the ritual activities
associated with the annual Feast of the Madonna, to whom the parish church
is dedicated; at the height of these events, several thousand elderly former
residents and their families crowd around the sixteenth-century fountain
dominating the square. But many come at other times as well, to sit and
chat in the spring or autumn sunshine with the few remaining residents of
the old population, their Romanesco cadences, languorous reminiscences,

and salty jokes contrasting with the clipped, fast diction of mostly younger people walking straight across the square with determined steps and briefcases in hand.

Then there are the "cat people" (*gattari* and *gattare*), usually older men and women who feed the many stray cats that happily wander around the neighborhood. Rome has a fascination with cats; at the Largo Torre Argentina, on the far side of Piazza Venezia, an enormous cat sanctuary coexists with ancient ruins; when the state archaeologists threatened to remove the sanctuary, the outraged reaction caused them to beat a hasty retreat. A Monti newspaper vendor who regularly feeds the local cats solemnly informed me, "Better [give] to the beasts than to humans" (*Mejo a'e bestie che ai cristiani*), a phrase in which, by using the old-fashioned "Christians" for "human beings," he invoked their shared burden of sin, adding, "There are quite a few people who are truly disgraceful."[20]

In pre–World War II times Monti was controlled by two *capi rione*, rival bosses and clan chiefs who made it their business to see that neighbors were not cheated or robbed and that women were not molested.[21] One clan stalwart described himself as "a doorman for the district"; his clan had never tolerated protection rackets or drug dealers, he asserted, "and we always had to send them packing." People knew their local roles; until recently men and women were often known by their professional identities—*er macellaro* (the butcher), *er tassinaro* (the taxi driver), and so on—rather than by name. Even when several members of a profession lived close together, some unique professional label would ensure recognition. Among those so labeled a deep complicity against the interference of predatory outsiders, including state officials, prevailed. This complicity, akin to the mafia rule of silence (*omertà*, a term sometimes invoked in such contexts), was nevertheless remarkably fragile. In a city where the local police were drawn from the ranks of the Roman working class, it could easily be penetrated by informers and persistently inquisitive officials.

The fragility of social life often evokes contrasts with a nostalgically reconstituted past. A male jeweler lamented the difficulty of getting artisans to cooperate with each other in defending their collective interests: "There's no longer the unity here that we used to have." This nostalgia consolidates a strong sense of class identity. That district was much more overwhelmingly "popular" (*popolare*, working-class) in the remembered past. The few truly wealthy or aristocratic individuals who were considered to be true Monti people once comfortably coexisted, so present-day residents claim, cheek-by-jowl with the working poor. The importance of such assertions is to decry the current situation, especially the adverse effects of gentrification. They also obscure memories of a Catholic mutualism that was anything but egalitarian.[22]

One such aristocrat, the nineteenth-century Marchese del Grillo, remains a particularly important figure in Monti myth and memory—an irascible aristocrat, a favorite of the Vatican, who nurtured working-class retainers in the area around his palazzo dominating the upper reaches of the district, high athwart the road that separates Monti from the ancient forum. A popular Romanesco comedy about the Marchese del Grillo still plays to appreciative audiences. Yet such figures were not as benign in life as comedy may make them appear today. The politeness that eased interaction between the few aristocrats and wealthy merchants on the one hand and the working-class artisans on the other was never mistaken for an expression of equality. Even the humorous recollections of past interactions are tinged with the violence of another age. I was told that the marchese once asked the pope for permission to throw stones at passing Jews; the pope told him that the Jews were under the Vatican's protection and should not be put in so much danger, so the marchese, apparently without exciting papal disapproval, decided to throw raw potatoes at them instead. Protection, whether as petty extortionism for a parked car or as papal paternalism toward a conveniently cowed religious minority, can be a heavy burden for those who have no choice but to accept its dubious benefits, and popular accounts are tinged with the realization that the difference between aristocratic and ecclesiastical attitudes to the Jews and to the working classes, respectively, was one of degree rather than of kind.

Modernist understandings of class, by contrast, refract it in spatially more direct and clear-cut fashion. The ownership of space itself becomes a marker of class identity, with what were once the apartments of the poorest inhabitants now becoming symbolic markers of cultural distinction. As a result, the continuing presence of the poor and the uncouth in an area undergoing gentrification has come to strike the new arrivals in particular as incompatible with their pretensions. A pitiless market drives this process. As a result, no fondly recalled former standard of civility now protects the weak against the uncivil courtesies of wealthy speculators—known, appropriately enough, as *palazzinari* (apartment block people).[23]

Agonies and Agonistics

Rome is now an elegant national capital and international center. At the same time, however, it faces a housing emergency so dire that even the

United Nations has seen fit to intervene. The ever-accelerating pattern of eviction has, in two short decades, transformed the city's historic center into a tense stage for confrontation among a wealthy and highly educated stratum (many of whose members treat it as a dormitory town), poor immigrants from Eastern Europe as well as Africa and Asia, and an increasingly bitter and fast-diminishing remnant of the older denizens.

The situation is a tragedy, not because of change (Rome has never been a static city and since ancient times has often absorbed varied cultural influences), but because the displaced families are bewildered and disoriented; easily fall prey to racist and neofascist social demagogues; and see their familiar places "restructured" to make way for people who usually have little interest in the spaces of collective memory. With the pattern of eviction, the old economy also collapses. As one man, a printer, pointed out, the *forestieri*, the "outsiders" who are now buying up the restructured residences, ignore the local shops: "But here they don't spend anything; they just come here to sleep." The rents they pay, he added, have pushed the overall level far beyond the means of most workers and merchants. And the money goes mostly to absentee landlords.

It is a tragedy because it erases all alternatives to the neoliberal vision of the good life. It is a tragedy because its prime movers prefer to keep decent housing vacant rather than allow existing residents to remain at affordable rates, perhaps hoping that isolation and physical neglect will finally drive this riff-raff away for good, especially as building decay constitutes a legal reason for refusing to extend a rental contract under the 1998 law; and because in the same process proprietors shut down artisans' workplaces in the expectation that their patience may be rewarded when high-end restaurants and boutiques replace the artisans at vastly inflated rents.[24]

One shop space was left empty for two decades and attracted the interest of a bicycle repair mechanic. The proprietor repeatedly agreed to appointments, only to stand the mechanic up repeatedly. "He's making a mockery of people," scowled the disgruntled artisan. One property—a palazzo in Via degli Ibernesi that was the site of a ferocious decade and a half of resistance to eviction by the remaining tenants—was only equipped with running water in 1997, and that only after considerable legal and political pressure by those still living in the building. Proprietors apparently calculate that the rents they lose in even two decades of disuse will be amply compensated when they finally rent to a wealthy tenant, a circumstance that dramatically illustrates the rapidity with which both rents and real estate prices are shooting "to the stars." The systemic neglect that results has devastating consequences. In the vacant spaces thus created in at least one building, the proprietor, a bank, sent workmen deliberately to squash all the piping so that the apartments themselves became completely uninhabitable and could therefore not serve as squats. Wealthy proprietors are willing and able to pay the higher taxes levied on vacant properties. The voices of former residents now silenced, these deserted apartments now trumpet the speculators' message that the only viable cure for degradation is gentrification.

All this is a tragedy, too, because it happens with the complaisance of left-wing authorities who have surrendered to the allure of neoliberal market logic in virtually every aspect of city management,[25] thereby handing an easy victory to the so-called social Right that had itself evicted many thousands of citizens during its heyday under Mussolini.

It is a tragedy because it builds on the practices of a church that preaches generosity, the avoidance of unnecessary luxury, and tolerance for those whose circumstances are different, but practices none of these things despite the indisputable goodwill of individual members of its sometimes genuinely dedicated clergy. (Another view I heard expressed held that the church was active in charitable works and parish organizations because this gave it a capillary presence at the community level and thus also "a reservoir of votes.")

And it is a tragedy because, in the Eternal City, the bureaucratic denial of any relevance or dignity to the personal sufferings of decent women and men takes on a global resonance that cannot but have far-reaching effects in time and space. It did not escape my friends' notice that at the very moment when, in the Jubilee year of 2000, the pope was calling on Romans to take the poor and needy into their homes, churches and confraternities throughout the city were evicting long-term residents. Secular owners, too, evicted residents to make quick money from the wealthier pilgrims expected to flood in that year, as happened in one stretch of Via del Boschetto right in the heart of Monti. The city authorities wrung their hands but, beyond a few symbolic gestures, failed to intervene.

Perhaps some readers will notice that my words have taken on something of the tone and rhetorical cadences of an Italian political speech. The last few paragraphs could easily be rendered in Italian with the rough lilt of Roman diction. That is not coincidental. I write with all the anger of identification, and it would be disingenuous to deny it. The struggle against eviction is a struggle against vastly stronger economic power, and even those whose ideological leanings might predispose them to sympathize often just shrug their shoulders as if accepting as irresistible the implacable march of the market.

There is, to be sure, resistance at every turn; I well recall the quiet fury of the man who had paid a pittance in rent to an aristocratic proprietor whose heirs, having no interest in the old tenants of their newly acquired property, were now raising the rent to a level callously designed to produce immediate flight: "Now we are at war" (*Mo' stamo in guerra*). And my friend Paolo recalled the moment about a decade before he was himself finally evicted after a long struggle, when he overheard the agents of the real estate company of the Bank of Rome politely reassuring an aristocratic neighbor that the leakage of water from the neglected palazzo where Paolo lived, and which the bank owned, would stop once they had at last kicked him and the other tenants out. He retorted, "You'll have to come with all the armored vehicles of the Warsaw Pact to chase us out!" Evoking an alliance that had so ignominiously fallen apart was an unfortunate choice of metaphor, if, sadly, a prescient one. These struggles rarely end in victory for the tenants.

Failure seeps in everywhere, and helpless anger is never far behind. I have watched elderly Romans, humiliated by the abstruse pontifications of property dealers' lawyers, forced to sign away the stains and cracks of their dilapidated homes—watched them as, with tears in their eyes and pain in their trembling voices and hands, yielding to the harsh indifference of bureaucratic formality and having exhausted every last possibility of appeal, they surrendered their consent to that to which they could never in their hearts agree: the rupture of lives they had expected to conclude with some tranquility amidst the familiar places and people. I looked around at the glass and plastic ornaments and the carefully placed photographs and souvenirs of someone's visit to the Holy Land, testimonies to a bourgeois sentimentality that symbolized the residents' reaching for respectability. Where would those objects go in the predictable confusion of the distraught retreat from their homes? As I recall the tenants' slumping shoulders and the heavy tread of their feet on those once casually familiar floorboards now about to be abandoned to the wreckers' blows, I feel again the incandescent fury of helplessness shared.

But tragedies are rarely one-sided; and while some of the people whom I saw signing their homes away are my friends, I can also understand that there are other individuals enlisted among the forces that have brought them to this humiliation who nevertheless weep with them; who laugh and joke with them to ease the pain—a bailiff, a policeman, a municipal administrator—and then shake their heads as if to try in vain to brush away the indestructible miasma of disgust with their own roles. Morality and long-standing friendship were, in the familiar social universe they shared, no less vital for them than bureaucratic or civic obedience. They, too, are caught up in the dislocation that sudden and massive change brings in its train, leaving entire lives to peter out in a sour reek of failure and disruption.

I can also see that some of those who are being evicted have good homes awaiting them. I am aware that localist sentiment can be a festering ground for its own forms of racial and religious intolerance, and that one ironic side effect of the intense battles being waged for the spaces of historic Rome is a rising (if not unchallenged) tide of intolerance toward those who are different. Human life is complex, and in Rome the wages of original sin are paid with extraordinarily high rates of moral interest. No one is innocent of the ordinary social ills of jealousy, dishonesty, and trickery.

The story of these transformations is all the more tragic because it is not a sentimental story of cardboard heroes and villains. If I tried to tell it that way, I would be guilty of the sensationalizing "folklorism" that is the bane of the residents' experience of media attention. It will remain a complicated story precisely because not all the officials and entrepreneurs were necessarily evil or callous. Some were deeply conflicted, even hurt, by their own actions—actions from which there was, perhaps, no convenient social form of absolution.

That circumstance deepens the sense of tragedy, giving it the resonance that allows us to recover the powerful human emotions that inform the baroque forms of Roman life and that belie any contention that performance and commitment must be mutually incompatible. I cannot pretend to be dispassionate. I do not accept the argument of one speculator who claimed that by converting the homes of the working classes into bijou apartments he was improving and even perfecting the urban fabric while, he claimed, the overwhelming majority of those evicted "were given economic help in finding a place to live." He acknowledged the psychological damage to those who must leave homes of long standing. Nonetheless, his primary goal was clearly to make a quick profit; the money he arranged to accelerate the tenants' departure was simply part of his overall calculation and investment. Even so, I can recognize the commitment, perhaps even dangerous sincerity, that might motivate such claims of urban improvement,[26] just as I can see the strategic calculation that led some defenders of their homes to suggest that they were now the last of the ancient Romans or to accept the support of politicians whose ideologies they despised.

All this inextricable interweaving of interests and attachments makes the tragedy still more profound, its sense of inevitability all the more shocking, and its probable effects all the more likely to last for many decades, perhaps centuries, into the future of this city with its aged marble hands—

worn, cracked, and stained like so many of the homes and lives now being destroyed—feverishly clutching at the fraying fragments of its tattered and soiled eternity, tearing at the last loose threads in the desperate attempt to remain attached to a social world now vanishing into the deepening gloom and soon to be erased altogether by the pulsing lights and raucous beat of bars and pubs and discos.

The Cadences of a Cultural Preserve

It might seem strange to introduce the ethnographic core of this study with remarks about language instead of the more conventional themes of neighborhood, work, or family. But Romans guard their cultural intimacy through a profession of complexity that holds that their dialect is a "way of life" rather than a speech form alone; and this attitude manifests itself in several modalities that reveal the intensity of social relations in this most localist of localities. Prominent among these is a form of conventionalized punning; greeting an acquaintance after a long absence, for example, instead of remarking, "I haven't seen you [in a while]" (*non t'ho visto*), one might say, "I haven't 'lived' you" (*non t'ho vissuto*).

Such jokes serve as boundary markers, recalling a time half a century earlier, when relatively few people spoke standard Italian and the local dialect offered one effective means of exclusion. One elderly man insisted that that the Fascist regime actually reinforced Roman localism by insisting that if, for example, you were Sicilian, "you had [to have] a permit from the police station to stay here in Rome" (*tu avevi un permesso d'a questura pe' stá qui a Roma*)—an ironic observation, in view of both Mussolini's strenuous efforts to impose the national standard everywhere and of the speaker's own noticeable shift to dialect forms even in the course of this one sentence.

The dialect also exhibits a nearly impenetrable semantic subtlety when it comes to intimate gossip. "Where are you going?" can be asked in at least four ways, for example: *dove vai*? is the neutral form in standard Italian (one does hear it from time to time!); *ando vai*? is old-fashioned dialect for the same thing; *'do vai*? is its even more casual variant; and *'ndo vai*?, with a leering pause on the initial *n*, asks the same question with suggestions of trickery, evasiveness, or illicit adventure.[27] Going places is not a neutral activity; finding one's way through Romans' social worlds requires a baroque semantic sensitivity.

A Roman friend recounted that he had followed a sign at the main (Termini) train station, only to find that it led to a dead end. So he turned around and went in the opposite direction—which was in fact correct. He mused that foreign tourists would be confused, not understanding, as he had done, how to deal with such vagrant signage; but when he suggested to an employee that perhaps, for their sake, it should be replaced, the employee retorted that the station staff could hardly be expected to change the signage all the time! Such antic mystification of the ordinary is far from rare, and, like the dialect, sometimes serves to shield the collective intimacies of a capital resentful of the cultural contempt in which the rest of the country holds it.

That curious relationship reflects the persistent incompleteness of the project of Italian nation-building.[28] Among European states, Italy is arguably unique in the extent to which it is tormented by powerful separatist movements and torn by conflicting local autonomies in culture and politics. Its longest lived post–World War II government (2001–2006), under Silvio Berlusconi, was a paradoxical coalition of ultra-nationalist rightists and the perhaps even more extreme separatists of the passionately anti-Roman Lega Nord (Northern League).[29] Romans themselves express a surprising degree of sympathy for those northern separatists who accuse Rome itself of robbing them—meaning, in this case, that "thieving Rome" (*Roma ladrona*) is a bureaucratic parasite.

Even Romans concede that their city, home of *ministeriali* (government employees), allows for too much surveillance by the authorities. They also resent the extent to which such interference has shaped the cultural forms of everyday interaction. A furniture restorer was particularly incensed that police officers would come with warm professions of friendship, only to be subsequently revealed as snoops whose task was to identify and punish the kind of everyday cheating that makes life economically and socially bearable. As a result of this resentment, as well as the inconvenience of playing host to a vast population of bureaucrats and diplomats, there are many—including some in surprisingly high places—who would prefer the capital city to be elsewhere. At least two special Roman associations are dedicated to precisely that goal, or at least to reducing the effects of the city's capital status on the lives of its inhabitants; the president of one was also the vice president of the city's transportation system at the time. As the literature of his group (*Identità popolare*, popular identity) claimed: "The less we are the capital, the more of a city we'll be" (*meno capitale, più città*). These attitudes are also not uncommon in less exalted circles or among the young. The son of a local newspaper vendor reacted to my comment that even Romans might sometimes harbor separatist attitudes by unhesitatingly responding, "I'd secede!" (*Me staccherei!*)

The paradox of Rome's ambivalent relationship to the country reflects and reinforces the opportunistic play of localism and nationalism among the major political parties. The political Left is increasingly identified with the trappings and logic of nineteenth-century nationalism; former president Ciampi's enthusiasm for the national anthem and for military parades evidently emerged as a counterweight to the histrionics of the Lega Nord and its strange nationalist bedfellows on the political right. These same northern separatists have repeatedly shown their contempt for the capital. Perhaps the most remarkable incident was an attempt to exclude its citizens, as putative southerners, from holidaying in bungalow hotels they had built in an exclusive section of the island of Lampedusa—which happens to be south of Sicily![30]

Romans, in a country whose northern separatists profess to despise the south as an uncivilized backwater (while more recently encouraging the south's own separatist ambitions), do not necessarily reject the southern label. On the contrary, they profess admiration for Neapolitans, claiming that the latter have a more sophisticated humor, better coffee, and a more cosmopolitan outlook on life. And the southern stereotype serves them well as an excuse for those intimate areas of local life in which *la bell'arte d'arrangiarsi* (the fine art of fixing things) offers the only relief from a cumbersomely inefficient bureaucratic state.[31]

Romans were nonetheless somewhat bemused when the Lega Nord, in 2000, organized a massive "march on Rome." The symbolism of this event, which recalled the exploits of Mussolini rather than of Garibaldi, did not escape Roman townsfolk, some of whom even expressed sympathy with the marchers—but were careful to point out that the disaffection with which they sympathized concerned Rome as seat of government, not Rome as their beloved home. They were not particularly upset when the marchers burned an Italian flag, and they could sympathize with the graffiti that evoked, right there in the city itself, the charge of "thieving Rome." Their own feelings about the bureaucratic nation-state were not necessarily more positive.

Once Rome acquired capital status in 1871, it immediately became the site of one of history's most extravagant explosions of speculative urbanism. Huge areas were developed, the value of real estate shot up with destructive rapidity, and whole streets were cut through the existing urban fabric to accommodate the rapidly accelerating movement of human and vehicular traffic. Some areas still retained charmingly inappropriate rustic names; Prati ("meadows"), for example, became the seat of the Palace of Justice, the preferred office zone of the legal profession, and a bourgeois residential quarter. The image of the *burini*, the bumpkins from the Roman hinterland who, since Unification, have migrated to the city in search of more lucrative work than the countryside can offer, remains a presence drafted into attempts at explaining the uncouth manners of some diamond-in-the-rough citizens.

These are, so to speak, papal pagans—the word *paganus*, like the English "heathen," meant a rough countryman in ancient times, and the condescension of urban Romans for their country cousins persists to this day. Nor is the link with paganism merely the shadow of a lost past. The unease of the Vatican about the dangers of pagan revival have something to do with this amiably uncouth presence: not only do graffiti proclaim "Rome is pagan" and "out with the priests!" but the very term *pagano* recalls the rustic— that is, "uncivil"—associations of the old religion that Christianity sought to replace with its own urbanity.

Hence, perhaps, some of the embarrassment about the Roman dialect, an attitude that once led a former Communist, a man one might have expected to delight in using working-class speech, to apologize to me for letting dialect color his criticism of the present left-wing leadership. Another man, describing a Chinese immigrant who had accused him of Fascism and racism, remarked, "Excuse me if I express myself in Roman style," even though the expression he seemed particularly embarrassed to have used— *morto di fame* (dying of hunger), evidently in reference to the Chinese man's state when he first arrived as an immigrant—was perhaps impolite but certainly not dialect-inflected; his squirming embarrassment seems rather to exemplify the view that Romanesco is more a matter of attitude than language.

Such discomfort exhibits a pervasive awareness of the notably low status of Romanesco and its country cousins. Using dialect in a moment of anger is a sharing of intimacy that a Roman may suddenly, and retrospectively, feel is inappropriate when speaking with outsiders.[32] For my part, I take such usages as a sign of trust and friendship. But the growing influence of bourgeois and nationalist values becomes apparent when inadvertently slipping into Romanesco embarrasses a working-class leftist, even though some leftist politicians still use the dialect in media appearances. My interlocutor's voluble discomfort at being accused of racism reflects the same bourgeois fear of the disreputable, a fear also expressed in the frequent disclaimer, "I'm not a racist, but . . . ." (*Non sono razzista, però . . . .*)[33]

These disclaimers are highly significant. Many Italians view openly racist attitudes as incompatible with current ideals of civic harmony. Redolent of the discredited Fascist past, such attitudes conflict with the new cosmopolitanism and its norms of political correctness as well, for those who genuinely care about such things (and they are many), as with the pursuit of social justice. But accusing minority groups (especially Gypsies[34]) and immigrants of failing to adhere to local standards of law, hygiene, honesty, and the like provides a framework of self-justification for those who continue to espouse racist views; one resident claimed that people became racists by being "too civil" (troppo civili) and being rewarded only with rudeness, but this, again, seemed to be a version of the disclaimer just mentioned and to indicate how far people instrumentalized the ideal of civility to exclude the unwanted. A carpenter offered a slightly more elaborate version of the same self-exculpating device, acknowledging that some of the immigrants work for "the cost of earning themselves a piece of bread" (er costo der guadagnasse un pezzo de pane), but then immediately invoking the stereotype of the criminal immigrant.

In short, new and globally diffused forms of civility provide a means of undermining the civic project of including the newcomers in the social mainstream. The politically correct courtesies, a variety of cultural capital that also marks a certain level of affluence and education, favor the emergence of a polite discourse of subliminally Fascist orientation.[35] What is more, they absorb forms of politeness and reserve already available in the Italian language. I shall return later to the contrast between civil and civic, a distinction that can illuminate emergent forms of social conflict and cooperation. For the moment, however, I simply want to signal its value for challenging models of globalization as the unequivocally beneficial spread of liberal, democratic values.

The relationship between language use and ideals of civility is complex and is grounded in class formations. For many bourgeois Romans, the use of the dialect is associated with a horrific image of incivility, while their working-class fellow citizens, by contrast, engage in much more localized forms of civility using that same speech mode, and even sometimes employ ritualized rudeness and sarcasm as expressions of affection. Knowledge of the standard language, like mastery of politically correct terminology, is a matter of cultural capital; a woman architect said that whenever she used her professional jargon (l'architettese, "architectese"), people asked her whether she was from the north, the ultimate topos of formality and high culture! From the perspective of working-class Romans, by contrast, the use of especially salty phrases and distinctive dialect forms shields a richly intimate cultural world from inquisitive and often contemptuous outsiders.

Bourgeois expressions of distaste for the Roman dialect are almost as common as disclaimers of racism, and similarly represent claims to a national or cosmopolitan identity. Middle-class residents, especially those who are upwardly mobile, actively deny the existence of a distinctive Roman dialect, while also, somewhat inconsistently, affecting delicate horror at its distinctively swooping cadenza, its gleeful scatologies, and its sexually suggestive metaphors. (They often resolve that paradox by complaining that modern Roman speech is not the elegant Romanesco of the caustic dialect poet of the nineteenth century, Giuseppe Gioacchino Belli, and insist on calling the modern speech *romano* rather than the more stylish *romanesco* or the affectionately familiar *romanaccio*.) Once, when I was dining with a woman furniture restorer, two other women at the next table started talking about how only those who had a very low level of education and did not know correct Italian would speak the dialect. My dinner companion was fairly sure these two were themselves Roman; their attitude is common among the higher bourgeoisie, and especially among the inhabitants of such prosperous and right-wing quarters as Parioli, a district originally created to house high-ranking functionaries of Mussolini's regime.[36]

Nor is this attitude a prerogative of Roman birth; a graphic designer, originally from Treviso but now living and working in Monti, praised one or two older residents' speech for its charming capacity to conjure up old-time attitudes, but saw most Roman speech as simply the "fallen" (*calata*) idiom of a bourgeoisie made arrogant by the arrival of new prosperity. This postlapsarian imagery, part of a larger discourse about the corruption of pristine tradition, reflects the privileged nostalgia and cultural snobbery of cosmopolitan professionals, many of whom did not grow up in the city but came there in search of prosperity and assumed an aesthetic posture to match their social ambitions.[37] The graphic designer's attitude should be contrasted with the comment of a university professor and professional linguist, a left-leaning Monti resident of long standing, who habitually spoke Romanesco with his immediate family and urged me not to forget that "for us, Italian is a second language."[38]

Precisely because Romanesco is relatively close to standard Italian, it is more easily dismissed as simply corrupt or incorrect than are the more distinctive dialects of, for example, Friuli and Sicily.[39] At best its critics recognize its former literary glory but shake their heads with nostalgic distaste over the corrupt argot into which it has supposedly declined. One Monticiano recounted that his wife, who was from Ferrara province, had seemed to him to speak very musically, but that she had been corrupted into chewing up words just like any Roman. Even highly educated academics and civil servants tend to acquire the local dialect of their place of residence, and Romanesco still exercises a sufficiently powerful influence to achieve that effect.[40]

One way of dispelling the embarrassment is to claim that Romanesco is not so much an acceptable speech form as it is a reflection of ignorance and insecurity resulting from decades of papal rule; but that even in its ugliness it is, in some ineffable way, *simpatico*.[41] But that perspective, as ironic as the language to which it is addressed, argues a deep bond concealed behind the usual affectations of urbane distaste: Romans enjoy their cultural intimacy in a space largely defined by the way they talk.[42] Dialect, obscenity, and insult can all convey affection; for example, calling a close friend *fijo de 'na mignotta* (whoreson) or a *stronzo* (turd) or cursing *li mortacci tua* (your dead) is an index—or a test—of true intimacy.[43] So, too, is the studied churlishness of the carpenter who peremptorily told a bar proprietor, "Make me that cappuccino, you!" (*Fammi er cappuccino, á!*) That abrupt final syllable, which also introduces the familiar Romanesco vocative (*á Miché*, "hey there, Michele"), would give offense to any but a close friend. It is both an affirmation of true closeness and yet remains, the barman subsequently grumbled, a sign of *ignoranza* (being badly brought up). Such semantic ambiguity conveys the indeterminacy of everyday social relations; not for these Romans the precise pedantries of grammarians!

But such tests of social agility logically also carry risks; swearing at the wrong person, or at the wrong moment, can have catastrophic consequences. Moreover, a man takes care not to use her first name in addressing an unrelated woman who is not a social intimate, as he would with another man, but instead calls her *signora*. He thereby intimates to the woman's husband, explained the (female) owner of a boutique specializing in exotic furnishings, that he should "rest assured that I am not eyeing your wife."

These usages are remarkably precise indicators of the extent to which intimacy is being extended and controlled. But it is also important to be alert to ironic play. Dialect, for example, offers a means of pretending humility while teasing those with greater power—particularly, perhaps, those whose left-wing political credentials are belied by either their use of power or the legislation they support. When then prime minister Massimo D'Alema once entered a jeweler's shop, the owner pretended to treat him like a passing mendicant, combining the polite form of address with dialect morphology: "*Vole un bicchie' d'acqua?*" (Do you want a glass of water?) In the discussion that followed, D'Alema offered the jeweler his compliments on maintaining an important tradition, but the jeweler forthrightly replied that a government that did not support the resurgence of apprenticeship would be doing nothing for his trade.

As I began to get to know people in the neighborhood, I particularly noticed that surnames were almost studiously avoided. People introduced themselves, or were introduced by others, by their first names; further intimacy was given a public airing by the breezy hailing of friends in dialect (for example, *a(hoo) Miché!* [for *eh, Michele!*]). The use of first names is considered "friendly"—a concept that is not necessarily always positive in its implications but that, for exactly this reason, defines a social space in which even hostile relations can be transacted with minimal damage to the larger social context.

An elderly carpenter's observation that people used to introduce themselves more readily with their surnames, and that the use of first names on their own was a form of disrespect (*dispetto*), does not necessarily conflict with this view; he was speaking of the distinction, which has become rarer in recent years, between people of different social rank. Indeed, today surnames are occasionally used in irony, to hail an acquaintance of some standing to whom one nevertheless does not want to show excessive deference. Thus, a local notable greeted the Sicilian president of the artisans' union in this way, as does one of his more aggressively working-class neighbors; by accepting this mode of address, he neutralizes what could otherwise have become a mild but insistent form of mockery. With intimates, however, people are otherwise reluctant to use surnames. Most first names are drawn from a relatively restricted common stock; when they are used on their own, they also therefore protect their bearers from being identified as "legal persons" and thus as accountable in some formal sense. Truly tough individuals, especially the old-style local bosses (*capi rione*), are known by a nickname, sometimes, perhaps for ironic effect, consisting of a feminine noun preceded by the masculine article *er*.[44]

In the standard language informal modes of address can serve as markers of inclusion and collegiality. Generally speaking, for example, even when speaking formal Italian—as lawyers, doctors, and academics are usually expected to do—professional colleagues will quickly adopt the informal pronoun *tu*; rejecting this by responding with the formal equivalent *lei* is a snub. At the very least, the polite form can convey a sense of social superiority, as when a bourgeois landlady addresses the local plumber as *lei*, combining this usage with the plumber's first name to ensure that the hierarchical implications of the polite address form remain unmistakable. When, on the other hand, male police officers use the informal *tu* to a well-educated Latin

American immigrant woman, and she remonstrates that this is inappropriate (especially as her papers are completely in order), the officers tell her that this is because she is from the third world; their contempt is woundingly casual.

In other contexts, it is the polite forms that wound. When the lawyer for a big real estate company carrying out a major eviction addressed the tenants' advocate with the polite form, the latter reacted angrily: he was a youthful but not inexperienced professional, a close kinsman of one of the residents and thus personally interested in the affair, and he felt that he was being deliberately put at a social disadvantage when he should instead have been treated as a nominal equal.

These usages have material as well as social implications. Tipping a waiter or barman who has used the informal idiom with the customer can be an insult; it rejects a gesture of equality and friendship and reinstates hierarchy. Bars are in fact important sites for the negotiation of masculine companionship, often through such linguistic niceties.[45] An intimate—one who is *de casa*, literally, "of the house"—is charged only for drinking while standing at the bar even if he is seated at a table, where the official prices are higher. There is a rite of passage for achieving this desirable status; it entails getting someone who already has it to let the newcomer treat the veteran to a drink and so claim nominal equality. Both parties speak Romanesco; formal Italian would imply avoidance or rejection.

Even among those whose speech habitually comes closer to the national standard, a tiny change of accent—what linguists call "lenition" (a reduction of sonority) in the *t* in *ti saluto* (I greet you), for example—can signal intimacy beyond anything conveyed by the phrase itself. That phrase can also, in a formal accent, be a warning; a jeweler explained to me that he used it to mean "be well," but with the hint that the conversation should now end. "*Ci vediamo*" (See you!) is, he observed, a nicer (*più carino*) way of saying the same thing. In the same way, "*Dica*" (tell me, a polite formula used to invite an order), said in a Roman accent and with a formal mien, can be a subtle device of exclusion rather than of friendliness.

Saying something apparently friendly but with slight tinges of potential irritation fits the Roman self-stereotype of collusive but occasionally tense social relations. Perhaps the most interesting example of this is also the shortest: *Boh!* is an expression of skepticism and perplexity. The jeweler, an astute commentator on dialect usage, suggested the gloss of "*che ne so?*" (literally, what do I know about it?) or "*che me frega?*" (what the frigging hell do I care?), but then pointed to an example right before us: a traffic policeman, faced with no less than three rows of illegally parked car, shook his head in despair and expostulated, "*Boh!*" before hastily taking himself off so that he would not have to attempt the impossible and risk a humiliating loss of authority—he evidently found the whole chaotic situation beyond him.

While teachers ensure that children will not grow up speaking only dialect and learn quickly to avoid using it outside the intimate family circle, parents will occasionally use formal Italian in speaking to their children as a way of threatening the withdrawal of affection. Among adults, the double-barreled tactic of the formal pronoun and standard Italian is far more effective a barrier than rudeness. A furniture restorer, an amiable man who had been a chemist working for a state agency, decided around the age of fifty to retire and turn his hand to his long-suppressed artisanal passions. To his dismay—which did not prevent him from sending up his tormentors in a hilarious imitation of their hostility—he encountered precisely this form of exclusion; although a native of Rome who had grown up speaking the dialect, he could never persuade the working class artisans of Monti to speak it with him. They responded to his friendly overtures with a wall of formality. While this might superficially have seemed respectful, and certainly gave him no viable grounds for complaint, he experienced it as intentional exclusion. Behind their hostility lay a real sense of grievance, which I also encountered in reactions to another gifted amateur; those who only do this work to amuse themselves, the older artisans imply, can afford (or perhaps are compelled by their relative lack of experience) to offer lower prices and so take the bread out of the mouths of those who exclusively live by it. To such inconsiderate competitors a true artisan may deny the expression of intimacy with a sense of righteous indignation.

These exclusionary attitudes remain strong among working-class Romans. Yet there is more—so much more—to Rome. Here one can also encounter the elegant, the famous, and the fabulously rich. Here, too, one can listen to the frequent evocation of the city's historical and cosmopolitan status as the head of the world (*caput mundi*, revealingly, a Latin phrase recalling ancient imperial glories). It is, moreover, a talking head, a *chiacchierone* (chatterbox), as Romans bemusedly acknowledge—so much so that a woman once remarked to another woman whose dachshund had started barking wildly at another dog that obviously he too needed to talk—that he was a chatterbox himself! A disposition to chatter that infects even the dogs is doubtless a great boon for any anthropologist.[46] It is also something of an embarrassment for more self-restrained Romans, as when their fellow citizens accost unknown northerners and offer well-crafted orotundities on everything from climate change to the deficiencies of government; this un-

affected delight in talk also opens up some of the most intimate areas of social life and makes a public spectacle of gossip and social judgment. Romans
are, in short, an ethnographer's dream. And Monti offers an intense refraction of this seductive perversity, concentrating within a relatively narrow
space artisans, merchants, and intellectuals and politicians.

CHAPTER TWO

Popolo and Population

M onti is now undergoing the greatest demographic transformation in its history. What the various enemies of Rome did not succeed in achieving, neoliberal economics and especially a rampantly speculative housing market, along with a declining birthrate, are now putting into effect. Older Monticiani often remark, with only partial exaggeration, that one no longer sees children on the streets; the restructuring of old palazzi has brought into the zone a considerable number of absentee landlords and small, wealthy families, while there is some evidence to suggest that the declining population actually reflects a deliberate policy of gentrification designed to turn the entire historic center into a preserve for the privileged. What was once a popular (that is, working-class) district (*quartiere popolare*) is today noted more for its depopulation (*spopolamento*), a process that began with Mussolini's attempts to reorganize the historic center and that is now, ironically, recuperated by a city administration that claims left-wing credentials.

The Artisans

While Monti prides itself on a working-class identity, its stance is not the purist proletarianism of industrial workers in cities such as Turin. It is a distinctly artisanal identity—often loyal to the Left up to a point, to be sure, but nevertheless socially conservative, suspicious of technological change and innovation, and conscious of a long history of coexistence with the upper bourgeoisie and the local aristocracy. Today, moreover, the Left is more visibly represented by intellectuals, party activists, and artists, and local artisans and shopkeepers are often infuriated by the insistence of these newcomers on traffic-free zones and the other appurtenances of gentrification that, they claim, impede their ability to conduct their trades.

The artisans themselves are changing. Ever fewer are those whose work is basic and practical: ironmongers who can fix a lock or a grille, carpenters who will make a new door, plumbers, glaziers, builders. Artisans in this category have an increasingly hard time of it. Not only do their raw materials continue to rise in price, but so do the taxes and social security that they must pay. If they have apprentices, the social security payments become truly ruinous. But most say they cannot afford that expense, and few young people are interested in artisanal work anyway—so artisans resign themselves gloomily to the demise of their profession as they struggle to make ends meet for the last few active years of their own lives. The only exceptions are those who can persuade their own offspring to join them in the work, and such situations are also increasingly rare. Other factors have also worked against the hiring of apprentices. A carpenter no longer needs a junior assistant to make up glue as the work proceeds, for example, since, like many other materials, it can now be bought ready for use. As the national education system provided alternative skills, moreover, young people have generally avoided manual labor. The often secretive atmosphere of artisans' workshops has little appeal: suspicious masters who fear their apprentices' ambitions can generate continual tension, while conditions are cramped and the hours are long.

A few of the humbler artisans still remain in Monti, able to do so only because they belong to the minority who have long owned their own houses or were able to buy their rental properties at affordable prices. The new wave of artisans is decidedly artistic and expensive, and even they face difficulties. A glassworker, for example, must spend considerable sums on raw materials and cannot compete against the commercial power of designer brands even of relatively mass-produced objects. More and more, the shops reproduce the pattern of other former concentrations of artisanal skills; the artisans are restorers rather than creators, or the objects they create are individualized, each piece a unique and expensive work of art. Restoring an art object already belonging to a customer brings little income; but one restorer told me that if instead he bought the object for himself and then restored it, he could sell it at double the original price. Such secondary artisans, some of whom fled to Monti because they could not compete with their upscale colleagues in places like Via Margutta and Via de' Coronari, are now themselves retiring, yielding to even more upscale successors.

Few of the artisans find work with those responsible for "restructuring" the old palazzi as apartment blocks, while the strict control of all such work—at least as regards house exteriors—restricts it to the relatively few artisans who are deemed competent to do it. There is a sense of something

Fig. 2. Reflecting on past and future—a Monti glassmaker. (Photo by Michael Herzfeld.)

closing in on artisanal life—almost literally, since the erection of metal fences (*recinti*) around some monuments in some parts of the historic center and the designation of limited traffic zones imposes a further grid on the spaces of everyday life. The city administration's plan to gather as many artisans as possible in the old slaughterhouse (*Mattatoio*) in Testaccio seemed to some to be the last straw—a means for bureaucrats to fence them in while destroying their means of livelihood throughout the rest of the city, Monti included.[1] The increasingly rigid demarcation of monumental space disturbs residents' habitual use of streets and squares for debating the issues that most affect their lives.

There is a sad irony in this accelerating alienation. Artisans and small shopkeepers have long been the economic backbone of Monti. Artisans are generally regarded as conservative loners, although it is important to distinguish those who provide essential services at what is often a rather basic level—carpenters, ironworkers, and builders—from those who present themselves as artists who make original works that are aesthetic rather than functional.[2] The latter can command the more substantial income that comes with a clientele that is not purely local. Some also have their own Web sites; there have also been attempts to create more inclusive Web sites that would project the weaker artisans' work out into this larger environment. The more specialized and artistically innovative artisans are best equipped to survive in the competitive arena of the new economy. Among the latter, two glassmakers (*vetrai*) are especially prominent; they are also intellectually active, and one is involved in left-wing politics. Most of the humbler artisans are not so much hostile to the political Left as indifferent to it, both because their individualistic style of working sits uneasily with cooperative social action and because the Left itself has always favored factory workers while regarding artisans as marginal and conservative.

Artisans are also notoriously reluctant to enter into cooperative arrangements beyond those between close kin—in our street two brothers repaired upholstery, while on the other side of the road a jeweler worked with his partner and relative, a retired clockmaker. Even the upholsterer brothers had their rough patches, because the one who did more of the design work found his concentration weakened by the other's love of listening to the radio all day; for no very obvious reason, he blamed the latter for a delivery of fish intended for the restaurant next door but dumped at their doorstep instead—it would, he insisted, create a lasting, distracting stink. Partnerships involving unrelated individuals are even harder to sustain, and relatively rare; they are subject to ever-increasing economic pressures that add to their instability. In 1993, when a four-person furniture restoration team split up, the single artisan who wanted to continue the rental agreement for their workspace had to negotiate a new contract; the owner more than doubled the rent established in the previous contract eight years earlier.

Attempts to mobilize the artisans against these processes repeatedly foundered on their mutual suspicion. One Monti goldsmith participated in 1988–1989 in the creation of a citywide cooperative in which two out of the twelve participating firms had their workshops in Monti; but this body collapsed after five years as a result of disagreements about the relations among those who were productive artisans and others who only sold jewelry made by others. Had they stayed together, they might have succeeded in organizing exports to the United States and reaping considerable individual profits from this venture. But most preferred to concentrate on immediate, local sales from their shop windows. This was a safe, familiar conduit; outsiders who happened to see something they liked were not a dependable source of income.

That attitude worked well enough as long as the district remained predominantly working-class, but it has proved disastrously maladaptive under present conditions. With the exception of the few artisans who have focused on beauty rather than utility, most find themselves marginalized by their social as well as their technical traditionalism. They are ill prepared for the new forms of market economy. Their work lacks the regularity of production-line industries, since they mostly work to order; they are not always in a position to repay their increasingly expensive suppliers promptly, and thus, lacking the collateral they would need to get bank loans, easily fall into the arms of rapacious usurers. In some cases, the suppliers may themselves be usurers who are especially well positioned to take over their defaulting clients' entire establishments.

The few artisans who might instead consider asking their union for loans must demonstrate that, even if they lack personal resources, they can turn to relatives or friends with fixed incomes in case all else fails; in addition to whatever reluctance their potential guarantors may feel about taking on such a risk, the latter must also expect to waste a great deal of time in interminable bureaucratic procedures. And if the indebted artisans default, the law now allows the few banks that do exceptionally underwrite the loans to confiscate their goods in compensation; while in theory a creditor may not confiscate a debtor's means of livelihood, in practice it is the equipment that goes, since most artisans own little else.

Artisans are poorly served by legislation that protects the wages, safety, and health insurance of factory workers. At the same time they are also in ever-increasing competition with factory owners for the loyalty of customers. Although they are categorically protected by the Italian constitution,[3] their livelihoods and working styles fare badly in the new economy, a transformation paralleled and deepened by the effects of gentrification. The advent of this hard modernity has also meant devastating changes in patterns of consumption. Artisans, as (appropriately enough) a garage mechanic pointed out to me, do not only create objects; they also repair them. Those who produced artifacts for daily living could depend on the owners' desires to keep these objects useful and attractive—useful because replacement was relatively expensive in a tight economy, attractive because their local reputations depended on appearances. But repair is also expensive; this is especially true in an age of planned obsolescence, the principle whereby goods are deliberately produced for short-term use so that replacing them entirely would be significantly cheaper. Even in as delicate an artisanal trade as a goldsmith's or a jeweler's, moreover, artisans cannot easily compete with a large firm's ability to organize repair work on a more efficient and cheaper basis.

Mass production has thereby turned Rome's self-ascription as a "southern" and thus under-industrialized place into a considerable economic burden. At the same time, the idea of artisanship has itself been diluted; a consumerist reading has caused numerous "artisanal" ice cream shops to sprout all over the city, for example, while the prices of hand-made goods have contributed to the recasting of artisanship as a privileged activity patronized exclusively by the rich—a transformation that was only possible for the most skilled and adaptable of artisans.

A further problem arises from what many artisans regard as the overregulation of their working conditions. One rule requires workshops to have ceilings of at least three meters' height, a virtual impossibility in most of the buildings in Monti. Further rules on ventilation and sewage create additional problems in these old houses. Restricted access to motor vehicles, welcomed by a few, was greeted with fear by the majority, who thought that customers would be discouraged from entering and shopping, to say nothing of the difficulties that would be faced by anyone attempting to load or unload goods. Quality controls have added to their woes, forcing on some a precise standardization that sits ill with their professional ethos and reconfigures the civic order, which has ancient and medieval roots, as a pedantic obsession with modernist bureaucratic procedure.

Ironically, however, it was the growing valorization of "historic" properties that dealt perhaps the lowest blow to both the self-esteem and the economic viability of the old artisan class. Under increasingly severe legal provisions for the restoration of historic buildings, especially churches, responsibility for overseeing the work shifted from parish priests to the Inspectorate of Fine Arts. From an archaeological perspective this was a desirable change inasmuch as priests' concerns were usually less with historical accuracy than with the greater glorification of God (according to their rhetoric) or the embellishment of the church itself (if one believed more cynical interpretations).

Surely less necessary, however, was the relentless deskilling of the older artisans, who were displaced by formally trained and bureaucratically credentialed restorers able to command vastly higher prices—twenty-five times as much, in one estimate. Responses vary between despairing surrender and creative adaptation. One carpenter ceased work altogether except to produce occasional and very expensive small items of furniture for wealthy local professionals such as architects and engineers; as a result, he now enjoys a comfortable lifestyle himself. But he is a rare exception. Economic survival is increasingly difficult; most male artisans' wives now take paid jobs rather than assisting their husbands, while the latter are forced to work ever longer hours. Humbler, jobbing artisans have found themselves increasingly squeezed out of work or relegated to the most mechanical tasks, their very status as artisans threatened by the new pressures and concomitantly

by the dilution of the once proud designation of *artigiano*, itself now gentrified beyond the point of no return. Even the various promotional schemes to
use the Internet intensify the process of gentrification, producing clusters of
more affluent, educated merchant-artisans and virtually eliminating those
who lack the skills, finances, or interest to participate.

These less adaptable or skilled artisans, who in an earlier age would
have enjoyed both respect and a steady income, have thus found themselves
facing a downward spiral of disaster. They must now compete with others
holding more bureaucratic credentials, especially as it is now fashionable for
well-educated people to take courses in some of the artisanal trades. A real
apprentice, one furniture restorer sourly remarked, would learn by observation in the workplace; the widespread idea that an apprentice should "steal
with the eyes" is widespread in Italy and indeed in many parts of the world.[4]
The very idea of a formal course, with its panoply of wordy explanations and
principles, is anathema to most artisans, whose few remaining apprentices
earn too little to afford such an indulgence even if they desire it but must
work solely "for the love of the objects."[5]

The courses have very small enrollments, often with a quota reserved for
foreigners, and, remarked another restorer, applicants must come "highly
recommended through political connections or on account of some [instru-
mental] friendship"—to say nothing of the tuition fees. Participants thus
start out from a position of privilege and are generally interested in only the
most upscale of the artisanal trades; they are also expensive to hire because
they have union-protected salaries based on their formal qualifications, and
most older Monti artisans will have nothing to do with them. But it is often
from these courses that new restorers emerge, frequently without the benefit of ever having worked with an experienced old-style artisan. Of those
few who do manage to get taken on by more experienced artisans, most
work illegally (*in nero*, literally, "in black"). This further intensifies the
competition with which the older artisans must contend.

Arguably, the coup de grâce to old-style artisanship, embedded as both
production and consumption in community life, was the sudden upturn in
rents in the late 1980s. Had this not occurred, craftsmen producing window and door frames, for example, might have been able to hold their own
against less attractive prefabricated products. When rents started to rise ex-
ponentially, many relocated their homes rather than their workspaces. This
disaggregated the old economic unit of the *casa e bottega* (house and shop), a
unit that had provided the further advantage of enabling residents to keep a
collective eye out for potential intruders, and so cut the artisans off from the
unpaid labor of family members.[6] The ratio of floor space to earnings, along

with the advantages of producing small objects when the pace of pedestrianization began to accelerate, favored the goldsmiths. But the very gentrification that is driving other artisans away also means that increasingly the
only clients who will appreciate handmade objects—and be willing to buy
them at the prices that the artisans must now charge—are living in what
were once their own streets; people in the suburbs, I was assured, would not
invest in such expensive items. And so all the artisans are, in this sense,
condemned to stay in the places from which they are also being driven away.

Some, too, have succumbed to changing views of what constitutes a
public nuisance. A carpenter, for example, found himself expelled from his
workshop because of the noise his work created, even though the subsequent
opening of a pub nearby produced noise of much greater volume (and during
the night hours, at that) and even though his old boss continued to work,
noisily and in contravention of the new zoning rules now in force, at the
same workshop.[7] A woman who worked for a survey firm, evidently a new
arrival in the area, sent an anonymous note complaining about the noise
made by some young musicians, but, said their irate father, "she didn't have
the courage to sign [it]"—an indication of the social distance between many
of the newcomers and the local artisans and merchants.

One restorer who had moved his business into the area and had started
off with a workspace attached to his shop soon faced legal challenges to the
arrangement and agreed, regretfully, to desist, arguing that laws should be
respected. Having hitherto felt that "those who make objects should not
be selling them," he now became a merchant himself, specializing in cute
manufactured goods of which a basset hound welcome mat seemed representative. In this, he partially followed a pattern already well under way in other
areas of the historic center where many artisans succeeded in maintaining
their presence only by turning their hands to the sale of antiques and tourist
items.

Gentrification thus hurts artisans in at least two different ways: it makes
their continuing residence ever more untenable—"restructuring" being,
from their perspective, a particularly ironic form of structural violence—
and it fails to provide many of them with replacement work in the new
conservation economy. While many artisans had belonged to local rotating
credit associations at least until the late 1980s, these organizations began
to disappear, leaving the artisans trapped between the intransigent refusal
of banks to offer them loans and the equally intransigent (and sometimes
violent) insistence of loan sharks on ruinous interest rates.[8]

Artisans thus had to seek new forms of professional identity if they
wanted to remain in their old workplaces. Above all, they needed work that

would pay higher and faster dividends. One adaptation was for carpenters to become restorers and repairers rather than producers of original pieces; this work, which is often quieter than building new furniture, could also yield relatively rich economic rewards. One restorer admitted that he could work for just a few hours cleaning a nineteenth-century marble plaque that he had bought for 250,000 *lire* and then resell it at twice that amount. Some sold off their businesses; but, as a former heating installation mechanic pointed out, the woman potter who took over his premises was not necessarily in better economic shape than he had been. He, at least, had been able to rely on people's practical needs, whereas she would need to establish a much wider network in a notoriously fickle and competitive market.

A garage mechanic compared the secretive ways of southern artisans, among whom he included the Romans, with the northern trend toward the creation of artisans' cooperatives. The latter, he said, was the only way for artisanship to survive; but he doubted whether Roman artisans would be able to overcome their mutual suspicion quickly enough to be able to save their professional lives. This remark is especially revealing, not only of the "southern" image of the Romans, but also of the tension between intrusive ideals of civic management and older models of civil secrecy.

The Shopkeepers

While some artisans have become shopkeepers, there is an imaginary line that separates the two categories. Merchants, in contrast to artisans, are supposedly right-wing, ingratiating with customers, and determined to provide their children with a prosperous inheritance and social advancement. There seems to have been considerable truth to this division until the 1980s. With gentrification, however, has come a considerable degree of variation in patterns of business. While there is still a plethora of small shops, some of these are innovative ventures, such as herbalists and computer suppliers. One such merchant, a young woman of generically leftist inclination and with a passion for proselytizing about the virtues of the new alternative medicines, was often too busy tending to her customers and focusing on increasing the variety of her products to waste much time in idle conversation. Even owners of more conventional enterprises, some of them relative newcomers to the area, turned out to have relatively progressive political attitudes. And even some older merchants were famous for their left-wing views, if not always for the corresponding business and civic attitudes.

Food suppliers faced an uphill struggle with the arrival of small but efficient supermarkets. Rumors that at least one of these new establishments had underworld connections may have reflected nothing more than local fear of the kind of competition they provided; with the enormous variety of products they could field at any one time, they represented a challenge, not only to the older grocers' economic viability, but to norms of reciprocity. These norms nevertheless remain so strong that even customers with diametrically opposed political ideologies continue buying from the familiar old shops.

It is in these domestic forms of commerce that we see one of the main sources of the accommodation and complaisance that Romans claim as their distinctive social style. Politeness, ostensibly an expression of communal solidarity, works in practice as a key ingredient of genteel competition; a rude response sends customers elsewhere. Showing a lack of interest can be fatal; a clothes merchant said that he would cease to put on a smiling face only for the kind of customer who kept returning but never bought anything—a "ballbreaker" (*rompicoglione*) with whom, in the end, he has lost all patience. When business is precarious, politeness becomes unctuous to the point of self-abasement. As an exasperated older shopkeeper put it, "Commerce is cowardly" (*Il commercio è vigliacco*). And he added, with a meaningful appreciation of the role of gesture in determining social hierarchy: "The good merchant should never look the client in the face [that is, be anything other than demurely polite]." His rhetoric reveals deep currents of anger beneath the face of accommodation: "I must submit to the violent. I must submit to the ill-behaved. I must submit to the clever. I must submit to the ruffian and to the one who is mildly mannered. I must submit to all, both Italians and foreigners."

His voice weary with humiliation, the elderly shopkeeper—no friend either of immigrants or of predatory policemen—articulates the price of living in this society that is the lot of small shopkeepers and artisans. To be sure, his air of resigned humiliation may disguise something more calculating; when a friend of mine bought a single tomato from his shop, the shopkeeper's daughter, whom my friend had known since childhood, calculated the initial weight on the basis of an inflated price per kilo and, when my friend remonstrated with her, made some vague gesture and recalculated the amount without further comment. Whatever the motives and practices that underlie such accommodating humility of manner, it certainly makes it difficult to object when a small fraud of this kind has been attempted by an old acquaintance and neighbor—everyone, after all, must make a living, and all but the most confident and capable fear the usurers awaiting the carrion of failed enterprise.

Intellectuals and Politicians

If I had followed the prevalent traditions of anthropological writing about Italy, it would have been all too easy to confine the description of the population to the artisans and shopkeepers. A colleague once remarked to me that her friends in Monti did not seem to know of my presence. Yet I did in fact encounter many intellectuals, politicians, and artists, and participated with some of them in the activities of the Monti Social Network. The intellectuals, many of whom treated my importunities with as much generosity as the other residents, may not have encountered me as a daily presence on the streets in the way that many others did, because for the most part they do not engage with quite the same intensity with the artisans and merchants, or for the same reasons, as I habitually did; beyond their own relatively specialized social gatherings, their range of contacts is much more widely extroverted beyond the district and even beyond Rome itself.

Departments of two of Rome's universities provided a considerable academic presence, which perhaps sustained the fairly numerous and well-stocked bookstores in the district. A sign of the new gentrification, however, was the increasing inability of some academics to sustain their residential status; academic salaries could not keep up with the rapid rent increases. Students, too, did not live in the district, but flocked to classes on foot, bicycle, and motorbike, sometimes blocking the narrow streets with their passionate arguments and carefree flirting.

Those intellectuals who tried to establish a business presence in the district, like those who became artisans, encountered some reserve. A former journalist who opened an antiques shop was dismissively informed, "You're a friend of [moderate left-wing mayor Francesco] Rutelli"—meaning, he thought, that he was simply "not one of them." With a foreign business partner who also teaches in a provincial university, and a shop still sufficiently unusual in this district to offer a contrast to those of the restorers and carpenters, he did not fit the mold.

The one powerful and intensifying link between intellectuals on the one hand and established artisans and shopkeepers on the other is urban activism. Some of the intellectuals have pioneered a new grassroots engagement among a hitherto suspicious population. Among those engaged in the Monti Social Network, for example, and indeed one of its foremost protagonists, is a political economist—Riccardo Troisi. Troisi, critical of the crass manifestations and destructive effects of globalization, represents a politically nonviolent position springing from his active engagement with

Christian-oriented popular movements. He is very much the peacemaker, disliking conflict whether in condominial meetings or in the Network's activities, where he has sometimes appeared to other members to be too willing to pursue consensus at the expense of hearing out a full range of options; but then he is a practical man, perhaps more so than the thoughtful glassmaker who claimed to enjoy the psychological contrasts that these meetings brought to the fore.

Troisi nevertheless speculated that it might be possible to pursue a form of local revival that would resist what he called the "post-Fordist" globalization of the present age—a community of artisans and intellectuals who would not yield to the economically driven forms of gentrification that have predominated worldwide and who would not accept the museological urban vision of the current administration. In seeking an alternative development, Troisi does acknowledge the importance of reconstituting the kind of intense political activity that formerly occurred in the district committees of, especially, the left-wing political parties; he calls for a reconstruction of a social and political linkage (*legame sociale politico*) that has, he argues, become unstuck (*scollato*) under the pressures of the new order. It is not only in Africa that neoliberalism has attempted to muzzle political life by taking over its rhetoric and deliberately misrepresenting critique as hostility.[9]

Such a process of reconnection appeared to be underway during the course of the following year when, after the violent clashes between No-Global activists and police in Genoa during which one demonstrator was killed, a large graffito appeared on the face of the Ukrainian Catholic church: *G8: GUARDIE ASSASSINE*. The inscription was in blue paint; a white background had been applied first, obliterating the existing graffiti, most of which were about soccer. In the eyes of two left-wing friends who commented on it in lively fashion, the new inscription had a double significance: on the one hand, it appeared to allude to the fascist behavior of the *carabinieri* who harassed immigrants on the square, calling them "guards" in an evocation of the Mussolini era rather than using their official name; on the other, the white background not only signaled a departure from football obsessions in favor of a more political engagement but provided a space for locals to append their signatures—which many did. This was the first time in many years, it transpired, that there had been such a lively form of local political engagement; it was not a party-directed activity, but an expression of collective outrage and solidarity. For those who wanted to see the emergence of a new sensibility that drew on existing social connections rather than tamely yielding to the neoliberal format, this was an encouraging sign indeed.

While this protest was apparently not a Network initiative—the Network itself operates strictly on legal principles—it did appear to herald something of the lively concern that the Network's leading activists hoped to revive. These activists are very aware of the pressures of time as neoliberal management styles erode the social conditions that favor critical debate. Riccardo Troisi is one of the more engaged Network activists. Another is the urban planner Carlo Cellamare. Both have contributed enormously to my understanding of the local dynamics—Troisi as a resident, Cellamare as a nonresident who teaches in the locally based department of urban studies of the University of Rome–I ("La Sapienza") and who has become a key player in articulating the complexities of reducing traffic noise and pollution in ways that respect the interests of merchants and artisans. There are many others, including numerous students. Mentioning them now rather than in the formal acknowledgments alone is, like a zoom lens spotting some key feature in the physical landscape and bringing it to the foreground, a way of underscoring the enormously creative role they play in reshaping the local environment. The identification of Monti people as either colleagues or informants blurs into a shared bustle of engaged activity. The intellectuals are very much a part of the ethnographic picture.[10]

CHAPTER THREE

The Wages of Original Sin

The presence of the church and its bureaucratic panoply deeply affects the daily lives of Monti residents—even those who, as members of the old Jewish community or as Muslim immigrants, or again as self-declared atheists—do not worship in its halls. It is an inescapable presence; simply in terms of the number of churches and of houses owned by religious institutions, it commands the spaces through which Monticiani move on their daily rounds. Artisan and intellectual, honest merchant and crooked moneylender: all must reckon with the pervasive odor of a somewhat decayed sanctity, even if they do not accept either its doctrinal principles or its self-appointed guardianship of public morality. They see formerly leftist politicians, once elected to civic office, coming to terms with the extraordinarily persistent power of the papacy; and, with shrugs of resigned cynicism, they recognize in such accommodations the model that has for so long dominated their own everyday lives.

Accountability and Accommodation: The Pragmatics of Original Sin

In this chapter I want to explore the implications of this extraordinary dominance of the church—at once revered and hated, saintly and sinning—for what is happening in the city today. This will necessitate an exploratory foray into questions of doctrine. At times in tandem, at others in discordant rupture, theological and political moralities have guided the management of the city—as well as the lives of its inhabitants—for many centuries.

Most prominent, although rarely invoked in name, has been the doctrine of original sin. As a taken-for-granted etiology of ordinary human imperfection, it provides a framework for blame and accountability. Because the world is full of evil, moreover, idioms of respect, courtesy, and mutual

regard provide ways of compensating for the imperfections of the social order and managing relations from day to day. These express the pragmatic
face of another doctrine, that of mutualism, whereby an apparent reciprocity
of gifts and courtesies disguises, but does not suppress, a hierarchical reality that has often—as in Spain, for example—allowed church and state to
reinforce each other's power structures over long stretches of time.[1] Poorer
Romans know full well how things work: the rich, "they're in charge . . . they
have the money, they have the power, they have the lot." In this context,
civility—here the antithesis of civic engagement—is a means of maintaining
inequalities in the name of stability and mutual dependence under the banner of the church, and even its charitable works take on a more instrumental
and oppressive hue.[2]

Commentators on the recent vagaries of Roman civic life often express
great astonishment that a relatively left-leaning administration should accommodate itself so easily to both the demands of the religious Vatican
state and the demands of neoliberal ideology. To understand how this came
about is to perceive the enduring presence of certain assumptions about
human imperfection—the necessity of political compromise, the ineradica-
bility of corruption, the improbability of altruism—that persistently appear
in the practices of the all-too-human representatives of both church and
state. Attempts to explain these phenomena away as forms of backwardness or underdevelopment are a sad reproduction of condescending foreign
critiques; they explain nothing, but they illustrate a great deal about the
global politics of value.[3]

A generic model of original sin, by contrast, informs the long Roman
conjuncture of corruption and civility. It helps us understand how remarkable architectural glories and a robust politics could emerge from, and indeed
exemplify, centuries of illegal construction and underhand governance. The
aesthetics of both personal interaction and artistic creativity spring from an
urbanity (civiltà) in which elegant appearance always trumps a too-literal
adherence to the rule of law.

Original sin is a theodicy, grounded in that originating eviction of Adam
and Eve from Paradise, through which both Orthodox and Catholic traditions explain how, in a world divinely ordained, human life is still subject
to deep and ineradicable imperfection. Rome defines itself as a city of Christians (although many other religions are represented there); and Christians
are, by their own definition, sinners. This is not merely a theological conceit, but has social resonance; to call others "Christian" is to recognize them
as decent folks who, like the speaker, are forced by the wicked world around
them to lie, steal, cheat, quarrel, and fornicate, often at the expense of the

rich and powerful and thus also in solidarity with close kin and neighbors. Since J. K. Campell's remarkable account of the Sarakatsan shepherding community of northern Greece, anthropologists have recognized the significance of this moral alibi for reconciling ideals of deep religiosity with the inescapable fact that everyday life always falls short.[4] Italo Pardo has similarly noted the working-class Neapolitan view that commonplace sins can be expiated through the sufferings of this life or a passage through Purgatory in the next.[5] These attitudes represent a vague but powerful etiology of petty evil that reflects, none too precisely (as its all-purpose ubiquity perhaps requires), the tenets of an ecclesiastical doctrine.[6]

Monticiani proclaim their sinful condition in loud, public prayers as they walk in solemn procession during Holy Week, calling on the holy Virgin to "pray for us" (prega per noi)—this plea for intercession being repeated in sepulchral unison by predominantly female voices, led by the incantatory invocations of the priest over a portable loudspeaker and periodically interspersed with the solemn music of a brass band. These prayers remind the entire community of the burden of sin that all must carry, and of the central importance of hierarchy (in its double sense of priesthood and inequality) in mediating its alleviation. The rite of confession absolves a declining population of faithful Catholics of the burden of particular infractions; because it does not cleanse them of their shared sinfulness, however, the price of such complicitous communion is the maintenance of the church's authority.

Even those who do not go to church acknowledge, in a shrug of the shoulders or a complaisant wink, the inevitability of human imperfection. The very buildings around them, many deliberately neglected by their owners, with cracked or fallen plasterwork in the hallways and unkempt clumps of weeds in the courtyards, attest to the impermanence and suffering of this life. While ruined buildings appeal to a romantic aesthetic, they also testify to the ceaseless attrition, the recurrent mortality, of history. Conservationists' attempts to perpetuate and generalize their time-stained appearance long into the future ironically undermine their more focalized significance for the people who have lived in them, and have put up with their flaws, for generations. The encompassing irony is that the capital of the Catholic world should be known as the Eternal City, given the romantic ruins that so fascinated the eighteenth-century artist Piranesi, the now frequent condemnations of old houses as collapsing (fatiscenti), and the moral corruption of Rome's political life. Its inescapable temporality is at once theological and social, and in both senses is inseparable from the inevitable decay of all things material.

Theologically, original sin is seen as a debt to the devil;[7] and debt is by definition a condition that accentuates the sense of time, through repayment, the process that is, significantly,[8] called redemption; Christ is the Redeemer because it is Christ who, through suffering, redeems the sins of the human race and brings the hope of a return to eternal bliss. He also, and concomitantly, allows humans to achieve a state of forgiveness, their souls purged in that limbo between Hell and Paradise. Socially, this process is economic, and is rendered more so by the ability of the wealthy to pay for more masses, erect more holy images and monuments to their own piety, and bestow more gifts—especially as bequests—on the institution, the church, that represents the divine will on earth. The church's practice of issuing indulgences for a faster passage through Purgatory effectively converts temporality into a new hope of eternity, which is tantamount to final and comprehensive redemption. On the way, each person must be absolved of the many minor sins committed during the temporal sequence of a lifetime or risk eternal damnation.

The debt that is thereby redeemed has its counterpart in the earthly life. The repayment of a debt should ideally be disinterested—that is, literally without any interest payments—and be voluntary and unrelated to time. In practice, economic life could not function without the recognition that financial loss can only be tolerated to a certain degree; economics in this sense is the sign *par excellence* of human mortality. At least from the time of Marx, economists have recognized that the inequalities created by both theft and usury spring from some original condition or event that should never have occurred. For Marx, that event was the colonial expropriation of the natural resources of what became the colonies of Western states; such was the original sin, as he explicitly but ironically termed it, of political economy. The idea of an incurable original sin was thus, like the doctrine of the church, a convenient fiction for those who actually controlled the resources in question, whereas the indebtedness it represented was not necessarily irreversible; this view, appropriately modified, has been extended by modern economists to the fiction that emerging nations are incapable of borrowing in foreign currency—a mystification to which there is nothing, say these economists, that compels such countries to surrender their independence as they so often do.[9]

Debt is about redemption, a temporal process. The church holds out the promise of eternal bliss in exchange for a carefully paced process of expiation. The state does so through its management of a legal system that frequently—sometimes through the actions of corrupt officials, who allegedly use their authority to extort bribes—reduces citizens to the status of offenders. Romans have no difficulty in articulating this parallel: "We are guilty as soon as we are born. No matter what! Whether in dealing with the state or in dealing with religion," as one shopkeeper put it, adding that it "seems like a prison, because it has to be oppressive" in forcing people to live "with a sense of guilt" but without actually knowing what they have done. On the other hand, they also enjoy the security of knowing that this "excuse" (scusa) will bring certain forgiveness in its train. The everyday sense of original sin thus ensures compliance through constant reminders of human imperfection and of the necessity of expiating its stains.

Punishment consists in the payment of fines, but delays can sometimes buy redemption from the state. Not so with usurers, who enslave people to debts that spring from their own economic incapacities. Usurers thus reproduce the universal human indebtedness to the devil, incurred at the time of the expulsion from Paradise. Because indebtedness involves the payment of interest, and because interest is calculated on the basis of time, this common form of social distress—which leaves debtors at the mercy of events they often cannot control—injects a viscerally painful temporality, of real time with all its uncertainty and unpredictability, into social experience.[10] The barrier to eternity is the temporality of moral and financial debt, its redemption forever deferred to reinforce the maintenance of real power.

The church formalizes redemption for minor offenses by issuing indulgences—documents awarding a specific (and finite) degree of relief from time in Purgatory, where sinners are cleansed of the remaining miasma of original sin before entering Paradise. The Italian state adopted a virtually identical model in its practice of issuing pardons for unpaid fines in exchange for the immediate payment of a small fraction of those fines, and this, as we shall see, allowed for the ongoing construction of a city that ultimately can be read as a palimpsest of consecutive and overlapping violations of all sorts of laws, but especially those pertaining to zoning, traffic control, and historic conservation—that is, to the very fabric of the Romans' inhabited space.

Original Sinners or Elder Brothers?

In this sense, the material presence of the historical past is the temporal record of the wages of a form of original sin made inevitable by the fact that the laws thus violated are of human, not divine, inspiration—and are therefore made by legislators who, all too human in their desires, are themselves entrapped in the decay of mortal flesh. Those who legislated against usury, for example, were often also capable of profiting from it; the church fathers themselves found numerous casuistic devices for enabling the lending of money at interest, even though they were often uneasily aware that such exceptions entailed a questionable moral stance, and so the church eventually also became involved in this activity.

In part, it did so by demonizing the very people whose own religious injunctions against usury provided the bedrock of the church's arguments against it: the Jews, a presence of deep historical record in Rome that forcibly reminded a hostile hierarchy that the church's own original sin lay in its dependence for moral precepts on a people it regarded as damned to all eternity. It is ironic that Pope John Paul II, soon to be imitated by the parish priest of Monti in a genuinely moving ceremony of recognition for a local church's role in the forced conversion of Roman Jews, sought the forgiveness of the Jewish people, whom he called "our elder brothers"; the Israelite condemnation for usury was expressed as a rejection of ensnaring one's "brothers" in debt.[11]

In Monti the Jewish presence is a weak echo of the Ghetto's nearby presence and of a past when Monti was the place where newly converted Jews, from 1634 on, were forcibly isolated in a convent-like structure—now a seat of one of Rome's secular universities—adjoining the parish church and a few paces from the Church of San Salvatore, formerly the seat of the parish priest. Here, in rigid isolation for a ritualistic forty days, they were indoctrinated in their new faith. In the parish church, too, lies buried a rabbi who not only converted but also served his Vatican masters by trying to bring his erstwhile followers into the Christian flock with him, his tomb marked by a Hebrew inscription that, like the bilingual text from Isaiah over the doorway of the Church of St. Gregory at the entrance to the Ghetto, marks the ongoing attempts by the Vatican to incorporate the Jews while marking even those who converted as forever tainted by their collective past.[12]

Recognition of the historical relationship between the two religions, and even the shared doctrine of original sin, was not to come until the twentieth century, when the Jews who died at the hands of the Nazi occupiers were eventually commemorated in a simple but deeply moving memorial as "Roman citizens of Jewish religion"—claimed, that is, not as indwelling outsiders nor yet as citizens of the nation-state, but as an integral segment of the city's very soul.[13] Two black-shirted neofascists assured me, individually and on separate occasions, that the Roman Jews were truly the last genuine Romans.[14] Some Monti Jews certainly owed their survival during the

Nazi occupation to the willingness of nuns—and even, in one case, an active Fascist—to hide them at considerable risk to their own lives. Such incidents are often held to demonstrate that anti-Semitism is foreign to the Italian way, despite the fact that others (including one entire Monti family) were betrayed to the Nazis by local informers; and that Mussolini's racial laws were entirely the result of pressure from Hitler and the Nazis.[15] While such self-exoneration has come in for some long-overdue rethinking,[16] the Jewish presence—despite hostile mutterings among right-wingers who blame the Jews for letting Chinese immigrant entrepreneurs buy out their properties in the nearby Esquilino district—is now largely viewed with equanimity and affection. The Monti parish priest was clearly serious about recognizing the importance of reconnecting the church with its Jewish roots, and his enthusiasm for this subject was manifest in his unflinching lecture, preceded by a formal ritual of prayer and followed by a historical exegesis of the role of the Church of San Salvatore in the forcible isolation of Jewish converts, on the wrong that the church had committed against the Jewish people—although, as he insisted, this wrong sprang from a sincere if misguided desire to save souls.

The Jews were often hated in earlier days, as they had been elsewhere in Europe, because of their reputation as extortionate moneylenders—a role into which the Christain faith propelled them, and not only because the authorities forbade them to own rural land. St. Thomas Aquinas and other medieval church leaders claimed that the Jews could serve as usurers because they were damned anyway; this would not only save Christians from the venal sin of usury, but would protect the desperate from the hardly lesser sin of complicity in the usurers' wickedness, since to ask another Christian for a loan at interest was to place that person's soul at risk of eternal damnation.[17]

Over the centuries, and especially as it began to countenance money lending on a limited scale by members of its own flock, the papacy increasingly persecuted the Jewish community even while continuing to exploit its financial services, thereby tacitly admitting its indebtedness to a population it regarded as diabolical. Its cynical expropriation of Jewish law at once allowed it to depend on and to repress the Jewish community, a tactic that can partly be traced to the hostility of the Franciscan order in the fourteenth and fifteenth centuries,[18] and served as a template for the continuing cultural ambiguity of the Jewish presence, and the equally persistent moral ambiguity of commerce, in Rome. As Renata Ago points out, "the intermingling and reciprocal influence between the two cultures—that of the theologians and that of the merchants—is strong and continuous."[19]

In practice, the church tolerated certain forms of usury and deployed some adroit casuistry in its defense.[20] By the end of papal rule usury was certainly not a Jewish monopoly; indeed, by that time it had become normal for local priests to engage in limited forms of low-interest money lending, and there are still instances of this in some areas.[21] Thus the Vatican eventually approved the lending of money at rates that were fixed by law, and this process accompanied the gradual downgrading and disappearance from public view of the Jewish community, formerly the bankers as well as the scapegoats of a Vatican prepared, even compelled, to tolerate its continuing presence.[22] As the fortunes of the Jewish community declined in the two centuries before Unification, the Vatican increased its own financial activity. The arguments in favor of this shift appealed to social relations and practical necessity as well as to the risks that an honest lender always assumed. Debtors sometimes felt enormous gratitude to usurers who, at risk to both their souls and their mortal lives, had saved them from immediate ruin; moreover, the church also recognized that forbidding the restitution of a debt with interest was also a denial of basic forms of reciprocity.[23] Faint indeed was the echo of the medieval church, which had even argued that lenders should not stipulate deadlines for repayment, and that even the expectation of reciprocity represented the morally illicit hope of material gain.[24]

Such reasoning brought minor usury morally into line with relatively trivial misdeeds like tax evasion and bribery; just as some priests began to lend money as an act of charity (and pawnshops, the famous *monti di pietà*, were openly permitted to do so), so corrupt officials often appeared as saviors who facilitated the everyday survival of hard-pressed citizens.

Usury, whether as an avaricious form of opportunism or as a helping hand, did not endear those who practiced it to their debtors, who suffered social stigma as well as a terrible financial burden. Some of the most vicious forms of extortion appear in Rome, and usury has come to be regarded, in the secret spaces of the city's sense of cultural intimacy, as a peculiarly Roman problem, the church as one of the institutions that perpetuate its presence. The Vatican's involvement in banking led to major embarrassments, among which the collapse of the Milan-based Banco Ambrosiano in 1982 was the most dramatic.[25] Such scandals fueled the cynicism of the Italian public just as Vatican influence over electoral politics went into sharp decline.[26] Anything and everything became believable. While nothing ever came of repeated attempts to convict Cardinal Giordano, the archbishop of Naples, of usury and extortion, many Italians seemed to believe that this demonstrated only his enormous local power. Whatever the truth of such unverifiable allegations, they were enormously damaging to the church's moral authority.

The Dialectics of Casuistry and Tolerance

Usury has continued to proliferate in Rome and more generally throughout the country. Because it necessarily entails the timing of interest payments, the church condemned it as especially heinous on the grounds that time, as a common good, was the property of God, and, as such, could not legitimately be appropriated for human use.[27] Usurers' precision in recalling debts parodies the theological calculus of the confessional but extorts redemption instead of bestowing it. Moreover, usurers measure the amount of interest in proportion to the lapse of time, but are—in practice and by reputation— opportunistically willing to compromise that precision and relax their stranglehold just sufficiently to force debtors to find some way of paying them off, usually by going into further debt to other usurers.

People who fell into usurers' hands directly confronted the imperfections both of their own souls and of the social world in which they lived. Rome is not only the capital of the church and of the Italian state; it is also, for many, the capital of usury.[28] The state's internal divisions and structural weaknesses are perhaps most clearly illustrated by its spectacular failure to curb this evil, the wages of a collective original sin. By comparison with usury, the state's own practice of forgiving fines in exchange for a partial payment is more redemptive than punitive (although it was also advantageous to a system of government that was, and is, chronically strapped for ready cash). But the failure of the state to control the banks and their operators in an effective way has driven many a poor merchant and artisan into the hands of the usurers, making the state and the banks complicit in the perpetuation of a practice that is also the source of profound and unending distress. If, as James Aho has argued, the emergence of precise bookkeeping in the form of double-entry accounting was an extension of the careful accounting of sins in the confessional, leading to the emergence of post-Reformation idioms of accountability in civic management, an equally careful but socially and theologically pernicious form of calculation insidiously reasserts temporality through the downward spiral of debt that characterizes the practice of usury.[29]

While Italy, a predominantly Catholic country, nevertheless later turned to post-Reformation models of civic virtue as these have been articulated in powerful countries to the north, real life offers alternatives that are more compatible with the intimate needs and religious practices of local society. This is what produces the sometimes cynical, and always practical, recognition of divergence between civic ideals and social practice. People watch the activities of supposedly civic-minded authorities with an eye jaundiced by experience, for they know that bureaucrats, like priests in the confessional, do not always practice what they preach, and that the call for ethical self-examination is no guarantee of compliance. In this, too, the church's earthly regime serves as a template for people's understanding of the modern secular state that has succeeded it.

While usury is formally a mortal sin, because it represents an antisocial act tantamount to cannibalism according to many of the medieval preachers, its social utility and the professions of friendship that accompany it effectively render it more like the redeemable features of fallen humanity—that is, the consequences of original sin. The casuistry of exceptions opened up vast possibilities for those willing to risk their souls in the pursuit of profit. By the end of the sixteenth century, at least one prominent theologian was arguing that gratitude was the mark of "civility" and "urbanity"—and from here it was a short path to accepting some forms of profit and the circulation of value "on condition that this value be effaced by the gesture of the giver."[30] In this privileging of civility—which in turn obscures the inner motivations that had been the particular concern of those who condemned usury in an earlier age—we can discern the emergence of the rhetoric of manners and friendship that often softens the violence of usury today, and is indeed the principal disguise for an entire range of socially recognized actions that violate formal rules both religious and civic.

Such casuistry, however familiar, leads many Romans to feel that the church has too often failed to live up to its own precepts. At no time was this sentiment more strongly expressed than during the year of the Jubilee, an event that since medieval times has recuperated the imagery of Old Testament debt forgiveness and offered the church numerous opportunities to advance the salvation of its flock of sinners.[31] Romans instead saw the Jubilee as a business opportunity that the Vatican would cynically exploit to the fullest; it did not escape the notice of critical observers that the sudden proliferation of routes to forgiveness for the consequences of original sin through the sacrament of the confessional coincided with a new building boom and what struck some as a routine apology for the church's own past sins even as they were being replicated in the present.[32] In Rome, which encapsulates the capital of a vast theocratic commonwealth while also serving as that of a secular state with strong left-leaning tendencies and a bitterly anticlerical working class, a history of ecclesiastical oppression and scandal offers the clearest possible evidence that no human being is exempt from the failure to stand up to temptation.

In particular, the church's evasive and casuistic handling of both usury and the ownership of real estate, with the consequent victimization of debtors and tenants, is a lightening rod for all the resentment that centuries of cruel and rigid control have accumulated. The Jubilee year saw a massive rebuilding of much of the city's fabric and a huge expansion of property speculation in anticipation of the arrival of the pilgrims; local commentary generally saw in these developments an economically profitable collusion between the city government and the church hierarchy. The Jubilee did not seem a blessing to many; even a relatively religious shopkeeper with a royalist past called it "this damned year 2000"—damned, because many hoped to make a financial killing and most were doomed to bitter disappointment. Only the churches and the tourist agencies, he predicted, would do well. The holy Jubilee itself, in other words, was imperfect, riddled with the all-too-human flaws of an event of historical significance; at least the pious shopkeeper's bitter reaction was in this sense consistent with doctrine.

This was also a year in which rights to the city were arguably more sharply contested than ever before. In particular, the huge World Gay Pride demonstration that summer tested the limits of the much-touted virtue of tolerance and found them exceedingly narrow. Agreements with the Italian state notwithstanding, the Vatican claimed Rome as its peculiar responsibility, arguing that the procession should not take place there in the Jubilee Year.[33] The Vatican leadership tried, unsuccessfully in the end, to pressure the city authorities into banning the entire event—one of the few major issues on which Mayor Rutelli refused to yield to ecclesiastical pressure. The Vatican argued that the demonstration would be an insult to the pope as well as an exercise in bad taste; a local right-wing newspaper, *Il Tempo*, collected signatures in support of the ban.[34] In the end, however, the march went ahead, much to the highly public disgust of the church and its sympathizers. Even the threatened attempt to head it off from the approach to the Colosseum failed. While the flamboyant antics of some of those adorning the floats in sexually provocative poses, with lurid body paint and revealing costumes adorned with huge feathers, seemed designed to taunt the self-designated protectors of good taste, the orderly crowd, the strong representation of powerful political parties, and the solidarity shown by many who were not themselves gay during the parade on that long, hot July afternoon offered a strong response to the increasingly strident objections of the clergy and their right-wing supporters.

In another act that seems to suggest something other than tolerance, the Vatican had the Jewish vendors of religious paraphernalia removed from Via della Conciliazione, the road connecting the Vatican to the rest of the city. Ironically, these vendors were—perhaps in a faint echo of their money lending forebears—handling the commerce for which the church itself affected such distaste, but from which it clearly profited both materially and in the propagation of its symbols; their signature items were statuettes of the Madonna. The Vatican also enlisted the help of the Italian police in forcibly expelling the homeless people who were sleeping at night in St. Peter's Square. Here, too, the irony did not escape local critics, who were appalled that such an action should coincide with the pope's calling on Roman families to extend their hospitality to the homeless.

Not coincidentally, the most visceral issue concerning rights to the city was that of housing. Here, the connection with the Vatican was more tenuous and much less consistent. Nonetheless, evidence of at least tacit church complicity in processes of eviction and gentrification was not hard to find. Families that had resided in the historic center of Rome for many generations received only a temporary stay of eviction by various church bodies. Such delays, mostly engineered to avoid the too-obvious irony of a brutal showdown during the internationally visible Jubilee year, could not disguise the fact that in this sacred year, with all its promises of redemption and the forgiveness of debt, many would be preparing to leave their old homes forever.

Rome, the flawed city called "eternal" but so deeply steeped in the history that is, we are told, the consequence of the Fall, is by virtue of that paradox an ironic echo of Paradise on earth. The expulsion from Paradise is, among other things, an allegory of the presence of temporality in human life: aging, the pain of parting, the decay and collapse that is built into every aspect of human experience—corruption of the flesh and corruption of the soul. For a city dubbed "eternal" to host the headquarters of a religion so concerned with the transience of all things earthly requires a ceaseless reckoning with materiality; as buildings decay, so souls backslide.

Absolution is doctrinally banned to those who committed their offenses in the full expectation of obtaining a formal absolution for future derelictions and without any sense of contrition. But that is only the view from dogma. In practice, who is to know whether another is contrite? How does one judge such an invisible condition, especially in a city where people are often afraid to take each other's professions of friendship at face value? Religion has an efficient answer to this dilemma as well: that what other people think is irrelevant, since it is only at the Last Judgment that a true assessment will be recorded—and will indeed be eternal.

Such a position is crucial in a city whose lifeblood is small-scale trade. The fathers of the church taught that no financial transaction should be conducted with a view to profit; the mere desire to reap profit was sinful in itself. Repeated insurrections against the central authority by poor orders of monks and nuns, and the final revolution that led to the emergence of Protestantism, never succeeded in deflecting the enrichment of the church, which appointed itself the guardian of all the evil instruments of temptation, including wealth itself. And since one source of its wealth was the system of indulgences, it was hardly in a position to question the motives of those who sought its blessing even as they contemplated the attractions of new backslidings.

This inbuilt complicity pervades the negotiation of all relations of power in Rome. The apparent impunity of high officials of the church illuminates two of the most important dimensions of this dynamic. First, even the most elevated prelate—and, by extension, the most powerful and apparently incorruptible public servant—cannot be presumed innocent, since all human beings are subject to temptation and none are capable of resisting it absolutely. Second, repeated acquittals—significantly, defendants who are acquitted are "absolved" (assolti) in Italian—reinforce already existing power. To take a secular example, senator-for-life Giulio Andreotti, seven times prime minister during the post–World War II years, was acquitted on charges of conspiring in a political assassination.[35] One of his bitterest local critics in Monti admitted that there was simply not enough evidence, and that, because that evidence had all been provided by recanting (pentiti[36]) mafiosi, it could not stand up to the imposing distinction and imperturbable self-confidence of this national leader (a man, not coincidentally, of well-advertised religiosity). They might, said his critic, have been able to do it to "some other kind of person" (un'antra persona)—a clear indication, this, that accountability has less to do with what happened, or even with what people think happened, than with the relative social position of the players. Thus, an elderly lady of rightist views (and a former student of Fascist-era anthropology) declared that Andreotti was far too intelligent to have been mixed up in such affairs, whereas she could believe anything of the late Socialist leader Bettino Craxi. Blame and exoneration emerge from hierarchy, ideology, and the situation of the moment, not from justice in an abstractly civic sense. Romans also understand that, as a hardware store proprietor wife sagely observed, politics is "the art of the possible" (l'arte del possibile).

But this attitude may also favor accommodation—or surrender—to external powers, notably the economic forces that increasingly bear on city management. The resulting changes have an inevitable impact on the prevailing sense of temporality. In particular, the new civic order requires a form of accounting that is less embedded in social experience than in a theory of management by measurement—what one group of anthropologists has aptly called "audit culture."[37] Such a system may be no more able than others to regulate people's sincerity than is the penitential rite of confession, although its rhetoric may suggest otherwise.[38] In Rome it finds a precedent in the precise accounting whereby a penitent's time in Purgatory is reduced through indulgences and pious acts signifying contrition. But it parts company from local perceptions in rejecting the idea that human imperfection makes compromise a necessity and deferring perfection to an eternal afterlife, aiming instead to create an aridly ideal-typical society in real time.

This managerial ideology treats eternity in a very different fashion. Instead of glorying in the partly rotten and forever pulsating fabric of society and architecture, it aims to fix cultural form for all time. It arrests and dissolves the process of material corruption (and claims, speciously, to abolish political corruption as well). Above all, it routinizes the management of blame and responsibility, reducing ethics to a numerical audit and history to an aseptic chronicle of names and dates. Rome's eternity, thus managerially reformatted, is reduced to a taxonomic device that spreads classification across the ground in the form of fences and labels. By defying the corrosive passage of time, it parts company from Catholic doctrine and social experience, since it opposes to both the hubris of permanent preservation. To achieve that goal, either it must expel the present inhabitants (messy sinners that they are)[39] and replace them with fewer residents, all committed to the same calcified order.

Ironically, it is now the most rightist segment of the parliamentary political spectrum, steeped in a peculiarly Italian version of "social Fascism," that especially objects to the replacement of society (società) by a museum (museo). As a relatively moderate, locally raised councilor of the rightist Alleanza nazionale (National Alliance) party put it, "it's not right that the historic center should become a museum where only a few people can be allowed to live in the historic center." His anger was doubtless partly directed at a plan to remove Via dei Fori Imperiali, Mussolini's grandiose ceremonial road built at great architectural and human cost across the sites of the ancient forums.[40] But the social framing of his objections laid claim to a wider political constituency.

A Passion for the Past

If history is the chronicle of human mortality and the corruption of flesh and soul alike, it is also a source of shared sociability and pride. Its very sinfulness renders it a space of familiarity and indeed of intimacy. Monticiani are deeply engaged in their past; they are proud of living in perhaps the oldest extant red-light district in the world.

I came to develop a close friendship with two taxi drivers—*tassinari*, a category closely associated with modern Roman identity but now fallen into some disrepute.[41] Both were avid collectors of old books about Rome, prepared to resort to many a ruse in their pursuit of knowledge about early editions. One day they plunged into a passionate discussion of the relative merits of different editions of an old book of which one had a facsimile edition. The same man, with an indicative air of self-congratulation for his devious intelligence, sometimes boasted of how he had taken my business card and used it to get past the supercilious librarian at a certain institute that housed the only extant copy he could locate of a seventeenth-century poem about one of the infamous *bulli* (toughs) of Rome. It mattered to him to check his facsimile copy against the original printing. But it also mattered to him to score points off his friend "the professor"—me—as well as the snooty librarian. He also took great pleasure in instructing me in the literary history of Monti; he was wonderfully generous with both the information he conveyed and the ironic put-downs with which he reminded me that, in Monti at least, he knew a great deal more than I did. Although he is the son of Neapolitan migrants, his passion for history has assured him the status of a true Monticiano—he particularly delights in relating how Monti escaped the general slaughter that followed the sack of Rome in 1527—and his speech is deeply inflected with the local dialect.

Although the conventional wisdom has it that true Romans are those who have been in the city "for seven generations," there is also a widespread perception that few such people actually exist. Even those who grew up in the city's environs and speak a thick Romanesco dialect are often dismissed as mere bumpkins. As an antiques dealer pointed out, however, all residents of the city are surrounded by the inescapable accumulation of history's material remains; and this, he claimed, gave them a sense of security. He himself, a Sardinian by birth and formerly a much-traveled journalist by trade, said he felt neither Sardinian nor Italian but Roman. He had only to peek out of his shop on the nineteenth-century main street and he would see a medieval tower, a paleo-Christian basilica, the edge of the imperial forum,

Fig. 3. The Colosseum from Via dei Serpenti. (Photo by Michael Herzfeld.)

solid bourgeois palazzi from the period immediately following Unification, and, rising high in the background, the Capitol and, beyond it, the antiquarian chariot atop the nineteenth-century Vittorio Emmanuele monument past which runs Mussolini's ceremonial passage through the forums to the Colosseum.

The past is inescapable in Rome, and nowhere more so than in Monti; it is hard to ignore the Colosseum. A woman who with her husband ran a restaurant nearly opposite our house told me that the ghost of Messalina, the emperor Claudius's flamboyantly promiscuous and politically disloyal wife whose execution he eventually ordered, occasionally roamed the street. Curious passers-by were more interested in learning from this would-be clairvoyant whether it was true that the famous filmmaker Mario Monicelli still dined at their restaurant; indeed he did, she responded—such famous public intellectuals, who occasionally participate in civic affairs, can have no privacy since they, too, have become part of the collective heritage. Monicelli once attended a news conference organized by some local activists in a wine bar to generate more active involvement in the district's future, and although he said very little his presence, along with that of a locally well-known journalist and writer, generated much excitement and optimism. When Romano Prodi moved into his Monti apartment, the residence staff showed it off to passing tourists, even though the great man was rarely actually there and used the apartment as a *pied-à-terre* for those brief occasions when Prodi had to return to his own country and its capital. The fascination of association was apparently enough to draw a thin but persistent stream of curious tourists. ("Poor Prodi!" remarked a British anthropologist who lived nearby at the time.)

Such associations perpetuate the presence of even the more actively famous scions of Monti; the physicist Enrico Fermi's old laboratory is often pointed out as a site of special interest.[42] A protracted tussle between the Ministry of the Interior, which wanted to use the building to store old files and claimed to have nowhere else to put them, and a local group of academics who wanted to see the local hero honored nicely illustrates the very different priorities of state bureaucrats and local activists. For the locals, modernity may be more immediately appealing than the ghosts of the ancient past. A restaurateur even tried to persuade me to buy real estate, claiming (erroneously) that prices had recently halved in a short while and arguing that the arrival of a good class of residents would help to preserve the local "culture" as represented by Fermi's laboratory.

This fascination with notable personalities somewhat belies the impatience so often expressed with the rich and famous. The Bosio coffee shop and bar boasts of having been the favorite spot for Fermi and his associates, and hands out little slips with a Romanesco poem celebrating the fact that Pope John Paul II, when he was still a seminarian at the nearby Angelicum, used to come by for his regular cup of coffee here: "Stop by to enjoy a cup and a smile / and, if even the Pope goes to taste it, / perhaps it will be the coffee of Paradise!"

But the ancient past does have resonance for locals. The street where we lived ended at the forum, at the massive stone wall Augustus built to contain the fires but also the disreputable people of the Subura. Monti, like the rest of central Rome, is profoundly and at times perplexingly stratigraphic.[43] Beneath our feet lay streets created in the ancient past, and paved over with self-consciously traditional diamond-shaped cobblestones (*sampietrini*, the stones of St. Peter) that cause taxis to rattle and bounce just like the hansom cabs of two centuries earlier.[44] A local architect asserted that the older houses on what may be the oldest continuously inhabited street in the world, Via Madonna dei Monti, reproduced the structure of the ancient *insulae*; while it seems improbable that specific buildings had reproduced the ancient model over several demolitions and fresh constructions, the general principle may be affirmed by the persistence of internal courtyards, external balconies, and workspaces giving onto the street.[45]

But the district is rich in the echoes of other eras as well. We lived in an apartment in a solid eighteenth-century *palazzo* acquired by our pious and kindly landlord's grandfather, an engineer of Florentine origin who worked in the Vatican state apparatus, in 1890, two decades after the final incorporation of the city into the national territory. Diagonally opposite crouched a more modest home, perhaps four centuries older. Here a printer preserved an older press that his son was now rendering completely obsolete by switching to computer-based technology, which left him shaking his head in bemused but affectionate wonder; the father deliberately gloried in his Romanesco speech, peppering it with phrases that underscored his attachment to the dialect, while the son's diction, still slightly inflected with a Roman accent, nevertheless more easily adapted to the national standard language whenever he had to deal with outsiders.

Much as some dialect usage is self-consciously antiquarian,[46] attention to objects once discarded as useless has become commonplace. Around the corner from the print shop, a bar still sported the old 1940s-style wooden refrigerator of a previous owner, while in a barber's shop further away a shelf of old cameras still reminds us that tourists and anthropologists are not the only recorders of visual reality, and in the nearby Bosio bar an old coffee-grinding machine, bulky and squat and almost at shoulder height, and fully visible to all comers (which sanitary law forbids for the current equipment), anchors the store in local history at least as solidly as the rather self-conscious framed dialect poems that line the walls. Yet another store, a pharmacy, simply displays its date of foundation (1740); the previous owner, who still visited from time to time, was happy to give me a coffee-table book on the historic shops of Rome, his pharmacy prominent among them.[47]

Along the street from our house stood the sixteenth-century church and neighboring hostel used to house newly converted Jews dragged from the Ghetto but isolated here so they would not contaminate their fully Christian neighbors; the side-street was triumphantly named Street of the Newly Converted (*Via dei Neofiti*), a name it still bears. Beyond it lay an old printing house, once responsible for producing the paper money of the Bank of Italy but subsequently ruined by scandal. Beyond that imposing structure lies the incongruously Fascist war memorial and the baroque parish church, while, on the opposite sidewalk, a flower vendor plies her trade from a stone slab thought to have been in place for at least the past thousand years.

Huge green garbage dumpsters, often overflowing with decaying refuse, block the main street as one turns down toward the Colosseum; a little higher up, in another side street, a stone inscription (one of many to be found throughout the city), dated 1749, threatens fines and other, unspecified punishments for anyone who defied the authority of the "Monsignor President of the Streets" by leaving any kind of refuse there. The problem has not gone away; at one point an irritated resident put up a handwritten sign nearby begging people not to block the doorway: "YOU ARE REQUESTED TO THROW GARBAGE IN THE DUMPSTERS, NOT BENEATH OTHER PEOPLE'S WINDOWS!!" It was soon torn down, and garbage soon began to reappear.

Monti, it is clear, is embedded in a remarkable *longue durée*. I hesitate to call it "history." It is too palpably present, immediate, an inhabited reality; and, at the same time, it has an aura of the fabulous because local residents can rarely resist dramatizing its intensity or its duration. I often found myself seduced into the same rhetorical enthusiasm, and still delight in remarking that "our" street had been in more or less continuous use for two millennia.

Residents' historical awareness, profoundly felt though it appears to be, cannot be divorced from the more obviously operatic productions of historicity. Lower Monti ends at the Colosseum, where until recently red-plumed centurions with blunt modern swords wheedled visitors into having them pose for expensive photographs. For years these centurions were tolerated by the authorities despite a law that forbade virtually all commercial activity on archaeological sites; in a fine demonstration of the Roman capacity for compromise, they were allowed to continue on account of their "antiquity of service" (*antichità di servizio*). In the spring of 2005, however, it turned out that the current incumbents were actually a band of local toughs, operating under the command of a minor boss of the Roman underworld who had recently emerged from prison and was now directing operations; under his command, the interlopers had chased away their rivals with serious threats of violence and were now extracting a plentiful harvest from some of the more impressionable tourists.[48]

Tourists with a more independent imagination might have chosen to do without their often rather clumsy ministrations in any case; not far away, for example, visitors can see the unreconstructed, ruined foundations of the original gladiators' training school. The only plastic there is the rubbish thrown away by careless passers-by as they head out of the ice cream shops and pizza parlors. But the false centurions have also been part of Rome's modern scene, along with the graffiti that deface the walls; like the graffiti,

they spoke a heavy Roman dialect, appropriately enough for these henchmen
of a latter-day minor local potentate.

Other moments evoke a more national sense of the past. I can recall
an occasion, right next to the Colosseum, when the brass orchestra of the
carabinieri struck up the tune of "*Va pensiero*," Verdi's famous chorus of
the Jewish slaves exiled in Babylon, which became the unofficial second
anthem of the Risorgimento state and was recently also claimed by the
northerners aiming to establish their own state independently of Rome.[49]
Listening to the swelling brass chords I found myself reacting with powerful
emotion, despite an official presence for which I did not greatly care and an
ideology that has been expropriated by unpleasant forces of reaction. But
such is the operatic stage: you suspend your most cherished sense of how
the world should work, and another reality supervenes for just long enough
to afford a glimpse of the strange alchemy whereby what many locals regard
as an unworkable state and an unmanageable city have maintained their air
of infrangible glory and cohesion.

The sense of permanence that such performances produce is itself temporary, if infinitely repeatable. But the fragmentation is equally unmistakable. At one level it has been recognized as the persistence of "micro-
quarters" by local sociologists charged with returning the rapidly modern-
izing city to a scale of human interaction that would reclaim social space
for ordinary activities. At another, the same expression (*micro-quartieri*)
has, like *cultura*, become an everyday descriptive term in itself; Romans
may be steeped in history, but they are also tireless sociologists. Sociologi-
cal research, some of it commissioned by the city authorities, has focused
heavily on the internal differentiation of small segments of the various administrative districts; the sociologist Lorenzo Bellicini gave the concept of
the micro-quarter a more precise and academic definition, but its appeal lies
largely in the fact that it does in fact correspond closely to the perceptions
and experiences of local residents.[50] An electrician friend, after reeling off
a list of streets, each with its defining features, explained that just as each
segment of Monti had its own character, loan sharks also patrolled specific
small localities of the city in ways that reflected the economic and social
peculiarities of each.

Of particular interest in his account is his inclusion of Celio, an area
that was split off from the Rione Monti by papal decree in the 1921, half
a century after a similar act had severed Esquilino from the district (1874).
The earlier reduction is still resented; but this, in the relativistic logic of
localism, does not stop those who have been forced by eviction to live on
the Esquilino side of the new border from resenting the tragedy of their

exile. These administrative acts of reorganization could never entirely eradicate the locals' collective sense of belonging to both the largest and the most important district of Rome as well as to the only one never to have been completely depopulated in the course of foreign invasions—this last, a source of historical pride that rings hollow today in the face of the rapid demographic decline and disappearance of the older families of the district.

CHAPTER FOUR

Refractions of Social Life

Across from the imposing building of the Bank of Italy, and tucked away behind the main road, a small side street contains tiny apartments barely able to accommodate the prostitutes and their furtive customers. Above it runs Via Panisperna, a street made famous by the former laboratory of the physicist Enrico Fermi and his associates. Their laboratory is a modest unit in a complex of notably old houses. Indeed, the houses on this street are all several centuries old; some are beginning to show all too evident signs of imminent collapse. At right angles to Via Panisperna run two parallel roads, both connecting Monti to the busy Via Nazionale above; one is a busy thoroughfare that filters traffic into the nineteenth-century Via Cavour and the ring road around the Colosseum, which is framed by an imposing block of Renaissance ramparts culminating in the church of San Pietro in Vincoli, famous above all for housing Michelangelo's *Moses*. The other street, Via del Boschetto, is a more modest thoroughfare, named for a long-vanished wood but now fronted with small shops and prey to asphyxiating traffic that seems to burst its narrow confines asunder. At many points molded or painted medallions of the Madonna bespeak a popular devotion of many centuries' standing, uniting the disparate segments of this socially and architecturally fragmented district in a shared iconography.

If virtue is represented by the portraits of the Madonna at many street corners, vice, its necessary antithesis in Catholic doctrine and practice, is thus similarly refracted through the same complex built environment. Portraits of the Madonna cluster far more thickly in places of ill repute—and nowhere more than in Monti and the other Roman district with which it is still locked in a tradition of deep and irrevocable rivalry, Trastevere.[1] Vice has its own geography, no less than virtue; to this day, for example, different parts of Rome are known for different styles of prostitution, which today are also marked by ethnicity.[2] As with prostitution, so too with usury, its modalities refracted through the latticework of micro-quarters. Money lending at interest was a problem in ancient times, and it remains so to this day; as one exasperated merchant put it, it is "like 'the world's oldest profession'"—and indeed prostitution and usury are often interlinked.

Segmentation and Subsidiarity

This localization of virtue and vice encapsulates a principle of social organization that, perhaps not coincidentally, harmonizes surprisingly well with the administrative doctrine of the Vatican. It does so in two ways. First, there is the pragmatic recognition that social life will always encompass both good and evil, and that it is often far less productive to combat corruption than to engage with it—and that it will always leave a residue: as the proverb has it, "The baker is always dirty with flour." In this regard, clerics are no better than anyone else; their very humanity is defined by weaknesses they share with others, and another Roman saying has a priest admonishing his flock, "Do what I say, not what I do." The Vatican expects its priests to wrestle with their consciences and recognizes that some must inevitably fall prey to the allure of temptation. Within this understanding, a pragmatic reading of the doctrine of original sin, there is plenty of room for creative interpretation and calculated mischief.

The second area of convergence is structural. This is the system of levels of identity whereby each district fractures into smaller units, either because hostilities break up the surface unity or because responsibilities must be delegated so that the community as a whole need not collectively bear the brunt of all its denizens' sins. The moral economy thus follows existing principles of social relationship. The proliferation of shrines in such areas as Monti can perhaps be explained in terms of the district's relative autonomy from ecclesiastical supervision, both through its resistance to papal command in the sixteenth century and through its perpetuation of its self-image as a lowlife backwater. Wickedness, no less than good, can be refracted through such earthly distinctions—especially in Rome, where the fusion of cardinal virtues with what we might describe as cardinals' vices is a recurrent refrain.

Micro-quarter organization and ground-level social relations thus reframe and subvert the ideals of a unified as well as an eternal city. An artisan who has been particularly active in local civic affairs remarked that the ideal of civic life should be "a healthy sociability" (una socialità sana), a social world in which he could casually encounter precisely those people, the "bad" (*cattivi*) in particular, with whom he otherwise preferred to avoid more intimate contact. Intellectuals similarly recognize the importance of not avoiding the conflict-laden quality (*conflittualità*) of many social interactions—even, perhaps, of building upon it.[3] Conflict becomes a cultural "property" in its own right, an intimate facet, as the Italian anthropologist Berardino Palumbo has sagely noted, of the local community as it challenges the rigid uniformity urged by official state and municipal discourses.[4] Viewed as a sign of backwardness by outsiders, and sometimes used by officials as an excuse for denying local interests a serious hearing, this roiling fractiousness actually signals a lively degree of local self-appreciation, indeed of cultural intimacy, in the face of massive and often externally imposed regulation and change.

Thus, Enzo Scandurra, an urban planner at the Monti-based department of urban planning at the University of Rome–I ("La Sapienza") who is deeply engaged in resisting the official cooptation of cultural diversity and especially of citizen participation,[5] reminds us that residents' needs include "fraternal love, the desire for relationships, but also envy, jealousy."[6] Such ethically generous stances are not only stereotypically Roman acts of accommodation; they also, and concomitantly, acknowledge social realities and resist as inhumane the bureaucratic tendency to reduce all social experience to a legalistic and conformist separation of good from evil.

The destructive presence of envy has long been taken as especially characteristic of southern Italian society, at once a consequence and a product of an endemic inability to cooperate for the collective good. This cultural determinism has had a long history in Italy; instantiated by the charge of "amoral familism" leveled by Edward Banfield and historicized and modulated by Robert Putnam, it has also become something of an article of faith among Italian scholars, although a younger generation has begun to question it.[7] Putnam's treatment represents a significant departure from earlier work; rightly acknowledging the panoply of cultural factors and historical forces entailed in the emergence of civic transparency and engagement, he nonetheless incorporates, not the judgmentalism of Banfield's approach, but certainly the assumption that a lack of associational life signifies the absence more generally of all forms of cooperation among families and other groups. The somewhat schematic north-south divide that emerges from his work is also partly a result of its dependence on surveys, in which respondents evidently share the researcher's prior assumptions and embed them in "officializing" answers, reflecting positions sometimes shared by foreign scholars and local intellectuals alike.[8]

No anthropologist could reasonably take exception to Putnam's assertion that the moral values of local communities account for differences in
the implementation of state-initiated practices of local governance. Indeed,
I would go further; local *practices* also reuse, as in bricolage, the *values*
of the state; the way in which, for example, Cretan mountain-dwelling
shepherds recast the institutions of democratic elections in terms of clan
loyalties, linking the latter to a network of powerful politicians at the local level, dramatically illustrates this type of reuse.[9] Such adaptations take
place over long periods of time, necessitating, as Putnam rightly observes,
careful attention to historical precedent and process. I would therefore recast his insistence on the importance of history, making a larger space for
agency than he does; older practices are "sedimented" in practices and even
in bodies,[10] but people use them selectively to frame interpretation and
determine political futures.

Where we especially differ, however, is over what I read as Putnam's Weberian assumption that the efficient deployment of democratic institutions
for the greatest overall benefit of the citizenry—a civic ethos that Putnam
traces back to Tocqueville and others—constitutes the definitive telos of
modernity. Here we are back, albeit in a much more sophisticated variant,
to the kind of evolutionist thinking represented by Banfield's evocation of a
"backward" society. This is the language that James Ferguson has criticized
in his account of "development," but that also appears in Norbert Elias's
notion of a "civilizing process"—and, as we shall see, it often conflates the
civic with the civil, with disastrous consequences for our understanding of
political *practice* in relation to prevalent but changing forms of ethos.[11] The
attempt to identify a single, persistent ethos rather than a shifting congeries
of practices is one for which anthropologists must unfortunately also bear
their share of responsibility; it results in a deterministic reasoning that pre-
cludes the possibility of alternative modernities and adjusts the very notion
of modernity to an orientalizing discourse: "southern" is reconfigured as
"backward," "rural," and, indeed, "oriental" or "African"—a perspective
that conflates an impressive range of Eurocentric prejudices and solidifies
as science an attitude that already has considerable respectability in everyday discourse in Italy.[12] Many Italian critics would gladly accept Putnam's
formulation that the north of the country follows the rulebook where the
south pays more attention to the pocketbook.[13] But to equate civic management with the rulebook entails the questionable proposition that those
who are governed more by the pocketbook are less interested in social rules;
although Putnam denies that this is a legitimate extension of his argument,

it certainly appears to be a commonplace assumption in Italian public discourse.

Moreover, Putnam does appear to endorse Banfield's contention that the defense of familial interests in southern communities is at once "amoral" and "backward." Ethnographic research in the south reveals instead both an intense concern with morality and an emphasis on the value of civility as its performative face (as well as more ramified civic institutions and attitudes than Putnam acknowledges). Romans, as we shall see, express a great deal of skepticism about the efficacy and relevance of formal civic models to the moral conduct of everyday life, but their skepticism is still grounded in a desire for good governance.

The Civic and the Civil

It is vital to build some critical and analytical distance from evolutionist models that are clearly embedded in the logic of colonial and capitalist expansion. The fact that many Italians endorse such models is mainly interesting inasmuch as it shows that social-science discourse is not hermetically sealed off from its objects of analysis. Assumptions about the superior qualities of one intrusive kind of civic ethos should be resisted; the tension between ideals of the civic and the civil, respectively, is masked by the kind of semantic slippage that comes from an excessive sense of familiarity, not unlike what happens when we are careless in translating etymologically linked, cognate terms between Italian and English.[14] By "civic engagement" I intend a willingness to engage in a variety of political modalities of active and general participation, no matter whether these are acrimonious or polite or whether they follow imported or domestic prototypes. Civility, on the other hand, can on occasion be little more than the courteous style that oils distasteful inequities. Scandurra's call to recognize envy as a part of lived social life is also a considered response to the bland social antisepsis of a new managerial style of local government, exemplified by former mayor Francesco Rutelli, in which, for example, the civic bureaucracy tries to organize "neighborliness festivals" as a way of investing petty conflict with the taint of inefficiency and bad faith. ("Competition," needless to say, is another matter entirely.)

As Franco Lai has pointed out, moreover, the kind of cultural determinism that rejects conflict as dysfunctional reflects as much the assumptions of anthropologists and others as it does the actions of particular local people who find it convenient to blame the envy of others for their own failures.[15]

These local people, too, are engaged in a war of stereotypes, which they use to strategic and sometimes violent effect,[16] and this influences their decisions and actions. Social actors are often well aware of the political value of being able to deploy stereotypes of themselves by way of explaining away perceived weaknesses or claiming particular strengths. In this sense stereotypes, like invocations of "culture," are interesting for what they tell us about the relationship between daily social life and the intellectual imagination.

The actual practice of the law and its various realizations—taxation, regulation of zoning and traffic, and so on—both borrows from ordinary social life and infuses it with its own rhetoric. Ecclesiastical casuistry about when lending money at interest was reasonable or when the forcible baptism of Jewish children was a virtuous act provided a convenient template for the secular management of legal principles.[17] The very rigidity of the law provides a shield for those who know how to manipulate its language; the knowledge that it contains intentional ambiguities—it, too, is the product of mortal minds—allows social actors to assume its flexibility in advance, at least up to a point. This widely shared knowledge, which allows every citizen to calculate the probable costs of various infractions, is the key to practical survival; its illegal dimensions borrow the rhetoric of law, while the operators of law in turn depend heavily on a real-life flexibility that is nowhere to be found in its surface discourses. Civic rules and the civility of social practices are deeply and reciprocally entwined.

The distinction I am making between the civic and the civil is thus an analytic one. It is not a description of two separate spheres of social action, and it is not helpfully reduced to the antinomies of new and old or foreign and local. The distinction is like that between official and folk religion, a misleading discrimination that serves only the church's hegemonic interests; ecclesiastical attempts to purify ritual practice of its vernacular elements are above all demonstrations of power that overlook the shared origins of both idioms.[18] Original sin, similarly, belongs as much to popular attitudes as to formal doctrine and makes nonsense of any rigid distinction between them except in a rhetorical sense. In the same way, too, the legal principles of civic management and the social practices of civility are mutually entailed. For example, legislators and police officers may benefit from the legislation against corruption—legislation created, moreover, by fallible human beings who live among the populace at large—because a compliant populace may be willing to offer them small inducements so that they will keep quiet about more egregious offenses. Sometimes such trade-offs are embedded in formal legislative and administrative practices, as when the comprehensive payment of a percentage of all fines owed brings a citizen absolution from the remainder.[19] Other arrangements, technically illegal, are classified as corrupt. But corruption is by definition a form of reciprocity; it is not about officials alone, but a mark of the shared condition of original sin—of what it means to inhabit the social world. Ironically, therefore, refusing its temptations is rarely a viable option for officials who care about getting their jobs done, a point that moralistic complaints about supposedly southern familism and venality fail to address.

Rome is an ideal location for studying these issues. Its citizens' conviction (or convenient article of faith) that theirs is a "southern" culture, the long history of northern aristocrats' as well as the Vatican's involvement in the management of the city's administration and social life, and Romans' ambivalence toward their role as the citizens of a national capital together produce a "mixed" culture with its own cultural specificities. Romans would certainly agree with Putnam's emphasis on historical explanation, as when they discuss their stereotypically "un-southern" avoidance of conflict in terms of the need to adapt to a harsh and pervasive papal regime that controlled every aspect of civic life; but that explanation then becomes a back door through which complaisance with underworld activity, bribery, and extortion enter as readily as do micro-political alliances, civility of social interaction, and practical expropriation of the structures of church administration.

In that Monticiani like to imagine their neighborhood as a village (paese), they create a specific version of southernness based on preformed images of peasant sociality. In this they reproduce with arresting accuracy what Maria Minicuci has observed for Italian anthropologists, who, she says, "presume [a fixed image of] the south and within it study the world of the peasantry," confirming the continuity of perception between intellectuals and others that anthropologists today ignore at their peril.[20] In short, these Romans see themselves as part of a cultural world whose values they feel they know and understand; but within that world, they also try to identify what makes them different from other southerners. Not only does the pattern that emerges confirm Minicuci's emphasis on the internal variety of social forms in any supposedly southern society,[21] but it underscores the importance of Scandurra's insight that embracing conflict, without essentializing it as "southern" or "inefficient," poses a serious conceptual challenge to dominant idioms of governance by stereotype.

Romans largely reject the ideal-typical models of civic virtue espoused by writers like Putnam. Yet they do not do so because of some persistent strain of "southern" venality, although they may claim it as an excuse; and this is a key point. It is true, as we see in the vivid portrait that Palumbo has painted of a Sicilian community,[22] that claims of a southern identity can serve to justify actions that, while they are of practical benefit to the entire community, are explicitly recognized as illegal—and, indeed, rest on the assumption that following the law simply cannot work in such a society. In this vision of southern culture, the pragmatism of everyday life rejects formal legality as a surrender to bureaucrats' delaying tactics and intransigence. In an imperfect world, so the reasoning goes, both humanity's fallen condition and its warm familiarity are amplified in the tactical skills that are the enabling condition of secular life.

While many Romans do resort to such schematic self-justification over particular actions, however, they do not categorically reject the hypothetical model of a civic life based on good management and fair play. Rome was long the site of a particularly strong tradition of rotating credit associations, the institution that Putnam especially invokes to exemplify the concept of "social capital" that, as he argues, is an absolute prerequisite for effective civic life.[23] On the other hand, Romans do not assume that such perfection is attainable; in this, their logic retains at least a hint of its theological underlay. They opt instead for compromise that reflects and embraces the reality of envy and other consequences of human imperfection. After working on Greek social relations for so long, I was often struck by the relative ease with which most Romans appeared to avoid discord, and a Spanish woman told the daughter of one of our neighbors that she was astonished to see Romans who had staged a big fight then go off to dinner together in apparent amity. Rather than complain to the point of being disagreeable (although they actually do a great deal of complaining), Romans take the long view. When one asks a Roman how things are going, the response is often a shrugged *nun ce lamentamo* (we're not complaining) or, more formally and positively, *ci accontentiamo* (we're reasonably content); and once a man I had asked how things were going replied, "*Mi adatto*" (I adapt).

Indeed, being content is relative to ineluctable realities. Many Romans are inveterate skeptics, refusing to believe—or at least refusing to admit that they believe—in the possibility of honest, decent administration. By the same token, however, they also readily accept that this refusal is itself strategically useful inasmuch as they often need a justification for the illegality of their own actions. Thus, for example, a man whose job was to supervise workers' safety and compensation reported that the city authorities were guilty of using undocumented immigrant labor—Romanians working for illegally low wages (50,000 *lire* for fifty hours of work) and without the safety protections that are required by law—as a shortcut to completing all the numerous building projects timed for the Jubilee celebrations. When government breaks the law like this, he demanded, what can one expect of private operators?

His exasperation shows that civic honesty remains more of an ideal than an experienced reality. People may even be genuinely convinced that it is unattainable. But it is useful, at the very least, as a stick with which to belabor an authority that clearly, and often, fails to meet such an exacting standard. A disgruntled former shop proprietor went to the garbage collection authority to find out why there were no bins at one location where he had gone with his disposables when he could find none next to his own house. This good citizen was seriously told in response that the bins had been removed to make way for a political demonstration. Apparently, demonstrations being a regular feature of Roman life, it was too much trouble (*fatica*) to keep replacing the bins! On another occasion, the city police said they "could not confiscate the big umbrellas"—used to shade an illegal extension of a restaurant into the public space of the roadside—"because we have nowhere to put them!" With that kind of official response, conditioned as it probably is by the expectation of substantial bribes for delaying action, offenders not only feel able to commit offenses but, in doing so, make their immunity to legal pursuit ostentatiously evident: it is, remarked an infuriated leftist councilor, "a display of arrogance ... like a dog marking a tree with its piss," and one that has its own instrumental logic in warning away anyone audacious enough to conceive of challenging their actions. Under these conditions, Roman cynicism about the possibility of a clean and industrious bureaucracy can only flourish.

The sudden burst of anti-corruption activity at the national level during the 1990s produced both idealistic enthusiasm and, especially as the justice system proved unable to overcome all of its own endemic corruption, cynicism about the motives of those who rode to political prominence on platforms of honesty and good government. One local supporter of the disgraced Socialist Party went so far as to argue that the system of bribes and favors (*Tangentopoli*, Kickback City) that had engulfed his party had actually been a means of creating new economic opportunities and employment, especially as it encouraged government officials to connive at the unregistered subcontracting of small companies. This argument, while it resonated with local attitudes and practices (and specifically with the experience of the goldsmiths, who did very nicely because they were paid with ill-gotten cash for making gold ornaments for politicians' and officials' lovers), did not resonate well with the vast majority of citizens who felt themselves marginalized by all the wheeling and dealing in high places. It may have reinforced the growing cynicism that soon overwhelmed the idealism of the anti-corruption drive, souring the brief burst of enthusiasm for a new ethical universe as much at the local as at the national level.[24]

In Monti, however, local intellectuals and community leaders are now seeking a more optimistic and proactive adaptation of this same realism. Instead of resigning themselves to strategies of compromise and collusion, they try to probe beneath and beyond the superficial assumption that elegant manners and rhetorically smooth performances are the essence of social harmony. They embrace the rough edges of human life as a necessary prelude to civic action, encouraging the expression of dissent and carrying the energies thus generated into blunt but sometimes productive engagements with elected politicians and municipal functionaries. Their rejection of a superficial notion of civility—the assumption that the absence of conflict is the most desirable end of government—gives the lie to the idea that their lives are all beautiful surfaces without depth.[25] Above all, their insistence on the importance of incorporating legitimate conflict and embracing the occasional rudeness of fellow citizens is clearly conceived in direct opposition both to the managerial rationalism of audit-culture civics and the repressive courtesies and elegant menace conventionally associated with "southern clientelism."[26] In both cases, they elevate a rough pragmatism above a comedy of manners—in the first case a traditionalizing one, in the second a new managerial style.

These local thinkers reject older models of the civilized life in which there was no place for the wild-eyed prophet of gloom or the irritating social misfit; they also reject the arbitrary authority of administrators. At one point an archaeologist with the Fine Arts Inspectorate saw someone who appeared to be a third world immigrant using the top of a Renaissance stairway as a toilet. Instead of calling the police or one of the social service providers, such as the Catholic relief agency, Caritas, she appealed to the director of her service, and together they blocked the passageway—the most direct route from Via Cavour to the Church of San Pietro in Vincoli. Local residents and shopkeepers were furious. Instead of accepting the inconvenience, as they might previously have done, they organized a petition and collected signatures. One of the organizers, an antiquities dealer, remarked, "It's an example of a civic intervention (*un intervento civico*)"—something, he added, that was extremely rare in the area, but apparently a harbinger of attitudinal changes in the making.

Association Life

We cannot understand the new forms of civic consciousness without taking the established conceptual templates into account, although it is equally important not to see in them a rigid determination of all future action. The forms of conflict and alliance among the micro-quarters that compose each district also surface in the history of the many associations that, over time, have sought to address local problems—but the fact that such initiatives have existed at all, and that they also probably derive some inspiration from the rotating credit associations operated by artisanal guilds, belies any stereotypical representation of this population as "traditionally" incapable of civic solidarity.

In fact, in addition to the various religious confraternities there have long been numerous associations of various kinds in Monti. Of these, the so-called mutual aid societies (*società di mutuo soccorso*), or rotating credit associations, were the most numerous and have the longest history. In the twentieth century, and especially since World War II, there have been sporting clubs (notably for fans of the Roma soccer team), artisans' associations and street associations, and one social club on the main square where (mostly) men gathered to play cards, argue about sports and politics, and organize festive events such as the annual October feast (*ottobrata monticiana*, an evening of music, dancing, and feasting in the square). This association, which claimed to be so apolitical as to have refused offers of contributions in the form of fruit and other goods for the annual feast from ambitious politicians, was nevertheless rumored to be a nest of Fascists; its members were, to be sure, many (but not all) of rightist political persuasion and especially anti-immigrant sentiment, and it seems to have been they who most actively tried to end the gatherings of Ukrainians and other immigrants who gathered twice a week, on Thursdays and Sundays, before the Ukrainian church on the opposite side of the square.

If the Association did have rightist support, it was of little practical value; soon after a rightist alliance took control of the regional administration of Lazio (which includes Rome) in 2000, it sanctioned the eviction of the club from its centrally located premises. The struggle dragged on for a considerable time; the lawyer for the private citizen who had now bought the building (and perhaps expected to sell at a huge profit) said that he thought the club was a place for "four little old ladies who just play cards" (*quattro vecchiette che giocano a carte solamente*).[27] The lawyer for the club explained that, to the contrary, the club had been a major source of social activity for the district for two decades, organizing sporting events and an annual October festival. His plea was nevertheless ignored; and, eventually fearing that his father, the president of the club, would not only offend powerful operators in the city and regional governments, but would also have had to pay the expenses of a trial if they lost, he retreated and the club leaders found alternative and less visible premises. The club was not in a strong position to argue; the city authorities had not asked it for rent for many years, and, although one suggestion was that it should now pay the arrears in order to gain the right to stay in place, that was clearly beyond its means.

The soccer clubs represent something of the factional dualism that, in Monti as virtually everywhere in Italy, has inflected social relations and political rhetoric ever since the end of World War II. The Lazio team was traditionally more right-wing, perhaps because its base was in the rural hinterland; but in recent years the fan groups of both clubs have been taken over by extremists with anti-Semitic slogans, Fascist salutes, and a taste for violence. Monti fans of both teams regard such developments with great distaste. An optician who became a Lazio supporter, he said, out of pure happenstance—as a boy he had gone with an itinerant peddler on his rounds and had simply acquired his soccer allegiance by osmosis from this man— admitted that it was not a matter of passion (he was much more devoted to opera); but he also said that fandom, once set, could not be changed—he joked that it would be easier to change one's wife! He expressed great distress about the emergence of the ultra-Right in the club, saying that it was "as if something ugly had happened in the family." Until the very early 1960s, after a match between the two teams, the local supporters of the victorious team would parade down Via Baccina bearing a coffin marked as containing the corpse of the other side. The Roma club has the more visible presence, perhaps because of the more left-wing traditions of the district, and its premises on Via Baccina remain a place for men to go and play cards and organize fan support for the team when it travels abroad. When the Roma team won the Italian national championship, the entire city erupted in wild demonstrations of joy, and for hours Monti was full of honking cars and streaming club banners and scarves.[28]

Soccer unleashes enormous passions. But it also provides a relatively harmless space for political bantering. An old clothes vendor, commenting on Mayor Rutelli's known support for the Lazio team, growled that the electorate would turn him into the mayor of Frosinone instead![29] Once I was speaking with a belligerently left-wing and pro-immigrant friend, a bar proprietor, when a right-wing restaurateur entered. The bar proprietor announced provocatively that the other man was the shame of the *quartiere* because was a supporter of the Lazio team.[30] Not to be outdone, the other man responded that Roma was the team of the lowest social class—doubtless an allusion to Monti's "popular" status, and amusing in part because this man is decidedly local and speaks predominantly in Romanesco. The bar proprietor then made a rude gesture at what he thought was the restaurateur's car, only to discover that someone else was driving it! The restaurateur ignored this gaffe, simply responding—in what is an interesting attempt to claim a special form of marginality—that the Lazio supporters were "few but fine." The exchange remained light and cordial throughout. Roma enthusiasts admitted that they were pleased that the Lazio team—rather than a team from some other part of the country—had won the national tournament in 2000, but would have preferred to carry it off for themselves in that Jubilee year.

The practical problems of the district require other idioms of interaction and organization. The street associations were often created to address particular issues. The Via Baccina group, for example, which ended by coalescing with an artisans' group of much wider geographical range and eventually was absorbed by the Monti Social Network, began as an initiative by concerned citizens to revive the languishing district market, down around from thirty or more active stalls in its heyday to a mere three or four now. An attempt to get artisans to join the food sellers in these spaces attracted some generic interest but produced no new leases. The market remains largely deserted.

On the other hand, the group spent an inordinate amount of time bickering about its name, much to the irritation of some of the more practical members. One vocal member alienated the younger artisans because of his right-wing background and his pompous delivery; two other members, a goldsmith and a bookseller, protested that when others claimed that the association would be "apolitical" they were already making a political choice—a fine point, perhaps, but one they were prepared to argue down to the last moment against those who wishes the association's constitution to include that very claim. As the bookseller pointed out, there is a world of difference between being non-party-political (*apartitico*), which the association could reasonably claim to be, and truly apolitical (*apolitico*). This group was especially complex in that it brought together a remarkably diverse group of people: intellectuals, merchants, artisans, artists, and retired bureaucrats. Yet in the end it was probably its riotous complexity that enabled it to play a formative and transitional role in the emergence of the most successful district-wide initiative to date, the Monti Social Network.

There were many other such small associations, each covering little more than a single street. One of these, in a little side street off Via Cavour that was connected with another road leading down to the Colosseum, had a fairly typical history. A former journalist, who had been asked to lead the group, described its goal as "defending the identity of Via del Cardello, to defend it against illegal parking." Parking was indeed a major concern, not so much because the presence of so many cars undermined the antiquarian feel of the little subdistrict, but because the city police were constantly fining the local shopkeepers rather than those outsiders who dared to park here. The ex-journalist, who perhaps did not realize that his newly acquired sphere of influence had been under the protection of a local underworld boss, soon discovered that he lacked the necessary political acumen to manage such a motley crew. One local resident, a surveyor, wanted to close the road off altogether, which provoked a mixture of hilarity and anger from the other members; another resident, an architect, wanted to place plaques with historical information on virtually every building, which struck many as an exercise in megalomania. Bureaucratic procedures (such as finding a willing notary to approve the association's documentation and deal with the city authorities) proved too onerous for this fragile group, the members of which also showed no inclination to pay the dues on which they had previously agreed. "The association died at the moment of its birth" (*l'associazione è morta sulla nascita*), observed its reluctant president, noting that the jealousy (*gelosia*) that motivated such associational antics, much like the multiplicity of post-war national governments, could only lead to anarchy. Most local associations have collapsed amid such disagreements.

Their instability reproduces the pattern of national politics. At both levels, instrumental and provisional alliances overcome commonality of principle and long-term planning. "Defending one's own doorway" (*difendere il proprio portone*) leads local social actors to accept provisional alliances for the pursuit of immediate goals, but ultimately, also in the same way, creates the conditions for fission and disarray as well. People of broadly similar political outlook often make common cause and together seek legal intervention against a specific source of trouble such as noise or pollution. But these acts of solidarity do not outlive the causes they emerged to fight, and indeed, given the delays that beset Italian legal practice, often dissolve before they can achieve their goals. One club created in the early 1980s to raise funds to protect poor Monticiani from eviction never really got off the ground; one can easily imagine what role was played by such factors as mutual suspicion, lack of a tradition of collective philanthropy, party-political

squabbles, and the desire to be personally and visibly identified with whatever financial sacrifices one made. Some people, especially some of the older
artisans, simply distrust collective initiatives on principle. One loner who
refuses to join any kind of collective activity sourly asserted that people
only joined because of "fear, because there's some friend [mixed up in it],"
or because they stood to gain a discount.

Finally, some initiatives fell afoul of the incompatibility between the social needs of their members and the conceptual ambitions of an increasingly
neoliberal civic administration. Most dramatically, an attempt to create an
artisans' association failed to get off the ground when the municipal officer
in charge of labor tried to corral an entire group of artisans in the old district market on Via Baccina. The problem was that the officials wanted the
artisans to reproduce the "ancient professions of Rome," regardless of their
current activities. "You were expected to do your work in a shop window,"
recalled a carpenter, marveling at the sheer stupidity of a plan that would
have been more appropriate, as he pointed out, to actors than to active artisans with their own existing and specialized trades. The day the authorities
called for elections to the association's governing committee, no one showed
up, and it died stillborn.

That most of the older formal associations have succumbed to the ero-
sion of daily conflict at the local level does not erase their significance, but
exemplifies the forms and dynamics of social relationships in Monti (and
more generally throughout Rome). Far from representing failure—as might
appear from a managerial perspective—it permits a constant flow of rein-
vention and dissolution, a pattern that remains both recognizable and predictable because it incorporates the instability of ordinary social relations
into productive if ephemeral social action. The relative success (and apparent durability) of its most recent avatar, the Monti Social Network, springs
in large measure from its members' refusal to institutionalize their activities
or to demand any sort of conformity—a stance of pragmatic flexibility that
not only sustains the Network where a more rigid structure would crack
under the strain of incorporating so many conflicting perspectives, but also
keeps the municipal authorities healthily on their toes since they can never
point to a single political grouping as the source of proposed reforms.[31]

The Premises of Conflict

The complex ways in which the Monti body politic splits and reassem-
bles reflect its ability to adapt to changing political and economic interests.

This reversible fractioning, in which we can reasonably see the temporal realization of the Roman capacity for compromise and accommodation, was already a striking feature of eighteenth- and nineteenth-century Monti society. The entire *rione* united in symbolic opposition to other such segments of old Rome, sometimes in ways that materialized as real violence. Rivalry with Trastevere was especially fierce. Stone-throwing fights (*sassaiuole*) and lengthy drunken brawls pitting Monticiani against Trasteverini were celebrated in poetry, prints, and popular memory; it was only when the Napoleonic forces invaded the city that the two neighborhoods forgot their mutual enmity for long enough to pelt the French soldiers together. Violence in homes and streets remained a common occurrence until after World War II; an elderly lady who had grown up in a more genteel district recalled the horror with which she heard loud brawling and threats of mayhem during her first nights in the area. One of my book-collecting taxi driver friends drew my attention to a passage in Stendhal, who described the people of Monti as "terrible people" who matched their rivals in Trastevere murder for murder.[32] Within Monti, similar but more localized rivalries often erupted between sections of the area; while some of these rivalries were rather generic (between Upper and Lower Monti, for example), others pitted single streets against each other. People took collective names from their localities; the Ciancaleonini, for example, were named after a small side street (Via dei Ciancaleoni)—"as if," said one resident of a nearby street, "it was a whole family." (In fact, their sense of collective identity may reflect a common history, since the buildings on this street had been donated by one of the Ciancaleoni family to a confraternity, which was bound by the terms of the bequest to rent to handicapped people at low cost, while the monetary part of the bequest was dedicated to the care of orphans.) Each of these streets asserted its identity through sometimes violent confrontations with the others. But, added the same resident, "If there was any argument with other districts, there was always the coalition"—that is, of a larger group of streets, united in the face of a common rival.

The rivalries among districts of Rome were entirely real, as early-nineteenth-century prints by Bartolomeo Pinelli make clear.[33] Today they are more the material of jokes than of actual hostility, though the persistent groaning of one shopkeeper about how she disliked Monti and how badly she missed her native Trastevere (although she also admitted that she would not return to live there as it has now been overrun by foreign residents) suggested that a sharp sense of mutual distrust persists even amid all the apparently good-humored banter. Indeed, the banter itself is indicative of the spectacular ease with which hostility and alliance, like vice and virtue, merge and split with the needs of the moment.

The relativity of conflict is a striking example of what anthropologists call "segmentation," which they have usually taken it to be typical of non-European people who lack state-based forms of governance; the absence of a strongly unified sense of the nation-state perhaps accounts for its prominence in Roman life. This social logic, so reminiscent of the idealized tribal structures of certain African and Middle Eastern peoples,[34] is neither necessarily tied to the structure of unilineal lineage systems nor incompatible with centralized forms of government, especially when the latter are relatively weak, and it is certainly not unknown in Europe.[35] One dramatic instance brought a lineage-based society into confrontation with the Italian nation-state at arguably its most ideologically unified moment: the colonial war between the Bedouin of Cyrenaica and the Fascist Italian government of Mussolini. Evans-Pritchard, the anthropologist who did most to emphasize the importance of this phenomenon as a form of social organization, brilliantly demonstrated how the emergence of the Libyan nation-state was in large measure the result of a process of segmentary fusion as the warring tribes united behind a religious leader to confront the menace of the Italian invasion.[36] The Romans' collaborative attacks on Napoleon's occupying troops represent a small-scale version of this process. More recently an Italian anthropologist, Marino Nola, has invoked the same principle, explicitly derived from Evans-Pritchard, to explain the nesting-box structure of devotional loyalties and political geographies in Naples.[37]

In invoking this model to analyze Roman social arrangements, I do not wish to impose a formal model on a dramatically informal idiom. Romans are not typically organized in unilineal clans, although some underworld elements certainly are and the grand families of the Renaissance and later who gave modern Rome something of its baronial structure represented that tendency.[38] But a social ideology of compromise produces a remarkably similar effect: groups form and disband with sometimes alarming rapidity, around interests that from one moment to the next may be defined as held in common and then as mutually conflicting. Again there is the echo of that curious symbiosis of vice and virtue: Romans acknowledge that factionalism is both destructive and morally reprehensible, but they often openly enjoy the drama it brings to everyday interaction even as some of them decry it as incompatible with civic management.

Throughout Italy, moreover, patterns of factionalism are often based on districts or quarters, as in the famous *palio* of Siena; in many Italian settings they are often also expressed as "wars" between patron saints or even between images of a single saint.[39] In such cases, the unity of the church and its images is refracted through the social turbulence of everyday life; the relative autonomy of individual parishes and confraternities contributes a religious authority to sometimes quite bluntly material causes.

In pre–World War II Rome this relativity of hostile relations began early in life. Children learned the principles early, throwing watermelon rinds at each other while their parents dined in the open air on the street. But when they graduated to stone-throwing, matters became more serious; one could "get hurt." And it was here that the segmentation began to emerge in earnest: "When I went out of our home I'd quarrel with my neighbor. Then together we'd fight with those of the floor below . . . and then together with them with those from the house [literally, door] right opposite. . . . And together we'd fight with those of the next street." Eventually such fights would spread to even more inclusive levels—Lower Monti against the Celio hill, for example—until they eventually erupted between representatives of entire districts. It was not so much that children's play determined the shape of future social relations as that the play provided a context early in each resident's life for learning just how relative loyalty and solidarity could be.

In this guise, localist factionalism emerges as central to the political organization of everyday life; the idiom in which it is expressed is spatial, relative, and often tied to the notion that particular segments of the city were under a specific saint's protection or associated with a particular relic or holy image. The sacred spaces of Rome, which reproduce such religious dramas of spatiality as the Stations of the Cross and processions to all the shrines of the Virgin Mary, have today largely given way to secular, street-based organizations of artisans and shopkeepers, and now—with the help of computer technology—to the Monti Social Network. The Network has come the closest of any to achieving a semblance of unity—by rejecting it as a political format. Scandurra's thinking is shared by many of its members, some of whom can recall too many instances where calls to unity ended up as consolidations of power and thereby provoked collapse.

The instability of social relations is all of a piece with the fragmentation of the lived urban fabric, expressed in the city's baroque aesthetic, a promiscuous stratigraphy that is tolerant of the remnants of other eras even as it incorporates new ones and thus challenges the purism of most state-supported scholarship.[40] Such political liability also fits conveniently with the Catholic model of authority and administration known as subsidiarity.[41] That model holds that all matters should be handled by the smallest and most localized segment of the administrative system; the Vatican, for example, does not consider it appropriate to intervene in parish affairs. By logical extension, subsidiarity thus recognizes the autonomy of each parish priest, and indeed of every member of the religious hierarchy, from interference by others of equivalent rank, since this would imply an encompassing and higher level of authority; issues are considered appropriate to particular levels, and each cleric, representing a specific level of competence, must arrive at a disposition to the best of his ability and in accordance with the promptings of his conscience.[42]

The segmentary quality of Roman social life fits neatly with the subsidiarity principle. What goes doctrinally for the church also applies sociologically to the laity, whose collective sins are embedded in an unstable moral geography of material interests, and who make a practical virtue of minding their own business—or, at least, of telling each other to do so. By the same logic, they affect indifference to others' curiosity about their own affairs; they "couldn't care a fuck" (me ne frego). And even this principle of studied indifference—often expressed by a corresponding physical stance of insouciance[43]—is subject to a segmentary logic: the cautious avoidance of interference in others' affairs by one's own side becomes the indifference, the "couldn't care less" attitude (menefreghismo), of those with power, and especially of the officials of state and city. When one thinks that the city police should target those who break the laws regarding opening times and parking, their failure to do so is taken as indicative of this indifference; when it works in one's favor, it merely shows that the speaker is an adept survivor who can evoke a similar respect for others' socially recognized rights even in the most pedantically legalistic of bureaucrats.

Menefreghismo and subsidiarity are two sides—the social and the ecclesiastical, respectively—of the same coin. The often rough expression of indifference that Romans express toward to others' affairs has no obvious religious justification in itself; the idea that one should not intervene in others' escapades with the law is largely a matter of tact—that is, of everyday civility. Just as priests can ignore the sufferings of parishioners facing eviction by other churches on the grounds of the subsidiarity principle, neighbors can loftily refuse to get involved in the plight of evictees because one is supposed to mind one's own business—particularly if they happen to be of a different political ideology.

This internal fragmentation of collective interest makes it extremely difficult for police and other authorities to gain much purchase against minor crime, even if they wished to do so—and that commitment is constantly subjected to public scrutiny and doubt. Fragmentation, whether ecclesiastical or social, weakens any sense of collective responsibility along the lines of individual self-interest. A tax evader would presumably not wrestle with torments of conscience as a priest might do over some gross act of greed, but the end result is the same. All are left to their own devices; all must face the consequences; and all try to anticipate those consequences through a calculus of material cost and benefit—the tax dodger because such offenses may eventually be amnestied, the priest because sins can be expiated through a range of deprivations from the monetary cost of an indulgence to fleshly mortification.

Catholicism is deeply concerned with the material world. This seems surprising only from the perspective of a Cartesian distinction between the material and the symbolic—the same socially disengaged dualism that views theatricality as necessarily superficial and virtue as absolutely opposed to vice. Such readings distort the lived experience of the people of Rome. Without vice and its material temptations, and without the unceasing aggravation of conflict, virtue has no opportunity to shine. But a world without wickedness is in any case doctrinally unthinkable.

Through the concept of original sin, which is also the single cataclysmic event that brought temporality and history into the human condition, Catholicism accords enormous significance to the presence of temptation in everyday life. It is both a moral alibi and a test of virtue. It thus encompasses the daily sins of the faithful and at the same time provides the means of alleviating the consequences of those sins in the afterlife. If the historical sensibility thus embraced by the church provides the sole antidote to the culture of death represented by criminal forces such as the mafia, as one religious apologist argues,[44] this same sense of temporality and its attendant imperfections provides a theological exoneration of real-life peccadilloes. A historicity that charts the path from a state of original sin to the ultimate redemption is no less capable of carrying countless individual tales of abject backsliding, and there is no more dramatic physical illustration of the wages of such sin than the profusion of aesthetic styles and the palimpsest of broken rules that together constitute the historic center of Rome.

Indeed, the shoulder-shrugging acceptance of minor sin is the expression of a cosmology that also informs the organic development of the city itself, inasmuch as urban space here is a complicated palimpsest of multiple infractions of often evanescent and ill-defined laws. But the sinful condition of humanity also poses very practical dilemmas for the representatives of the faith itself. Thus, for example, a priest assured me that the inability of concerned clergy to prevent some of the more harrowing evictions carried out by various churches and confraternities reflected the necessity of not interfering with each priest's individual struggle with the temptations of the material world. (An older colleague of his had already pointed out that many of the properties once owned by religious bodies had been sold off to raise funds for charitable causes, so there was also a historical reasoning behind the Vatican hierarchy's repeated insistence that it was not competent to intervene in particular cases.) Nor was this something that could be corrected from above; the doctrine of subsidiarity leaves the burden of responsibility weighing on the individual priest's soul.[45] Each member of the clergy must face the consequences of his own actions alone, in his conscience in this world and before divine judgment in the next.

Subsidiarity might be thought to provide a moral alibi, but it is also clear that some of the speculative use of real estate conducted in the name of the church emanated from the highest echelons of the clergy. Four years before the Jubilee, in 1996, the Vatican itself attempted to fire and evict the peasants farming the land in the agricultural zone of Acquafredda, in the hope of turning that land to an economically more profitable use.[46] Whether the pope himself was actively involved, and whether he even knew what the officials of the church bureaucracy were attempting to achieve, does not alter the fact that as an institution, the church seemed to care little about the lives its economic policies affected; after all, was poverty not of those afflictions sent to test the souls of the flock; and did not the principle of subsidiarity mean that the individual cleric or layperson must bear the moral burden of having ordered the eviction? The care of the church's material endowment, moreover, is a sacred end in itself.

Residents experience this use of subsidiarity as undiluted buck-passing. One elderly couple, living in a house owned by an confraternity of lay persons associated with the Church of the Most Holy Name of the Virgin in Trajan's Forum, appealed to the archbishopric for help when the old rent of 250,000 *lire*, which in 1993–1994 had been raised to 400,000 (half of what the confraternity had originally demanded), now suddenly went up to 1,200,000 *lire*—a sum so out of their range that building a new home in one of the more distant suburbs, which they decided to do, would eventually prove an economically more feasible alternative and also gave them legal grounds for obtaining a temporary extension (*proroga*) of their current lease. Their offer to pay a rent of 600,000 *lire*, presumably made on the logic that they had been able to halve the original rent once before, was summarily refused this time. The archbishopric officials told the couple that they knew nothing of the case, because it was only the affair of the confraternity to which the building belonged. But the confraternity sent them back to the archbishopric! The wife, puzzled as to the source of her woes, and perhaps reluctant to voice accusations while they were still living in the building, told me, "I don't think it's really the priests who are kicking us out." Other residents disagreed, and could cite numerous precedents; priests' and lay brothers' moral responsibility is always diffused among their own all-too-fallible consciences.

Far more relevant is her puzzlement itself, especially as she was described to me by a local intellectual as alert and intelligent. It reflects an effect, intended or otherwise, of that structure: the residents are perpetually baffled and frustrated in their attempts to appeal to higher authority, both because doctrinally it may not interfere and because practically it is nowhere to be seen. As the distraught woman pointed out, the church had no right to sell these properties, because they were bequests (*lasciti*) explicitly made to the church—but in practice, while the terms of the bequests were that the houses should be made available to the needy, "they want to do them up for people who can pay [a high rent] instead." The churches and confraternities can resort to a series of legal maneuvers to achieve such a goal. For example, a confraternity based in Bergamo got around the legal restrictions on the sale of a similar Monti property by arguing that they needed extra money to restructure their headquarters, which they successfully argued should be considered a charitable use of the resulting income; after they had sold the property in question to a large real estate company, the rent went up to five times its starting amount over a period of ten years. In yet another case, one of the evictees told me, "If you could see with what a phalanx of lawyers I went there [to the court appeal against eviction]," I would have realized that the confraternities and others possessed "powers that cannot be touched."

In the case just mentioned, in 1995, the couple had been technically well-qualified to compete for one of the apartments made available by the city authorities. They could demonstrate need: the husband was unemployed, the wife earned little, the children were young, and they faced imminent eviction. But without the right connections, said the wife—a recommendation (*raccomandazione*) from someone with authority in city hall—they were unable to compete. "It's always that way," she lamented. Because the overall population of Monti was dwindling their grocery business was withering away as well, which meant that they did not have the funds to finish the work on their suburban house. Meanwhile, the church authorities maintained a consistent stance of blandly polite disengagement, making it impossible for her to know where to turn and whom, specifically, to blame. Work went forward on the restructuring of some of the other apartments in the building; but progress was extremely slow, the apartments being more or less uninhabitable as a result of years of perhaps intentional neglect on the part of the confraternity. Some were simply left vacant.

It is certainly true that neither the casuistry of conscience nor the rhetoric of the Jubilee and its attendant notions of forgiveness and tolerance cut much ice with ordinary Romans. The church attracts a great deal of dislike simply because of its special privileges. While the church has always defended its exemption from paying property taxes on buildings used for religious purposes, for example, its definition of those purposes may have stretched ordinary credulity beyond tolerable limits; it has certainly allowed itself a generous interpretation, to say the least, of the law allowing it to accept bequests of real estate tax-free as long as these were used for charitable purposes. What is more, the church has lately found itself confronting charges of tax evasion on its revenues from rent income and calls for the imposition of the municipal property tax (*Ici*) for the first time since their introduction in 1992.[47] Such calls find a ready audience in working-class Rome and among the city's left-wing intellectuals. While the hierarchy urges tolerance in general terms, moreover, its practices—notably its opposition to the World Gay Pride procession—suggests a selective understanding of tolerance at best. Critics have also attacked its calls for tolerance toward immigrants as a disingenuous argument for allowing cheap labor to invade the housing market and work force to the detriment of Italians' interests.

The persistence of expectations of material rewards for social pressure, however directly it may seem to contravene the values of a pre-Reformation Christianity, is not antithetical to the established practices of the church in everyday life; indeed, it is the church and its appointed allies (the so-called black aristocracy) who are deemed worthy of owning significant real estate, rather than those Weberian upstarts who might consider themselves entitled to show themselves the elect of God by actually working for such material evidence of their condition.

The burdens of property management, however, also create ethical dilemmas that are deflected from the central power of the Vatican by the doctrine of subsidiarity, much as the same doctrine is deployed to justify the capital accumulation and ethnic exclusivism championed by the European Union's most right-wing politicians. In an Italy governed during much of my fieldwork by a right-wing coalition and shadowed by a church both

extolling what it regards as the Christian basis of true European identity, and
unprepared to compromise with notions of ethical or cultural relativism, the
physicality of the church's presence in everyday life maintains venal temptations that test the ethical will of citizenry and priesthood, sinners all. How
can a protestant sense of the civic emerge and survive here? The observable
failure to pass the test, to resist temptation, repeatedly confirms the wisdom
of the doctrine and especially the logic of the indulgence—the anticipated
forgiveness for petty crimes yet to be committed. If we are truly sinners, we
cannot live without that endlessly repeatable promise of salvation. Even the
pious rhetoric of disgust seems at times to perpetuate the civic corruption
that it decries.[48]

Rome, the center of the Catholic world, is also deeply anticlerical. The
political Left has habitually opposed corruption that it associates, in the
post–World War II era, with the rule of the right-wing Christian Democrat
party (Democrazia cristiana). One example of political graffiti in Monti
proclaims "DC = mafia," perhaps an allusion to the trial of Giulio Andreotti,
today a senator-for-life and one of the most vocal exponents of loyalty to
the values of the church. Even leftist mayors of Rome, however, have gone
out of their way to make their peace with the Vatican, leading residents to
shrug their resignation: "But here we have the pope, don't we?"

Power, like sin, is a burden of the human condition, its corrupting
presence rooted in the city's streets and buildings. In Monti, the old printing press, one street away from the spray-painted attack on the Christian
Democrats, produced the paper money of the Bank of Italy until scandal
abruptly ended operations. Despite its ignominious end, the press holds an
honored place in residents' affections. One friend, who moved away from
the district but was constantly seeking to return, proudly showed me a
chair with the faint mark of the factory still on it, sold off when the firm
collapsed and kept as a relic of Monti's past. Today the old printing works
again bears the mark of Cain. It was put up for sale; but then, suspended in
mid-transaction, it languished for a few months under official seal, because
its ownership was under investigation by the Anti-Mafia Commission. No
one knows exactly how this came about; no one seems to know when the
seal was removed. The official notice of suspension of the sale disappeared
long before work on the building resumed. Evidently nothing—of course,
the neighbors nod, what did you expect?—was found against the owners,
and the sale eventually went ahead. The old factory thus serves as an ominous reminder of the irrepressible and familiar undertow of evil, leaching
perpetually into the operations of ecclesiastical, state, and civic management.

Most suspect that the impending sale of the building was intended to launder—or "recycle," as the process is locally called—dirty money. Nobody in the locality actually knows that this is the case. Nor, more generally, can anyone be sure that any of those flashily dressed real estate speculators operating in the area are true underworld figures, as all suspect. Suspicion is nevertheless informed—if not by facts, then by the recognition of mafia-style politeness whenever and wherever it appears, whether as elaborate manners and ostentatious dress or as the aggressive acquisition and restructuring of once working-class apartments or industrial property as elegant homes for the wealthy and privileged. The assumption of underworld involvement is a self-fulfilling conspiracy theory.

But residents still reserve their greatest anger for the churches and confraternities. An elderly gentleman, facing eviction from his house by a religious order, spluttered with fury at the priests' "terrible commerce" (*commercio terribile*): "For mortality they want money, for marriages they want money, for baptisms they want money!" And the supposedly secular state colludes: "And the state doesn't care in the least because those guys are priests and they are the ones who give the orders." Angry graffiti proclaim that "[the] Vatican evicts." The city authorities, in particular, play a double game, deflecting and even amplifying anger against the ecclesiastical powers (and occasionally sending letters of solidarity and protest) while, through inaction, protecting their own cordial relationship with the Vatican. This in turn enables the church to protect its interests and its ability to operate without constraint and enhances a sense of fear and helplessness that further deflects all but the most courageous critics. As in the terrestrial world, so too in the spiritual: the same local entities that are responsible for administering the material dimensions of Rome's sacred geography also control the sites of possible contact between the mundane and the divine, its holiness refracted into multiple hues and intensities like light through the shimmering patina of a twisted piece of old glass through the multiplicity of holy relics, body parts emblematic of a fragmented body politic.[49]

The social fragmentation of Roman spaces is consistent with this moral economy; each subunit is responsible for its own collective actions, and the level at which such coalescence occurs is determined by the needs of the moment. In pre–World War II times, the local bosses oversaw the good conduct and solidarity of small tracts of the *rione*—typically, two or three streets. Then as now, any unwelcome interference in another's affairs was usually met with an angry "Do your own shit!"—perhaps, given the shifting nature of solidarity, from someone with whom, in a different context, one has just acted in concert. The *ciga*, the secret deal, is the closest the

self-admittedly garrulous Romans usually come to the kind of massive silence that characterizes the operations of mafia thugs.[50]

Indeed, a certain kind of silence is widely regarded as the "first seeds
of mafia"—the kind that does not itself entail physical violence, although
it may presage violence if its implications are not heeded. A flower vendor
agreed to talk with me about her open hostility to the immigrants crowding
the main square. Later, however, when the opportunity to chat seemed ripe
(she was reading a newspaper and there were no customers in sight), she
decided that she could not talk. Since she was clearly much less busy than
usual, this was as clear a brush-off as could still remain within the bounds of
civility. Commenting on her reaction, an exasperated artisan of some formal
education, a bemused observer of the behavior of his more traditionalizing
colleagues, supposed that she had been afraid she might have given too much
away. As he remarked, "No one speaks, no one hears, no one sees, no one
knows." In a city where domestic quarrels and screaming matches between
enraged prostitutes once provided vivid street theater, serious violence must
first ensure the hermetic silence that generalizes menace: uncertain fear, not
certain knowledge, keeps the cowed in line. People nevertheless continue
to observe, draw conclusions, and keep out of the way. Knowledge is a good
to be gathered, not imparted. Faced with any kind of inquisitiveness, each
person thinks, said my artisan friend, "I have to live here," and fears that
volunteering information, even if it is not dangerous, might provide some
unforeseeable advantage to a competitor. Those who benefit from spreading
fear are happy to encourage such a silence, one that also draws on stereotypical models of strong-and-silent masculinity (omertà).[51] Those models at
first seem irrelevant to the usual cheerful garrulity, especially when no obvious interests are threatened by light-hearted talk. But even chatter must
respect the sensitivities of those who might have something to hide, and
should not contain jokes that are too heavy (pesanti)—that is, personal and
invasive.

Minding one's own business is a prized moral precept precisely because
few actually follow it. When serious matters are at stake, it can be enforced.[52]
Usually, however, it is a contrived performance of non-engagement that permits one "to lighten one's own responsibilities" as a citizen (as my artisan
friend sourly observed) while counting on a similar form of tact in respect of
one's own illicit activities. There is a dour civility in ignoring one's neighbors' activities, a form of connivance that is also thus a rejection of formal
civic ideals.

Neighbors' sins, whether against divine law or against the regulations
of the state, are thus always their own business, and theirs alone. While

few Romans would hesitate to complain to neighbors about a violation—for example, of the building code that caused them discomfort—reporting it to the authorities is another matter altogether. For one thing, it carries a serious risk of long and complicated involvement, possibly entailing expense and countercharges. Those who do bring such charges often do so more as a diversionary tactic than because they are themselves innocent of similar infractions. Moreover, just as the confidentiality of the confessional is widely viewed as a fraud that can nevertheless be effectively used to gain easy absolution from complicit priests,[53] in secular life wrongdoers can invoke the imported civic virtue of *la privacy* to protect special interests and local secrets against government intrusion and the rule of law.[54]

Monti, then, is a space of vibrant social life, rich in the human weaknesses and divisions, the poverty, and the intimacy of a people accustomed to alternating between accommodation to the power of the ecclesiastical state and resistance to its incursions into that intimacy. Their religiosity was similarly both accommodating and fiercely local. Italian self-characterizations may be helpful here; a phrase of Gramsci's about the local forms of Catholic devotion—"the Catholic working class's passive and indolent-rascal (*lazzaronesca*) concept of grace"—echoes in a left-wing shopkeeper-artisan's remark, as he tried to explain the role of banks in perpetuating the practice of usury by refusing loans except to the wealthy and landed, that "Italy is a land of idle rascals (*lazzaroni*)!"[55] The parallel is surely no coincidence.

Theaters of Piety and Peculation

The intimacy of the street and the theatricality of everyday encounters provides ongoing witness to a powerful mixture of devotion and delinquency. The Monti women of old were notorious for their loud, public fights, which even culminated in a highly dramatic striptease "to embarrass the husband" on one occasion still fondly remembered, and Stendhal noted with some astonishment that Roman women who fancied particular men made no secret of their interest or saw themselves bound to constancy for life;[56] this is not Greece or the Middle East, or even a southern Italian village, but a comedic and operatic space for the baring of emotion and physicality clearly framed as performance: "They do it as a kind of theater." Quarreling prostitutes would try to tear each other's hair out. Women who got into especially dramatic screaming matches would contrive to take the whole show down to the Piazza del Tritone, where they calculated that there would be more people to watch the spectacle.

Moments of dramatic female self-assertion still occur, although in a more urbane tone, on a much smaller scale, and usually for less disreputable ends. Nor are they particularly about neighborly relations among women. Women's willingness to speak out, which was also characteristic of the various association and condominium meetings I attended, is often about the assertion of rights and propriety. Once a taxi driver complained volubly because, he claimed, he could not drive past a car parked in a narrow side street. The owner of the car, a woman, came down and declared that there was room for a truck to pass and that she herself would drive his taxi past her car—which she proceeded to do! Having made her point with great aplomb, however, she clearly thought that discretion—the famous Roman accommodation again—was the greater part of valor, and drove her own car off in search of a more legal parking spot. The taxi driver had threatened to call the police and she did not, she admitted later, want to make a public fool (*figuraccia*) of herself by having to deal with them. There was satisfaction enough in having put the aggressive male in his place; now she also denied him the pleasure of revenge.

The mixture of exuberance and discretion that we see in this incident displays in an exemplary moment the peculiar calculus of consequence and pride that colors all social transactions in these streets. A woman of non-Roman origin who ran an antique shop noted, with some irritation, that vans would stop at all hours of the day to unload goods, blocking the narrow streets: "These are everyday occurrences, even banal ones . . . it's a compromise . . . that's what's so hard to take." In such little moments we see the constant reenactment of a model of social interaction that allegedly informed relations with the papal authorities of the past, and that, in a minor key, continues to inform commercial relations in an economic world in which the niceties of courtesy can make the difference between survival and bankruptcy.

Accommodation does not automatically mean that an abject act of surrender to the arrogance of those with power or money is sincere. But shopkeepers, in particular, do abase themselves when the alternative would be economically disastrous. Every social interaction entails some calculation of risk; self-assertion can snatch dignity from the most humiliating encounters, but it may also result in economic disaster, harassment by corrupt officials, or a legal penalty that self-abasement might have averted. This experiential context colors people's sense of eternity itself; no wonder, then, that the late-eighteenth-century inscription accompanying one *Madonnella* on Via Baccina should offer sinful passers-by the option of reciting a few

Fig. 4. Indulgences written in stone: two hundred days off, "also applicable to souls already in Purgatory" (1797). (Photo by Michael Herzfeld.)

prayers "with the heart at least contrite" in order to shorten their stay in Purgatory![57]

The *Madonnelle*—portraits of the Virgin Mary and sometimes of other holy figures—are the most visible physical reminder of the segmentary fractioning of local identity. Embedded as they were in the ebb and flow of social relations, protected by particular families and subject both to weather conditions and to the whim of proprietors who wished to alter the appearance of their houses, many of the *Madonnelle* simply disappeared. Shortly before Unification, in 1847, they passed from the old Prefecture of Waters and Streets of the papal administration to the control of the city council, and this began a process of rationalization and monumentalization—as well as a concomitant privatization of devotional practice—that culminated, ironically enough, in a formal exhibition devoted to the shrines and the social marginality that they expressed. One of the responsibilities that thus came into the hands of the municipality was the supervision and prevention of the use of public space (*occupazione del suolo pubblico*), a function that today provides the legal and bureaucratic basis for resisting the illicit privatization of sidewalks and squares by restaurateurs and bar owners in their purveying of packaged charm to tourists. One of the most important effects of this administrative shift was, first, to formalize the shrines as part of a public heritage, and then, gradually, to dismember the raucous open-air homage that had previously filled the streets.[58] The church has repeatedly attempted to "purify" such popular devotion on religious grounds as well, rejecting its sociability as alien to church writ and dogma. Especially perverse from an ecclesiastical standpoint is the association, in Monti and Trastevere, of the most intense concentrations of *Madonnelle* anywhere in Rome with an equally prominent reputation for disreputable behavior and petty crime.[59]

Everyday sanctity is thus perpetually stained with everyday sins. In this city so engorged with corrupt beauty, piety, like courtesy, draws sustenance from a rich night-soil of cunning and violence. Monti, physically submerged below the bustling nineteenth-century city and overshadowed by the fierce architecture of San Pietro in Vincoli, embodies the delinquent intimacy of the city's daily life. Residents, who in the sixteenth century defied a pope's orders to surrender their most sacred image to the Vatican, later refused to remove these sacred images from the invading troops of the Napoleonic forces in the eighteenth century or from those of the national army at the time of the Risorgimento. Such intense localism perhaps reflects a sense that the poor houses of the neighborhood "hardly defend the inhabitants' intimacy" so that "a space is thus designed in which there is no real break between outside and inside."[60] The habit of dining on the street, each *fagottaro* contributing a package of food to the sociable scene, similarly brought neighbors together in the space of a conviviality still warmly alive in residents' recollections.

Inevitably, too, as state and municipality increasingly took over the management of public order, sanitation, and planning, the surviving shrines lost some of their intense association with locally remembered events and persons.[61] Some disappeared simply because the families that had preserved the memory of their miraculous original appearance—for such was the alleged origin of many of them—had died out, leaving no substitute in the new bureaucratic landscape. Objects of pious veneration that had long resisted both the oppressive propinquity of the Vatican and the newly acquired status of national capital, other *Madonnelle* survive today, emblems of a still persistent and willful marginality, only through their adoption by the very institution they had so resolutely defied.[62] Many factors contributed to this radical change in their significance. Once the sole source of illumination at night, for example, their lamps were routed by the new urban lighting

Fig. 5. A Madonnella adorns a Palazzo

that arrived with Napoleonic planning; then again, the rationalization of city street names was but the prelude to the fury of "sanitization," spatial cleansing, that arrived with Mussolini's Fascist administrators, who sought to gut whole segments of the city, especially in Monti.[63] Thus began a drawn-out upheaval in which the newly monumentalized private homes that survived the slaughter—"little gems" in a guidebook of the Fascist era—came, in the hands of today's entrepreneurs, to be refractured as minute luxury apartments. The real estate agents' aggressive sales patter and brash banner advertisements drown out the fading laments that accompany the final, despondent trickle of departures. Today's battles are again particularly about noise, traffic, and the ownership of public space. The Madonnelle have become symbols of a lost past; they are recast as monuments to virtue rather than as the persistent stains of sins now forgotten.

All these changes have disrupted, but have not immediately destroyed, the strong sense of local belonging among the relatively few, comparatively prosperous individuals who have been able to buy out their old abodes or purchase new ones. And so it came about that the local priest, born in Rome of parents from Friuli in the northeast of the country, could recapture for

a modern and less locally focused age the traditional forms, suitably redi-
mensioned, of local devotion. He recognized as the defining paradox of the
shrines their testimony to a sanctity that could only subsist in a world of
carnal desire, but recast their significance in terms that emphasized today's
norms of respectability and religiosity; where once this devotional practice had been a means for the teeming poor of Rome's crowded center to
transcend the meanness of their houses but also to protest the heavy hand
of clerical rule, today the priest's followers are decorous middle-class citizens who see themselves as defending the Vatican's presence in their midst.
The "purification" of popular religion objectifies it as an activity set apart
from the sacredness of the church itself.[64] On the one hand, this process
reinforces the church's paternalistic supervision of the working poor and
their bourgeois successors. On the other hand, by orchestrating pilgrimages to the shrines, the priest has reified their significance in ecclesiastical
terms that also fit well with the monumental pretensions of the municipal
authorities.[65]

A published historian, the priest has recast the popular forms of worship
in terms of both historical accuracy and respect for local tradition. His
"affective tie" (legame affettivo) with the physical space of the parish and
its churches has intensified through his study of "every block of stone"
(ogni mattone) of which the parish church, in particular, is made.[66] His
historical studies are also motivated by a desire to know more about his
predecessors in the parish. But he also acts decisively to tie the monuments
of popular veneration more tightly to the parish church and thereby to
reinforce and perhaps even extend the sense of a community defined in
religious terms. In particular, he has made it his business to encourage
local reuse of the shrines as objects of veneration and to enhance their
centrality to the historical sensibilities of his parishioners. Through regular
miniature processions or pilgrimages to the district's principal Madonnelle,
organized down to the most meticulous detail, he has emphasized historical
depth as well as powerful local sentiment. Emblematically, participants in
these processions now sing a hymn locally composed in the eighteenth century.

His attachment to the sites of this religiosity manifests an intriguing
tension, one that perhaps draws on the working-class history of the shrines
but that at the same time addresses paradoxes within the current doctrines
of the church. On the one hand, by incorporating explanatory lectures, and
by thereby producing a philology that occludes older understandings of the
shrines, he seems to endorse the ongoing gentrification and monumentali-

zation of the district. On the other, his intense focus on the physical spaces of his parish represents a doctrinally sanctioned displacement of physical desire. The priest must deploy to the sites of his church the sensuality frustrated (as an outsider might interpret it) by what for him is a willing acceptance of the sacred charge of celibacy: "I was speaking of the connection of the priest with the physical place of the church. So there we are talking of a discourse of affect that is tied to the choice of celibacy and to the way of living, that's the point, the realities of sentiment—the sentimental realities, so to speak."

On the one hand, he said, his role as parish priest was an administrative one. On the other, however, he described with sparkling warmth the pleasure he felt after he had cleaned out the previously abandoned little Church of San Salvatore and removed the accumulated garbage; this, he said, was "a very beautiful moment." And then, after he had performed the ritual of the Eucharist in this newly cleaned church, his eye fell on a set of prayers for deconsecrated churches in his breviary. The church had never been deconsecrated but had simply been ignored and allowed to fall into disuse, but he was beset by a sudden urge: "At that moment I felt the need to pray, to have everyone there pray, and to reflect, on the place, on the physical space as . . . on the church as a building, and as a metaphor; and this was a moment of great intensity for the people, I realized—and nor was it a moment of lesser intensity for me." Such moments stand out far beyond his administrative role; they are the truly spontaneous expressions of a deep and consuming love.

This sublimation of the sinful condition that he shares as a member of the human race deflects temptation into a materiality that ultimately reproduces and celebrates the passion of Christ. It grounds this physicality anew in the sites of local devotion, but in the process also "purifying" these sites of older associations with the erstwhile notoriety of Monti social life. This connectedness, "a slightly strange relationship" (una relazione un po' strana) between the priest and the physical space of devotion, also moved him, for example, to spontaneous prayers of contrition for the church's past cruelties to the Jewish population, in a space—the Church of San Salvatore, the Savior—that had played such a key role in their persecution; acknowledging that cruelty but also explaining that it had been intended as a benign act of saving souls, he spoke to a new kind of redemption that was consistent with the revised teachings of the Catholic church about its relationship with the Jews. In the same vein, he also thought that it would be good to have a weekly prayer service both to ask for God's pardon for what was done by the church to the Jews but also to give thanks for their physical salvation inasmuch as the church, both as a built space and as a local institution, became, like other such sites, a refuge for numerous Jews during the Nazi persecution. He would also like to add the Easter (Good Friday) prayer for the inclusion of the Jews in God's redemptive plan, but, politically sensitive as he was, insisted that this prayer would be "very discreet, very fraternal." He also emphasized to me the negative image that the role of the Church of San Salvatore in the treatment of the Jews had created for our own epoch, a fact that complicated his commitment to the recovery of historical knowledge. But such is the burden of sin and the past.

The priest can thus embrace an entire religious community that his church had hitherto disdained as an ineradicable reminder of its sin-begotten origins. It is within the same framework that he also subsumes popular worship within the ritual space of the parish. Such acts make it easy to forget that, in an earlier and earthier age, the yoking of religiosity and carnality might not have seemed as strange as it often does in our own post-protestant times. In this sense, the priest's historically grounded progressivism is itself paradoxically conservative. It hearkens back to established doctrine, one that also recognizes history itself as a consequence of humanity's fallen condition, and to the ultimate desire for a universally Christian world.

This conjuncture has its own pragmatic logic in the present social context of Monti life. The presence of the church, architecturally ubiquitous, is also socially embedded through the personal commitment of this popular and well-respected parish priest. But his very humanity constitutes something of a threat from the point of view of those who continue to oppose the church's presence in their everyday lives, or at least to express discomfort about its ubiquity.[67] The materiality of his commitment to his parish, a source of great enthusiasm to the faithful (an enthusiasm, in his own judgment, that sometimes far exceeds the demands of a more reflective religiosity), means that the struggle is joined in the real time of daily political conflict; the spiritual is thus thoroughly embedded in the material, not only theologically, but also politically. Treating these various elements separately would thus distort the experienced realities of Monti life and belie the often-expressed Roman desire for compromise and symbiosis.

The procession to the *Madonnelle* offers a dramatic illustration of the significance of place, sanctity, and history in reinforcing localist sentiment within the universal claims of the Catholic faith. It gives Monti a distinctive materiality that marks it off from the rest of the city of which it is nevertheless a vital and resonant part. The procession is heavily gendered;

most of those who participate in the procession are women, and the hymns are an often discordant but restrainedly enthusiastic paean of female religiosity, over which the priest's voice, amplified by a portable loudspeaker, soars with occasional but unmistakable authority despite his recent arrival in the parish—sometimes leading the singing, more often explaining the historical antecedents of the procession and its stations. In a city where taxi drivers are history buffs and book collectors, this parish priest is notable for his several studies of local devotional history, works that he compiled after only a few years in office.

His miniaturized pilgrimage, an invitation for locals to rediscover in their home terrain a model of what millions of pilgrims have sought in Rome for centuries, purges the urban fabric of some of its notoriety (and perhaps also of his own unease at so sensual a reminder of the constant struggle with materiality in his pastoral life). It thus creates a moral trajectory that, for an incandescent moment of hope, also both sublimates a sinful past to a rationalized present and symbolically overcomes the threatened tragedy of the neighborhood's impending social dissolution. Such moments of heightened effervescence also occasionally highlight local struggles—in town meetings about traffic problems or the sometimes violent disagreements that sometimes erupt between older and younger condominium residents—between the values and practices of a civil but sometimes oppressive society and those of an idealized civic model of participatory governance.[68]

Monti's boast of being the "first *rione* of Rome" encapsulates the key paradox of local specificity and temporality on the one hand and the centrality of both the Universal Church and the city's brooding eternity on the other. In the city's ecclesiastical sites, its people can attain direct experience of the divine.[69] But the popular shrines, as material embodiments of everyday life, are also sites of moral corruption as well as of resistance to corruption from above. A religiosity that demands engagement with the material can itself be turned against papal authority when the popes or their representatives display an excess of arrogance, venality, and hunger for power—or simply refuse to accept the autonomy of a local parish or confraternity as part of the divinely ordained condition of the city.

Monti, proud of a deeply venerated image of the Madonna in the parish church, rose in revolt in the sixteenth century when Pope Gregory XIII, apparently out of fear that a local cult could subvert theological doctrine (but ostensibly because the locals wanted to keep it in the humble house where it had been miraculously discovered), tried to have the image surreptitiously removed to the Vatican soon after its miraculous discovery.[70] A heavy rainstorm persuaded the local people that the Madonna did not wish to leave. Not only did the local gentry rebel; the image itself resisted relocation, threatening to dissolve in a pile of dust at every attempt at removal. Eventually the pope was persuaded that nothing could be done and relented even to the point of giving his blessing and ordering an appropriately magnificent housing to be constructed in the form of the church. The present parish priest himself pointed out the house, then already a couple of centuries old, where a local notable had organized that resistance to the central power of the church.

Roman history is thus not a simple story of contests between ecclesiastical and anticlerical camps clearly defined and drawn up for battle. Fighting the power of a pope does not mean disputing the moral authority of the church but, on the contrary, subjects the exercise of that authority to divine arbitration. Such continuities persist today in improbable forms; the postwar political history of Italy, with its strident opposition between Communist and Catholic parties until the early 1990s, might seem to favor a starkly dualistic reading, but, as David Kertzer has shown, the sworn enemies of the church adopted its symbolic forms and strategies and so increasingly came to adopt some of its attitudes.[71] The breaks are never as clear or absolute as modern political discourse makes them sound, mainly because the moral struggle does not take place so much in the political arena as also in each individual conscience and according to the particular circumstances of each moment of confrontation. Every resident of Monti can see, reflected in the ambiguous gaze of the countless images of the Madonna that overlook the streets, the ceaseless tension between heartfelt piety and the inevitable taint of sin that necessitates and nurtures it, between a perfect and transcendent universal faith and its broken, corrupt materializations on earth.

A Clergy Scorned

Cynical recollections of the less edifying parts of papal history are thus not necessarily irreligious; they simply show that no mortal, not even a pope (and certainly not a priest who must manage the earthly goods of his parish church), can escape that agonizing oscillation between good and evil or the passionate debates about where the line should be drawn between them; such is the nature of original sin. Local religiosity may even offer moral refuge from a Vatican perceived as having betrayed the values of humility and charity. Eviction from Monti led the scion of an old Communist family to take part, with his sons, in the parish church confraternity's religious processions, a participation that allowed him to perpetuate a local identity from which he had been physically "exiled" to a home just a few meters away from the *rione* border. Loyalty to his natal parish church and respect for its very personable priest, however, in no way diminished his biting resentment of the Vatican for what he condemned as its hypocritical intolerance—notably its hostility to gay activism in Rome.

Echoes of such battles between local piety and the encompassing secular power of the Vatican reverberate down through the centuries. One of the taxi-driving historians and a left-wing butcher, for example, recalled with ill-concealed glee the exile of the popes to Avignon in 1309—although, the butcher caustically remarked, "it's now two thousand years we've lived with the popes . . . we've tried to send him to Avignon [in exile], we've tried sending him to Viterbo—but the pope always comes back—don't ask me why, he always returns to Rome. I don't know why! I don't know why! The pope keeps coming back to Rome!"

Anticlerical sentiment has found a new source of anger in the large population of eastern European immigrants, given great visibility in Monti by crowds that regularly converge on the Ukrainian church on the main square. A minor incident nicely illustrates the connections that local people increasingly perceive among immigration, government, and church. A local resident who one day saw me being attacked by a group of Gypsy children using a large sheet of cardboard to try to block my way and confuse me—a common device of petty thieves on Rome's sidewalks—thought that nothing could be done to stop these incidents. Revealingly, he blamed the lack of seriousness (*serietà*) in the application of the law on the Vatican's repeated calls for tolerance (*tolleranza*). Prejudice against immigrants and Gypsies, which this man clearly and unequivocally expressed, feeds the anticlericalism of those working-class people who, in an earlier age and as yet innocent of much contact with immigrants, would mostly have supported the Communist party. One retired old man, apparently a member of a vigilante group, made a point of hanging around the areas in which Gypsy children allegedly attacked tourists and tried to rob them, and experiencing great delight whenever he was able to thwart these youngsters and earn the grateful praise of their intended victims. The church's call for tolerance does not resonate well with these self-appointed guardians of public safety.

Anticlericalism is reinforced, more strongly today than ever before, by the frequency with which churches have been evicting working-class tenants from their homes, sometimes, if rumors are to be believed, in order to house much more densely packed populations of immigrants at inflated rents. Several of the confraternities responsible for recent evictions are based abroad, or in places—such as the Lombard city of Bergamo—known to despise Rome and considered scarcely less foreign by many Romans. For most locals, all these religious bodies are thinly disguised proxies for "the Vatican."

One local observer of a particularly cruel eviction by a religious confraternity remarked bitterly, "I'm a believer—but I'm also anticlerical, because it's just not fair." On another occasion, he justified having hung a little portrait of the cult figure of Padre Pio on a wall of his own house by again affirming his fundamental belief in his religion, but said that he would not visit the saint's shrine because he disliked the "business" (he used the English word) that went with such pilgrimages, as opposed to the selflessness of priests who went to Africa to care for the sick and destitute. Such disaffection from the institutional church is a centuries-deep tradition in Monti. It does not necessarily conflict with personal religiosity; on the contrary, religious values provide the yardstick by which the entire clerical structure is judged and found wanting.

Such dislike of "the priests" (i preti)—especially for their callous disregard of the local poor, sick, and aged—is far from new. Recall the young Trastevere barber with whom Stendhal liked to converse, and who, whenever he recalled some absurdity perpetrated by the papal authorities, exclaimed, "What would have us do, signore? We are under the [authority of the] priests" (Che volete, o signore! siamo sotto i preti).[72] There has been little recent evidence to suggest that the authoritarianism and avarice of the church have abated with their temporal authority.

The local Alleanza nazionale activists are quick to exploit the resulting disaffection and resentment. The connection between the Vatican and immigration is the subject of a writhingly active conspiracy theory: that the Vatican, particularly under the Polish pope John Paul II, in addition to urging tolerance for the immigrants, has actively encouraged them to migrate from eastern Europe and must therefore bear a significant share of the blame for the heightened level of petty crime. Since one part of the party's base is a strongly Catholic bourgeoisie, its leadership promotes good relations with the Vatican at the official level; not so its local chapter, which increasingly benefits from an anticlerical attitude once much more typical of the Communists whose constituency the neofascists are trying to capture. In this, the neofascist Alleanza nazionale reversed expectations, much as did the leftist coalition that controlled city hall, but in the opposite direction: the leftists, under Rutelli, had begun to make very warm overtures to the Vatican, and shared with the Vatican an interest in converting the entire historic center into a depopulated area of museums, residences for the wealthy, and lucrative service industries. Together, the secular and ecclesiastical authorities were prepared to sacrifice archaeological treasures to cement their oddly convenient alliance.[73] Some of the most sophisticated residents are convinced that city hall and the Vatican are conspiring to evacuate the social life of the historic center.

CHAPTER FIVE

Life and Law in a Flawed State

The hubris of the nation-state is, as Giambattista Vico noted so long ago,[1] that it lays claim to an impossible permanence and antiquity. In Rome, that antiquity seems almost tangible; yet Rome is the one capital where the nation-state's agelessness seems most vulnerable to empirical disproof. The religion of the Vatican seems to have stronger claims on eternity. As the capital of a nation-state that has great difficulty in articulating a common culture, Rome is also the site of the promulgation of laws that illustrate how far the state lies from representing a lofty and timeless detachment from human self-interest.

Laws and Regulations

Some brief examples will illustrate how little the state influences the actions of its citizens. Almost opposite the house where I lived was a little side street that gave onto the bustling Via Cavour. It was a one-way street, yet frequently drivers boldly drove straight into it in the illegal direction. Several cars came through this way when the left-wing councilor held his street meeting to discuss, oddly enough, traffic control. No one took the slightest notice of the offending cars; no one seemed at all perturbed about the illegality occurring under their eyes while the politician spoke about the necessity of following legal procedures.

Nearby, a shopkeeper surreptitiously kept under-the-counter tabs for his best customers. The practice is illegal, as he acknowledged with a disdainful shrug. He was more concerned about keeping his customers. Such a performance of trust was an important way of securing their loyalty—perhaps even more so than the economic flexibility that the practice gave them. Residents sometimes seemed to live in genuine fear of the tax police (*Guardia di*

Finanza), whose gray uniforms and threateningly parked cars were a source of uneasy glances and whispered mutterings. Rumor had it that people were being stopped on the street to have their machine receipts for purchases checked. The state would have had good reason for this; many shopkeepers, barmen, and restaurateurs produced very incomplete receipts, while the prices their customers paid were also substantially below the official rate. The arrangement was convenient for both sides; the customers paid less, while the entrepreneurs were able to avoid paying full taxes—although, at tax return time, they, like others in the artisanal trades, would improvise receipts for a set of fictitious (and significantly smaller) payments so as to convince the authorities that they were in fact obeying the law. If they got away with it, they paid lower taxes, and were also able to treat their favored customers to reduced prices.

These minor misdemeanors were almost always a matter of common knowledge. Unlike outsiders who stole from Monticiani, the perpetrators were not considered any more immoral than the officials whose rapacity—itself, some sagely averred, forced on them by their terrible salaries—allegedly compelled them to resort to such practices in turn. On the contrary, failure to take advantage of the state's weakness would only earn a merchant a reputation for almost culpable innocence and an antisocial attitude.

Such openness does nevertheless entail a measure of risk; spies exist (local people betrayed at least one large Jewish family to the Gestapo), and people who feel slighted may take their revenge by bringing illegal actions to the attention of the authorities. The dominant ethos, however, strongly rejects betrayals of neighbors to the official state. Openly illegal transactions exemplify a fragile trust, performed in an atmosphere of partial fear that failing to read a customer's real intentions can result in serious trouble. The state is perceived as a watchful presence, made all the more damaging by the corrupt practices, especially extortion, of its officers; among one's neighbors, by contrast, constant testing can reduce the risk of betrayal to manageable proportions.

The sense of living under oppressive and unrelenting inquisition, perhaps a relic of papal rule, is still remarkably widespread: "You're forced to keep things under wraps and you can't get ahead [as a result]." The resulting intimidation takes the form of a constant fear of snooping informers who exploit the dialect and gestural style of friendly interaction while actually either doing the work of the state or, worse (and perhaps more common), feathering their own nests. The miasma of potential extortion induces compliance without, usually, the necessity of resorting to actual physical violence or to the use of legal provisions. All become complicit, because there is no other way to operate in this society. But that does not mean that anyone can be prevented from complaining about it. The point is precisely to keep options open by complaining that, in effect, local and national government give one no choice but to cheat and lie; politicians (and priests) are human too. People work best with the state when its representatives act in ways that ordinary citizens can understand, and indeed see as normal. As a local tag has it, "for citizens the laws are applied; for friends, they are interpreted." This attitude creates a high degree of ambiguity, especially as professions of friendship can actually be intimations of a coercive presence. Officials often do not trust each other either, which is why some categories of police, following a series of scandalous disclosures, were ordered to watch others for signs of bribery and extortion.

Cynics also point to widespread evidence of corruption in the highest echelons of civic administration; there is a paradoxical sense that "in Italy [only] the dishonest are politically credible!" The shopkeeper who offered this ironic observation had lived some years in the United States; he also said that in Italy everyone participated in the game. Thus, to use one of his examples, a butcher who gave his customers receipts for half the amount paid thereby made them tacitly complicit in his tax evasion; not for these Romans the stern Christian prohibition of involving others in one's own sinful failures to resist temptation.

The predictable sins of the powerful, moreover, furnish both a model and a moral alibi for those of ordinary people. A district councilor inveighed against city hall's plans to replace the famous Roman cobblestones with asphalt, suggesting that this kind of work was simply a way of spending money by farming contracts out to loyal supporters. The policy's supporters could point to the damage that cobblestones did to motor vehicles; they also raised the noise level—one of the most familiar night sounds in our street was that of wheeled suitcases bumping over the diamond-shaped *sampietrini*. Given the choice, however, people usually assume the most cynical of the available explanations. And tales of work created to serve special interests abound; the constant resurfacing of sidewalks is a common example. Such stories reinforce the self-justification of ordinary citizens. Corruption and its benefits, so the implicit argument runs, should not be the exclusive privilege of the rich and powerful.

The political leadership at all levels, from local council to city government, must perform its Romanness for an electorate that, as all politicians know well, includes a constant litany of complaints about the leadership's failures of civic decency. They are trapped in the social imperative to demonstrate precisely the kinds of intimately recognizable trickery or simple disobedience that they officially oppose. When Francesco Rutelli began his tenure as mayor of Rome, for example, he allegedly made quite a point of refusing to wear a seatbelt in his car. To have done otherwise would have been an admission of weakness.[2] When the leadership is trapped in this kind of logic, citizens see no compelling reason to follow the laws themselves. In the intimate spaces of their local culture, they see their politicians, not as the embodiments of a civic ideal, but as eminently human tricksters whose social strengths often lie in what civic or religious morality would treat as their moral weaknesses. Adherence to civic ideals sometimes thus clashes directly with distrust of the state's representatives; the formal precision of the state—as opposed to the social engagement of its corrupt officers—is a poor substitute for the warm sociality of local relations.

The Limits of Law

Italians often lament the inadequacy of their legal system to deal with current social problems. Laws are numerous and mutually contradictory, each successive reform being at best a patchwork response to the most pressing difficulties of the existing legislation; and many are written in such a complex way as to encourage highly creative tactics of evasion. Those charged with the enforcement of the laws are underpaid and mutually suspicious; the several police forces operating on Italian soil are frequently goaded into mutual suspicion and surveillance. Some of the laws lack penal teeth; others, so critics maintain, are deliberately framed to obstruct the forces of law and order in the pursuit of their legitimate duties—as, indeed, some of their severest critics concede.

There is a striking convergence of ideologically very diverse perspectives on one key issue: that the mechanisms of state do not favor the consistent enforcement of the laws. On the Left we hear the charge that the multiplicity of laws written with special interests in mind allows abuses on every side. On the Right we hear complaints about the failure of the state to provide adequate salaries and to equip the authorities with sufficient protection from agile lawyers defending dishonest foreigners as well as citizens. But the consensus across the whole political spectrum is that the defects in question produce the indifference known as *menefreghismo*. And it is clear that these defects originate, at least in part, in the compromises that were made in the formative years of the Italian state in the late nineteenth century.

From the start, the state's leaders struggled to reconcile a perceived need for a strong, centralized state authority with the persistent demands by local political elites for exceptional treatment—concessions to local special interests in the writing of national laws—in exchange for their overall structural compliance. The result was a legal tangle that combined the rhetoric of civic disinterestedness with practices reflecting relations of patronage and favor peddling. This was a key aspect of the political opportunism known as *trasformismo*—here, an idiom of adapting abstract and generic laws to the exigencies of local power.[3] It left a lasting heritage even at a time when local authorities gradually began, after the end of World War II, to wield more power in the management of citizens' everyday concerns; the idea that laws should be constructed so as to incorporate the calculation of benefits and favors dies hard and meshes perfectly with the popular assumption— an assumption grounded on the everyday understanding of such religious instruments as confession and penitence—that all social action entails some sort of calculus of future benefits and exonerations.[4]

The state, many Romans conclude, makes its own calculations. These may include a measure of expendability, applied as much to people as to principles. A retired police officer accused the state authorities of indifference to the economic plight of those who enforced the laws at some danger to their personal safety. The state, he suggested, did not really care—beyond a symbolic gesture of mourning—when officers were killed in the line of duty; it calculatingly treated them, not as human beings with families, but as replaceable cogs in an official machine. Such assertions represent a widespread perception; moreover, the state's alleged indifference provides the ethical alibi—and, in a moral economy of small reciprocities, the model—for acts of callous and self-interested disregard for others.

This disgruntled ex-policeman's account, however partial, shows that law enforcement is as compromised as the laws themselves. Neither can be reduced to a set of abstract rules or norms. Frequent scandals engulf the judiciary, the various police entities, and the banking world. Statutes of limitation, as well as an overworked judiciary and a widespread assumption that judges and advocates have everything to gain by procrastinating indefinitely, render the management of criminal accountability an arena for tactical creativity. Most citizens reason that it is better simply to accept the realities of the situation and to try to draw the maximum benefit from these.

The apparent illogic of the legal situation therefore begins to make better sense when we move away from analyses based on idealist models and formal projections, and consider instead the calculations of lawmakers, bureaucrats, and citizens as occurring in a shared social context. We must remember that those who enact new laws, as well as those responsible for their enforcement, are themselves members of the society over which they exercise these forms of authority. Rather than reading the laws as model texts and their infringement as instances of failures in practice, which prejudges the situation in terms of decontextualized concepts such as efficiency and democracy, I prefer to examine their content for evidence of what we can call "structural collusion": the mutual engagement of legislators and citizens in pragmatic compromises that allow life to go on—not always satisfactorily, to be sure, but at least comprehensibly. In this perspective, even the complaints themselves form an important part of the larger social universe of which the laws themselves are only one component.

There is some evidence, moreover, that legislators act to anticipate possible damage to their own interests in the way they write the laws. In this regard, they act just like other citizens, who calculate probable fines and other punishments in the total cost of their illegal building or restoration, their business practices, or their parking violations. As a local joke has it, a government official visited a prison, and kept telling his secretary to make a note that the kitchens needed improving, showers should be installed, and so on—until the secretary got the point that he was preparing for the moment when they would find themselves in jail! Assuming a clear distinction between legislators and citizens distorts the collusion that occurs even before the laws are passed and applied.

These laws and regulations, moreover, enacted in Rome, must make practical sense in the capital. Between the writing of these laws and rules and their application, only the formal legal language masks the structural collusion that binds legislature and populace together in a convoluted synergy. That synergy converts civic principles into a civility that has more to do with the easy command of courtesy and with the obligations of friendship and neighborliness than with promoting abstract principles of governance. It preserves much of the *trasformismo* of an earlier age—and perhaps also the casuistry of a medieval church trying to come to terms with contradictions between generosity and profit—through the reinforcement of an idiom of political tact. However desirable the immediate social effects of such civility may sometimes be, it does not necessarily favor, and in practice often actively subverts, the technical application of the law. New laws are often intended to fix problems created by previous legislation. That is the intention behind the various *sanatorie* (cleansing laws) by which punishments for previous infractions are reduced and their residue forgiven; city plans are produced to correct the disasters of earlier planning; and rent increases are regulated and deregulated with a calculation that is easily misread as caprice. These devices are socially grounded, necessary, episodic, and circumstantial compromises between formal principle and social reality. A clothes merchant described the state-citizenry symbiosis succinctly and, on the whole, accurately: "The state is fully aware that any merchant, right? is a tax evader.... So, on the state's side, there's a tacit agreement, right? that it will make you pay again later, with other taxes." This restless process, nicely captured in his self-checking speech style, never ceases.

The *sanatorie* are the most obvious examples of the state's adjustment to the habits of its citizens. Sometimes known as *condoni* (pardons), especially in the context of building regulations, they allow the state to collect a small but certain percentage of overdue fines in exchange for the cancellation of the remainder. They have provoked vociferous objections, largely on the grounds that they legitimize and perpetuate violations of the laws designed to protect the historic fabric of the city—which ironically derives its rampant beauty, as we have seen, from the proliferation of such infractions through the centuries.[5] In particular, they have allowed already wealthy speculators, and perhaps also individuals with the convenient power to obtain advance notice of such announcements, to buy and "restructure" substantial properties without troubling themselves excessively about the relevant regulations.

On a broader scale, ambitious city plans (*piani regolatori*) have emerged at various points in the history of modern Rome; each is designed to correct the errors of its predecessors and of other, more localized interventions.[6] By their very nature, however, they incorporate the special interests of current administrations. While some have undoubtedly been better conceived than others, they have also remained very much on the level of general possibility; few of their recommendations are ever translated into a consistent, enduring planning practice. In this, they give reality to the capacity of the Italian language to recognize a distinctively high level of abstraction in planning (*progettualità*, "projectuality"). Such abstraction lends itself to what one might call the alibi of inevitable concreteness; faced with the seemingly ineluctable difficulties of planning Rome's future with any degree of confidence, planners can blame the special interests for which provision is already implicitly made in the plans—indeed, that is the burden of their complaints.

Paolo Berdini's analysis, published when the Jubilee was still in motion, holds enormous interest for any attempt to make anthropological sense of the relationship between legislation and its translation in practice.[7] His focus on various political and ideological forms of culture (*cultura*) and the ways in which they changed not only utilizes a concept central to the discipline; it also permits a comparison with the role of this concept in the intellectual discourse of the political Left on the one hand and the popular adoption of the term as an explanation of attitudes and practices on the other.

Berdini's analysis is a trenchant but also nuanced and judicious dissection of the way in which the supposedly leftist and environmentalist Mayor Rutelli replaced any notion of concerted planning with a piecemeal approach that permitted the intensified resurgence of special interests—including the

Vatican's—in shaping the city's future. But it is also a highly accessible illustration of the explanatory force with which Italians, particularly those of broadly leftist conviction, invest the concept of culture. In this regard, it also helps us to understand how a measure of cultural determinism in public discourse has encouraged the persistence and exaggeration of practices associated with a particular political orientation: clientelism and favor peddling on the right, civic regulation on the left. But his account also shows quite clearly that even professions of a leftist culture do not always stand up to the temptations of power; civic morality yields to the demands of a contingent civility.

For Berdini that contingent civility is apparent in the return under Rutelli to the practice of *pianificar facendo* (planning as you go)—an abandonment of any kind of central plan in favor of dealing with each occasion as it arises. This effectively surrenders the initiative to wealthy and unscrupulous speculators. It is marked by the cult of particular monuments chosen for their extraordinariness (*straordinarietà*) rather than by a sense of the organic wholeness of the city; and this, too, not only serves monumentalization at the expense of local populations but also invites the highest bidders—bankers, construction magnates, media tycoons—to determine many of the important decisions. Such ad hoc arrangements to suit the wealthy and powerful have a long history in Rome.[8]

The (Disreputable) Origins of Legal Loopholes

Construction magnates are especially important players. Berdini's comments on their destructive impact on attempts to maintain a consistent planning policy are matched by the experience of a courageous archaeologist, Andreina Ricci, who risked professional isolation as well as possible danger to her life by exposing the connections among some segments of the conservation bureaucracy, certain construction firms, and private archaeological "consultants" who undertake excavation (excluding the professionals in the process); by officially declaring that it had exhausted the archaeological possibilities of a site in the semirural outer edges of the city (and thus far from the concentrated interests of the tourist industry), such a ghost firm (*ditta fantasma*), usually run by a close relative of someone in the conservation bureaucracy, would open the way to massive construction, with the consequently irreversible destruction of significant ancient remains. By daring to disobey the authorities on several counts, Ricci also exposed their weakness; they did not stop her when she began to excavate again in spite of an interdiction that had been slapped on her. It seems that certain individuals were both angry with and afraid of her because she had managed to undermine their deals.[9]

But the example of the city government was hardly more edifying: Berdini particularly points an accusing finger at Rutelli for his disdainful treatment of Rome's Superintendent of Antiquities, Adriano La Regina, who dared to oppose a planned underpass in front of Castel Sant'Angelo. This project, while relieving heavy traffic congestion, also entailed the destruction of an extensive and well-preserved ancient villa with priceless wall paintings and important architectural elements.[10] By that point, it had become abundantly clear that powerful forces in the city government were determined to please the Vatican, the construction magnates, and the banks—and would treat with contempt any who dared criticize its actions. Given long-standing local irritation with the power of archaeologists to stop ordinary construction and repair work in the historic center, these moves enjoyed considerable popular support—even though, again, Romans often complained about such forms of official vandalism as the destruction of old trees and favored spots for long, sun-drenched chats amid the ruins.

In arriving at their decision on the underpass, the mayor and his team undoubtedly benefited from the increasing lack of clarity in the framing of the city's future. By reworking existing plans, they were able to advance other schemes in which they, the Vatican, and the major construction firms all shared vested interests that were of questionable benefit to the local population. Indeed, it seems that they aimed at the further depopulation of the historic center. When one university professor, unable to cope with the rapidly rising rent on his apartment, went at a friend's urging to ask the church authorities if they had housing available (many of the houses in the area are owned by various churches and confraternities), he was treated with great politeness and encouragement until he reached the door of the administrator: "I entered. Ice and polar cold!" The administrator, a high-ranking cleric, demanded, "Who are you and what do you want?" So he explained that he had heard that the church owned a number of properties in a state of near-collapse (fatiscenti) and that he would be interested in taking such an apartment on and assuming responsibility for all the necessary repairs—an arrangement that church authorities sometimes adopted. The response was a haughty inquiry as to why he was bothering them: "We do not provide houses. . . . There is an appropriate office at city hall; go there." Despite the professor's puzzled insistence on pursuing the matter, specifically emphasizing his interest as a Monti resident, the prelate simply reiterated, "We do not provide houses."

Contemplating this "absolutely disproportionate" reaction, the professor suddenly began to realize that the tactic of sending him off to the city authorities was meant to convince him to move away altogether; and that behind this lay a strategy of discouraging residents from remaining in the historic center. As he remarked, there were "so many politer formulae for saying 'No.'" In a society where even menace is (especially) polite, the cleric's frigid response conveyed a clear message: in their ignorance of our plans, our underlings misled you; we do not want any but the wealthiest people staying in the historic center. The professor, not a man to stand on ceremony, was nonetheless thoroughly disconcerted by such icy rudeness and is convinced that its cause lay in an increasingly consistent policy, at the highest levels of the Vatican administration, of encouraging the depopulation and gentrification of the ancient heart of the city.

That perception accords closely with the indictment that forms the core of Berdini's study. There is a historic irony of massive proportions here, inasmuch as a self-styled leftist and people's mayor was spearheading a policy the closest precedent for which was Mussolini's dismantling of a large segment of Monti in order to build Via dei Fori Imperiali. Mussolini hoped thereby to further his goal of urban sanitization; for the Fascists, Monti and Trastevere were breeding grounds for the criminal classes, Communism, and anarchism. In Trastevere in particular, the streets had gradually been reorganized locally to provide cover for any inhabitants who wished to evade the eyes of authority. Such secrecy was intolerable to a regime bent on total regulation. Surveillance and the program of civic hygiene initiated by Mussolini went hand in hand; suspected Communists were relocated to apartment blocks with few entrances, ensuring the direct policing of residents' comings and goings.

The destruction originally committed in order to create this road was certainly enormous. Among the buildings demolished were important antiquities—most from the imperial era!—as well as medieval, Renaissance, and baroque churches. The ancient remains were dumped along the Via Ostiense, the modern road leading to the ancient port of Rome at Ostia, now a suburban zone but at the time a malarial swamp that the Fascists thereby hoped to sanitize. Architectural historian Italo Insolera writes with undisguised astonishment, "Malaria fought with the dust of ancient Rome: that was one of the most extraordinary things about that insane era."[11] A significant segment of Monti's inhabited area, notably the subdistrict known as Marforio, was also obliterated. Mussolini's intervention, with its obsessively literal and exclusive derivation of *romanità* (Romanness) from the days of imperial glory, caused great hardship among the living population, forcing many of those evicted for his self-aggrandizing scheme to migrate to unpleasant, distant suburbs.[12] It was, surprisingly, a neofascist architect who pointed out the irony that Mussolini's ceremonial roadway was probably the greatest disruption ever made to the urban plan of ancient Rome.

There were thus powerful reasons for Rutelli's administration to obliterate this embarrassing past. But the new archaeological restoration project now proposed oddly echoed Fascism's own preoccupations with the grandeur of *romanità* and with the creation of clean monumental spaces. It was widely viewed, not as an attempt to rescue an important archaeological site from Mussolini's depredations, but as a leftist act of revenge. Even my relatively moderate landlord, the grandson of an engineer who had worked for the Papal State until Unification and then had become a functionary of the new Italian authorities, sniffed that the only reason for it was hatred of the Fascists' memory, and he suggested that this was all of a piece with their fussy regulation of such matters as the colors used to paint house facades. Archaeology has become a problem of excess and nuisance in the eyes of those conservative souls who simply want to continue to live as before. "A modern city can't be a museum city," he fumed. While he hankered indulgently for the Fascists' entrepreneurial modernism, he had little stomach for the bureaucratic modernism of today's political Left, with its rendition of historic conservation as an exercise in audit management and boundary building.

Even relatively poor residents were often surprisingly adamant in their opposition to the demolition of the road and the extension of the archaeological park to cover a much larger area. It was particularly ironic to hear Monti residents inveigh against the Rutelli administration for daring to contemplate the removal of Mussolini's grand processional way. Opposition to the scheme, in the mouths of the descendants and former neighbors of those evicted under the Fascists, shows how the policies of the Italian Left—at both the city and the national levels—had alienated its traditional supporters; these working-class citizens all but forgot their hatred of Fascism as their dislike of the "radical chic" in the city administration intensified to incandescence, fueled, in many cases, by an epidemic of evictions that came to rival the "disemboweling" (*sventramento*) of the historic city center during the Fascist era. As the debate raged on, arguments favoring archeological restoration and air quality improvement (the area was supposed to be cleared of traffic) were increasingly ignored, and the Rutelli administration eventually lost interest—much to the disgust of critics like Berdini, for whom the lackadaisical, piecemeal approach to Rome's problems is nothing short of a surrender to the power cliques that dominate policy decisions.[13]

Some of those who locally criticized the original plan may have been especially inspired, or lured, by opportunistic right-wing politicians' support for the victims of present-day evictions, despite the fact that it had been Mussolini's urban reconstruction that triggered the first major wave of evictions

from the district. The issues of rent control and eviction have followed a legal trajectory as piecemeal and as riddled with instrumental compromises as
the path of historic conservation. A 1998 law liberalized proprietors' rights,
especially through its establishment of a variety of four-year contracts, renewable for a single further four-year term; proprietors could then demand
termination of the contract and, when tenants refused to leave, could request police intervention to enforce their rights. Free of rent control and
of finite duration, this contract type encouraged a virtual epidemic of rent
hikes and consequent evictions.[14] Here, too, we are dealing with legislation
that incorporates features perhaps intentionally designed by the lawmakers
in Rome to undermine its impact and divert it from its ostensible goals.
Legislation providing for strict rent control and a greater balance among the
rents paid in a given building—the so-called *equo canone* principle—had
been introduced in 1978. A scathing critique of its intentions and deficiencies is to be found in Corrado Giustiniani's *La Casa Promessa* (The Promised
House).[15] This work anticipates, in a different context, Berdini's criticisms
of gerrymandered regulation and built-in surrender to special interests.

What Giustiniani demonstrates is that a law intended to resolve some
of the worst inequities of existing conditions produced exactly the opposite
effect. Lacking penal sanctions, and couched in a complex array of cross-references (not to speak of an arcane language marked by an extraordinary fertility of legal cant), the law had the ostensibly unintended consequence of
encouraging underhand deals among the richer proprietors and an increasing
openness to gentrification. Clearly new laws were needed to protect the poor.
Such, on the surface, was the goal of the 1998 law, which specifically protected
tenants from being evicted without due notice. But it also protected the rights
of proprietors against those tenants who had become defaulters (*morosi*) and
gave them a freer hand in determining rents; significantly, it also led to more
comprehensive evictions by encouraging proprietors to sell to builders and real
estate agents or to speculate for themselves, notably on the basis of a stipulation that renewal of a rental contract could be denied because of the projected
"integral restructuring" of an entire building by its current owner.[16] These
developments had disastrous consequences for the poorer residents.

Taken together, the two studies illustrate a more general aspect of Italian
legislative history. As in most countries with parliamentary systems, politicians emerge from a popular base—either representing its class concerns,
or linked to it through vertical ties of patronage, or both. Even so, a few
legislators have not only adopted important causes but have also invested a
good deal of serious effort in them.

Thus, Luciano Violante, a former president of the Senate, has been consistent and active in developing legislation against usury. His efforts are as deeply appreciated as they are frustrated by the tangle of countervailing laws. Listening to Violante speaking at a major anti-usury conference, at which he attacked the tradition of treating the debtor as complicit in the crime itself (much as the church considers borrowers to be theologically culpable for having lured their creditors into the mortal sin of usury), I was struck both by the practicality of his position and the extraordinary amount of legal and social obstructionism he faced. The widow of a victim of usury who had been assassinated for reporting his situation to the authorities warmly declared on another occasion that Violante was an exception to the entire state apparatus, from politicians to *carabinieri*, in his commitment to breaking the vicious circularity of crime. Yet that was precisely why his efforts seemed unlikely to bear fruit. He has actively engaged in interrogating some of the mafia *pentiti* who claimed to have links with the Roman usurers, and has courageously pursued these connections in the hope of discrediting the local subordinates as members of a criminal network now, since the Clean Hands campaign, far more vulnerable to prosecution than ever before. Aside from the predictable obstruction of self-interested politicians, however, the victims of usury are terrified of speaking out. He must thus overcome structural blockage at both the national and the local levels.

More generally, separating legal judgment from its social context of personal favors and special interests—the goal of civic ethics—makes no sense either analytically or from the residents' pragmatic perspective. Not only are existing reciprocities stronger than the moral authority of a poorly respected state but they provide a key resource in the struggle against its perceived depredations. They are also literally embodied in the built environment. We have seen that the old buildings of Monti (and of the entire historic center) testify to the decay that constitutes the tragic core of the human condition. They also testify to the illegality of their own construction, and in multiple layers at that; each layer creates an aesthetic against which its successors innovate though further violation. Once aesthetic concerns are written into law, moreover, as in the powers vested in the Fine Arts Inspectorate, they become an affront to the informal social management of the built environment. The culture of legal practice is often diametrically opposed to legal prescription; like politics, it operates largely within the constraints and enabling mechanisms of everyday life, and cannot realistically be viewed—except insofar as this provides useful excuses for some of its perceived failures—outside that context.[17]

Indulgent Complicities

From a windy rooftop offering a glorious view across virtually the entire historic center of Rome, an architect friend sardonically surveyed the panorama. There, and there, and there—he pointed, we looked, and there, indeed (as he said) everywhere, were the skimpy scaffoldings shaded by umbrellas that signified the start of haste-driven, illegal construction: a new apartment, a store, a bathroom. But the culprits would have looked hurt had they been able to overhear us; they were just putting up some trellises, nothing of a permanent nature, they would have said; and we would have nodded understandingly, signaling our own complicity in this social reality. But there was no one to hear us, and the roaring wind made it difficult for us to hear even each other. Nature too, it seemed, preferred to encourage discretion.

Then, directed by the architect's didactic finger and his counterpoint of complicit chuckles, we saw the next stage: construction work beyond a doubt. And occasionally we could spot examples of the third and final stage, though this—thus was its success made material—was usually hard to discern: once a structure acquires a roof, the bureaucracy finds itself caught in the web of its own regulatory passions, for domestic structures that are recognizable as such may not be demolished at all without complex procedures that offer little hope of anything more than a financial slap on the wrist—a fine for creating an illegality that will now remain, forever embedded in the architectural fabric of the Eternal City. And of that fine, only a small portion will—perhaps—be paid at long last, in a deal that will help the state out of its persistent skirting of bankruptcy. Meanwhile, the offending structures will themselves merge with the cityscape, absorbed into its monumental fabric like countless other illegalities before them.

After all, mused the architect, the entire city is in one sense an illegal construction site. When Napoleon illegally built the balcony of the Palazzo Venezia for his empress Josephine, he was conniving at a practice already old, one that today continues at an accelerated pace: "In Rome abuse of the building code is almost a historical tradition!" (*tradizione storica!*). Or, as a bar proprietor summarized the situation on another occasion: "Rome is built out of illegally constructed houses!"

The architect's eyes traveled across the horizon with knowing indulgence—complicit affection, one might say—over layer upon layer of legal history and its splintered works. He had built his own share of illegal constructions, and had submitted his own complaints about those of others. He knew this world intimately. So, we may be sure, did all his colleagues and clients. There is nothing new in his complicity. The aristocracy had set a bad example at a still earlier date, especially in the seventeenth century, when they thought little of damaging neighboring houses to the greater glory of their own and in one instance, when checked, vindictively getting the pope to forbid the neighbors to have any windows or doors facing the offended party's palazzo.[18]

Such power forces others to into a sometimes unwilling resignation. An influential media tycoon, rumored to wield as much authority in Rome as the Vatican itself, wanted a door cut into the Renaissance building where he lived—an act of sacrilege against the architectural heritage that, as an enemy of his remarked, would have put an ordinary person in jail; as it was, when his foe tried to protest to the officers in charge of the building's condominium, they pointed out that no formal complaint had been lodged at the time—and so not only would the work proceed, but the condominium would have to pay for an irreversible disfigurement of the past! Thus is collusion forged out of the very bedrock of opposition even as it reconfigures the built environment yet again. As a retired laboratory assistant from one of Rome's universities remarked, "Here in Italy what is provisional lasts for so very long!"[19] It lasts long enough, in fact, to contribute to the sense of a living, breathing city, one that accretes layer after layer of historical departures from previous norms. A few examples of law enforcement make for spectacular exceptions; helicopters spot the illegal constructions, and the bulldozers move in. Many of these interventions occur far from the historic center; they are expensive and therefore necessarily also rare.

Nor is there much popular enthusiasm for them. A furniture restorer, a man both ideologically and professionally much taken with the idea of preserving antiquities (but also one who did not shy away from profiteering through the creative reconstruction of minor art objects), pointed out that one of Italy's endemic problems lay in a besetting preference for construction over conservation; the prevailing pattern of patronage required the immediate gratification of short-term projects rather than the painstaking investment of time and effort in continual refurbishment. The evidence is everywhere; the repeated laying, removal, and replacement of sidewalk cobblestones testifies, in most citizens' opinion, to the corruption that allows crooked contractors to do shoddy work precisely so that they will then be paid for removing and replacing it.

In short, Rome was certainly not built in a day; but it was (and is) built and rebuilt at a tempo and according to rules that have rarely been those approved by officialdom—or, more accurately, by officialdom acting officially. It is an architectural monument to something more furtive and yet also more lasting: the capacity to thwart the arid admonitions of the law by generating in their place, sometimes out of unpromising materials, a warmly sensual, inhabited, and ecstatically illicit beauty.

In this, the city is consistent with the a church that views the peccadilloes of its endemically errant flock with an indulgent eye. Indulgent indeed—for it is in the practice of offering documents so named (*indulgenze*), as a documentary guarantee of accelerated passage through Purgatory for the faithful,[20] that facilitates the advance calculation of the material cost of sin and allows people to adjust their moral budgets accordingly. In a society where cleverness counts for more than saintliness, any gain in social stature is underwritten by theological guarantees against eventual perdition. Little acts of cunning tip the balance decisively in favor of social standing; a butcher who was unable to find enough chicken livers to satisfy an exigent and extremely wealthy client from a nationally prominent family proudly showed off his cleverness to his assistant—and to me—when he announced that he would mix what he had with some rabbit livers so that the client would never notice the difference! And jewelers save money by filing off small quantities of gold from each object and by beating rings and other objects to a larger size after they have first been shaped.

Minor peccadilloes are the very stuff of social life. Even devout Monticiani know that they can always ultimately count on the sacrament of confession to absolve them from small offenses made necessary, they would argue, by the brute inequalities of everyday social experience. The secular as much as the religious authorities also reject the idea that such deals should become precedents, but in fact know perfectly well that they will. Indeed, public debate about the state's repeated recourse to these measures emphasizes the dangers of habit-forming conveniences for the long-term health of the polity.

Thus, artisans rely on the state's willingness to engage into tacit reciprocity whereby social security payments remain low and are payable in small installments but the pensions are also small. This connivance is "an unacknowledged fact" that the state tolerates, said one (relatively prosperous) restorer, "also because it is just"; as an artisan, he "could never be a major tax evader." Indeed, most tax evasion by artisans is small-scale, and is similarly grounded in shared, tacit understandings. Customers often do not ask for receipts, knowing that in exchange the artisan will not pass on to them the state and other taxes such as *Iva*, or value-added tax (although a dishonest shopkeeper can as easily take advantage of the related practice of providing a receipt without listing the actual goods so that no one can later check the price); artisans say that for their part it is virtually impossible to survive without a certain proportion of illegal (that is, unreceipted) work. One maker of metal stamps and signage told me that his problem lies in working with too many government offices, all of which demand very precise accounting; his accountant tries to talk him into giving fewer receipts in order to reduce his tax bill, but he simply cannot do that in transactions with any official bureau.

Occasionally, on the other hand, if too many private customers ask for reduced prices in exchange for unreceipted work, an artisan has to invent some transactions and declare earnings from these, simply to establish credibility. A carpenter said that he was forced by private citizens to work without a receipt as a way of avoiding value-added tax; he then had to produce imaginary receipts at least to the amount of 40,000,000 *lire* for the tax year, as this is the minimum that the state simply assumes the artisan must be earning. The financial consequence of declaring his real income would be far worse, forcing him to close down for good. The tax officers presumably recognized the ruse for what it was; they are complicit in what everyone recognizes as a performance and an invention. Such performances have clear and substantive consequences, since, when they are successful, they deflect the bureaucrats' attention away from minor but useful derelictions while saving the bureaucrats a great deal of work into the bargain.

The pattern, then, is of a state system willing to countenance a fairly high degree of defaulting as long as, in the end, it can reclaim a sufficient part of what is owed to it. With the *condono edilizio*, moreover, the practice is recognized in a systematic and institutional framework, which grants individual absolution under cover of a generic law.[21] The authorities established a special office to administer the paperwork of what are, in effect, prefabricated plea bargains. For Rome alone, nearly half a million requests from the *condono* of 1985 were further inflated by a sudden influx of another ninety thousand almost as soon as the neoliberal Berlusconi government took power—a great boon to the construction magnates who immediately rushed in to take advantage of this new windfall, but in reality quite a serious financial blow to a municipal administration that now had to clean up the resulting mess. To make matters still more complicated, the older habit of simply adding illegal construction to existing and entirely legal buildings now spread far beyond the confines of the historic center.[22] It seems that even the goal of restocking the state's and city's coffers was not well served by the *condono* policy.

A senior official of the new *condono* office was quick to point out that the practice followed the Catholic model of the indulgence.[23] As with the ecclesiastical doctrine of original sin, moreover, those responsible for administering this program are thoroughly aware of the pressures that drive the poorer segments of society, especially, to commit offenses that can then be cleansed, increasing the functionaries' power in the process. For this official, the parallel with the confessional and the indulgence gained further credibility from the fact that the *condono* did not only benefit the homeowners; the contractors who had undertaken the illegal work could now likewise request similar relief in exchange for paying a predetermined proportion of their residual fines.

The official spoke of the presence of "an enormous illegal real-estate heritage" (*un enorme patrimonio immobiliare irregolare*). This terminology is richly suggestive; the collective inheritance of illegally constructed buildings is a consequence of the practical difficulty that poor and middle-class citizens face in trying to create decent homes (as the official conceded). Just as the church is as burdened with inherited sin as its flock, so the government inherits its predecessors' debts and the state as a whole inherits a "patrimony" of illegal housing that it would be both cruel and impracticable to demolish in any significant measure. The historic center is less liable to excesses of illegal construction than the outlying and poorer suburbs, if only because major new construction among the monumental remains and baroque streets has now become very rare. The fact that the city police write observational reports (*verbali*) but have little power to intervene when they do not actually see the illegal construction being carried out, however, allows the owners of the mostly small older houses in the historic center to make changes in infinitesimal increments, and so to evade detection with relative ease as long as they do not interfere with the facades. The entire *patrimonio* of the old city is thus, as the architect pointed out from the rooftop, riddled with effects of centuries of accumulated illegal construction; the sins of the city fathers have truly been visited on successive generations—a logical corollary, albeit one that would not be evident to the stranger's unknowing eye, of the Vatican's monumental strategy of enfolding the present consequences of original sin in an architectural forward march toward eternity.[24]

It is also an inheritance that carries within itself the marks of a temporality that is embedded in social life rather than in the rule of law. Indeed, the 1985 law itself recognized the problem, and the official remarked that with this law the state created "the moratorium on this heritage that was called "sub-spontaneously [*sic*] construction heritage"—a curious term, as he admitted, and used to describe the vast agglomeration of illegal building that it would now be virtually impossible to dismantle. The law sought to legalize this "sub-spontaneity" retroactively, thereby ensuring that yet another layer of illegal construction be added to Rome's already massively encrusted architectural history. The official described it as " paying a sum of money as an oblation, and then not merely oblation money [but also] a sort of fine, of punishment, that made it possible to render licit the fact of not having had a building permit." The metaphor of oblation—a gift to the church and its charities, for which the primary model is the offering of the bread and wine of the Eucharist—reinforced the religious imagery with which he conceived of the entire operation. The money thus rendered paid for the additional services the city government had to provide for areas, usually in the outlying and less salubrious suburbs, that were entirely made up of illegal construction.

The city authorities accept this pattern with some alacrity. When a Franco-Italian research team looked at ways of improving suburban conditions, moreover, the French were apparently shocked to discover that the Italians had in place a fully articulated system for acknowledging the ownership rights of those who had built illegally and for authorizing their active participation, on the basis of these illegal constructions, in the process of self-regeneration (*auto-ricupero*). Carlo Cellamare, who was a participant, recalled that the French partners were utterly astonished by the Italians' "culture of sin" (*cultura del peccato*) and their application of a system of pardons whereby the state, far closer to Catholic models than the self-consciously secularist French republic, allowed offenders to pay off their misdemeanors while also incorporating the illegal constructions in successive phases of planning.

Forgiveness and Calculation

The practice of giving indulgences was one of the major causes of Martin Luther's break with the Catholic church. Luther's objections, which sometimes find a sympathetic echo in modern Italy, centered on the monetary aspect; indulgences were sold to further the Vatican's earthly goals, and the church's alleged greed made it virtually certain that a pretense of penitence would suffice to bring about the desired pardon. The discomfort of the Left with the practice of the *condono* has a distinctly "protestant" feel to it, but it is also grounded in a reluctance to let the old masters of corrupt government—with their well-known ties to the construction industry[25]—continue their shameful deeds.

The theme of forgiveness came into particularly sharp focus during the Jubilee year, especially with an acrimonious debate in parliament about whether and to what extent state prisoners should receive acts of clemency, as urged by the pope; the very root of the word Jubilee (*Giubileo*) is a Hebrew term denoting a ritual time for the forgiving of debts—and this fact also acquired considerable resonance in a city more than ever conscious of the role Jews have played in maintaining its specific identity. The traditional Left also became increasingly angry with Mayor Rutelli because, having seemed to promise no cooperation with the big construction firms (many of which are reputed to have mafia ties), he then proceeded invoke the emergency of the Jubilee as a reason for developing massive projects in conjunction with precisely this category of operator-entrepreneurs.

The general attitude to the pope's call for clemency appears, nicely satirized, in a cartoon accompanying a message from Pasquino, the talking statue. The pope's face is shown overlooking the Regina Coeli prison, and to the left appears the inscription, "*Ammate, ammate, ammate, fili mi'; ammate, arirrubate, stuprate, Dio ve perdona*" (Love, love, love, my children; love, rob [and] rape; God pardons you), and to the right, "*Qui commanno io*" (Here it is I who commands) and an apostrophe "*a li fedeli ammaestrati*" (to those trained in the faith) and the "signature" of Pasquino. The disapproval is clear: pardoning convicted criminals appeared to exonerate criminals of extraordinary influence and wealth while also encouraging permissiveness toward street crime. But it also signals rejection of the Vatican's paternalism, with its pervasive expropriation of charity and mercy for suspect political ends.

The bureaucratic adoption of the indulgence principle and the secular cooptation of the rhetoric of the Jubilee are both consistent with a conspicuous process observed by David Kertzer in the festive ceremonies of the old Communist Party (*Pci*), which strategically adopted the forms of Catholic ritual as a way of reassuring those who feared the church's threats of excommunication for all Communists.[26] But the *condono edilizio* represents more than simply an expropriation of ritual form. It is also deeply rooted in Roman understandings of the spaces of their city; the translation of moral accounting into architectonic space is literally grounded in doctrinal practice as well.

For the church acknowledges as a microcosm of the divinely ordained universe the sacred geography of a parish, of which Rome as a whole is exemplary and of which individual parishes then serve as further refractions. That reproduction of the presence of the divine is further cemented by the devotion of each priest to the physical spaces of his parish. But those spaces are themselves both scarred and ornamented by the less devotionally motivated imperfections of all who dwell therein—and who rebuild as they dwell.

The principle of the indulgence is literally written in stone in Monti. Not only does the late-eighteenth-century inscription on Via Baccina still promise a reduced passage through Purgatory in exchange for penitential prayers, but the accumulated effects of the *condono* policy are visible at every turn: a bathroom stuck out on a balcony, windows that break the rhythm of a facade, pipes and cisterns on the outside of much older walls, the ubiquitous sproutings of umbrellas gaily marking the start of new abuses and disguising an enormously complicated calculus of risk and opportunity.

Calculations are precise; once, when I met an upholsterer dragging a heavy mattress along the street, he explained that using his car would have cost him too much in fines for illegal entry. But many fines are simply never paid. Unpaid fines are initially added to one's tax bill. If a citizen stalls too long, the authorities may show up and try to sequester the offender's more expensive goods, such as a television set, at which point the citizen pays up and the bailiffs go away again. But the citizen may also be in luck; the clerks who must transfer the information about unpaid fines to the tax office may dawdle too long, at which point the citizen is relieved of further worry by a generous statute of limitations.

This is a guessing game in which timing—the rhythm of response and action—is both crucial and unpredictable. The law is notoriously slow, and this fact creates some space for creative management. Bureaucrats, too, have their characteristic *tempi*, say the locals; indeed, a city policeman admitted that delaying procedures could be an effective way of extracting a present (*regalo*)—that is, a bribe. A performance of choreographically staged foot-dragging and sudden alacrity also allows the bureaucrats' superiors to stay above the fray by "looking good, looking calm."

The concept of *tempo* as elaborated by Pierre Bourdieu is as relevant to the practical management of taxation and the administration of fines as it is to the study of flamboyant masculine performances.[27] It is not by chance that Romans also use the term *tempo*, with its implications of musical style. While the city administration tried to convince its public that time was a matter of punctuality and efficiency, both necessary appurtenances of the new economic and civic order that these administrators envisioned, most Romans experienced—and connived in producing—delays, prevarications, and creative ways of buying time in the hope of fending off legal consequences indefinitely.[28]

Legal process bristles with examples of creative time management, both through the constant media reports of long delays in judicial process and in the minutiae of court practices.[29] In a system in which some actors may be both legislators and suspected malefactors who create laws in anticipation of the possible future need to be able to use convenient loopholes, the legal culture would seem to be a refraction of larger cultural values through a formal system that these actors have learned to operate to their own and their allies' advantage.[30] They buy time to meet a debt or in the hope of an amnesty such as the *condono*. While there may indeed be no direct evidence that economic players reinforce this system in anticipation of the day when they may in turn need to defend themselves from charges of debt or incompetence,[31] the suspicion itself—like the similar charges laid against legislators—forms part of the cultural environment.

In some ways, these temporalities are not unlike those of the Roman kitchen, in which a sense of precise but embodied timing, based on experience rather than formal recipes, is valued over abstract calculation and complicated ingredients. What matters is less whether an action is slow or fast than whether the actor is able to bend and shape the timing enough to demonstrate effective control over it.[32] Romans take enormous pride in the simplicity of their cuisine, attributing this feature to the deprivations suffered under papal rule; but that simplicity also serves, like a humble or unsophisticated manner of speech, to frame and emphasize the timing that bespeaks dexterity and wit. A simple dish of parboiled chicory, rapidly fried with garlic and chili in an extremely hot, heavy pan (*padella*), is significantly known to locals as *cicoria ripassata*—that is, the vegetable has been rapidly "passed through" the hot oil, and mistiming can result in a flaccid mess rather than the crisp and spicy delicacy that this dish should be. Coffee, too, is all about timing; not for the Roman barista the clocks and beepers of the American coffee chain stores, but a public performance of instinctual dexterity amidst a host of other tasks and social graces, the latter including a stream of witty, ironic conversation. These transient but intense pleasures help us understand the embodied and serendipitous opportunism of Roman life more generally and remind us that in legal life, too, a good performance in and out of court may count for far more than a knowledgeable but dull reading of legal prescriptions. All social transactions, legal and illegal, entail the playful but consequential manipulation of tempo.

Usurers exemplify this temporal creativity. Ostensibly intent on holding their clients to precise payment schedules, they actually stretch and pull these schedules when that seems the likeliest way to regain their loans and collect the promised interest. Since time is theologically a divine property, to calculate realistic rhythms of debt repayment marks usury as an offense against religious as well as secular law. But usurers, who are already considered lost to eternal perdition, are unlikely to entertain qualms about such a detail.

When illegal actions meet legal practice, moreover, the play of rhythm and timing can extend over surprisingly long stretches of expiation and self-exculpation. Charged with usury when his associates deserted him and absconded with most of the money, the manager of an informal rotating credit association initially tried to get his trial postponed in the hope of a timely amnesty, although, when it became clear that this was not about to happen, he decided that a couple of million *lire* would be an acceptable punishment. When I sympathetically observed that the collapse was hardly his own fault, he replied with practical stoicism and striking candor, "I know. But these things are illegal"—that is, in the eyes of the state, which now had no choice but to prosecute, since the collapse had made the original illegality of the rotating credit arrangement too visible to be ignored according to the usual compromise. This man's sense of pragmatic calculation excluded fighting a hopeless battle on indefensible grounds, no matter how supportive the moral judgment of local observers might have been. But then he began to hope again, at least for a measure of relief, thinking that the pope's Jubilee call for clemency might help him. There was even a chance that the left-wing parties would force through an entire amnesty, in which case he might never so much as be tried on these charges. But he also continued to count on the lawyers' delaying tactics, since the chances of amnesty in fact appeared to be very dim. Such battles take place on many fronts at once.

Some may appear to be more fortunate in their machinations, even if, in the end, they must appear to cede gracefully to the inevitable—itself an important recuperation of social capital from the jaws of financial disaster. Thus, a wealthy participant in a Monti condominium found himself threatened with a lawsuit when he failed to pay his annual fees; but he and the condominium administrator who served the writ clearly had an understanding that he would now pay up all his arrears, having gained a substantial amount of interest through the delay. A close but cynical friend noted with both admiration and a measure of malicious glee that his delaying action had been effective but had now come to an end: "It's been years since he paid up. But now he does." (It is probably indicative of a very comfortable mutual understanding that the defaulter subsequently offered strong support to the administrator when a group of the residents wanted to fire the latter.[33]) Evidently, however, the tactic was a repeatable act; and the same man, who employed the friend's daughter, only paid her wages under pressure and then with a check postdated by several months.

For those in arrears with their taxes and fines, the ability to manage time with a certain insouciant flair pays off handsomely. As with the confessional, moreover, sometimes quite nominal slaps on the wrist can—if the payoff is sufficient—provide complete absolution from any further guilt. It is in this context that the widely reported priestly abuses of the confessional as a site of wheeling and dealing provide a significant model. One would not have to prove that priests are always so outrageously corrupt—indeed, I would very much doubt it—in order to see that the widespread assumption that they are provides a familiar template for understanding the institutionalized venality of the bureaucratic state as well.

In avoiding the payment of fines, timing is crucial; the citizen will try to figure out when the next *condono* is likely to arrive. Beyond the general expectation that some such amnesty will eventually appear, however, prediction is wildly uncertain. The citizen must try to calculate the probabilities of getting a new government within a short time; if the prediction is accurate, the citizen has a better chance of getting off with a vastly reduced fine and comprehensive absolution from future prosecution. Such calculations form part of the accounting that each householder must do, much as parking fines are calculated into a citizen's monthly expenses. (In fact, citizens often simply ignore them, calculating, at minor risk, that the authorities will never follow up.) Citizens have learned to compensate for their own imperfections by relying on the similarly inherited weaknesses of the authorities. The parallel with the doctrinally grounded pragmatics of the Catholic church seems inescapable.

Priests, as human beings, are as subject as their parishioners to the consequences of original sin; in a district favored by such a notorious libertine as the Borgia pope Alexander VI, it should probably come as no surprise that even priests have frequented the brothels of Monti in recent memory. Like their parishioners, too, priests find reflected in the Roman landscape the evidence of their flawed condition; and if they do not see this clearly, lay people are more than willing to point it out, as in the frequent anticlerical graffiti that litter the walls. There is also a punning Roman proverb that ironically lampoons the church's presumed venality: "*a Roma Dio non è trino, è quatrino*" (in Rome God is not triune, He's a *quatrino* [a coin formerly issued by the Vatican State]).[34]

Conversely, the Vatican, like many bureaucracies, shares much of the culture of those whose lives it regulates, and the church has trained the population well in the practicalities of moral accounting. The recurrent prospect of absolution from taxes and fines at a minimal immediate charge thus materializes, not so much a high-minded morality, as a practical and earthy orientation—an ethical calculus—in which ecclesiastical and secular models converge. Could it be that the Romans' reputation among other Italians for salty, ironic directness owes something to their proximity to the all-too-obvious moral fragility of the church and its personnel, and, by extension, of these clerics' lay counterparts in the local and national bureaucracies of this complex capital city?

Violations of the building code are frequent and varied, but they all seem to follow the tripartite temporal structure indicated by my architect friend. Rome, remarked a Sardinian resident, is like a beautiful woman: you love her and hate her at the same time, particularly because, amidst all the beauty, the city has "grown badly"—and even as he and others complain about this, they themselves continue to challenge the laws. The relatively new institution of the *condono* is only one of the measures that ensure the survival of Rome's riotously hybrid built environment and perpetuate a far older artistic vision of Rome as a city of beautiful fragments. Piranesi's prints, for example, display artful ruins that emerge as architectural models of Rome's fractured claims on eternity. Piranesi was active during a time when many of Monti's palazzi were constructed. But there are still older corners of Rome—Michelangelo's archway across Via Giulia, for example— that today, with their drapery of foliage, seem to imitate Piranesi rather than the other way around. In this sense, his prints represent a convergence of foreign visitors' love of picturesque disorder and the ongoing practicalities of Romans' everyday lives. In his day, the city's claims on eternity were already well and truly fractured and refracted—sometimes much more violently than they are today.[35]

In the modern age, neoliberalism and cheap mass tourism have brought about some unprecedented changes. These notably accelerated at the time of the preparations for the 2000 Jubilee. They have largely worked against the promiscuous vision of Rome as a kaleidoscope of fragments; they represent a more bureaucratic and "protestant" view of the city. The newspaper kiosks, for example, were all required to adopt a visual format not unlike those of their Parisian equivalents. Such homogenization, energetically pursued by Francesco Rutelli,[36] sits uncomfortably with Rome's hitherto piecemeal development.

Against that vision, however, conservation regulations have had unintended consequences. Because digging new foundations is highly likely to lead to new archaeological discoveries, bringing construction to a complete halt, most property owners prefer to continue to "restructure" the existing buildings rather than start completely new construction. This process involves sometimes massive changes to the internal disposition of space; houses that have changed little since bathing was done with a sponge or in public baths require drastic refashioning for occupancy by wealthy new owners or renters.

Other objections to the historic conservation regime of the state have focused on the official insistence on using standardized colors for restored older palazzi. A barman expressed deep disgust that a wall facing his establishment was left in a state of dilapidation because the conservation authorities would not permit the use of new colors more in harmony with modern taste; the frustrated proprietor then apparently decided to leave the wall as it was, prompting the barman's irritation. Regulation thus paradoxically attempts to preserve the picturesque confusion and dilapidation of the city, but in a way that removes it from the social and aesthetic agency of the citizenry, erecting little fences around monuments and other features of note: Piranesi's ghost in the age of mechanical reproduction.[37]

Romans are not hostile to preserving the remains of the past, but they object to the excessive regulation that they attribute to the bureaucratic state. That state forbids even internal changes. Yet one furniture restorer told me that when she removed the parquet in her apartment and found a layer of concrete underneath that, she excavated further and found an attractive early-twentieth-century decorated floor that led her to remark that she had been walking on stars without even knowing it! While such modern artifacts might be of little interest to the conservation authorities, moreover, and while her action in digging beneath the parquet could have been construed as a violation of the rules, she clearly felt that, as a Roman "of ten generations" (*da dieci generazioni*),[38] she had a right to decide what was worth preserving.

Sacred Images and Sinful Spaces

The calculation of moral debt and forgiveness is written into the very streets. The convergence between secular and sacred power is ineluctable; it was the papal authority that imposed fines "and other punishments" on those who dared leave their garbage in inappropriate places—a restriction that was apparently as cheekily defied then as the environmental laws requiring differentiated garbage collection (*raccolta differenziata*) are today. These were secular offenses; but they were framed in the same language and style as the inscription that promises accelerated redemption from Purgatory in exchange for reiterations of the *Ave Maria* before the Madonna's image.

The Mother of God, thus entreated to mediate on behalf of the humble sinners who have already calculated what her intervention will cost them, is indeed everywhere. We meet her in the little shrine plaques and figurines, the *Madonnelle* that adorn so many houses around Monti, evidence of a constant and pressing need for intercession. Thus it is that we also meet her, as one somewhat cynical friend noted, in the pose struck by a mother perched demurely on a bed and holding her child, a woman who was acting her part in a real estate scam as the pious tenant who hopes that the new purchaser will remember her need when the deal is struck. She is young; but hers, no less than that of the youthful prostitutes whose antecedents plied their trade in the same location in antiquity, is a very old and recognizable presence here. The iconography that she evokes is even perhaps pre-Christian; many archaeologists argue that the Madonna imagery follows that of the imported Egyptian goddess Isis nursing her son Horus.[39] But these Romans were disinclined to take her meek appeal to piety as anything more than the prelude to a scam. Given their conviction that such, too, is the moral standard of the ecclesiastical establishment itself, one wonders why she even bothers—but there are women similarly holding out their hands in a piteous gesture of seeking alms on the main street nearby, and, yes, some take pity on them and drop a few coins in their outstretched hands.

Religious syncretism in the art of fixing and muddling through? Why not? Roman Christianity is a very practical religion, its adherents sinners by self-ascription and thus adept in the arts of self-justification and moral cost-benefit analysis. Invocations of piety for material reasons are unlikely to be challenged when many are convinced that the Vatican colludes with the mafia, where confession has been shown to have served venal political ends, and where papal calls to show charity and hospitality to the homeless seem to coincide, tactlessly but revealingly, with dramatic cases of eviction by churches and confraternities. On the secular authorities' appeal to the citizens to provide paid accommodation for Jubilee pilgrims, a banker reckoned that an ordinary householder could make 10,000,000 *lire* that way in the course of a year; but his friend, a picture-framer, retorted that a local priest would *only* do it for the money!

So what Romans see in the figure of the Madonna is not simply the immaculate Virgin, but the comforter of sinners, and especially of those whose greed for money exceeds their needs and so risks placing their souls in danger of eternal perdition. In Italian society more generally, the mother figure remains the pre-eminent symbol of indulgence, the bearer of spoiled and sometimes violent males[40]—those whose actions require the unending redemption offered by the sufferings of Christ, and, more trivially but also perhaps more magnificently, whose infractions against the building and conservation codes pervade every nook and cranny. Cause and effect merge here in a terrible synchrony.

CHAPTER SIX

Scandals of Sociability

Usury represents one source of the hidden viciousness that occasionally disrupts the social pleasures of Monti life. Once the territory of minor underworld clans, Monti began to open up to much more powerful sources of crime, notably the global drug trade, from the 1950s on. The massive anti-corruption drives of the early 1990s weakened the remaining areas of local reciprocity without necessarily defeating the protection rackets that continued to thrive. Throughout these changes the presence and exploitation of fear have persisted. And it is this fear that partly explains the relative invisibility, amid the sun-drenched monuments and shaded alleys of Monti, of the considerable suffering that organized crime has brought in its train.

Usury, for example, is a hidden presence in Monti; some residents might be surprised at the prominence I give it here. But the surreptitiousness of its local presence and the way in which it feeds on idioms of social relationship and temporal control illuminate the production of fear in the most intimate spaces of social life. Usurers represent both an evil and a need; as such, they emblematize, in an extreme and sometimes terrifying guise, the dilemmas and paradoxes that all Monticiani face.

Friends Who Strangle

Usurers have an extraordinarily ugly reputation. They are known as *strozzini* (stranglers) and *cravattari* (from *cravatta*, necktie, apparently because they can draw a debtor's pocket tightly just as one ties a necktie around one's neck), and they are ubiquitous in Rome, where, as an electrician said, "there's an ocean of them!" They are feared, but they are also known. Most people go to moneylenders who operate at an extremely local level; it is hard to track down usurers except through word of mouth among trusted friends, and the usurers themselves prefer to find clients whose reputations for economic solvency they can hold hostage to local public opinion. To be known as a chronic debtor is socially calamitous. It also initiates an ineluctable, endless downward spiral as each new failure of solvency forecloses other sources of loans and even of moral support; the usurers themselves, among whom there is what one commentator called "an iron pact," will conspire to discredit a chronic defaulter socially, punishing the hapless artisan or small merchant in exemplary fashion as a warning to others.

Suicide is often the only escape from such crushing debt. Such was the fate of one bar proprietor and manager of a football fan club. This entrepreneur ran a rotating credit association and accepted as pawn articles of value that belonged to members who were unable to pay their regular quotas; he then sold off these objects at prices considerably below their market value,[1] finding local customers with ease. He was able to do this under the very noses of the tax police, the *Guardia di Finanza*. Its agents would come to check on his cash register—ironically, they did once discover that it was issuing receipts without recording the amounts and fined him 5,500,000 *lire* for an infraction of which he had probably been completely unaware!—and reportedly overlooked, or did not care to understand, the evidence before them that he was simultaneously running an illegal (but frequently tolerated) type of operation; his members would be brazenly writing up the association's accounts while the tax inspectors were still checking on the cash register. Even this operation, however, did not rescue him from his own growing debts, so he in turn, having exploited the economic distress of some weaker members in his association, was forced to borrow money from a still more powerful usurer. But he became the ultimate victim of his own machinations; his debts continued to increase, and there were now no other sources of money to which he could turn. When he realized that he could no longer break free of his increasingly precipitous fall, he shot himself.

Each usurer has a distinctive beat, a unique clientele, and locally recognized idioms of threat and violence for extorting the prompt payment of high interest charges. Their deep-rootedness in local society makes them relatively immune from prosecution, both because betrayal is considered a blow against local solidarity and because the reach of their retaliation is immediate, swift, and exemplary. One or two Monti usurers have maintained ramified business interests in the district so that their power was further enhanced by the secretive whispering of cowed neighbors—neighbors who knew of threatening phone calls in the night or saw the daily impunity with which such people violated building codes and other laws. The only power their debtors had over them was the threat of being unable to pay up at all.

One barman even claimed that the banks were worse than usurers, because, whereas banks would crack down on defaulters without mercy, the usurers would generally extend deadlines to a certain extent if that ensured that the debts would thereby be settled; they had no legal means of enforcing payment, and thus tended not to use violence unless they thought that it was the only way to get results.

The dislike of banks is certainly pervasive and intense; one official of an artisans' union suggested that usurers occasionally even saved poor artisans from complete ruin when the banks refused to help them. Most regard banks as the true usurers. Even working for a bank as a lowly employee carries social risks, as I learned when one of my friends teasingly called a bank clerk a thief (ladro) in a jesting tone that nevertheless carried more than a hint of opprobrium. Artisans' solitary work habits lead other, more educated colleagues to assume with a knowing air that, in order to survive, such wretches must indeed be getting loans from usurers. A bank that had demanded payment of a considerable amount of interest on a loan to a merchant hastily agreed to halve the amount when it became clear that the merchant knew that the bank had used a dishonest consultant to value the merchant's collateral at double its real worth. The consultant's cousin told me about this incident, remarking that a consultant's capital was purely a matter of credibility (fiducia)—a social rather than a factual attribute, often subsisting in dishonest complicity rather than generic trustworthiness.[2] Among friends, the consultant could always claim to have miscalculated in order to allow for the kind of recalculation I have just described, perhaps by hinting that real estate values were unstable. "Even the banks are usurious," sighed the consultant's cousin, although he did not seem to think that another consultant would have acted differently in a similar situation. The system works because the standards of social capital are largely a matter of consensus.

As a result of this wider sense of shared involvement and the fear that debtors generally feel about reporting acts of extortion, usurers get caught only very occasionally. One young woman, a merciless extortionist and the daughter of a local prostitute who had built up a substantial capital from her trade, found herself trapped by her victims when she went to demand her payment at a time when she knew them to be in difficulty; she started screaming at them, and a pair of carabinieri who happened to be strolling past at the time (or perhaps had been alerted in advance) demanded to know what the fuss was all about. On learning that she had loaned the shopkeepers 10,000,000 lire and was now demanding 11,000,000 from them, they hauled her off in handcuffs and went on to discover a large stash of gold, watches,

and other precious objects that had evidently been offered to her as pawn to
stave off her terrible demands. A jeweler thought that the capture of another
woman who had been caught in the same way must have been set up "to
hide the fact that someone denounced her."[3]

Such occurrences are in any case very rare. In this instance, the woman
was soon out of jail and returned to live in the district, fully at ease with
her nasty reputation and with the neighbors' resentment; indeed, she needed
that reputation in order to enforce payment by her customers. She nevertheless also represented a necessary evil, she was local, and she evidently continued to provide her dangerous services for those desperate enough to accept
them. In this sense she exemplified the fundamental paradox of usury: it is
particularly heinous to profit from the miseries of those who are socially
closest, be they kin or neighbors, but it is precisely over these same people
that usurers can exercise the greatest degree of social and moral pressure
even as they present themselves as friends who have come to the rescue in
a moment of dire need.[4]

Usurers are nothing if not practical. If they know that their debtors are
unable to pay but scent the possibility of a reasonably profitable compromise, they can sometimes be induced to accept such an arrangement; this
usually entails renegotiating the deadline for repayment. A couple who ran
a bar expanded their business and opened a restaurant; lacking both experience and financial knowledge, however, they immediately plunged into
debt. As their situation worsened and they approached more and more
usurers in order to pay off existing debts, it seemed as though they would
never be able to reverse the spiraling collapse of their fortunes. One of the
usurers, a Gypsy from a family of well-known criminals with alleged connections to Sicilian mafiosi,[5] had a ferocious reputation that he enhanced
with threats of kidnapping children and setting fire to homes; another, a
drug addict with mincing steps and heavy gold jewelry, simply told stories
of his crimes without directly threatening his debtors at all. The couple became desperate, fearing for their lives as well as for their economic survival.
But a brother-in-law intervened, with the help of a lawyer (who profited by
getting the entire clan of Gypsy moneylenders as clients, a very lucrative
arrangement); they brought all the moneylenders to the table with the distraught couple, and the brother-in-law agreed to help settle the debt—but on
his terms, which meant the return of the original loan plus the compound
interest to date, but without any further interest payments. The creditors
agreed because they saw that this was the only way they would be able to
make any money at all out of the situation (and they gained an adroit lawyer

in the process). The couple eventually went into partnership with the brother-in-law; he also borrowed money to advance their now-joint business, but on far better terms—from several friends, including a prostitute who—like many of her older colleagues in Monti—saw financial generosity as a way of buying friendship and compensating for her fallen status; and a cousin (mother's sister's son), who was willing to help for reasons of kinship and affection. The brother-in-law's hard-nosed approach had saved the entire family from ruin, while his affluent local contacts allowed them to improve their fortunes dramatically from then on.

The Cultivation of Fear

Usurers generally keep a low profile. They rely on their victims to be complicit in maintaining their relative invisibility, as they, too, have too much to lose through the exposure of their indebtedness. The very difficulty I experienced in trying to elicit information about usury in the district signified, not the absence of such practices (as some residents rather defensively claimed), but the presence of fear—fear of social ostracism, fear of a loss of social as well as financial credibility, fear of violent responses to any kind of exposure. An official of an artisans' union said that the victims of usury experienced it as shameful, much like drug addiction, and would usually only speak of it when they were at last emerging successfully from the nightmare. The taint of having fallen into a usurer's hands is, he noted, treated as an incurable disease, so that even an artisan who can produce collateral will not get a bank loan; the manager will have no faith in the artisan's ability to stay clear of the usurers and may suspect that the loan will be used to pay them off rather than to advance a new business venture. Once a debtor has reached this stage, the outlook is truly bleak: the fear of humiliation and even of ostracism complements the fear of physical violence.

Under the sunny surface of Roman life, fear is a common and corrosive miasma. Outcomes are rarely as terminally violent as they are expected to be, but fear feeds on uncertainty, which the very failure of some criminals to inflict violent reprisals increases rather than reduces. Some forms of fear have become systemic and even institutional; one of my key non-Monti informants very recently wrote to me that the church created fear—both of material reprisals in this world and of eternal damnation in the next—as a way of protecting its financial interests; and that she, having initially been reluctant to share certain information about the ecclesiastical management of real estate in the historic center, had now liberated herself from the fear to the point where she was prepared to fax me the documentation overseas and to request that I publish all the names mentioned therein.[6] A bar manager who wanted to make some quite general comments about the circulation of dirty money and the use of real estate to launder it abandoned his habitual seat behind the cash register to mutter, "They have some big capital to recycle." Even in a self-avowedly gossipy society, in some domains discretion is wise.

Fear is often deliberately cultivated, and people who have lived or worked in Monti for a long time claim that its seeping presence is increasing insidiously but perceptibly. Partly this is a matter of intentional acts of intimidation. A former union organizer wanted to create a private coffee bar on his terrace, entirely within his own walls. This did not sit well with another resident, who used his connections to create interference. There was evidently nothing illegal about the proposed construction, because no legal measures were taken to make him desist. Instead, a *vigile* showed up and told the first man, "Leave my friend in peace!" Then the night-time telephone calls began, full of menace. Instead of yielding, however, the union man called on his own connections; having enjoyed the protection of a special security force in Sicily, where unionists often went in fear of their lives, he resorted to its local representatives in Rome. The threatening phone calls stopped immediately.

This incident demonstrates—twice—a common source of fear: those with enough arrogance (*prepotenza*) are able to impose their will, at least temporarily, simply by demonstrating their own sense of immunity. With the rising tide of eviction has come an equally disturbing increase in the incidence of pressure tactics to speed up the old residents' departures—again sometimes with phone calls in the night, or offers to help with moving possessions out of the house accompanied by unmistakable if inexplicit threats of dire consequences if the tenant fails to cooperate. And even at the moment of eviction, timing often responds to the exigencies of a particular legal provision; speed often trumps decency. An elderly couple was hastily evicted before a new regulation protecting the old could take effect—the city policeman who told me about the case said it was carried out by a "company no one has succeeded in identifying"; the wife was allowed to organize a search for a lost ring before finally leaving their home of several decades, but only on condition that the husband remain waiting downstairs.

Sometimes, too, fraud is involved, and a crooked official in the family can be useful in these cases; on one occasion a proprietor persuaded his brother-in-law, a policeman, to show up in uniform and represent himself as authorized to evict the tenant, an elderly woman living alone. She did not know enough to challenge the imposing presence of a uniformed representative of the law. Because the primary victims are the elderly, the less well-educated, and more generally those who do not know their rights, there is a pitiless, self-fulfilling quality about the neoliberal speculators' and real estate agents' claims that they are upgrading the neighborhood: the weak do not so much go to the wall as get tossed carelessly outside it.

In all these operations, knowledgeable operators play on the fears of those who lack the necessary information. They also play on a profound reluctance to involve the official authorities in any local matter. Those who feel cheated are able, and indeed are technically supposed, to file a complaint (*denuncia*) about threatening behavior or other kinds of pressure; indeed, without such a document, the authorities will not act, because the law very clearly places the responsibility on the citizen to initiate proceedings. This, once again, reflects the practical implications of a model of inherited sin; in the days of the Inquisition, those who were caught deliberately failing to file a *denuncia* against any practitioner of magic or similar heresies were denied the confessional and thus the only available means of relieving their consciences of the burden of even the most trivial of their own sins.[7]

Filing a *denuncia* is thus a historically resonant, formal requirement of law; the consequence of failing to do so is a complete refusal by the authorities to take further action. But in practice it is viewed as antisocial and uncivil; older residents in particular speak harshly of those who report any but the most outrageous legal infractions. Even a relatively young and supposedly left-wing resident picked a quarrel with a friend who reported someone else's infractions to the police, ostensibly on the grounds that such acts play into the hands of the law-and-order state bureaucracy, but in reality—so it is alleged—because the critic, too, finds it convenient to maintain a social pact that tolerates his own minor infractions. All citizens share the inheritance of generic wickedness, but ultimately the decision—to denounce or not to denounce—rests with the individual. Conscience, here in the sense of knowing one's civic duty, only manifests itself through the specific act of filing a complaint, much as the "contrition" entailed in reciting prayers before the Virgin's divine image is only knowable from the performance itself; failure to denounce, like all socially acceptable sin, may make everyday life easier, but, at least in theory, it locks the citizen in the purgatory of blockage maintained by the power structure.

On the other hand, it reflects a practical awareness of the limits of official power as well. When a car near our house was vandalized (one of several such incidents, it turned out), a small crowd of local artisans gathered to debate whether they should do anything about what they had seen. A carpenter described it as "an act of disrespect" (*un dispetto*) of the kind that one might expect from a mafioso. Then a friend of the owner rode up on his motorbike and said that, although a purse had been stolen from the car, he did not think it was intended primarily either as a theft or as an act of underworld reprisal but was simply a commonplace case of vandalism. It struck me as interesting that the owner's friend had arrived so easily and so rapidly at this conclusion, but it would have been impossible to decipher what lay behind his glib response. The carpenter had already insisted that the locals should file a report; otherwise, he said, the authorities lay the blame on those who have failed in their duty as citizens. When a resident fails to report a burglary, he said later, the police may suspect a scam—such silence can be truly damning. But the ironworker who shared a workshop with him demurred: "What's the use?" he grumbled, disdainfully.

Indeed, most such reports produce little action and may create problems later on. A woman who filed a report about a robbery and replaced all her personal documents was then surprised to receive all the stolen documents, neatly packaged in an envelope. She did not feel capable of pursuing the matter further: "I'm not sufficiently Italian to do such things," she observed, revealing an association in her own perspective between being culturally Italian and preferring the civil to the civic (as, indeed, the thief had certainly been remarkably civil!). So she went to the police to ask for advice and was told to destroy the whole set of new documents in their presence; no one wanted the bother of processing them all over again, and the thief had kept his side of an implicit bargain and did not deserve to be persecuted further. He was now, ironically, protected by the original *denuncia* against him, a virtual guarantee of inaction. Her husband later remarked that she should simply have thrown the old set into the garbage container and kept quiet.

In reality the effect of the requirement that the citizen formulate a *denuncia* in order for action to occur at all is a device that effectively absolves the authorities of any pressing urge to investigate. It provides an internal control so that a commanding officer who encounters too many discrepancies between citizens' complaints and the reports filed by a particular officer can call the latter to account. But most people claim that the requirement really serves the officers' own interests, especially in the breach; without such a document, they have every reason to do nothing at all. On the other hand, once they have insisted on having the citizen file a complaint, they can also claim to have completed all the necessary bureaucratic procedures, beyond which further action is now their business rather than that of the injured citizen—and is thus also immune from the citizen's inspection.

The *denuncia* thereby also provides what a retired journalist described to me as a "self-defense." Suspects can bring charges of defamation against any journalist who dares to suggest that they have done anything wrong, even if the journalist has good evidence; the inaction of the authorities itself becomes the effective basis of the suspects' public claim to innocence. The journalist cited as an example the case of Archbishop Giordano of Naples, accused of having fixed up a network of usury with the connivance of a bank manager, and claimed that no one ever spoke of the case any more.[8] The *denuncia* can also backfire against the plaintiff. A jeweler who resisted demands for kickbacks (*tangenti*) and reported the crime, for example, was not offered any protection by the authorities, but instead was advised by a senior *carabinieri* officer to shut down his shop on the grounds that the alternative would have been an endless series of acts of sabotage. In situations such as this, public officials effectively connive—whether intentionally or otherwise—in maintaining a climate of fear.

The assumption that police indifference constitutes a practical declaration of immunity for wrongdoers thus provides a reinforcement of underworld fearmongering, the goal of which in turn is to discourage citizens from speaking out. Moreover, one did not gratuitously report "the butcher" or "the carpenter" because these were members of a social order in which mutual protection (*ricambio*) was assured among people who would only introduce themselves by a first name and who would never expect or offer a receipt for a small local purchase. Outsiders, by contrast, were considered legitimate victims of both criminal attacks—mostly theft and extortion—and denunciation to the authorities. Outsiders could also be cheated; neighbors, almost never. There was much disgust at an antiques dealer who boasted of selling sixteen fake pictures, not to a "person who was just passing through," but to a neighbor who was also a regular customer. Other social factors also underscore the contextual nature of business ethics here: a clothes dealer, for example, seemed quite at ease with the fact that, whereas he could not send a poor cleaning woman away without the pair of pants she so much wanted and so charged her 25,000 *lire* instead of 40,000, he would think nothing of "recasting himself" to overcharge truly rich customers.

Restitution and Redemption

Fear, friendship, and illegality: these define an intimacy that must be protected from outsiders and officials. As recently as the 1980s it was not uncommon for a local victim of bicycle theft to get the local boss to arrange restitution.[9] One man recounted how, when he had turned his back on his truck for a moment, a television set was stolen from it—so he found an underworld operator he already knew, paid him 50,000 *lire*, and got his television set back within two hours. A Monticiano who had gone dancing in Monte del Gallo got his purloined Lambretta scooter back within half an hour because he was able to identity the appropriate boss—who, he said, would interpret the theft as insulting his hospitality: "I don't allow myself to be robbed in my own home" (*non mi permett' a fá rubá a casa mia*[10]). Sometimes, the stolen goods have to be sought further afield, since the local clans are also connected through exchange networks. But even then a competent boss could bring about the recovery very quickly.

Residents' own bicycles and motorbikes were usually recognizable, so they would not be touched in the first place; this, I was assured, was a matter of respect (*rispetto*). People knew better than to padlock their bicycles to traffic signs, which could simply be lifted up out of the ground; they relied on the good faith (*buona fede*) of the neighborhood thieves. If residents did have to ask a local boss to recover stolen property for them (and to do that they had to know which of the local bars specialized in the particular type of goods in question), they also knew better than to tell anyone else of their misadventures, "for fear of retribution." Outsiders often never got their property back at all, especially if they did not have the right connections; locals professed to know nothing—"whoever does not wish to, does not know."

The solidarity that did exist locally, while never absolute, could at times furnish long-lasting benefits. At some point in the 1970s a Monti lawyer successfully defended a local thief in court. Since then, despite at least two previous break-in attempts, the visibly prosperous house of the lawyer's wife's uncle, where the lawyer's wife had grown up, has never been robbed. It also helps to have disreputable friends in other places. One night a member of the Trastevere *malavita* (underworld) realized that a raid being planned on a Monti jeweler's shop was aimed at a friend of his; in the end nothing happened, either because the jeweler's friend talked them out of it or because the criminals realized that someone had betrayed their plans.

Conversely, and predictably, going to the police was a virtual guarantee that one would never been able to recover the stolen property. Recourse to police intervention might be considered acceptable only when the mediator asked for too much money, in which case someone with police connections might be able to get some action. More often, the offended boss would make sure that the stolen object was burned or otherwise damaged as an unambiguous message of disrespect. But these were rare exceptions; most Romans understood the rules and played by them. The occasional act of violence was thus more of a threat held in reserve and used to maintain the system than a frequent occurrence. The mediators were themselves careful not to ask for too high a price for the restitution, since they knew that in many cases the stolen goods could not easily be fenced, or that they were objects of purely sentimental significance and no monetary value (in which case the police would not take the theft seriously in any case). A designer handbag recovered in this way around 1992 contained, in addition to some money, the owner's papers; after a neighbor intervened, she received a telephone call directing her to where the bag had been left with the papers intact but with her money removed. The thieves had evidently not been sufficiently up-to-date to realize the considerable value of the bag itself! All in all, the system worked well within the confines of the district; as one former policeman put it, the victim pays a reasonable sum, the property is returned, "and matters have been fixed up!"

The local bosses used these practices not only for profit but also, and perhaps more importantly, to assert their authority. They were often suspected of setting up the thefts themselves. Each *caporione* or *capobanda* (boss, gang chief) was in some sense a protector of his poorer neighbors, and the idiom of mildly extortionate and sometimes carefully staged property restitution must be read in the same framework as their harsh punishment of those who mistreated others in need. At one point, immediately after World War II, there were still two dominant Monti clans whose members would not speak to each other. But while they sometimes clashed violently (in one case allegedly murdering a Sicilian who was trying to muscle in on the turf of one of them), and while one clan was connected with the infamous *banda della Magliana*, they took good care to treat well-behaved residents in their respective sections with solicitude and respect.

Theirs was a moral code and understood as such. One boss made sure that a baker who refused to give free bread to paupers was repeatedly robbed; he chose to interpret the baker's churlishness as a sign of disrespect both to his own authority and to society at large—a rejection of decency. Relations were based on "a chain of respect" (*rispetto a catena*), and the stingy baker was ruined "because he deserved to be." The jeweler who explained the power of the local bosses in these terms also described the system as "a quick-fix/small-scale union." They also ensured that crooks from outside were kept at bay: intruders were immediately identified, and no boss could afford to tolerate such poaching. Car theft is still largely a local affair; the remaining local underworld operators are still apparently able to keep intruders out of that particular game—and the big-time crooks have much larger interests to pursue.

They are also able to keep up pressure on ambulant vendors. A Mon-ticiano who sold goods in many of the major markets of Rome, and who claims he bought off persistent pressure from police officers with gifts of socks and underwear, apparently knew the active thieves. That knowledge stood him in good stead. At one point his beloved van disappeared, complete with its load of clothes for sale. He phoned his numerous underworld con-tacts. At first, he found no trace of the van. Then one man, a fellow vendor, relieved him of his anxiety: "'I have it in hand. How much are you offering?' 'I'm offering one million!'" But, as the Monti vendor pointed out, "there's a 'why' [for this]." The other man, a fence for stolen clothing, wanted the Monti vendor's license for a market closer to his own home, and hoped to achieve his goal by showing off his skill as an operator and by offering the Monti vendor a much lower price (600,000 *lire*) to get his van back. He was prepared to go even lower in order to secure the license transfer (and invited the vendor to a cordial dinner in order to soften him up); but the vendor was extremely nervous because he was not sure of getting all the contents back with the van—in the event they were mostly restored to him intact—and so agreed to the price already on offer. He commented that the middleman's wife was "so very kind" (*tanto gentile*); she was evidently an active party to the polite exchange that masked a serious tussle over valuable resources. Some middlemen also frequently offer the Monti vendor a good price for vanloads of stolen goods, but he rejects these offers as, says he, he wants to sleep easily at night. Nervous though they make him, however, the vendor must keep his channels open to all the *capi*; they are still numerous in the world of the markets.

Aside from the moneylenders, underworld operators in Monti are now few in number, broken in spirit, and lacking in effective power. Their pre-decessors were fearsome characters who had managed to achieve primacy among the local toughs (*bulli*).[11] One of the best known locally went by the moniker of *Er Più* (The Mostest); one of his sons became a famous actor who played *bulli* in the nearby Manzoni Theater with huge success. In the transition from father to son, art did not so much imitate life as extend the performances of the everyday to the popular stage, whence it returned to source in the form of a newly proverbial expression for arrogant behavior and a reinforced romantic model of the local tough.

The role of these bosses in mediating thefts was symbolized by the em-blematic phrase, *Ci penso io* (literally, "I'll think about it"), which also signifies mafia involvement to many Italians. One man remarked that the typical attitude of such people was "*a me nun me frega un cazzo*" (Me, I don't give a frigging shit); their swaggering insouciance warned others not to take liberties with them. In restoring stolen property, moreover, they placed the victims of theft under a lasting obligation of respect.

Today this system is all but dead; the old reciprocities no longer work.[12] Around 1997 someone stole one of the side mirrors from a student's motorbike; the student told the man who repaired his bike that he would be prepared to pay the value of the mirror if he got it back. The repairman found him a mirror that was not the missing one. Probably, remarked the student in recalling the incident, this man had stolen the second mirror as well, in order to get the money. Two years later, someone stole the student's license plate; but this time, he said, he went straight to the police, as the plate was not something a local thief would have taken. A few years earlier a glassmaker had a camera stolen; he had noticed a young man hanging around near his shop, so he asked him if had any idea who had done this and whether he could help track down the camera; the youth replied that he knew (conosco) certain people and agreed to undertake the task—and showed up the next day with a camera, for which the glassmaker paid him 50,000 lire.

The victim was convinced that the young man was himself the thief; his assistant pointed out that the thieves could not easily fence such goods, so that this was their best chance of making some money from the theft. But the incident also illustrates how easily what had once been more of a system of reciprocity and authority among local residents could now be exploited by strangers who knew enough to apply the old rules to new and far less socially embedded forms of petty crime. What still persists, on the other hand, is the preference for negotiation over confrontation; the glassmaker resigned himself to the moral certainty that he was dealing directly with the thief, but pragmatically realized that this was the only way he could get his camera back. Anger would have gained him nothing. His assistant added that out in the suburb of Casilina, where she lived, someone stole a car radio, restored it to its owner, and then, two or three days later, stole it again!

Many Monticiani view the old pattern of controlled petty crime with affectionate nostalgia as a mark of the district's village-like social life, a mark of a southern idiom of social relations to be contrasted with the "cold" crimes—the deliberate violence for simple profit—that they associate with the north as well as with the foreign mafias that have come, so they allege, with the recent upsurge in immigration from eastern Europe. One man pointed to the killing of two child molesters in Torre Annunziata, near Naples, as typifying the certain dignity (una certa dignità) that also once marked the Roman bosses' refusal to tolerate the hassling of women. It is in this sense that the restitution of stolen property, while also profitable for the bosses, served above all as a boundary marker, an index of intimacy—so much so that even a boss with a reputation for financial greed might restore objects of sentimental value, such as photographs, at no charge while keeping whatever he wanted for himself.

Perhaps the last part of Rome where one could still expect to get stolen articles back was the popular quarter of Testaccio. A present resident of Monti who used to live there recalled that in about 1996, after she had been living in Testaccio for a short while, the local bookmaker stopped her on the street and greeted her. She asked him, "Do we know each other?" By way of response, he informed her, "I know your name, where you live, and which is your car. Nothing is going to happen [to your property]. But if something just *did* have to happen, just tell me." The confidence of this assurance suggests a more robust network than existed in Monti by that time.

The depersonalization of petty theft and the displacement of the local economy by the neoliberal organization of taste and consumption represent two facets of the same phenomenon: the suppression of old civilities in the name of a larger logic appearing under a variety of names including, especially, "the market" and "globalization." The gentrification of Monti, part of an encompassing commodification of the historic and the picturesque, begins within the same time frame that saw the arrival of a significant drug scene and the systematic organization of crime. Where once local bosses organized the restitution of stolen goods, today the police authorities will scarcely lift a finger to recover stolen motorbikes; crime itself has become a significant part of the Italian economy.[13] Such crimes are so widespread and visible, as a young politician observed, that "this creates a kind of indifference"—a banalization of crime, not unlike the effect of mass-media representations of violence.[14] Indeed, the media here stand in, much as myth did in ages past, as a paradoxical representation of, simultaneously, the conceptual triteness of universal truth and the specious excitement of local fiction. A *carabiniere* told the outraged victim of an unsuccessful burglary that there was no basis for taking fingerprints at the scene even though they had quickly apprehended a suspect: "Madam, you watch too much television—[it's] not even a murder!"

The market and criminality converge most obviously in the eruption, slow at first and then rapidly accelerating as the housing market also took off, of the drug trade. It began in the middle and later 1950s with a local émigré who was sending back cocaine from South America for comparatively wealthy local users and peaked in the 1980s, by which time drug use was widespread among the young people of the area. It was a key factor in the collapse of the old reciprocities in Monti; the drug market—which can be viewed as an early and illegal experiment in the liberalization of economic relations—recast the circulation of goods in the logic of supply and demand rather than of local social connections. Drugs have had the further effect of alienating people from their home communities; one bar operator, for example, was forced to shut down when he could no longer pay his electricity bills—and this was interpreted as a consequence of the effect of his habit on his financial situation. Theft, once the basis of a social hierarchy, follows the changes in the social order as much as any other pattern of social interaction; as a result, thieves now operate far away from their own districts, especially as those who steal to finance expensive narcotic addictions are completely uninterested in any kind of exchange network and only seek to satisfy their needs quickly. The new underworld is directed from outside and draws most of its income and impact from the circulation of drugs.[15]

In their day the old bosses were well-connected with the official world, mostly through kinship ties that also gave entire sectors of the district vertical connections. In the days before the anti-corruption drives of the 1990s, it was not uncommon for the errant children of a judge or a police officer to join the local gangs. Because their parents had to maintain at least a facade of respectability, however, they did not lift a finger to help them when they were caught. Today, even the most law-abiding residents would resort to at least the threat of violence in the face of some of the new forms of criminal activity. One outwardly rather gentle and quite elderly shopkeeper showed me a small knife that he had quietly placed on the counter when two obviously foreign customers he thought looked rather shifty entered his shop; when, on their way out, they helped themselves to a couple of peaches, he forced them to return, insisting, as he suggestively fingered the little weapon, "Either you pay or you leave it here!"

In this world of controlled violence, usury is not new; indeed, not only did it draw on the model of the rotating credit association, but it also characteristically claimed local people rather than strangers as its primary victims. Here the criminals, although not connected to the old moral universe of the bosses, are themselves necessarily local, although a few are members of larger gangs with ramified operations far beyond the confines of a single district.

The local economy is one in which, even today, small tradespeople run informal accounts to be paid on a weekly or monthly basis; this practice (known as *segnare*, "jotting") is now technically illegal, but it is very hard to discover because, although it is a classic instance of local accommodation with the law ("Yes, people do it, but you [technically] can't do it"), it necessarily only exists among those who have good reason to trust each other (and indeed is often a reciprocal arrangement, as, for example, between a restaurateur and a bar proprietor). Keeping a running tab in this way builds trust among merchants because, while the seller may get no direct financial advantage from it (although the social capital that accrues is considerable[16]), its illegality can encapsulate a form of tax evasion that leaves both parties open to mutual blackmail but that is more likely to establish a wary rapport between them. The seller starts the tab with a piece of professional equipment that buyers, all fellow merchants, can claim (even untruthfully!) to use for professional purposes, on the basis of which they can discount its price from the total value-added tax (*Iva*) to be paid on their own sales. To this tab are added all sorts of minor items until the payment on the tab comes due. These items are likely to be of no professional use whatsoever, but, as the seller writes an overall receipt (*fattura*) in which the original item is listed as having the total value of the tab, it is only the seller who pays the tax on these smaller items as well.

Today, some residents lament that such arrangements are disappearing because there is no more trust (*fiducia*)—a reason sometimes also cited for the collapse of the old rotating credit associations—or because customers are no longer afraid of losing face (*perdere faccia*), shame (*vergogna*) being the only instrument of debt recovery that occasionally did work for the associations. The complaint about current attitudes is familiar: "There's no longer any shame. When there's no longer any shame, people don't respect anything." But I also heard quite enough stories about customers who in the distant past had cheated local merchants to convince me that this tale of decline was really little more than nostalgia for the now-disappearing urban village of popular imagination. It seems more plausible to credit the changes to the larger shifts in the economic sphere and the attendant banalization of antisocial acts.

Interestingly, merchants still feel pressure to allow clients the privilege of a running tab: "You do it because you're obliged to—what can one do?" This presumption of obligation as well as the illegality of the arrangement, moreover, create an intimate collusion, made all the more piquant if either party happens to subscribe to the idea that trust is on the wane; betrayal would have disastrous consequences for both. From an economic standpoint, too, merchants only dare offer this service to customers they know well because the very illegality of the arrangement also makes it impossible, as

in the case of usurers or those who are left destitute by the collapse of a
rotating credit association, to take defaulters to court.

Friends Best Avoided

A common framework of friendship is central to all transactions. Even usury
is still almost always represented as an arrangement between friends (*amici*)
and, as such, is bedecked with unctuous courtesies—courtesies that conveyed a controlled, lurking menace. Usurers control their victims through
a cynical manipulation of the very laws that they themselves are violating:
often they demand an affidavit affirming that if the debtor fails to pay the
full debt with interest within a specified period the usurer will become the
owner of all the debtor's worldly goods. Many usurers are local merchants;
they only have recourse to underworld thugs as enforcers, and then only
when other measures fail. The moneylenders often locate these enforcers
just as the latter have been released from jail and are without work or funds,
so that these seemingly tough characters, too, are easily entrapped in the
usurers' snares. In their turn, the enforcers are themselves brutal and unforgiving in their dealings with defaulters: "They are terrifying mafiosi," said
an upholsterer.

Fear is effective only when both parties are engaged in the same social networks. Local victims have every reason to keep quiet; they fear the
usurers' revenge, but they are perhaps even more afraid of the damage their
reputations would suffer if the indebtedness became widely known. No
honest person would ever again lend them money, fearing their inability to
extricate themselves from the downward spiral of debt. Usurers have always
depended on local knowledge to identify potential victims and to play on
these corrosive fears, and this, too, has circumscribed the geography of their
actions.

As a result, I found it very difficult to find out about local cases; people
feared the consequences of recounting their difficulties to even a temporary
neighbor, while they also evinced great embarrassment at the very thought
that outsiders might discover Monti to be riddled with illicit money lending.
Some denied its prevalence outright; but the most vociferous of these also
said that he thought that small loans—the only kind most of the humbler
artisans are likely to need—were not really usury at all. Indeed, on another
occasion he commented that small-scale loans of the order of 100,000 *lire*
were more like prostitution; this, he said, was the work of the *strozzino*,
a profession that he categorically contrasted with the true *usuraio*. The
strozzino, in short, is not guilty of a mortal sin in the everyday sense of the

word, but engages in an ordinary misdeed that may also be of assistance to those to whom he offers his services.

This rhetoric clearly allowed the speaker both to define small-scale usury out of existence and to justify the practice as part of everyday social life. Whether those who follow this strategy do so because they want to disguise their own willingness to loan money at interest (as a local union official hinted to me) was unclear, but he evidently did regard the more massive forms of usury as something fundamentally immoral. There were also those who recognized small-scale money lending as a lifeline for struggling artisans, an unfortunate necessity of life, while yet others preferred to accentuate the talk about the disinterested (and interest-free) loans that are still relatively common among middle-class friends, especially women. In all these representations, Monti emerges as decent but, such being the human condition, flawed by temptations minor, inevitable, and recurrent. The most forthright admission of the frequency of usury in Monti came from a relatively recent and wealthy arrival who thus had little reason to be coy on the subject. But most residents do in fact recognize, with varying degrees of embarrassment, that such practices are commonplace.

Kinship is important to any financial relationship and may even, on occasion, outweigh the demands of neighborliness; a major restaurateur bought his meat from his prospective son-in-law out in one of the suburbs rather than going to the nearest (and much more expensive) butcher, and could justify doing so on the grounds that "we have this kinsman." Kinship is also a way of getting things done; our landlady wanted to get our electricity meter read immediately, as otherwise the utility company would make its own estimate, and getting reimbursed for any excess payment could become a nightmare. But that was a simple matter; the son of her sister-in-law's sister worked for the company—and so any problems would easily be resolved.

Neither friendship nor kinship, however, is a guarantee of honesty in financial loans. One man, of rural origins, gave his brother a large loan so that the latter could buy some land in the Roman hinterland. The brother offered to pay him back with interest, claiming to have found some profitable work; when the Monti resident refused, his brother sent him at least twenty bottles of preserved tomatoes as a way of showing his appreciation. That is the ideal pattern. But the same Monti resident's wife's brother cheated him over a promissory note (*cambiale*) for which the former had put down the original capital, repaying only 1 percent out of the 10 percent interest; my friend said that he would never again lend his brother-in-law any money but that, if asked to do so, would simply say that all his financial resources were tied up (*avvincolati*).

This man was relatively forthcoming about the presence of loan sharks in the district. On the whole, all those who felt free to speak at least generally about the subject were people whose own financial security had long allowed them to steer clear of such risky adventures. One man, who had left a rotating credit association because he never saw any return on the money he contributed, conceded that a few desperate debtors, unable to find solace in these associations, were forced to resort to the loan sharks. What few would admit was that usury was as common in Monti as elsewhere in Rome. The usual line of defense was a response that may have been truthful in a literal and personal sense: that they had never heard of such a case. But those who said this probably took care to mind their own business in general; outsiders, by contrast, scoffed at the idea that Monti might be uniquely immune to usury.

The neighbors' taciturnity on the subject—so striking in a city where talk is a treasured recreation—had a curious effect on my fieldwork. Locally, had one or two people not fearfully pointed out a single individual as a known usurer, a man who was detested for other brutalities, I could have imagined that usury no longer existed in Monti. Yet when I went outside the district, and in particular when I engaged in conversations with people who had already decided to throw their lot in with official campaigns against these practices, I encountered great willingness to speak out. Moreover, one student at the university, after hearing me lecture on usury one day, came immediately to my office, closed the door firmly, and proceeded to recount the story of her family's humiliation by a loan shark. She had finally found a safe way to exact at least a symbolic revenge.

It was thus not difficult to find such information outside Monti. Strangers could speak more freely—either because they had already gone public, so that my knowledge of their situations could not aggravate the danger to them, or because they felt that they could bare their feelings and worries to someone they would not meet frequently in the daily round. One such acquaintance was a woman whose husband, a fishmonger, had been murdered at his market stall in broad daylight for denouncing a usurer; the authorities then refused to help her, or so she felt, in her quest for justice. When I met her through a television feature on usury that I was allowed to attend and film, her story had already made a spectacular splash in several newspapers. Perhaps she felt able to open up to me in private with even more passion than she had shown before the television cameras. It is perhaps also revealing, however, that when I tried to call her a year later, her telephone had been disconnected and she no longer had a listed number. In the end there are few ways out of the labyrinth of fear beyond concealment and evasion.

A Family Friend?

In another non-Monti case, a usurer virtually imprisoned his debtor, my student's father, in his home. The entire transaction was framed as protection for his family. Although it took place in one of the more peripheral and "popular" areas of Rome, it illustrates the problems that people confront all over the city. The family—the debtor, a gambler who managed a bar in association with a friend, with his wife, mother, and two daughters—had been evicted from an apartment, apparently quite illegally,[17] to make way for the proprietor's son; in their new surroundings, they paid a rent that was seven times the previous rent for a much smaller space. Funds were therefore already tight. The elder daughter began to notice that something was wrong, because even though her father was working night and day, there never seemed to be any money for the family. Then the father and his partner dissolved their business relationship. Her father then acquired the management of another bar, a larger and more elegant establishment that he ran together with his wife. To do this, he paid with long-term promissory notes, as he had no ready cash. The younger daughter worked in the bar after school; the elder, who told me the story, took a part-time job elsewhere. After a while, she began to notice that something was very wrong, particularly because the father was putting pressure on the younger girl to leave school altogether, even though she enjoyed it and was doing well in her studies, and to work only for him. Even more suspiciously, he kept complaining that the bar was in bad shape although the daughters could see that it was always full of people. But then it slowly emerged that the father was losing money at cards and on the horses. The mother had not entertained the slightest suspicion of these habits, and was taken completely and horrifically by surprise.

He had tried to conceal the extent of the disaster from his family. At first he succeeded, in part because his wife, a woman of peasant stock from Umbria, was not in the habit of questioning her husband's statements. The elder daughter, however, had never hesitated to do so, especially as she was discontented over the way her mother was treated, and she began to argue with her father. Then the truth finally began to emerge. She in fact recalled that as a little girl she would sometimes take coffee to her father in a little tavern where he would be playing cards with local merchants. She thought that at first he asked these same playing partners for loans to pay off his gambling debts to them; a few of them, as it turned out, were full-time moneylenders. Eventually he borrowed a huge sum and, when the lenders ended up in jail (for an unrelated matter) he breathed an equally huge sigh of relief and thought he could now pay off his remaining debts and rest easily. Eventually, however, the lenders, released from jail, sold the debt to an accountant (*commercialista*) whose office was close to the father's bar. At this point the father shut himself up in his house and refused to face reality, sending his elder daughter to deal with the situation instead. The accountant, a white-haired and courteous gentleman whose secretary seemed (my source implied) to be his sexual slave, forced the father to sign a document transferring ownership of the bar to the accountant as compensation for the unpaid debt. The elder daughter, still a schoolgirl, talked matters over with "this damned fellow," who in manner was "very kind, very well-spoken," hoping to find a way out of the situation—until one day another gentleman, "very calm, very kind" and accompanied by a woman, called on her at school and asked her to arrange a meeting with her father. There she finally learned the full extent of the disaster.

The father was now heavily in debt. Once it became clear that he had lied to his family about the extent of his problems, which were increasingly dire, his wife's close kin stepped in with financial assistance, in some cases through loans for which they in turn assumed substantial debts. Although he reported his debts to the authorities, he avoided naming the primary lender out of fear of reprisals. The partial reporting of his debts relieved him of some financial burdens, but at the price of surrendering his civil rights (mostly to vote in elections) for five years, a penalty he was glad to assume in order to end the nightmare. He also transferred the bar to new management to pay off some of the legal creditors (including the original proprietors of the bar, who had ceased to receive the payments on the promissory notes). But the less forgiving usurers now began to threaten him with serious physical violence; some threats were well veiled, others less so. Although he was clearly afraid to walk about in certain parts of the city, he also continued to lie to his family about the depths to which he had sunk. Because they had to work long hours to meet the remaining creditors' demands, however, his wife and children were quickly disabused of their remaining hopes and illusions.

The threats continued. At this point one usurer appeared as a self-serving source of salvation. He was a classic underworld type, said the elder daughter, with a hard face and a brusque manner; "at a certain point, he was a creditor of my father, but in practice he put us on our guard against certain other creditors with worse intentions at, let's say, the level of physical [violence]." The father attached himself to this man, who had every interest in keeping him alive so he could recuperate his own loans and was convinced that those the father had denounced to the authorities would be looking for an opportunity to make an example of him. And so, one night, with all their possessions packed into suitcases, the entire family surreptitiously moved into the usurer's home, where, for a fearful three weeks, they remained. "Luckily it all went well. But we had put ourselves right in the wolf's mouth!"

The father was now confined where he could not lose any more money at cards; with the rest of the family working, and with some help in further loans from their close relatives, their grim host was evidently able to persuade the other usurers that sharing the proceeds would be more profitable—and perhaps less dangerous to them—than eliminating the debtor or his family. They then returned to their own home, whence they soon departed—in order to avoid the rent—to the house of an acquaintance in the provincial town of Pomezia, where the father was unable to find work but where at least the daughters could keep a close eye on him and make sure he did not gamble again. The elder daughter worked part-time when she was not at school and the younger daughter was employed full-time by a local merchant, while their mother took on a daily grind of twelve hours of mostly domestic work. Eventually, after the father had slowly extricated himself by working in various menial jobs such as dishwashing, they managed to settle the remaining debts, and the elder daughter ended up at the university.

While these events did not occur in Monti, children and other family members can become hostages to fortune anywhere in the city. Usurers protect themselves from being reported to the authorities through insinuating threats: "Remember that you still have your daughter. . . ." One resident of the historic center had gone to a usurer because, ironically, her appeal to a bank for a loan of a type specifically guaranteed by the state as protection against the need to resort to usury would have been too small. The state's inability to provide adequate protection springs primarily from the fact that people resort to loan sharks when they are already entrapped by successive debts. On the other hand, the presence of a larger family network can also be reassuring to a usurer who is willing to demand reasonable terms. One woman, then a baker, had to borrow a considerable amount of money; the bank provided a small loan because her family was sufficiently well established locally to be able guarantee the loan with collateral; an uncle (her mother's brother) lent her a further sum, charging only the interest that he himself had to pay his bank; but when she needed more, she did go to a moneylender, for whom the backing of a well-known local family was a sufficient guarantee of her good credit. By mixing the sources of her loans in this way, and despite the fact that the usurer's penalty for late payment was a doubling of the interest, she effectively eliminated the risk that she would end up having to borrow the entire amount all over again in order to pay off the first debt, thereby entering the most destructive cycle of all.

Local Narratives: Swaggering Victims

Occasionally I would hear an older tale of usury in the local setting of Monti. These accounts were usually presented as first-person narratives of a heroic victim's defeat of evil, and allowed the speakers to represent usury as a thing of the past both in their own lives and in the neighborhood at large. One shopkeeper described how, as a young man of 22, he had been lured into a small but, for him, crushing debt; eventually he was able to pay off half the debt and decided to take the risk of facing the usurer down over the remainder: "That's enough, I want to get off the train!"

It was a dangerous move. The real menace behind an underworld operator's oleaginous invitation to do business lies precisely in the non-reversibility of the contract that is thereby created. In this case, the loan shark, whom the victim characteristically described as "someone [known as] a friend" (una persona amica), tried to bluff his way into maintaining his hold over the victim, angrily claiming that he was still owed a substantial amount. At the crucial moment, as the voices of the two men rose, a police patrol car arrived. The loan shark hastily disappeared, never to torment this particular victim again. The victim's comment was laconic: "How do you get out? You have to have luck!" And he asked me whether I, too, believed in "divine fortune."

In another case, in another part of Rome, some thought that the timely arrival of the police when prompted by the loud ranting of a frustrated usurer may have been the result of a clever plot to entrap the latter. While it is entirely possible that the Monticiano may have similarly arranged something of the kind, he passed it off as an intervention by divine providence and denied that he had made any kind of formal complaint. A heroic tale was socially far preferably to any admission of dealing with the police, and it intimates that he is now uncontaminated by any lingering association with loan sharks; his social and economic credit, in other words, is good.

One Monti shopkeeper recounted a tale of usury in which he appeared as anything but heroic or wise. Unbeknownst to him, his son-in-law, while

ostensibly acting as his business partner, was siphoning off funds to buy a
boat and other forms of entertainment. The older man had no idea that this
was going on, but, in order to fend off the financial disaster that he could
already see looming, borrowed 5 million *lire* at a punitive rate of interest
from a local gang of loan sharks. In four or five months the debt had mounted
to 20 million, and he was less able than ever to pay it off; in further rising
increments—5, then 10, then 20, then 30 million—it rose to 85 million, and
soon thereafter to nearly half as much again. At this point his daughter, then
still married to the swindling son-in-law, figured out what was happening
and managed to recover enough money so that her father could pay off the
debt. This terrifying scenario played out from somewhere near the beginning
of 1989 until the September of that year—a detail that shows, not only that
usury was practiced in the neighborhood in very recent memory, but also
how quickly disaster can accumulate. At least one of the usurers was a local
man, although they apparently employed Gypsy toughs as their enforcers.

One difficulty I faced in trying to understand the role of usury was that
it was not always clearly separated, at least in the popular imagination, from
legally approved lending practices or from the socially embedded rotating
credit practices that used to form the backbone of the poorer residents' resistance to severe economic distress. This reflects a similar ambiguity in the
church's repeated attempts to make a distinction, or at least to operate as
though there were one, between extortion and money lending at reasonable
interest rates. Even priests had sometimes been known to lend money at
relatively low interest rates. The more inflexible ecclesiastical critics, especially from the sixteenth century on, had cited formal dogma in condemning
such practices; others argued instead that the papal pronouncements on the
subject allowed a considerable degree of latitude in interpretation. Ultimately the question remained a classically Catholic dilemma for individual
consciences faced with material temptation and unclear directives;[18] this
logic favored a relatively hands-off policy on the part of the papacy, especially as its own financial interests would not have been well served by a
complete suppression of usury.

The civic authorities, under papal rule as much after as before Unification, have tolerated and perhaps even benefited from a practice that contra-
vened both ecclesiastical and civil law and that offended popular morality
as well. We should view these ambiguities as practical accommodations to
the imperfections of the secular world by authorities and citizens alike; the
resulting arrangements facilitated the daily lives of the poorer citizens but
also strengthened the power of the elites over them. Comparing a rotating
credit club with the culture of the usurer (*la cultura dell'usuraio*), a jeweler

who was seeking membership—more for the sake of tradition and friendship than from need—claimed that the group in question had actively sought to protect its members from the far higher risks attendant on dealing with usurers.

Credit and Default

The rotating credit associations, like the pawn societies before them, skirted the edges of illegality and theological irregularity. So common in Rome until the last quarter of the twentieth century that they are often simply called "the famous societies," they still exist, although in greatly reduced numbers. In their heyday they ranged from well-organized groups of artisans, merchants, and professionals—one association had over two hundred members, but closed down as recently as around 1998 when the outgoing president could not find a replacement owing to the considerable amount of work involved—to the odd team of some ten waiters in a restaurant investing a small part of their meager wages in pursuit of an equally meager profit and the occasional minor loan. They should not be confused with what is still a relatively common arrangement in various government and company offices, where small amounts can be borrowed at the low interest rate of under 4 percent; this structure, the *cassa mutua* (savings group), has legal status.

The rotating credit associations functioned reasonably well as a source of support in dealing with the petty personal crises of a financially restricted lifestyle, less so when, as gradually happened more and more frequently, they were used to redress the difficulties of business ventures that were foundering, and least of all when members lent out their own loans at even higher interest and then failed to get the money back. The authorities were reluctant to close them down because they relieved an inadequate banking system of the need to extend credit to small artisans and merchants who lacked sufficient collateral. The banks' interest rate was also usually about 3 or 4 percent higher than that of the associations.

Lending to outsiders not only could trigger total collapse and the ruin of the members but also, since it was considered a form of usury (*strozzinaccio*), might well increase the risk of official intervention. It was thus profoundly antisocial both for the economic damage it could do to the group as a whole and because it threatened to expose its intimate secrets to the bearers of official power. The only tolerable exceptions occurred when the group as a whole was consulted and agreed on the principle that the outside borrower "is a friend of a friend" (*è un amico de un amico*).[19]

The members' social solidarity and collective amity were maintained by a series of dinners, usually in a local restaurant; one can still occasionally see such gatherings. Of one such group that I observed, entirely composed of men, the head cook at the restaurant quipped that their wives had told them not to eat and drink too much but that they were now taking care to do just that. The occasion certainly seemed both highly convivial and dramatically public. It contrasted with the memorable occasion, many years ago, when a group agreed to meet for Sunday dinner, only to discover in the morning that the restaurateur, who was also the manager of the association, had carted off all his tables, closed the restaurant, and disappeared forever with all the association's accumulated funds.[20]

In theory any member could leave an association at the end of the two-year cycle. Sometimes it was too late; especially when an organizer absconded with all the cash, safe in the knowledge that no one would openly admit to having participated in such an illegal activity, the association collapsed. In general, the risk of such collapse—as well as the potential profit for all as long as the members remained honest—increased with the size of each association; widening the circle, which could only be done under strict supervision of all those who were already members, meant going beyond the immediate confines of neighborhood and kin group, and this introduced categories of relationship that were considered to be less reliable by definition. With such expansion, it became harder to control the members' covert activities; when, for example, those who borrowed single units would not necessarily realize that another had borrowed five and then re-loaned four of the five units to a third party, a practice that was prohibited by the associations' shared rules and traditions. If the miscreant was unable to recover these secondary debts—a common occurrence in the tight economy of the local community—the entire association could go under.[21]

Even in the light of such relatively frequent misdemeanors, people were reluctant to accept the legalistic view of these associations as speculative conspiracy: "It's not a matter of usury," as one man remarked. By the closing years of the twentieth century, however, sudden economic pressures opened the way for genuine usurers to operate on an individual basis; the older ties had already weakened beyond the point of no return; and the rotating credit system began to disappear. Having operated along the segmentary principles of local social life in general, collapsing when they exceeded the range of a group of intimates but recoalescing around emergent new groups of kin and neighbors, they were ill equipped to survive in the face of competition from a free-for-all market and within the regulatory practices of a centralized bureaucratic state. Today, the sums people need to run a business are vastly larger than the tiny financial emoluments from membership in a rotating credit association, the status of an unofficial accountant carries little weight, and even the faintest smell of illegality scares clients away. At the same time, the intensifying pressures of the new economy push the less competent into the grasping hands of freewheeling usurers. Political opportunism can also blur the distinction between the associations and straightforward usury. At one meeting a leftist district councilor denounced a club frequented by some of the more racist elements in Monti as a lair of usurers—meaning, it was clear, that it was a rotating credit association, an institution now clearly increasingly stained by usury's extortionate taint.

The old associations usually charged an interest rate that varied between 10 and 12 percent—higher than that of the banks, but not as crushing as the interest usually exacted by usurers; loans had to be paid back, with the interest, over twenty weeks, but any interest left unused and all profits from its investment would in theory be shared out among all the members at the end of a two-year cycle. Those needing a loan would have to give twenty days' notice of their requests.

Recruitment to these associations was largely, but not exclusively, through kinship and neighborhood ties; a few were based on the old artisans' guilds. An unknown applicant would not ordinarily be able to gain admission; in the more competitive trades these would be very small, informal groupings of friends, willing to help each other with non-professional problems (such as an expensive girlfriend) but always on the alert for competitive moves from the other members. Even today these associations are useful in facing unexpected problems; one of them served to stave off disaster for the local butchers when the mad cow disease scare struck and local customers turned suddenly—if briefly—vegetarian. Their defenders defend these associations against charges of being a thinly disguised form of usury by arguing that, to the contrary, they provided a way of not being "suffocated" by real usurers.

For many Monticiani, however, the problem with the precedent these bodies represented was, as we have seen, that they also had a long history of malpractice. Quarrels would break out when someone was held responsible for having introduced as members kin who subsequently proved unreliable or dishonest; embezzlement was far from rare. One association, which had existed for at least two generations but broke up around 1992, had about 100,000,000 *lire* in play at the time. One of the most powerful of its 72 members lost some 12,000,000 when this happened; another, who was heavily in debt as a result of his construction of a huge new restaurant, owed 10,000,000 at the time of the collapse—and was not expected to pay back any of that money even if his business thrived (which it did). Part of his escape from indebtedness thus remains etched in local memory, but people apparently forgave him for this because, like so many others, he was not the sole architect of the collapse or even necessarily in any degree responsible for it. When the collapse began, he, along with nearly half the other members, was able to extricate himself hastily but without financial damage to himself; these survivors could hardly, in this sinful world, be expected to restore sums that no one had any legal means of extracting from them—indeed, had they done so, they would have been regarded as fools. They would also have risked bringing their own involvement to the attention of the authorities, with potentially unpleasant consequences. But they did leave the current head of the association, a man who had inherited his slot from his father, exposed to the wrath of the authorities and charges of tax evasion and usury; and this, not to speak of the 20,000,000 *lire* that he and his wife lost or of his legal expenses, was something he could not easily forgive.

Such embarrassing misadventures perhaps explain why it is actually very difficult to obtain relevant information from those who ran the associations in years past. Some scoffed at the very idea that there was any sort of formal organization at all, while at the same time reluctantly acknowledging the need for trustworthy "friends" at moments of economic difficulty. These arrangements were nevertheless clearly more structured than participants wanted to admit. One highly respectable and conservative individual I asked about a rumor that he had run one of these groups turned suddenly silent, clearly upset at the idea that his name might be associated with such activity, and dismissively blamed it on "chatty gossip" (*le chiacchiere*); but more than seven years earlier he had at least admitted to having participated in a credit association, so it seems either that there is more general nervousness about such things than before or that the specific role of the fund manager had come into such terrible disrepute. Perhaps, too, there was something disingenuous in the claims of a friend who said he had refused to participate in the association and that indeed he had retorted to the other man, "I eat my money for myself!"

The stench of suspicion haunts every recollection of these organizations, only partially deflected by a generic rhetoric about the relief they offered the truly poor in times past. Like the protection the *capi rione* offered the poor, these associations represented a systematic violation of both religious and legal ethics; justified by those involved in terms of the harsh necessities of economic deprivation, they trembled on the edge of discovery at all times, and as modernity encroached they became less and less viable. Embezzlement was always a persistent problem; even the "little old ladies" (*vecchi-*

ette) who ran some of the minor associations—one, the members of which were all women over 50, was apparently still going strong at the end of the twentieth century—were suspected of profiteering at the expense of their even poorer associates. Managers were almost always people with "the halo of the honest person" (*l'aureola dell'onesto*), local figures of some authority and economic substance, and their relations with the weaker artisans were clearly not egalitarian: "they turn the small-scale artisans into their subjects." But such unequal relations are always disguised as friendship—a friendship less violently extortionate than the usurers' and less structured than the mutualism of the church, but oppressive nonetheless. Fear, once again, bred a pragmatic resignation. If they thought they had been cheated, weaker members would generally let matters rest with the classic phrase *lascia perde'* (let it go).

That suspicion was nevertheless highly corrosive of social relations, which were also poisoned by the lingering smell of members' more specific guilty secrets—for example, the importuning of a child needing money to satisfy a drug addiction, or the fact that any transaction involving the payment of interest outside an officially recognized bank or loan agency was illegal. A butcher who had been active in one association told me that people would be reluctant to talk about these bodies; "they're a little afraid," even if the consequences were not likely to be as dire as those associated with the more sinister loan sharks. Even long-term residents of non-Roman origin have difficulty joining these associations, many of whose members have known each other since childhood and still do not feel that they can trust each other absolutely.

These attitudes show how insidiously the toxic experience of usury in Rome has leached into people's feelings about any kind of financial indebtedness. Creating a new organization, even a very visible and formally organized one with relatively transparent management and explicit links to respectable institutions, has to overcome the same persistent venom; this was a major obstacle in the way of the new artisans' union and its attempt to organize a reasonable system of loans for artisans.

Nor was this the only historical burden that the organizer of the new association had to face. Another—and formidable—obstacle to his plans took the form of his well-advertised links with the discredited leadership of the Socialist Party; the party leader, Bettino Craxi, had gone into self-imposed exile in Tunisia in order to avoid trial on corruption charges and had then died there. For many Italians, his name was virtually synonymous with *Tangentopoli*, the rule of corruption, against which there was a popular revolt in the early 1990s. During his ascendancy, some of his presumed political allies acquired substantial properties in Monti, a circumstance that kept their involvement in various corruption scandals before the censorious eye of the local public. The fact that Craxi's key local supporter, the artisans' union organizer, was Sicilian only served to fuel suspicions, always vaguely expressed and without any supporting evidence, of a mafia connection. Whatever the merits of such claims, which were widely voiced, the key problem remains that—as in the heyday of the rotating credit associations—involvement with the world of loans and credit will smear the most well-intentioned of entrepreneurs with the same clinging slime of presumed criminal association.

Banking on Fear

The banks are conventionally blamed for the persistence of usury. Given the difficulty of obtaining legal bank loans, an entire industry of lending agencies has appeared on the scene, printing advertisements in the newspapers and depositing flyers on the windshields of parked cars—anonymous approaches that implicitly also respect the rule of silence. But even these agencies cannot handle the many local merchants who have already begun the descent into a series of interlocking debts from which there is often no escape other than penury or suicide. By refusing to advance small loans to those without collateral, the banks have helped to create the conditions under which the only recourse is to usury, the very institution that will then make access to bank loans even more improbable—a dreadful quicksand from which few emerge.

The nervous preference for real estate over the uncertain value of cash is one obvious feature that even honest bankers share with mafiosi. But some bankers allegedly fit that image more fully still. Newly arrived in the local branches, they first entertain requests from relatively poor artisans and merchants from the neighborhood. They talk and jest with them, inserting a jocose question: "Do you have a piece of masonry? Do you have building stones?" Establishing that the visitors have nothing a bank could accept as collateral, the new manager dismisses these petitioners with unctuous regrets and good wishes. The jocular politeness of these exchanges actually disguises the fragility of the manager's position, since he will not stand up to a serious challenge. A jeweler, for example, told me that he simply told the manager to look at him and see in him a colleague for whom a loan would be as appropriate as it would be for the eminently respectable manager himself; and the manager, who had taken a liking to him (or at least understood the threat implicit in his emphasis on friendship and collegiality), agreed.

But the majority of artisans do not stand up for their rights, being intimidated by the manager's superior education and appurtenances of authority. They take themselves off, grumbling and unhappy. The manager then immediately invites promising prospects—those whose accounts are suspiciously large and active—to come in and discuss these accounts, to which he, alone aside from the customers themselves, has access. Settled in the privacy of a well-appointed office, he then remarks on the strangely impressive flow of funds into the clients' accounts; he delicately hints that he is aware that the source can only be usury and informs these clients that there are certain local artisans who are desperately in need of loans, which the bank cannot provide because the artisans have no property to offer as collateral. If these wealthy and distinguished customers would therefore simply help the poor artisans with loans—of which, it goes without saying, the bank manager would expect an appropriate percentage—no further investigation of their accounts would be necessary. He then sends the artisans to the usurers, explaining yet again that, as these poor applicants have no collateral, they represent an unacceptable risk for the bank, but that he just happens to know someone who might be able to help. The artisans do not tell the loan-sharks who sent them (although the usurers know this already), and this delicate tact has perhaps contributed to creating a convenient fiction that such occurrences are rare. But most residents seem convinced that they are not rare at all. An optician claimed to have read of such cases in the newspapers; and one artisan went so far as to say that all artisans ended up in usurers' hands at one point or another, and that bank managers' connections were the commonest link. Respectable citizens to all appearances, they thus supposedly entrap the vulnerable rich in order to exploit the desperate poor.

In an economy of limited options, debt is a moral and social stain from which redemption is all but impossible. The only recourse is to reliable friends, who do lend each other money for short periods without interest but in the expectation of reciprocation; this is especially liable to happen between small-scale merchants, and seems to occur with greater ease between women. A few men, especially those who see themselves as representing the culture of the old popular classes, also like to express their masculinity through their gracious consent to lend women, especially beautiful younger women, money without interest, in a spirit of gallantry. Loans between friends or close neighbors demand a high degree of mutual trust and esteem; indeed, the lender often proffers help precisely in order to gain a measure of social acceptance. One restaurateur who is locally regarded as something of a country bumpkin has found this a pleasant and effective way of compensating for his rustic ways in the eyes of his more urbane neighbors. In this way, he gains "a kind of intimacy, a kind of friendship." Loans actually create bonds between friends, but it is, remarked the same observer (a beneficiary of the restaurateur's desire for such relations), not without its social risks; she saw it as perhaps more typical of Naples than of Rome although it evidently subsists in both cities as "a solidarity that creates fear."

Friendship, in fact, is also the key metaphor for the relationship between usurer and debtor; this is an idiom that eases an almost imperceptible transition from social solidarity to vicious exploitation. A serious debt, especially one that the debtor may not be able to repay quickly, is likely to drive the debtor in search of ever more distant sources of financial help. This is when the usurers—local, but notorious for their ability to call on sinister outside forces—step in with their smiling protestations of a disinterested desire to help and their outrageous interest rates of up to 20 percent per month, their natty neckties and their insinuations of a friendship too useful to be refused but too dangerous to be defied. They often politely request small favors such as a gift of country produce. This reinforces the metaphor and pretense of disinterested friendship while reminding debtors that, in reality, defaulting is not an option—for these are people whose slightest request one can never refuse with impunity.

Every so often, the usurers' henchmen make an example of defaulters and welshers—those who have failed to pay up and those who have committed the ultimate solecism of reporting their distress and its sources to the authorities. The least violent response is the destruction of property, but it occasionally extends to an exemplary murder. For any large loan, moreover, usurers always cover themselves by making sure that the victim signs a promissory note; this not only ensures that they will be paid, but reinforces the usurers' good credit in the eyes of their banks.

Such stories of collusion grounded in fear and the hope of easy profit, frequently though they are voiced, are hard to verify. But quite recently such a ring, which also included a lawyer, was disbanded by the police.[22] The shopkeeper who told me of being saved by the arrival of a police car also recounted seeing his tormentor engaging in affable relations with the entire staff of a local bank: "he was greatly respected," he remarked, evoking the language of underworld ethics. Even so, it is not entirely this direct collusion to which Monticiani allude when they say that the banks are the worst usurers—far worse than the loan sharks themselves. Nor are they simply expressing a conventional preference for known neighbors, even evil ones, over institutions run by ruthless bureaucrats, although this, too, is a consideration.

They are, rather, talking about the institutional structures that make such collusion feasible in the first place. They are complaining about the absurdity of being asked for collateral when the whole point of taking out the loan is to try to create a more independent small business in the first place. Most Romans rent rather than own the properties in which they live and work, and few artisans are wealthy enough to start out in life as the proprietors of their workplaces.[23] The banks' policies, and the illegal practices of some of their officials, drive many poorer and less propertied Romans, first to try their luck with legitimate lending agencies that offer legal interest rates, and then with the "stranglers." A contributory cause is the fact that debts to the state agency (Inps) under which they are registered for social service payments are subject to rapidly compounded interest, which can go as high as 300 percent per year, payable after the first two months of delay. The artisans' reluctance to engage with the state authorities, whose punitive interest can itself be responsible for their ending up in the red and therefore being rejected by the banks, also puts them at a further disadvantage; many do not realize that they can pay in installments if they can demonstrate a temporary lack of liquidity.

The artisans' association already mentioned, recently created and with its base in Monti, developed a program of care (tutela) for artisans trying to deal with these economic difficulties and at risk of falling into the usurers' hands. The ambitious president thought that a workers' cooperative with an internal credit system might offer a just and workable solution. His goal was to create a group of consortia that would be financed by a bank, so that the bank would not have to accept direct responsibility for the loans to individual artisans but would be covered by the cooperative instead; eventually, since many an artisan with able hands "is mentally confused," he said, those who were unable to organize their finances so that they could repay the loans in cash might opt for a practical alternative: to surrender some of their products to the appropriate consortium for sale to the wider market to which the consortium itself would certainly have direct access. In proposing these schemes, however, he faced an uphill struggle against a deep skepticism on the part of Monti artisans, and he seems unlikely ever to persuade the majority of the viability of his scheme.

Tactful Silences

The porous fabric of national and regional institutions, and especially of banks, favors the refraction of a supposedly universal financial ethics through the privacy afforded by a multiplicity of local special interests and sufferings.

One electrician argued that the banks simply did not want any truck with unimportant customers: "If you want a billion it's easy to get the loans; if you want ten thousand, the banks won't give it to you!" Banks demand collateral in the form of real estate or a guaranteed state salary; artisans usually have neither.

The institutional framework, moreover, favors the alleged collaboration between bank managers and usurers. Privacy laws, designed to protect citizens' interests from the predations of state and business alike, in practice also favor such secret dealings and make their exposure all but impossible. In the sense that a banker has access to private information, as priests have access to secrets through the confessional, there is also a strongly felt parallelism between the actions of the financial establishment and those of religious authority. Bank managers are routinely moved from post to post every few years, which suggests that at least some of their institutions are aware of the temptations they face but would prefer to avoid confronting individuals; this seems to parody the situation of clergy operating in a system of subsidiarity that allows each to ignore the actions of all the others while all claiming membership in a common institutional and moral world. Again, many—perhaps most—priests and bankers are decent people trying to reach a workable relationship with a notoriously unreliable environment. But the widespread if unverifiable assumption that most are in fact corrupt means that those who are truly corrupt (and they are perhaps genuinely few in number) can rely, like other officials, on a common and locally recognizable code of winks and nods, the very obliqueness of which protects them from the exposure of deals offered and consummated.

Accommodation is written into the fabric of the city itself; beyond the palimpsest of amnestied architectural infractions, other inconvenient histories also persist. The Fascist insignia on the parish church's war memorial in this predominantly left-wing district, for example, were allowed to remain because their destruction, achieved virtually everywhere else, would have insulted the Monti families whose young men had died in an ignoble cause. Church and people are united at least on this one point, that the only viable approach to human imperfection is a pragmatics of compromise—and Romans pride themselves on exemplifying that feature in being, as they say, *accommodanti*. The city's appearance today is as much a monument to that spirit of compromise as it is to the grandeur of the officially recognized past.

Indeed, a furniture restorer argued that the local approach to the building code, and especially to the refurbishing of old houses protected by the conservation laws, was to "let things go" (*lascia correre*), an attitude that he specifically described as a "tacit compromise" (*un tacito compromesso*).

It is an attitude shared by the civic authorities, who, for a small consideration, are likely to respond to a request to make some alteration that would normally be considered illegal by granting permission, but take care to avoid some other alteration that might attract too much interest—a classic compromise, again. For the furniture restorer, his work is less a matter of historical accuracy than of fixing (*sistemare*) broken or damaged fixtures and ornaments in order to improve the quality of living conditions. It was not even necessary to make architectural changes surreptitiously at night when one could rely on the connivance of neighbors.

"Letting things go" is an expression of the noninvolvement that characterizes Romans' grandiloquent contempt for arguments they cannot win. A Communist butcher, faced with discussions about the existence of God, refused to be drawn, but avoided the question with a gesture that Italian viewers of my film *Monti Moments* consistently interpret as a refusal to take sides. He claimed that he did not possess the intellectual genius required to get to the bottom of such weighty questions: "I just let it [the issue] go" (*io lo lascio perde'*). His is not so much a stance of fatalistic resignation as a highly pragmatic assessment of political realities; one attempts to keep on good terms with all possible factions and to entertain even the most outlandish possibilities. In the stylistic promiscuity of house restoration, this accommodating attitude is also inscribed in the physical fabric of the city. Officials, as much as residents, sometimes find that is simpler just to let matters go by.

The awkwardness with which Monticiani discuss the question of usury illustrates, in a rather backhanded manner, their clear-headed realization that life must always be a series of compromises—and, above all, that human life is by its very nature riddled with imperfections. As with the priests' dilemmas of conscience over the eviction of parishioners, so lay people must search within their innermost selves to determine whether the loans they are making are acceptably free of the desire to profit at the expense of others. In the absence of desire for such profit the sin entailed in the gains themselves may be minor, a part of the original heritage of all earthly beings. But the line between acceptable and excessive profit is never clear. This allows a range of rhetorical postures, from protestations of pure intent on the part of the lenders to the charges of evil intent levied by debtors who find themselves unable to repay the loans. While the usurers themselves frequently resort to extortion, defenders of a policy of liberalizing lending practices—precisely the neoliberal arguments that also underlie the current epidemic of real estate speculation—argue that it is often the debtors who levy charges of usury as a means of avoiding repayment on debts incurred on genuinely legal loans.[24] For them, the banks may be guilty of bad manners (*scorrettezza*, a lack of civil decency), and perhaps of a hasty disregard for people's sensibilities, but not of criminal intent to defraud the poor.[25] Supporters of this approach attempt to justify the banks' actions on the grounds that loans to the very poor entail much larger risks, against which some minor incivility appears to be of little or no importance; and, while they recognize that the church has long held a very negative view of any kind of money lending, they draw a sense of justification from the inescapable fact that the papacy, too, was ineluctably drawn into the practice. Indeed, the standard argument seems to be that the disrepute associated with money lending is simply the result of historical accident, and was partially reversed by the rise, once in the Renaissance and then again in the industrial age, of families whose power and wealth derived entirely from banking.[26]

The fact that the papacy itself was implicated in, or at least tolerant of, usurious practices should be seen in conjunction with its attitude to the management of real estate in the city. In both cases, the ecclesiastical authorities are bound by the logic of both their theology and their bureaucratic organization to leave decisions to individual consciences. The intention behind each act is thus fundamental to the degree of its sinfulness; hence the early notion that even wanting to make a profit on usury was sinful.[27] But intentions are known only to the individual in question. The church thus essentially adopts a policy that, by respecting the necessity for each of its officials to wrestle with temptation alone, ultimately serves its goals by enriching its coffers while binding the people to it with a bitter potion made of equal parts of church disapproval and church involvement.

That, at least, is the local perception. The clergy are no less subject to the weakness of original sin than are those whose lives they are supposed to shepherd. Much of their business is conducted with great politeness: civility masks abuses rendered socially and politically palatable, if not doctrinally ideal, by theological hindsight. And their flock—not only the friendly neighborhood loan-shark but also every householder who wants to create a more habitable home—follows their example. Faced with imminent eviction, a resident nonetheless urges his uncle to stop haranguing the proprietor's lawyer. The prelate who comes to evict a group of tenants congratulates them on the hard work they have put into beautifying their building—which is what has now enabled the church to raise the rents above an affordable level. The loan shark claps the hapless gambler on the shoulder and warmly invites him, as a friend, to stay in his house until the latest loan is fully paid up (and only indirectly hints at the awful consequences of failing to comply). Because the church must operate in this material, flawed world, it thus also comes to terms with the necessity of usury—albeit with predictable expressions of distaste—and leaves the determination of intentions to the individual conscience.[28] Indeed, that is what it must do; temptation is the necessary burden of all, in a sinful world, and civility and a willingness to "let it go" together comprise the tact with which each resident respects others' inevitable entanglement in its snares.

CHAPTER SEVEN

Extortionate Civilities

It may seem strange, as well as romantically nostalgic, to claim that civility was ever a mark of the underworld. Nevertheless, the nostalgia that one does hear in Monti for the dour morality and measured extortion of the old bosses pays respectful court to the idea that these men (and they were all men) managed, if not a moral economy, then an economy of manners. One old woman recalled that the old bosses were respectful (*rispettuosi*) of neighbors, greeting them with an appropriate salutation (such as *buon giorno*, "good day"); it was to these same people one turned, recognizing the local power their grave dignity signified, when people "came to rob your house" (*venivano a rubà 'a casa*).

Almost all that is left of this petty protectionism (*pizzo*) today consists in extracting fees for guarding cars left in exposed parking lots. The term *pizzo*, which literally means "goatee beard," and thus a covering of the face, metaphorically signifies the polite gesture of generosity that actually covers up an expected bribe.[1] But in earlier times the bosses had a more respected role. So conscious are they of their emasculated power and of the values associated with the new civic order that one surviving kinsman of a formerly powerful local boss—the latter had been killed in a car crash following a dramatic police pursuit—mournfully denied that their family had ever been part of the underworld (*malavita*); they had instead, said he in a sepulchral tone of hurt and reproach, been people of integrity and humility who had enjoyed the respect of their neighbors: "We were never arrogant bullies" (*Non siamo mai stati prepotenti*). Yet such respect was, we should not forget, backed by a capacity for restrained but exemplary violence—because, said this same man of the typical petty crook (*mascalzone*), "if you do not intervene with these types, well, they'll continue to do [those things], to harass people's wives."

Accommodations Civil and Civic

In the sense that such practices are closely associated with urban life, they are also, paradoxically, marks of *civiltà*, of civilization, being *civile*. This concept, which gives free play to models of courtesy and social ease, is the subject of a justly famous discussion by Sydel Silverman, who considers a number of related terms in English—including "civic"—and concludes that none quite fit the Italian term, with its deep roots in the idea of the city and its manners as the ideal model for good living. Matters are further complicated by the evidence that in some parts of Italy the urban model does not get the respect Silverman found in Umbria; Anthony Galt's discussion of town and country in Locorotondo, in Puglia, shows with great clarity that peasants there even express a modicum of contempt for the ways of the town, although here the difference may be partly one that subsists between central as opposed to southern Italian culture.[2] Rome, one would think, should in any case be the ultimate exemplar of *civiltà*, a concept historically based on citizenship—being a member of the *civitas*—and thus also of civic virtue.

What we find instead, however, is that Rome, a self-consciously "southern" city, loses out to the great centers of Renaissance culture as the source of civil style and virtue. In Rome, moreover, the sense of opposition between the civic and the civil is often remarkably strong; civility often means the kind of urbanity that disguises (but also communicates) arrogance, power, and hierarchy, and that subverts the formal rules of governance in the name of sociability. That implies in turn that the civil may on occasion not only be compatible with what a civic conscience would dub "corruption" but can actually include it. In this sense, the underworld, with its attention to the correct comportment of men toward women and its active protection of the weakest members of the local community, can justly lay claim to the title of "civil society"—not, to be sure, in the sense that nongovernmental organizations are often so labeled, but still with a powerful implication of providing a morally coherent alternative to official, bureaucratic norms.[3]

It follows from this that, while ordinary violence is seen as contrary to the ideals of urbanity, regulated threats are another matter altogether; they are the instruments of a practical functionalism that underwrites and maintains a high degree of conformity to the perceived social order. It is not even clear that they are ever realized in the genteel surroundings of Monti today. But recall the middleman who invited the vendor to dinner in order to negotiate the return of his property; the ambiguity of who was threatening whom is sustained in the polite setting, and allows space for the negotiation in progress.

Threats may sometimes be pure bluff. A newly established greengrocer got a number of mysterious phone calls offering both protection against theft and help with ensuring that he could illegally park boxes of produce outside the shop without incurring fines. He told the callers that he needed nothing; after a while the calls ceased and apparently nothing else happened. The subsequent collapse of his business was a result of his failure to anticipate the switch from the *lira* to the euro rather than because of any hostile activity. Out in the suburbs, by contrast, the extortionists make their presence clear; they are prepared to slash tires or set shops on fire. Perhaps the knowledge that such things do happen is sufficient intimidation even in relatively tranquil Monti.

Discommoding Complicities

It is not even clear that submission, when it happens, is quite what it appears to be. Submission is usually expressed through the common avoidance of conflict: numerous phrases—*lascia perde'* or *lassa perde'* (let it go lost), *lassa stá* (let it be), *lascia correre* (let it run)—are all iterations of the complaisance that lets dangerous currents run past, as when rotating credit managers skim off personal profits with impunity.

Many Romans attribute this attitude to the years of papal rule. It is often described in terms of resignation or accommodation. Importantly, however, it is also an attitude that can imply a threat no less than expressing the acceptance of one. As an astute student pointed out, it can serve as a warning "not to compete with me" (*non entrare in concorrenza con me*). Indeed, the passivity suggested by these phrases is perhaps deceptive; intimates understand them as socially proactive. An outwardly religious attitude to the workings of providence can thus disguise a cynical willingness to avoid responsibility for failure: "Let it go; dear Saint, what are you doing [for me]?" (*Lascia perdere, Santo, che fai?*) An expression of insouciant indifference may thus conceal both the speaker's own unease and the cultivation of fear in others.

This ambiguous stance pervades the smallest gesture; it is the verbal equivalent of the expressive hunching of the shoulders and spreading of the upwardly outspread hands whereby Romans refuse to engage in compromising conversations or indicate the ineluctable authority of bureaucrats and clerics. It is, above all, an assertion of personal dignity in the face of overbearing power; its implicit egalitarianism, a fellowship of shared impotence and frustration, leaves scant room for tolerating any kind of impatience or authoritarianism among one's interlocutors.

One elderly lady used the phrase *lascia perde'* to slow me down when I became impatient to pay off a waiter at a bar; she also used it to express the uselessness of getting into an argument—using it, for example (*Dottore, lasciamo perde'*), to indicate her disgust with the modern attitude to marriage: "What is fidelity? Stupidity!" Disgusted she may have been; but she knew better than to tangle with young people convinced of their greater worldly wisdom.

The stance is clear: one cannot seize on every potential offense, topic of interest, or passing whim; life is quite sufficiently complex as it is. That is why the butcher preferred to assume an air of intellectual inadequacy when faced with thinking about the existence of God. Equally, however, one tries to avoid becoming entangled over the trivialities of everyday life. It may be best to compromise in true Roman style; when a Monti-based merchant collided with another's street awning (*ombrellone*) with his van, he asked the owner of the shop if he was insured; the latter said that he was but the he wanted some money right away. How much? Asked for 200,000 *lire*, the Monticiano offered him half and, in his own words, added, "If not, let it go, [go ahead and] make a formal complaint!" (*Se no, lascia perde,' faccia la denuncia!*) The bargain was struck.

The further implications of such accommodation ramify in capillary fashion through local power relations at every conceivable level. When it comes to bribery and extortion, for example, accommodation is the socially easiest way of dealing with a form of civility that dons the guise of friendship (*amicizia*), and that clearly anticipates an equally cordial idiom of response—even though, if a merchant rejects a policeman's approach, he may soon, or so locals assert, find his business in ruins, with permits withheld and a rash of citations for various petty but expensive offenses.

Collusion, on the other hand, would benefit officials and citizens alike. At least in the popular image, affable courtesies grease the wheels, protecting the minor extortionist from sustainable charges and reminding the victim that there is considerable benefit to be derived from cooperating. Reminisced a newspaper vendor, "My mother used to say, 'Eat so others can eat!'" (*Magna e fa' magná!*) A vendor who was twice stopped by *carabinieri* for some minor offense was delighted when they asked him whether he had heavy socks in his stock; "for me they were great. . . . A bunch of socks, and all is fixed!" This is, in short, an attitude that nurtures a commensality of corruption: eat and let others eat. Translated into indifference (*menefreghismo*), it becomes a more radical collusion with power—but also, sometimes, a means of keeping at least the pettier forms of power at bay and getting on with the ordinary business of life.

Officials quickly learn how to "let things go" when dealing with the people of Monti. An incident recalled to illustrate the former solidarity of neighbors also shows how the very reputation of Monti as "a bit delinquent" (un po' delinquente) helped to impress on police officers and others the necessity of respecting local ways; it also nicely illustrates the deployment of gender ideology in defense of a collective interest. An official had come to demand payment of arrears on a gas meter. The woman of the house did not have enough money to pay him; the neighbors in other apartments in the building tried to help, but together they could not raise enough money. When the official threatened to cut off the gas altogether, a woman living upstairs on the third floor came down and started screaming at him that he was "a turd" (uno stronzo). He tried pushing her out of the way, whereupon she yelled that he "had put his hands on me" (mi ha messo le mani addosso)— a grave offense from an unrelated male. Then her husband appeared and demanded to know who had done such a thing. When the others indicated the gas man, a violent fistfight erupted. At this point a policeman showed up; but, knowing the kind of people he was dealing with in Monti, he sensibly enjoined restraint and did not try to arrest anyone or issue any citations—it was better, he said, "just to let it go" (lasciamo perde'). Life in Monti was already too complex and dangerous; a policeman who did not understand the social realities might have proceeded with some sort of legal action, giving rise to even more violence and achieving nothing. "Let it go": sage advice, then and now.

Such phrases do not signal only a stoic resignation to the realities of daily living or to the inevitability of conflict. They also demonstrate a recognition that standing on principle can sometimes damage one's own interests. A pugnacious Pugliese, a bar proprietor, who had quarreled with a jeweler when the latter got too friendly with his wife, discovered the latter hanging around near his shop and looking around, so he greeted him quite cordially, and expected that the jeweler, duly abashed, would now be conciliatory. The bar proprietor could not afford to stand on dignity for too long, for "business is business." He added, "You can't brood over every little thing. . . . You have to let things go by. . . . I can rise above it. For me nothing's happened; he's the one with the regrets." And he explained that his mother had taught him that "if you let it go, the other side becomes your inferior." Of another petty cheat who failed to pay his bar tab, he said that the money was so trivial that "you [the cheat] are of no value" and that he would not dignify such antics by bothering to recover the money. What might pass for resignation to the whims of fate becomes, in this man's demeanor, quite the opposite: a proactive seizure of the moral high ground.

His tactics are thus a subtle reworking of the stereotype of the southern male. Rome represents an unusual variant on the pattern of gender relations in the wider Mediterranean region. Historically, for example, the women of Rome have certainly not conformed to the image of southern European female demureness. Displays of male aggression, conversely, are usually tempered with self-restraint; those who fail to control their tempers are often roundly criticized even by their most traditionalist neighbors.

The bar proprietor astutely stage-managed these partly conflicting stereotypes of masculinity and the south, tailoring an aggressive style associated with his home region to fit the very different self-stereotype of the easygoing Roman. A politician he apparently admired, the same councilor we have already encountered holding a street meeting on traffic control, complacently contrasted the Romans' attitude to problem-solving with the stereotypes of both north and south: "We're not neurotic, and that seems right to me!" The attitude of "letting things go" defuses some surprisingly tense situations, and the barman had to live among Romans; indeed, his wife grew up in Monti. His skill lay in managing to recast the avoidance of conflict as manly strength.

His forbearance served his business well. When two junior goldsmiths ran up a tab at his bar and kept evading payment, he showed the tab to another goldsmith who had asked why these two did not come to the bar any more—this category of artisans does communicate internally and a few routinely exchange useful information, despite the jealousies that inevitably subsist—and suddenly the two young men began appearing again, not entering the bar but greeting the proprietor with a cautious "*Ciao!*" and being greeted cordially enough in return. Had he confronted the defaulters directly, he would have lost their custom, failed to collect the debt, and been humiliated into the bargain.

Even deep anger—the overtly racist outcry against the immigrants who flooded into the Piazzetta every Thursday and Sunday is an example—generally does not lead to concerted action, and individuals similarly tend to hold back from any drastic actions of their own. Thoughtful locals expected this complaisant resignation, or at least a habit of compromise, to overwhelm the calls for hostile action against the immigrants in the long run; that is in fact what happened, after some mediation between local residents and the Ukrainian church authorities. Once a significant proportion of the population acquiesces in any kind of understanding, it is only the foolhardy who continue to stand against it, because civility demands a degree of conformity, or at least complaisance.

Uncivil Pleasantries, Unpleasant Civilities

A decidedly left-wing bar proprietor loved to bait police officers who, he thought, were harassing Ukrainians and other immigrants. His establishment thus became a gathering place for some of these victims of police intolerance—a source of profit that did not go unnoticed by detractors wishing to impugn the purity of his motives. He and his wife did also recognize some individual Albanians as known troublemakers, and would preemptively put "reserved" signs on all the tables—which at least discriminated against them as individuals rather than as immigrants-in-general.

This man was often extremely belligerent, especially toward figures of official authority. He attributed his stance both to his past as a left-wing street fighter and to his masculine and working-class identity. Yet the practical compromises that he made in excluding certain suspect customers, as well as the general assumption that his kindness to immigrants was actually good for his business, were examples of an operating modality that was perfectly comprehensible to his neighbors, perhaps more so than his sometimes flamboyant displays of aggression. Those, in fact, occasionally put the business at risk, much to his wife's visible annoyance. He got into a serious fight with an unknown man for insulting my wife during the New Year's festivities in 2000. He had told the man, rather politely, to "take his hands off" my wife and "let the matter go" and had received a powerful punch in the nose in response. Our two wives and I had to hang on to him with all our strength; he roared that he would kill the aggressor and afterward, when his wife tried to clean up his bloodied face, told her to go home on her own and that she should not have prevented him from going after the other man: "I can't stand you any more! Get out of here!" When I remonstrated that I too had helped to restrain him, with ironic courtesy he pointed out that I, after all, was not his wife—who, a convenient scapegoat for his failure to exact immediate and condign vengeance, could now be excoriated for saving him from humiliating himself further. "She comes from a working-class district" just as he did, he argued, so she should have understood how he was feeling.

The Pugliese bar proprietor muted his masculinity more carefully and tempered it with a more deliberate display of tolerance, perhaps because he had a much smaller establishment and thus much narrower economic margins. He was also more provincial in speech and manner, and thus had less cultural capital to squander. The performance of compromise and conformism is crucial to both economic and social survival, although the exact

balance will depend on social status and other circumstances. Italian notions of civility exclude nonconformist actions, including even justifiable
violence when the consensus opts for accommodation. In the past, behavior
deemed to be antisocial led to isolation in a mental hospital and rejection
by one's own family; it is still the subject of considerable anguish and social
disruption.[4] The pressure to conform, which also appeared in the old district bosses' maintenance of the local moral order, also generates a curious
solidarity against the power of the unitary state, nicely encapsulated in one
woman's observation that people were generally disinclined to obey the law
but that this was on the whole a rather good thing. This, then, is a rough
conformism even—or especially—in a capital not known for its obedience to
the laws and norms of the state; it is not the legalistic obedience demanded
by the state itself.

The alternation between amiable roughness and cultivated formality
links everyday actions with deeply embedded historical idioms. Stances of
friendship and politeness all allude to the very essence of what Italians call
civiltà, the quintessence of urbanity. But the practice is not always so civil,
and at times descends to pettiness; a customer might expansively treat five
people to a cup of coffee apiece, a bar manager told me, and then only pay for
four of them. One such occasion might be an innocent slip, but repeated acts
of this kind would give the game away. There are also not infrequent claims
to a heroic rejection of demonstrably insincere friendliness. A furniture
restorer, for example, told me that when he discovered that a police officer
was being particularly friendly because he wanted information about certain
neighbors, he told the officer that if the latter had come for disinterested
friendship, this was fine; but "if you have come to talk about such matters,
don't ever come back, get out of here!"

We do not have to take such masculine posturing at face value, especially as the speaker was also widely held to be responsible for absconding
with some of the funds of a rotating credit association, leaving the principal
organizer to face charges of usury; he himself says it was neighbors' gossipy accusations of usury that scared the members away in the first place.
His account of his response to the inquisitive police officer is nevertheless
revealing of the instability and insecurity that pervades some of the most
affable expressions of courtesy, and fairly represents what many men wished
they had the freedom to say. It also shows how easily any dealings with authority can undermine an artisan's or a merchant's social standing, and how
important it therefore is to deny any such connections.[5]

Courtesy is valued for its own sake. The merchant who complained
about being called racist by a Chinese immigrant explained his reaction in

terms of respect—which, he said, he is prepared to show anyone who demonstrates "a minimum of civilization, of sociability." Demonstrations of respect and good style facilitate communication and attest to a shared sense of
civilized conduct. They do not necessarily convey benign intentions. Only
when the pretenses wear too thin may one drop the veil of polite speech, as
when the outraged merchant chased his spying police friend away. This was
an explicit rejection of unwanted, false friendship—a too-obvious betrayal,
badly performed, of the fundamental social principle of minding one's own
business. The ideals of *civiltà* are about performance, good manners, and
tact.

But snooping is something that residents actively fear, and not only from
officials. Local gossip can lead to official interference; it can also be the mark
of an antisocial competitiveness. Although the tactic of "stealing with the
eyes" is a socially expected technique for craft apprentices, for example, it
can be extended into adulthood with less positive implications. A barber
with over four decades of work behind him (and a shop that started func-
tioning in 1923) recounted how, in his youth, a friend who was a women's
hairdresser would come and pick him up an hour early at his shop—not,
as it turned out, to engage in simple conversation, but because "he was
stealing my craft from me here." It would have been more honest (*onesto*)
simply to have asked for instruction, since women's hairdressing involved
quite different procedures than did men's, instead of "stealing with his eye"
(*rubare coll'occhio*).

Friendly civility, which sometimes has less to do with affection than
with the choreography of competition, also evokes the glories of a fiercely
urban national culture—a culture, we should remember, that has for centuries been steeped in oppressive forms of clientelism, torture, simony, and
sumptuous displays of the fruits of sin. A clothing merchant told me that
newcomers to Monti were often welcomed with professions of friendship
and offers of help but that this simply meant that the old-timers were "seeking to impose their will": "But it's not as though they want to help *me*, it's
that they only want to help themselves!"

Courtesy, which can subtly convey serious threats, conversely may often signify fear and nervousness, which also inflect its forms. One man
approaching retirement told me that he preferred to stand in buses, because,
while he was accustomed to offering his seat to the truly elderly and, especially, to pregnant women, he also preferred to avoid the offense that this
well-intentioned act occasionally caused in modern times. This detail illustrates the uncertainty that still, perhaps more today than ever before, clings
to acts of formal deference. It may also be that the Roman Jews' reputation

for having a less brusque manner in their dealings with others arose from the constant fear of persecution and their erstwhile dependence on a narrow range of trades.[6] A local Jewish merchant, attentive to the danger of reinforcing negative stereotypes, told me that he was careful not to accept many offers of coffee but always tried to pay for his own.

Today displays of exceptional courtesy are often the instrument of provoking fear in others rather than expressing unease about one's own circumstances. Some forms of civility are thus anything but civic in the uses to which they are put. Ruthless power-mongering can adopt smoothly pleasant manners. The rough side of Roman life is nevertheless an equally important part of the picture. Quarrelsome behavior, which may occasionally confirm "folkloric" memories of an earlier age, today provokes as much irritation and derision as it does amusement, particularly among the educated intellectuals who run bookstores, organize town meetings, and attend classical concerts and scholarly lectures.

While measured tones and ironic jokes may achieve the "accommodation" that is so central a feature of Romans' image of themselves, outside observers, who have their own experiences of exclusion to recount, often see the Roman style in less flattering terms. A Sardinian barman who had operated for a long time in Monti, and was proud of the agonistic interactions of his home island, expressed deep dislike both for the contempt that he sometimes encountered in Rome and for the opportunistic friendliness that he also saw as characteristic of Romans. Recall, too, the furniture restorer who allegedly chased away the police officer who professed friendship in order to extract information.

Aggression is rarely valued for itself, but a clever response to provocation often does elicit approval. In a particularly nice demonstration of poetic justice, a jeweler had discovered the mechanic from a different zone who had stolen one of the wheels of his rather luxurious bicycle. He forced the thief to pick up the stolen wheel and give him a ride on his own bicycle back to his own house, where the thief had to replace the stolen wheel and then leave with his own bicycle minus one wheel.

Culture and Custom

The Sardinian barman nicely captured the segmentary fragmentation of culture that still characterizes Italian life: "Union is fine when it's divided," he remarked, and added, "That means you aren't imposing a new culture on me." With such logic, in which culture itself becomes an explicit item of negotiation, the capital city is able to remain as determinedly provincial as any small town.

The concept of *cultura* is a useful device for explaining social and political differences, and for negotiating one's own position in social and political debate. It reflects a complex and historically deep relationship between social-science discourse and local ways of reifying identity, very much like the use of the term *kastom* in Melanesia.[7] To avoid the embarrassment of expressing racist attitudes directly, a relatively liberal merchant described Gypsies as having "a culture of theft, of non-work"; while he in principle favored the idea of offering them fixed employment he feared the effect of that supposedly endemic cultural trait and so "I don't want to be the first" (*nun vojo esse' 'r primo*) to take them on. Thus does the determinism of culture become a self-fulfilling prophecy.

This merchant also showed awareness of the disgraced genealogy of the concept of race (*razza*), a product of its incarnation in Mussolini's Fascist regime, but thought that the term *genetica* was less offensive. Yet his slide toward politically (more) correct language did not really change the underlying racial determinism of his position, as his rhetorical demand whether I thought it was easy "to disassemble my culture" (*smontar la mia cultura*) then made abundantly clear.[8] This innatism also has notable political ramifications. A politically conservative observer might charge the citizenry with a "culture" of refusing to take responsibility and blaming the state for all its ills; since citizens elect their leaders, one such person observed, they should not blame the state for its failure to reform the banks and eliminate the ubiquitous misery of usury at the same time. Here, however, culture itself becomes a scapegoat, a so-called explanation that in practice is more of an ideological standpoint. In this sense, culture is what others have; it is invoked as exegesis for their failure to adhere to civic values.[9]

But culture is also a positive term of political self-identification; those who share a party-political background tend to emphasize the commonalities that bind them. Thus, a Monti butcher whose family has lived in the same house since 1704 (and who are thus among the small minority who have "always" owned their own dwellings) described himself and his immediate kin as being of the *cultura* of the class of proprietors but of left-wing ideology. The term *cultura* is often used to describe and even explain the attitudes associated with a profession; a jeweler professed himself unimpressed by the "not inconsiderable cultural background" (*retrocultura non indifferente*) of those who used the fact of their families' having been in the business for five generations.[10] It may also stand for a political ideology;

the butcher shifted the term's meaning when he also described himself as *culturalmente de sinistra* (culturally of the Left) to explain why he objected to newspaper headlines that identified the nationality of Albanian but not of Italian criminals.[11]

More generally the term *cultura* describes a set of habits that signify a person's economic standing; poorer people, for example, might say that they never owned their own home because such was not their *cultura*. But it can also have much more focused meanings, as in the case of a man whose *cultura* was defined by his habit of reading newspapers all day long. The butcher's acknowledgment of a conflict between his class origins and his political ideology, an ideology that he absorbed from his immediate family as a child, represents in perhaps an extreme form the Roman capacity for political accommodation at the social level.

This feature continues into his own social world; he supports left-wing political groups but also speculates in small-scale property activities and provokes the ire of more puristic neighbors because of his willingness to cooperate with business associates of a more obviously speculative brand. Perhaps his shifting use of the term *cultura* reflects such accommodations. Despite his fondly remembered past as a leftist street fighter, many of his customers and friends are of firmly right-wing persuasion. In these matters, he is far from atypical; and I was often struck by the ease with which people of very different political stripe mingled and even collaborated. A left-wing restaurateur married to an immigrant had no difficulty in introducing me to a literally black-shirted Fascist of aristocratic origins, an admirer of Mussolini in whose house a family crest and a photograph of Mussolini greeting "his people" appeared to hold roughly equivalent places of honor. A vocally left-wing bar proprietor hailed an architect and former Alleanza nazionale district councilor and teased him as a "Fascist," then turned to me and remarked on how typical of Italy it was that here he was being friends with this Fascist—though it should be said that this is a phenomenon of perhaps only twenty years' standing. A barber's shop remains one of specific places where people of vastly different political convictions can drop by, read a newspaper, and, perhaps, have their hair cut. Occasional eruptions of political disagreement provide the entertainment, calmly presided over with studious neutrality by the stately barber himself; I met this politically conservative and thoroughly respectable citizen through a family with very different ideological proclivities. When I asked their son, an active local politician with the Democratici di sinistra, why the family also bought its groceries from a known neofascist, he replied, "Food doesn't have a color; it only has a smell"—and the neofascist had the best produce.

These enduring and practical compromises are important. We often read of the dualistic nature of Italian political life, and there is no doubt that the sometimes vicious battles between the two poles have left indelible marks on people's attitudes. For leftists, for example, memories of parents and grandparents tortured by Nazi collaborators or excluded from decent jobs because of their political past remain a source of considerable bitterness. For two decades after the end of World War II, street fights still erupted between the two opposing camps; some tell with pride of the violence they experienced. When I began my research I was struck by the relative ease of association I found between people who, a decade or two earlier, would have belonged to the mutually hostile camps of "Catholics" and "Communists" and who still tended to identify with these labels. These opposing political camps have now morphed into a pair of loose coalitions, the product of the reworking of political ideology after the collapse of the old Christian Democrat and Socialist parties in the aftermath of the corruption scandals of the 1980s and the demise of the Soviet Union in 1991. Memories still persist of violent street battles, in which right-wing toughs—now often identified with the neofascists of the Alleanza nazionale—brought clubs smashing down on the heads of the equally enraged Communist youths. These scenes have not been forgotten, but the memories are refracted through more evanescent and opportunistic political alignments.

In the course of a quarrel about the use of equipment posing environmental safety hazards, a couple of left-wing carpenters reported a local shopkeeper to the *carabinieri*. The merchant, himself a former Communist street-fighter, responded by telling one of them, "I'll send you my friends.... and I'll close you[r shop] down"—a form of intimidation that, said the scandalized carpenter, had been typical of the old Christian Democrats. He seemed more outraged by such supposedly right-wing behavior on the part of a fellow Communist than by the fact of the threat itself. For a Communist to have threatened his enemy with the intervention of "friends"—local city police rather than the national-level *carabinieri*—did indicate a startling reversal, especially as these city officers are known today for both their rightist sympathies and the ease with which they can be bought. On the other hand, the merchant's key protector is allegedly a left-wing ward politician who deserted the old Communist Party when it collapsed and then rejoined its successor, the Democratici di Sinistra, when their fortunes appeared to be rebounding.

In fact, the merchant's illegal activities were first brought to the attention of his neighbors by a local boss of known Fascist sympathies, who told the neighbors that this man was placing large flowerboxes across the sidewalk in front of his shop. The boss had no affection for the Communist tradesman, with whom he had tangled in the past, but he was also not prepared to commit himself to making a formal complaint in his own name, and the city police would do nothing without a formal complaint from a source outside their own ranks. Rather cleverly, then, the boss, one of the last of the *capi rione*, instead provoked other leftists into organizing the attack. Not only did this allow him to conceal his own role, but it set the Communists at odd with each other; and the tradesman's curt refusal to remove the offending flowerboxes drove an irreparable breach in his political as well as social relations, which were further damaged by the protracted quarrel about the environmental disturbance caused by some smoke vents that the tradesman had illegally installed.

Motivations are clearly no longer purely party-political, if indeed they ever were; but the language of hostility remains deeply inflected by the old polarity. Political identities become instrumental, losing ideological clarity in the process. Thus, dislike of a neighbor, or attempts to justify non-intervention in the plight of evictees, can take the form of political slurs: "He's a big Fascist" (*fascistone*)—this, of a committed left-winger, son of a prominent local Communist, who nonetheless married into a right-wing family and eventually found himself unable to avoid accepting the support of the neofascist Alleanza nazionale in organizing the barricades and other measures against eviction from his home.[12]

These slurs are nevertheless often temporary and situational attributions. Most of the time, people of very different political identities rub along reasonably well together, their affable greetings a (deliberately?) thin disguise for their never entirely eradicable mutual suspicion. Today there is sometimes an almost affectionate tone to many of the evocations of past conflict. Romans prefer to engage with and tease each other rather than avoid any contact at all. A janitor who had also been a policeman in his younger days was widely regarded as a Fascist; he constantly tried to probe my activities, and I got the distinct impression that he thought I was some sort of troublemaking agent; I later discovered that he had thought I might be a spy. Reciprocally, a left-wing friend who enjoyed baiting policemen told me that this man had actively provoked Monti leftists as part of a wider rightist plot to create unrest and so prepare the ground for a coup.

Political differences usually emerge less in violent confrontation than in this kind of gossip and teasing. Such indirect modalities allow considerable play to ambiguity and do not damage the surface civility of daily interaction. The abstract ideal was described to me by one literary-minded shopkeeper as that of the Three Musketeers: "one for all and all for one." The evidence for concerted, *rione*-wide action in the past is nevertheless quite scanty. Courteous accommodation creates a smooth surface, but it can contribute, at least indirectly, to the pervasive sense of fear, uncertainty, and internal division, since the desire to avoid unnecessary confrontation also leaves little space for sustaining any kind of concerted defense of collective interests.

Peaceful Politics

This local situation reflects political changes at the national level. As Putnam has noted for the country as a whole, direct confrontation between Left and Right has given way to a sometimes uneasy civility.[13] But local factors are also important. Activists for one leftist group explained to me that in Monti their party had failed to maintain its territorial control, in decided contrast with Campo de' Fiori—where the continuing presence of a party office has meant that even nonmembers continue to vote for the party because their families participate in its everyday activities ("the father came there to work [for the party], the mother came to cook the pasta"). The Monti office was closed down, allegedly by a cabal of party members, including a local member who was especially disliked for his alleged association with a suspected usurer and money launderer.

Some thought that this member feared he was at risk of expulsion from the party; and, that, having unsuccessfully tried to run for election with a different party, he knew that his continuing influence depended on being able to control the party's local representation. The result of closing the district office down altogether had been, not surprisingly, a progressive weakening of the party's local influence, which was already dwindling at an alarming rate in an area hitherto known for its "red" politics. Ironically, however, the closure may also have weakened the kind of personal politics that motivated it in the first place; the more civic-minded local artisans and workers were increasingly unwilling to tolerate even unproven cases of corruption, and found support among young activists alarmed at the party's precipitous—and embarrassing—local decline. Among the artisans, in particular, a reluctance to tie themselves to specific causes or individuals, and an appreciation of autonomy in themselves and others, worked in favor of the more civic-minded politicians and party workers, to the detriment of both some right-wing patrons (who viewed artisans as a category of merchants and thus as part of their own constituency) and those leftists who were trying to play the rightists at their own favor-peddling game; as a result, paradoxically, the artisans' conservatism served as a force for change. Even though the numbers of those concerned were small, they were enough to

tip the balance; leftist election posters appeared in artisans' shop windows
for the first time in living memory, heralding a growing rejection of some
of the old, self-perpetuating civilities. Those merchants who were unable
(or did not dare) to claw their way out of the offending member's clutches
presumably also voted for the left-wing coalition. In late 2000 Monti returned to its old political coloration, returning a solid majority for a locally
rejuvenated Left for the first time in a decade and a half, with a 6 percent increase in leftist votes over the regional elections a few months before, when
the Lazio region—like much of the rest of Italy—had lurched to the Right.
But the tone and content of political debate had changed on the other end
of the spectrum as well. Not to be outdone by the new purism of younger
leftists, local Alleanza nazionale Party activists increasingly sounded like
the old Communists, with a puristic rhetoric of workers' rights and clean
civic process and with their eager opportunism in support of those evicted
from their homes in the course of accelerating gentrification.

Political debate has thus changed, with significantly less emphasis on
the schematic ideological differences of earlier years than on how, and how
far, to dismantle the remaining sources of corruption in civic life. The much-
vaunted accommodation of the Roman social style now comes increasingly
into conflict with such participatory ideals of civic governance. The intense
localism that Berardino Palumbo calls "civic identity"[14] —but that here I
would prefer to dub "local civility"—is increasingly hard to reconcile with
the civic rationalism of either the state or of international institutions. It
is not clear that it will yield significantly to the appeal of these extrinsic
forces; those who operate with the polite corruption of earlier times have
certainly not been uprooted, and in some cases have been more brazen than
ever in their instrumental evocation of peculiarly Roman idioms of cultural intimacy. Even those who want radical change continue to operate in
a localist idiom; many of the youngest of the left-wing party activists, for
example, continue to emphasize their Romanesco speech and their embed-
dedness in local social networks—these are, after all, the immediate basis
of their ability to appeal effectively to voters. The debate is increasingly less
between the civil and the civic than between civic engagement and civic
acquiescence—a very different battle, and one that reproduces on a local
scale ongoing tensions between the desire for active participatory rights in
determining the course of local events and a global neoliberalism for which
such local self-assertion is threatening and inconvenient.

Italian neoliberalism, however, also invokes local idioms; this is the
underlying logic of gentrification in Rome and elsewhere.[15] In the same way,
the marketing of the national picturesque takes such localisms as *romanità*

and purveys them as tourist goods, new forms of folksy elegance, and the political posturing that one of the Monti evictees repeatedly condemned as *radical-chic* (parlor pinkery). Both left- and right-wing political alignments were caught between the desire to please local voters by involving them and supporting their causes, and, on the other hand, the powerful forces that favored the restructuring of social life according to the logic of the international market. That market in fact amplified a phenomenon that was already strongly present in Italian cultural and political life: the abiding tension between local pride and awareness that the very essence of *civiltà* entails a capacity to operate outside purely local interests and borders.

In Palumbo's analysis of Sicilian localism there is an important clue to the relationship between the civic and the civil in Italy more generally. It is clear that what he calls "civic identity," the collective pride that the denizens of a proud town and its environs take in their traditions of governance, feeds on strong sentiments of local attachment, which it nurtures by emphasizing "our" ways of conducting political business. Against official accusations that Sicilians had concocted a plot that somehow typified their insubordinate ways, for example, Sicilian leaders retorted that the plot was instead a "Roman concoction" (*pasticcio romano*), thereby recasting the state's rationalist and universalist logic to the level of just one among many local styles of (poor) governance.[16] This is a very different view of the civic than that promoted by the state or, for that matter, by some anthropologists and other social scientists.[17]

Because civility is as much about the mastery of form as it is about political engagement, and indeed privileges form over participation, it furnishes the idiom with which dissenters can be threatened into submission without a single violent blow. The current desire of intellectuals and educated community leaders to permit the expression of anger and conflict is thus in part an attempt to recapture the eccentric energies of those who have found themselves marginalized by a dire combination of the old civility and the state's unimaginative application of civic normativity. It is also a way of resisting the adaptive posture of noninvolvement that, if we are to believe the stereotypical history Romans repeat about themselves, kept potential dissenters in check during the days of the pontifical state, and that today serves the interests of neoliberal speculators and shadowy underworld operators.

There have been brave attempts to recapture the ideals of civilized behavior for the people of the district, as when the Monti Social Network information sheet condemned speculators' depredations against the older and poorer residents "in a city that wants to define itself as civil" (*in una città che vuole definirsi civile*). This move entailed turning the tables on those who claimed to have a definitive claim on the cultural forms of civility by suggesting that those who mistreated the less fortunate were in fact decidedly less civil than their victims; in the center of Rome, few residents are so lacking in the rudiments of good manners in practice that such a tactic would not carry some weight. But here the celebrated uncouthness of the Roman self-stereotypes works against the residents' interests; the speculators respond with haughty claims that by gentrifying the old buildings they are upgrading the neighborhood socially—that, they say, is their contribution to the improvement in standards of living.[18] With their massive injections of money, moreover, they are able to drive thick wedges among the remaining residents, dividing those who are simply holding out for the best deals from those who are resisting on principle or because they feel that no monetary compensation for the loss of their familiar spaces can suffice.

Condominial Civilities

As Monti gentrifies, its inhabitants increasingly reject older ways of managing their relations with each other and with the authorities. To find the roots of such changes, it is easier to explore small-scale local meetings and interactions than the grand political theatrics in which a rhetoric of "common good" tends to outweigh practical concerns.[19] A condominial meeting that I attended, a surprisingly dramatic affair, provides an exceptionally rich illustration.

The municipal administration has long been concerned about the often acrimonious conduct of condominial meetings. Members wrangle over the color of a newly restored facade or whether they should maintain scaffolding that is taxed for the use of public space; the expected answer to inquiries about the conduct of a meeting is "Terrible! (*Pessimo!*)" So, at a late stage in my fieldwork, the administration introduced the *festa dei vicini*, the feast of neighbors.[20] Such bureaucratic efforts met with predictable irony and cynicism; few Romans were inclined to go along with its cheerful rhetoric.[21] The administration touted its new invention as a counter to modern individualism. But a lively social life had long existed in central Rome; that it was now collapsing owed much, ironically, to the municipality's own helplessness and even collusion in the face of invasive speculation. There thus seemed to be something distinctly disingenuous in this celebration of an invented neighborliness.

The city authorities' categorical mistake was to confuse neighborliness with affability. In fact, such affability as they are able to promote may signal the collapse, rather than the resurgence, of older forms of social engagement. It is initiatives like those of the Monti Social Network that, by recognizing conflict as a necessary part of social engagement, stand a better chance of regenerating social interaction, given the disaggregation of the old population and its replacement by people sharing little more than some generic ideas about taste and style. The changes now sweeping Rome are reproduced on a small scale within each palazzo, with the older inhabitants moving away and the newly wealthy (and usually recently arrived) residents demanding new services, new standards of maintenance, and new ways of dealing with the bureaucracy and with each other.

Condominial meetings are thus an ideal context in which to observe such changes. These meetings are often true battles, with dramatic shouting, accusations and counteraccusations, all both promoting and intensifying strong intergenerational and interclass tensions. At the one such meeting that I was allowed to attend and film, I observed a microcosm of the larger conflicts over civic and civil values and the complex relationships among them. Conflict between older and younger partners had been brewing for several years. Of the older group, one elderly man—a fairly prosperous merchant of famously irascible disposition and salty language—was an especially vocal member.

Like others in this group, he valued social reciprocities over procedural niceties, although he was willing to give the latter a try if he thought they could be deployed to useful effect. His barber was evicted from another palazzo without warning, the barber's and his wife's belongings unceremoniously dumped in the streets, and they were at their wits' end as they had nowhere else to go. The merchant suggested that they could be given a small living space in the condominium at no rent if the wife would be willing to clean the common floors and stairways. They accepted the idea with alacrity, but the merchant warned them that the condominial partners would first have to agree; he knew that he faced a lonely fight to achieve this, but relished his role as a moral standard-bearer even when, as now, he had been deserted by most of those who more usually were on his side. In its extreme polarization, one man holding out against fourteen partners, the debate illustrates both the tenacity and the increasing isolation of those aging Monticiani who still uphold the old civilities and are prepared to defend them with, so to speak, marked incivility.

That earlier meeting, which I did not attend, was a stormy one that went on until 4 a.m.—unusual even in this city of compulsive debaters. The majority—all the partners except for the merchant—were against the proposal, on the grounds that they had just succeeded in getting rid of another cleaning woman who had stayed in the building rent-free and did not want to repeat the experience. But the merchant kept haranguing them: "Here's the point, here's the way I blackmailed them!" (*Ecch'er punto, er ricatto je l'ho fatto io!*) Or, as he put it, if they did not give in he was "prepared to kill them" and "strangle them one by one"—by which he meant that he had enough information about all of them to create serious trouble. One was raising pedigree dogs in the building without a license: "You'll be out of here!" Another, a fortune-teller whom he accused of fraud—"'You'll win at the lottery'—it's not true! 'You'll find a husband'—it's not true! You'll be out of here!"—because she had not paid any taxes on these dubious earnings. Another, who owned a vineyard in Frascati, brought his product to store in the building: "Are you authorized? You're out of here . . . don't bring the wine here!" After this long, rancorous, menacing harangue, the other occupants realized that they had little choice but to give in; the merchant was quite capable of carrying out his threat to expose them all.

A condition for their reluctant capitulation was that the merchant and a woman who had ended up agreeing with him would jointly serve as guarantors for the barber's wife's agreement to keep her side of the bargain. The merchant acknowledged that he had taken a significant risk, since he would have had to pay half the rent for any period in which the cleaning was not done satisfactorily; but he felt that he could have "faith" (*fiducia*) in her honesty. In the end, he was supported by the administrator, whose job was in any case not to argue with the partners but to carry out their wishes. This presumably did not endear the administrator to the younger partners in particular; they were already plotting to get rid of him. They argued that he too easily lent his services to such underhand arrangements; in this particular instance, procedure had been observed, but it had been hijacked, or so they felt, by one individual using unethical means and pursuing personal goals. (They may also have been aware that the barber's wife, fulsome with gratitude, now undertook to wash the old man's clothes on a regular basis and was forever bringing him plates of home-cooked pasta). The complaints against the administrator included procedural violations, irregular or illegal contracting of repair work, and a general attitude that was incompatible with the rule of modern law. And so the meeting that I attended was called.

This later meeting was held one wintry evening in the unheated offices of an organization run by one of the members. Many were wearing heavy coats, into which they hunched against the chilly current that crept into the room. Presiding was the administrator himself—a man who, like his protagonist, was more inclined to fix problems through personal contacts and gentle persuasion than by following the letter of the law. He had been able to evade all sorts of official inspections and requirements, and, in the process, had saved the residents a fair amount of money. He had expected to be left alone to do things this way, as he had for as long as the poorer residents and those with a more clientelistic view of how business should be conducted were in the majority.

His strongest supporter, the merchant, could call on several allies. While they had presumably been reluctant to support his championing of the barber's wife, seeing in it only an additional expense, the administrator's usual mode of operation had worked to their financial advantage. Their ironworker, plumber, and carpenter were all the administrator's friends; he would sometimes send his son to inspect the work, or do so himself, but he rarely saw any need to involve any of the partners in these evaluations: "There's tacit consensus. No one speaks, no one goes to law, no one makes a complaint, and all are just fine," as the merchant remarked.

In the eyes of the younger faction, by contrast, the administrator put the entire condominium at risk of both committing fraud and being prosecuted. Worst of all, it had now been four years since he had called a meeting, despite a legal requirement that this be an annual event. Suddenly, he found himself presiding over a meeting, one possible outcome of which was an exemplary exercise in civic procedure ending with his own dismissal and replacement. What was more, the rebels had their own candidate (as the old administrator's supporters had guessed), ready and in attendance at the meeting.

The younger residents were not simply being officious; they were defending a new moral order, although their methods were not without echoes of older modalities. Their candidate was well aware of what was at stake, commenting that the two groups "live in two worlds that are also culturally different." The dramatic years of *Mani pulite* (Clean Hands) in the 1990s had ushered in a new era of moral as well as political accountability, and this included a strong sense of civic duty.[22] The new civic sensibility affected all areas of engagement with state and local administrations. The younger faction in the condominium was led by a man in the medical profession, which perhaps also reinforced its commitment to a formal code of ethics and transparency. The older residents counted instead on ideals of civility for the common good among coevals of widely differing levels of education and social status. Among them, the organization head was a former ironworker who had gradually built up a career as a behind-the-scenes local political operator with ties to one of the most tainted of the older parties. One of his opponents described him in these terms: "a bit of a sweet-talker, a bit . . . [someone] who works underneath [i.e., in a concealed fashion], look, he tends to insinuate himself into those spaces where there's something to be gained, that's what I believe." The merchant, with whom the political operator quarreled all the time but with whom he nevertheless had close and affectionate ties, told stories of crooked doings in the markets that were a source of unending entertainment and instruction for me. He had lived in the building since the 1930s and was the longest-established resident; he was strongly backed by a woman whose mother-in-law had owned the apartment where he now lived and who thus also, with her husband, had a long-standing stake in the building. One of their critics remarked, "They continued to operate the building in their own way, making modifications and readjustments, even structural ones, with the administrator's support; the administrator always gave them his support."

The merchant thought the old administrator suited his style just fine: "He's a saint, Michael, and hey, off we go!" (*È un santo, Miché, e nnamo, ó!*) That kind of sanctity was hardly of the state's formal civic order, perhaps still less of the church's, and the opposition disagreed with this judgment; to make matters worse, the merchant and his friends had miscalculated the number of people who supported their desire to keep on doing business as usual.

It would be wrong to suppose that the older group was without respect for procedure; they simply did not view it in abstractly moral terms. Rather, they openly treated legal correctness as a strategic weapon (as the merchant had already demonstrated to devastating effect when he blackmailed the other partners over the deal with the barber's wife); and they also realized that the younger members were invoking civic procedure as a strategy for possibly quite self-interested (if unspecified) purposes of their own. The fact that the administrator was willing, albeit with a very worried expression during most of the proceedings, to preside over what was potentially a humiliation for him is itself an indication of some shared sense of civic responsibility. He was flanked by two of his supporters, the ironworker-turned-political operator and a woman who served as the condominium's record keeper. At various points in the argument, critics also came up to the front of the room to make their arguments more dramatically. The younger group also did not hesitate to engage in shouting and ironic backchat, and one of the loudest voices of all came from a young man who represented himself as defending clarity and simplicity—making sure, as became evident, that the central question of the administrator's future did not evade inspection as other residents became absorbed in their concerns over specific details of what had or had not been done to keep the building in a decent state of repair.

Much of the meeting was taken up with counting votes. This was not as simple as it might sound. The administrator initially tried to ram through a decision in his favor by claiming that the vote for a new administrator had failed since the number of shares (based on the size of the partners' respective apartments) gained by his rival's supporters was slightly lower. But his principal foe claimed to have won the majority vote required to name a new administrator under the condominium rules; "the partners," he observed with gentle irony, "are fifteen in number; eight are against [this decision]"; according to his reading of the procedural rules, the eight out of the fifteen members present, representing at least 50 percent of the shares, constituted a legal majority. There was a brief argument about the exact definition of a majority, but it soon fizzled as it became clear that the younger faction had made sure of their grounds in advance. Their leader then seized the opportunity: "The same people who voted 'no' to Giuliani [the old administrator] are disposed to vote 'yes' for another person," he demanded, and went on to say that, in that case, they could nominate a new administrator because—he hammered his point home—they constituted a majority. He then turned to his candidate for administrator, who—perhaps not surprisingly, but also with evident respect for the rules—concurred in his reasoning. To cap his triumph, he asked, "Is there anyone who would argue the contrary?" One woman protested, "The administrator," but was silenced by mention of the code of procedure, which required the administrator to accept the majority view.

Much more seriously for future relations within the condominium, there was a tremendous row about a proxy vote. The merchant had—obviously not without self-interest—agreed to serve as proxy for a foreign woman resident who had claimed she was unable to attend the meeting, and, he said afterward, had she really stayed away, the old administrator would have had over half the votes and could not therefore have been censured. In the end, however, apparently under pressure from the younger group—"They brainwashed her!" stormed the merchant—she did come to the meeting, and voted with this group ("She changed her face!" he raged). There was a furious exchange; the leader of her faction demanded to see the proxy document after the merchant had protested that she could hardly write a proxy and then expect to show up and vote.

In response to this act of distrust, which the merchant thought the younger man had no legal right to insist on carrying out, the merchant—who later threatened that "at the next meeting he would give him a good kick in the head"—told him that the proxy document was for the woman herself to show; she initially denied that she had given anyone a proxy, but the old administrator finally produced his copy of the document and she retracted her denial, especially after the merchant said he would sue her if she failed to do so and that he would demand that she submit to a handwriting test to prove that she had signed the proxy. There was a tense moment when the merchant challenged her to claim openly that the signature on the proxy was forged; while someone shrieked—from despair or outrage was not clear—the surprisingly imperturbable administrator simply handed the proxy to this woman and allowed to her retract her signature. The grumpy old merchant could be heard muttering, "Idiot!" (*deficiente!*) just loudly enough to ensure being heard. (Later, in private, he again threatened to take action against the various illegalities of members of the younger faction, thereby exposing their civic stance as disingenuous. He also admitted that he had signed another proxy, for another of the old administrator's allies; the latter had in fact not wanted to come and had authorized the merchant to sign his proxy for him, but became so concerned that the old administrator was about to be fired that he, too, decided to show up.)

Interestingly, although the critics rehearsed a whole series of complaints, it was the administrator who, most of the time, held the meeting to procedural rules; and it was he who enabled the one woman to retract her proxy and vote against him. Not that he had much choice; but he may have hoped to convince the younger group of his devotion to principle as well as to good manners; and he probably also sought to show that at least some of his compromises with legality were harmless and perhaps even beneficial.

In consequence of his adherence to procedure, however, he also found himself presiding over his own defeat. The complex public precision of counting shares in proportion to the square footage owned by each voting partner had the result that the old administrator had to accept the new man—who, as a further complication, was a resident, an active but discreet participant in the discussion, and also on good terms with the old merchant on account of their daughters' friendship—as his partner. In fact, however, he then took himself off, rather miserably, with the result, said the merchant, that various repair jobs that he simply arranged on the side were no longer being done. The merchant no longer greets the woman whose proxy vote he was supposed to cast, and is furious with the leader of the other group for having doubted his word.

During the meeting, one of the older men spoke up to say that for those who voted against the old administrator, "there must have been a reason." What, he wanted to know, if one were simply to say directly to the administrator (whom he indicated with some rather wild gesticulation), "You

are a thief!"—and so to avoid all the elaborate circumlocutions? To this
the administrator's critics could hardly object, but they did not like the
corollary—that they should enumerate the administrator's alleged derelictions before they went any further in the discussion. They feared losing the
force of their argument in a welter of detail.

The political operator intervened with a measured tone and a solemn
expression, every inch the elder statesman assuring his audience of his im-
partiality (which fooled no one) and admitting with deceptive transparency
that the reason for the current situation was indeed that there had not been a
meeting for a long time: "The reasons, I think, were dealt with, and a certain
rancor was created." He also pointed out that one could change one's mind;
by raising the hypothetical possibility of his abandoning his friend the old
administrator, he evoked an image of democratic argument and decision-
making that he certainly had no intention of following in practice. The
leader of the younger bloc did not in any case seem to fall for this diversionary tactic. The other older man, who had a rather obviously working-class
manner and spoke in Romanesco-inflected Italian, defended his desire for
explanation, but his plea—"Excuse me, be patient"—got short shrift.

A shouting match ensued. Both this man and the young rebel spoke with
a taut mixture of placatory smiles and evident anger, the younger man in a
light and even tenor that dominated the room, the older in a deep bass growl.
The younger man persisted: "At last we're all here, we can decide well. We
were always few in number, there was little participation [by the members],
you never came, you never came to the meeting—well, you didn't want to;
so now we're all, we're all decided that this is what we have to do." In fact,
the elder man was the one for whom the merchant had signed the proxy;
he was notoriously uninterested in coming to meetings and perfectly happy
to let the administrator take care of things in his own way—as the young
rebel well knew. In the democratic calculus of political advantage, failure
to take part in meetings, like the failure to place bids in public bidding for
spaces in the local market, is tantamount to surrendering to new economic
and political modalities.

The administrator, meanwhile, realizing that his best tactic would be
to entrap the entire discussion in arguments over matters of detail, politely
demanded to know what "these so-serious derelictions" had been. When
another of the other younger members answered this appeal for specific
information by starting to complain of the administrator's failure to respond
to any of his attempts to make contact, a by now more obviously agitated
administrator began to rebut him on details. The leader of the younger bloc,
alarmed that the argument would be completely derailed and thus fall prey

to the administrator's superficially civic-minded gesture of inviting specific criticisms, hastily headed his ally off and again seized what for him was the main thread of the debate.

He also presumably realized that the older faction's strongest suit was their conviction that, as the merchant put it, there had been no legal consequences of the failure to convene meetings, and that there had been no serious problems in the building—so what was all the fuss about? As the merchant subsequently reconstructed the previous exchange between the other older man and the leader of the younger faction, ornamenting his account with some editorial emphases of his own: "'Tell me what happened.' 'No! You didn't come [to meetings] for four years!' 'But what the hell's that got to do with you? But what's changed? Nothing's changed! There's been no, there's been no work [done on the building], nothing!'" It was precisely this kind of precise accounting, ironically, that the accountability-minded younger leader feared; clear evidence that in fact nothing consequential had changed might well have persuaded any waverers to forget about the administrator's derelictions—to let it go, in the familiar Roman way.

So at this point the young faction leader produced what can only be described as a passionately reasoned speech, oscillating adroitly between cordial civility and procedural punctilio. The emphatic repetitions perhaps appealed to emotion rather than reason, but the argument was an attempt to represent his own position as entirely a question of reason, and reason alone; it was also a strategic move, in that he understood that the administrator, given the chance to detour away from the most obvious complaint, could easily explain away some of his supposed derelictions and even turn the tables on his interlocutors—it was not as though they had always followed procedure either.

First, with a smiling expression of embarrassed sympathy on his face and after a jocular exchange with one of the others about my filming, the young man glanced down at the ally who had protested the administrator's lack of responsiveness and who was seated right in front of him; with a gentle hand resting briefly on this man's collar, he then turned back to the table where the embattled administrator sat with an increasingly defensive posture, and launched into his new peroration, emphasizing his points in a vibrant but controlled declamatory style, with downward, emphatic gestures of the hand that held his papers:

The problem is that for year after year the administrator never convened a regular meeting. This is the fundamental problem. Because then all the others are marginal matters and to discuss them seems to me to be a waste of time because it then leads to quarreling and answers about all sorts of things. [*At this point one of the older men began to protest again, but the speaker's voice rose just enough to prevail.*] Excuse me! No! Look, you did ask me what the problem was. The problem is fundamental. Always this matter, without which we wouldn't be here to discuss it, and it's this, that is: our administrator from 1991 to today has, actually for four consecutive years, not called an ordinary meeting [of the condominium]. The estimates for three consecutive years were not presented [to us]. So for years and years the estimates and builders' accounts were not presented. This is the problem! This alone! We all know it! That is, those who are in agreement [do], because there are some who are less aware of a problem [they regard as being] less disturbing; and there are those who instead would like to discuss the rules every year, to discuss the accounts every year, and nominate the administrator every year, that is, to follow the procedures laid out in the code. That's what we're talking about, not other, marginal questions that were presented a moment ago. That's what we're talking about! This problem has been presented several times to the administrator, and the administrator has never carried out his duty to convene a regular meeting. That's the whole issue! That's all it's about. About this, let's say!

The speaker's rhetorical techniques include not only repetition but also a sly hint that the administrator had a considerable self-interest in not calling regular meetings, given that one of the requirements would have been that his tenure of office would also be up for annual renewal. Note that on this point, and virtually on this point alone, the speaker avoided repeating himself. It would have seemed mean-spirited to dwell too obviously on such ad hominem considerations; but, by slipping the specific charge into his torrent of words almost as though it had been an afterthought, he reminded his hearers that this was actually a key aspect of the administrator's tactics, and he managed to do this without appearing uncivil.

His emphasis on procedure is not quite as transparent as it may have seemed. He restrained one of his own supporters from speaking out on a specific complaint, not only because the approved rhetorical style required conveying an almost obsequious respect for the rights of the other side (a tactic that the administrator and the office manager had mastered with great skill), but also, almost certainly, because he knew that the administrator would take advantage of a discussion of detail—which might in turn have reminded some of the practical advantages of the old ways, as perhaps the elderly merchant wanted to emphasize by ironically remarking to the administrator, "They haven't understood a thing, my dear Giuliani!"

The administrator's side did not surrender easily. The political operator swung into action again, from his position in the front of the room and beside the administrator's high-backed chair behind an imposing old desk: "Let's say that there's been a tacit agreement after so many years," by which apparently he meant a capacity to look the other way while the administrator skirted the edge of the law. He concluded his exposition by proposing that they retain the present administrator with the commitment (*impegno*) that he henceforth conduct annual meetings. A young woman at the back of the room erupted: "It's not that it's a commitment that he should make; it's a legal requirement!" (*Non è ch'è un impegno che deve prendere, è un obbligo di legge!*) The political operator and the new candidate began to talking about respect for the legal norms; but then the former reiterated the proposal to renominate the old administrator. To this, the young medical professional responded with a counter-proposal: to postpone the decision until the next meeting. Out of this, after much further discussion, was born the eventual agreement that the old administrator should collaborate with the new nominee in the intervening months.

The entire incident illustrates the mixture of civic and civil values that complicate the micropolitics of Monti life. On the one hand, the observation of procedure is directly linked to judgments about the extent to which the old administrator adhered to the requirements of law. On the other, the mixture of threats, cajoling, and pressure tactics by both sides shows that neither group had a monopoly of procedural purity. The civility that allowed the old administrator to remain in office, albeit jointly, seems to have been a face-saving device; the younger group, having essentially won its battle, had no interest in exacerbating an already disruptive tension, although the cordial relationship between the merchant and the new administrator would gradually restore a sense of cordiality and neighborly symbiosis.

That outcome would represent a striking victory for the Roman taste for social accommodation and belie the city administration's claim—which it made in defense of its much-touted "feast of neighbors"—that some sort of official intervention was increasingly necessary in order to bring peace to condominiums throughout Rome. The oldest resident was already on relatively amiable terms, albeit heavily larded with the sarcastic Roman speech, with the new administrator. The latter, himself a resident, readily admitted, "The rebellion started to form, in effect, after I came to the building, I'm the last of them to arrive. Because there were no accounts." The fact that the old administrator had long failed to convene annual meetings not only provoked the nascent rebellion but played into its leaders' hands, because they were entitled, under the terms of the code, to convene a meeting without the administrator if a third of the residents so wished. That quorum was easily reached as discontent came to a head. The old administrator's supporters suddenly became advocates of transparency: "They created secret societies, they met, they discussed, they deliberated, they spoke, they ratified—that Giuliani had to go—there, that's the truth."

Most strongly apparent in this entire confrontation is the apparent victory of a civic-minded group over the easygoing civility of the past; but it is a victory that still owes much to the civility that still prevailed among most of the main actors, and that entailed a measure of compromise in the final resolution of not actually dismissing the old administrator for the moment. A rhetoric of civic correctness prevailed overall; the rough language (much of it dialect-inflected) of the older group, its uncouth threats, and poor clothing placed it at a tactical disadvantage, especially as all knew perfectly well that its members were mostly interested in maintaining a convenient but illegal modality. Its cultural capital, which lay in a nostalgic appeal to an image of old Rome, could not stem the tide of change.

The younger group was equally strategic, and more successfully so. Its leader's demand that the proxy document be produced, a seemingly uncivil gesture among old neighbors, was—as both he and the old merchant knew— a way of making sure of a vote that had previously been firmly promised in support of the proposed firing. The younger group thus acted, as the traditionalists understood all too well, to impose their own will through the adroit manipulation of voting rules.

Perhaps, from their point of view, the tactical means justified the ends of civic order. They particularly objected to the fact that participation in decision-making had become extremely one-sided. "But what we are complaining about above all with the administrator was the fact that, that he has misled us, that he has managed all . . . the whole condominium in agreement with two or three [of the members alone]." The rhetoric is about democratic management, the concern it frames one of self-respect and authority.

The issue of the barber and his wife, now jointly responsible for keeping the building clean, was also still very much alive, since some of the younger members thought that they should pay some of the condominium costs as a matter of principle. Again, this view was driven less by economic considerations than by the perception that the younger faction had ignominiously lost out to the machinations of the merchant and his ally, the old administrator, and that perhaps it was now time to turn the tables on the two of them in this regard as well.[23]

The condominial meeting as a whole illustrates the dangers inherent in trying to create too strong a sense of categorical contrast between older and newer moralities. It makes no sense to treat some segments of the population as traditional, southern in their values and attitudes, focused on issues of respect and self-regard, and uninterested in civic order, in contrast to modernists with the opposite set of values. The contrast is a rhetorical one, between stereotypes that were both very markedly in play on both sides of the dispute. It is certainly true that the two factions sought contrasted kinds of advantage: the older a range of short-term benefits with an accompanying long-term assurance of sociability, the younger conformity with the law and with it more effective control over the way their money was spent. But these stances were stylized and exaggerated; in their proxy rhetorics of civic procedure and civil sociability, they proved not to be mutually exclusive at all. Instead, both factions drew on both models, although the traditionalists, clearly on the defensive, were forced to play the procedural game, while the younger group was not so much uncivil as insistent on maintaining a formal politeness that did little to warm the chilly room. In the microcosm of the condominial meeting, then, the impossibility of separating formal rules from the social environment of their authors and practitioners reproduces with focused intensity what we have already noted for the national parliament and for the forces of law and order.[24]

What mutual warmth remained among the membership of the condominium after this meeting came, to a significant degree, from the evident mutual respect that subsisted between the new administrator and one of the old administrator's most passionate defenders, the elderly merchant. Each spoke to me of the other with considerable affection and respect, and their exchanges even at the most passionate points of the meeting were somewhat sorrowful but never overtly angry. The day after the meeting the two of them encountered each other on the street and took careful steps to defuse the situation because, as the new administrator graphically remarked, "we can't walk about with guns on our shoulders." Initially the old man pretended not to see the new administrator, but the latter called to him and soon they began to chat.

The new administrator also immediately spoke with his defeated colleague, with whom, at least for a transitional period, he would need to work in some degree of amity. Meanwhile, he also had a couple of names up his sleeve as replacements for the old administrator. "I could do it myself," he remarked, "but I don't like it—I understand that this reason for the [bad] relations lingers from then on"—and, for the same reason, he was sure that others would not accept the option of letting the old administrator stay on if he showed himself to have adapted to the new rules. It was not that he personally opposed that option, he was careful to note; but again he emphasized the crucial importance of maintaining good relationships among the residents of the condominium.

In addition to the Roman concern with living together (*convivere*), moreover, the new administrator also evoked another factor that encouraged reconciliation, the nostalgia that Monticiani claim for a vanished past when he spoke about the merchant: "Underneath it all he's a good person. He's a good person [but one] who complains.... Let's say he has the style of old Rome, the Rome of the first years of the twentieth century." And, he hinted, it was this respect for the old ways that made accommodation possible: "We respect him for what he is, even if sometimes he behaves in a rather self-interested fashion, sometimes even a bit rudely." It is perhaps worth noting, too, that these sage remarks were accompanied by an openly stated awareness, marked by a familiar (if amiably enunciated) disclaimer, that the old man was Jewish, but (*però*).... The friendship and nostalgia were no less real, or mutual, for being qualified in such terms; the Jewish community's status in Rome is beset by this curious blend of alienation and centrality, a paradoxical mixture that affects all its members individually as well as collectively.

Indeed, the new administrator's observation encapsulates a virtual history of what has enabled Romans to manage to live for so many centuries under the punitive hand of the papacy, an outlook that now instead renders them more vulnerable to the modalities of a global, civic modernity. Even the delicate hint that perhaps the merchant's Jewish culture introduced a degree of tension was also, in the Roman context, suggestive of a past lived and shared. The rudeness that in other situations might have occasioned only dislike, hostility, and open prejudice here instead served as a reminder that what was being dismantled still belonged to the old traditional ways and thus deserved to be heard. That others might dismiss the merchant as too "folkloric" and thus as an unfit representative of local culture (to which it is worth noting that the speaker in question was a relative newcomer) only serves to show how, under circumstances requiring some degree of neighborliness, these diamond-in-the-rough qualities could instead be accounted a cultural gem. As happens more generally with the exaltation of such rude traditionalism, however, the end result is that its power to affect the course of events is marginalized and neutralized. Under the new dispensation, it is framed as "tradition"—as something ornamental, not intrinsic, to the dominant order of things.

In this microcosm of what is happening in the wider society, the spreading infusion of civic rhetoric and governance into the condominial meeting and the events surrounding it builds on the continuing presumption of civil relations among neighbors. The vociferous eruptions of the two older working-class men notwithstanding, the meeting was mostly conducted with an air of mutual respect laced with humorous asides and the occasional expression of true rancor. Members usually addressed each other with the formal *lei* and by surnames preceded by appropriate titles. Here, too, we see local sociality colored by national idioms of respect, but these are not in themselves indicative of a particular devotion to civic values. Nonetheless, overall the picture that emerges is that of a group of close neighbors who are skilled at managing the conflicts that divide them, with one side emphasizing this common social ground and the importance of saving money, while the other portrays itself as the champion of legality and of the longer-term maintenance of the condominium—moving, in effect, toward the more bureaucratic perspective, in which permanence and conformity trump provisionality, contingency, and social adaptability.

Lessons in Civic Civility

The story of the condominial meeting shows how sophisticated younger actors, some of them new to the district, engage with residents of long standing as well as with the nostalgic authority of the Roman self-stereotype. Because all social action emerges from a mixture of consensus and conflict, it is vital to understand the new civic pride in the context of preexisting structures of sentiment, loyalty, and identity, and especially of the deep tradition of civility and courtesy that constrains and channels the emergence of civic engagement. The civic does not entirely displace the civil; on the contrary, it must draw on it in order to be effective, and this means that norms of civility channel and constrain the uses of civic procedure as well.

Manners are vitally important; in business, they can make at least as much difference to a client's loyalty as price. Knowing how to talk to customers is an art in which politeness must balance jocular familiarity and even teasing, and in which informality can sometimes seem as studied as formal courtesy. Rudeness, conversely, can sometimes serve as a form of self-defense within a larger idiom of intimate civility. An elderly itinerant vendor who made a point of dressing in disreputable old clothes, his unshaven chin and aggressive speech emphasizing his refusal to play polite games, was charged double the price of a coffee in a bar belonging to a woman with whom he enjoyed a cordial friendship (and who would have charged him a mere 1,000 *lire* instead of the 3,000 the waitress was demanding). He was convinced that the staff wanted to discourage him from returning because of his scruffy appearance. The waitress did not answer his query about the price in words, but simply held up three fingers in a peremptory and disrespectful gesture; she also insisted that he pay right away. He could have called the proprietress over, but she was busy with customers at the tobacco counter at that moment. So when the waitress squeaked for help from the male waiters, he simply raised his voice even louder: "I want to see the price, [damn] your dead ancestors!" (*Vojo vede' 'r prezzo, li mortacci tua!*)

Behind the shifting balance between rough humor and formal courtesy lies a sense of movement, away from the clientelistic rhetoric of local friendship and familiarity and toward a modernist style of disinterested correctness and precision mediated by explicit and supposedly universal rules of civic action. Skilled actors can invoke civil charm and chilly correctness as alternating means to self-interested goals once more easily attained through the elaborately courteous application of guile alone. The transition is thus not the unilinear path from the courtly to the civic that theories from social evolutionism to the more self-congratulatory histories of European culture and the more recent trumpetings of unabashedly protestant forms of "civil society" might lead us to expect.[25]

The tension between civic principles and the demands of civility is, then, a complex engagement between differing forms of social and political management. Less kindly critics complain that Romans are not so much accommodating as hypocritical. Their supple response to power gives Romans' everyday interactions a curiously complaisant quality. Romans, as a jeweler who had grown up abroad told me, have an endearing ability to stand aside when someone of greater economic or social status tries to dominate a conversation. I had gone with the jeweler in the hope of discreetly entering the inner circle of a rotating credit association that met regularly in a bar in the upper reaches of the district. There we encountered a wealthy resident who was clearly not a regular at the very working-class bar and who, realizing that we were not laborers either, proceeded to monopolize the conversation we were trying to start up with some of the artisans, boasting of how Rome was the most beautiful city of all the many he knew around the world and claiming that there were no artisans left anywhere. The other patrons simply sat quietly, ignoring this embarrassing tirade. Afterward the jeweler apologized to me for having been unable to get us out of the situation, but expressed appreciation for the others' discreet retreat, which he saw as a distinctively Roman maneuver—and which would not, he said, have any effect on any subsequent attempt on our part to speak with them.

The self-stereotype of the accommodating but sometimes manipulative Roman has certain consequences for the struggle to establish more "rational" forms of civic life. Arguing that it is hard to get people to act in concert against crime and corruption, for example, reproduces, in the form of an abiding cultural determinism, the endemic resignation (*rassegnazione*) to which such passivity is conventionally attributed. The hatred often expressed toward these forces, moreover, does not exclude the principles of *civiltà*—principles that themselves bear witness to deeply entrenched hierarchies of authority and value—that we also encounter in small villages throughout the country. Indeed, harsh and uncouth speech are denounced as "not *civile*" in the sense of being incompatible with the successful conduct of civic affairs; the failure of some visitors or residents to close the front door of our palazzo properly—a serious security concern—was also so described by the landlord, albeit with a resigned expression that implied there was nothing to be done about the decline of interpersonal morality.

The downside of civility, its exclusionary side, is often clear from the use of language. As Inoue has noted for Japan, civil society merely masks the contradictions in the idea that difference and equality can coincide;[26] it creates textual spaces that "allow the other to speak," but only under strict control. In Italy courtly manners have long been associated with affectations of disdain and detachment. Such attitudes, once associated with ideals of austere simplicity and modesty, transmute under conditions of modern capitalism into the overbearing and ostentatious violence of the *nouveaux riches* who are displacing artisans and aristocrats alike. In Monti, the triumph of this essentially neoliberal ethos has especially painful implications and effects. Unlike the former Soviet Bloc, where economic restructuring often used new forms of civility to disguise the violence that in reality the restructuring had exacerbated,[27] Italy has long been home to a civility always potentially violent in both intent and effect. In both, however, new money amplifies the collusion of violence and courtesy to unprecedented levels, and this alliance conflicts directly with the civic values with which it shares a common language of moral outrage.

Spatial and Stylistic Violence

Competing reconfigurations of lived space lie at the heart of social change in Monti and throughout the historic center of Rome. An emergent sense of civic responsibility is usually not robust enough to shield against either eviction from domestic places or exclusion from public ones; it is also, arguably, undercut by hopes of increasing profit from the new arrivals on the part of those local merchants whose businesses have managed to survive the initial flurry of change. During the Jubilee year, some shops were protected from eviction by special edict. But the predominant motivating force is that of rapid reconfiguration and comes largely from outside the district. Regardless of their relationship with the locality, entrepreneurs who have little interest in the neighborhood in any socially meaningful sense, but who have plentiful money and political influence, can shape the new spatial configurations more or less with impunity, refashioning what were once artisans' shops and homes into brash tourist restaurants, bars, and pubs, private *pied-à-terre* apartments for movers and shakers, and bed-and-breakfast hideaways aimed at a supposedly discerning type of tourist.[28]

One of the most contentious issues arises from the bars and restaurants that have expanded their operations onto sidewalks and public squares. Tourists are usually charmed by this phenomenon; it allows them to sip their aperitifs amidst the beauty of the Renaissance and baroque buildings in the rich sunset warmth of a Roman spring or autumn. For local residents, however, it is a much more dubious blessing. The owners of these establishments are generally determined to push their luck as far as they can. Their defiance of an increasingly specific set of legal codes is self-confirming; the more they get away with breaking the ever more-visible legal restrictions, the more they can impose their will through a combination of unctuous courtesy and the fear that it engenders. The occupation of public space and the illegal extension into it of privately owned property for new kinds of economic gain provide the spatial and temporal frameworks for much of the conflict that now plagues the entire city.[29]

This is a process that draws effectively on a civility that is far from civic. One amiable rogue, I was told, "has no civic sensibility" (*non ha il senso civico*); this charge included offenses ranging from violations of sanitary and environmental regulations to a brazen attempt to take over a segment of sidewalk, ostensibly for the beautification of his shop but in fact in order to stop others from parking in front (with no greater legality than his own preemptive move, to be sure). Yet his social manner is certainly civil—so warmly and entertainingly so, in fact, that it contributes to the constant tactical discomfiture of his many detractors, as do his useful connections with people in power.

Taking over a sidewalk or a section of a square is not merely an act of territorial expropriation; it is also a threat, promising both more of the same and dire consequences to anyone foolish enough to resist. When cit-izens' complaints produce absolutely no effect, the message becomes even clearer; the fact that the perpetrators have never been charged with a crime protects both their reputations and their activities. Once they have suc-cessfully passed the initial risk of a serious legal challenge, audacity lends durability to their defiance of the law. Nothing succeeds like impunity.

The very names of some offending structures appear to offer referential force to the subtle architectural menace. Most Monticiani are convinced that two restaurants, belonging to a man local gossip portrays as a usurer, have been deliberately given names that suggest the romantic violence of bandits and cowboys. An artisan remarked that it was as though the propri-etor were announcing outright, "I'm an underworld character and I'm not hiding it." In reality these names are allusive, not referential, and the very deniability of their implied menace lends them even more sinister force, especially in a city where such a deliberate provocation is seen as Sicil-ian rather than Roman. (The Roman underworld style is instead for a local crime boss to make quiet phone calls in the night, suggesting to others that they should stir up trouble.) There was certainly nothing reticent about the restaurateur's tactics. The signboard for one of his establishments, for ex-ample, is clearly an imitation of the lettering of a Wild West sheriff's poster, but the (English-language) name is actually quite ambiguous and the Italian translation conjures up only its more innocuous meaning. Threat? What threat? One of this man's most regular customers was adamant that the criticisms were merely envious talk, and that all the restaurants in the area bore names that suggested the tough Roman underclass—"all the names are a bit in street-punk style" (tutt'i nomi un po' da coatti).[30]

All one can say with certainty is that these names are *perceived* as threat-ening by many residents, who experienced them as a demand for craven respect demanding "self-abasement on the part of the people"—an entirely plausible interpretation for local critics, yet entirely beyond the possibility of legal proof. The owner's personal demeanor reinforces the same message; he makes a point of smoking where it is forbidden, and, if asked to desist, walks away briefly and without speaking before quickly returning with his cigarette still lit. When a foreign woman demanded a receipt for a pizza for which she had been charged double the regular price, he simply walked past her car and then slammed his hands down on the bonnet in what she interpreted as a threatening gesture. She did not dare to complain.

Public opinion actually validates this kind of daring abuse; the more people talk about it, the more entrenched it becomes. One of the few local artisans who dared to criticize the owner despondently remarked of this public response, "They talk about it, but it becomes a way of exalting his acts." Sheer effrontery is a potent weapon: the longer the establishments in question continue to flout the law against occupying public space, posing risks to local traffic and causing environmental hazards, the more effectively their continuing presence creates the impression of invincibility and reinforces a despairing lack of faith in the law to do anything about it. This sad cynicism loses nothing through the rumors that the restaurateur is actually a police informer, nor is it diminished by such unrelated events as the physical drubbing a young policeman received, allegedly for daring to expose drug deals struck in the main square. Frequent media coverage of the state's inefficiency and of the slow pace of legal action further reinforces the message, which draws on a long-potent vocabulary of menace.

The law, moreover, is as complicated and apparently self-contradictory as the social codes that it regulates. A judge recently ruled that calling someone a "nobody" was an offense because it deprived that individual of a constitutionally sanctioned right to personhood; but the use of scatological epithets is simply an act of rudeness, socially acceptable in the code of Italian masculinity and legally protected because it does not demonstrably constitute an act of intentional menace.[31] A similar logic makes it illegal to "sequester" persons—so much so, that a householder who catches burglars red-handed and locks them in until the police can arrive may well be charged with sequestration, a charge originally devised as a sanction against kidnappers.

Such ironies, which frustrate the efforts of the most honest and well-intentioned of the police, simultaneously feed the righteous ire and electoral strength of the political right wing, with its frequent calls for tougher laws and punishments. Sequestration is in fact a serious and far from uncommon offense, but its most violent manifestations—as in the case of the usurer who persuaded his "friend" the gambler to live with him until the debt was fully paid—rely on blackmail (also illegal), masked by polite assurances of deep friendship that are themselves widely understood, but never legally identifiable, as reminders of what will happen if such friendship is betrayed. Locals call this potent mixture of lawlessness and courtesy "mafia behavior" (comportamento mafioso). Its basis is civility—the extreme antithesis of civic virtue, and a terrible weapon in the hands of the ruthless.

CHAPTER EIGHT

The Fine Art of Denunciation

Why do Italian law enforcement officials seem to be perpetually demanding that citizens "denounce" each other? Language can be a source of unexpected shock effects, especially when one is trying to make sense of official practices. Sometimes the appearance of translatability, which arises from shared etymological roots, can produce hilarious effects: *traffico promiscuo*, for example, means, not "promiscuous traffic," but a certain kind of mixed-function vehicle. *Case abusive* are houses that have been erected illegally; the phenomenon as a whole—which includes such misdemeanors as the illegal posting of advertisements and campaign materials and the equally illegal occupation of public land (*occupazione del suolo pubblico*) (usually in the form of a spread of restaurant and bar tables across expanses of sidewalk and picturesque squares such as that of Monti's *piazzetta*)—is comprehensively known as *abusivismo;* it is generally viewed as a systemic problem of Italian society.

Threatening though the *denuncia* sounds to English speakers (and often is for Italian speakers), it similarly has a rather different official significance: it is any formal statement—not even necessarily a negative one—made in one's own name to the authorities. (To be sure, it is highly unlikely that recourse to the authorities would ever be treated by Romans as an entirely neutral act. It is too uncivil. That is why, for example, the young man who turned on the loan shark preferred to avoid making—or at least admitting that he had made—a formal complaint, even though he did consider the arrival of the police at the crucial moment to have been a fortunate salvation.) Even the declaration about foreign residents or guests required of all householders under the antiterrorist laws comes under this category, which legally carries implications of a citizen's duty to keep the forces of law and order informed about any matter of official concern. It is also frequently, as it happens, a necessity for the victim as well. Insurance companies and other institutions bearing any liability toward a customer—such as a bank that has issued one's checks, for example—will only pay compensation for theft or damage if the *denuncia* has first been made to the appropriate police force.

The Logic of Denunciation

The *denuncia* is also hedged about with a complex set of prohibitions and limitations, ostensibly products of a concern with fair play but practically the cause of considerable obstructionism. A former student and present colleague and her husband visited my wife and me in Rome. When they were leaving the station for Austria, a thief snatched her bag. Somewhat sluggishly, a railway employee found a policeman, who directed us to the appropriate office in the station (and also claimed that functionally it would make no difference whether the report was submitted to the police or to the *carabinieri*). When I arrived at the office and revealed that I was a British citizen, I was told that I must make the *denuncia* in English, not Italian; and when it transpired that I was not the victim, but only a mere witness, I was told that in fact I had no right to make a *denuncia* at all! Since my colleague was now on her way to Austria, she should now make a *denuncia* to the Austrian police instead. I continued to argue that as a witness I should be allowed to submit some kind of report of what I knew; and, after first reminding me that the law was inflexible, the officer relented to the extent of saying that they could indeed make a report on the basis of my testimony—but that I would not be allowed to see that document. In the end, the police suggested, the best solution was for the colleague, a Greek citizen, to make a report to the Greek embassy in Rome, where I also had a good contact and could follow up if necessary. Nothing more was ever heard of the matter. Given that the *denuncia* often seems to serve only to shelve a problem forever, the citizen of a foreign state reporting on the misadventure of a citizen of another foreign state was unlikely to get much satisfaction.

For Italians, the *denuncia* is embedded in something much more dangerous than police procedure; it always entails a real risk of retaliation. Citizens who complained about illegal installations that were causing smoke pollution would be told in nocturnal phone calls that they were in serious danger, and complaints to the police produced nothing more than sympathetic shrugs and a practically meaningless official notation. These threatening calls are untraceable, especially because the victim would first have to go to the police station and make out yet another formal *denuncia* before the police could act, at which point it was inevitably much too late to find any trace of the callers' identities.

Submitting a *denuncia* can even be fatal, as the fishmonger who denounced his loan shark discovered. When the city official for commercial affairs asserted in a public statement that any victim of usury who failed to denounce the lender was complicit in the crime, the fishmonger's widow was understandably outraged (although the general principle that failure to denounce constitutes complicity actually applies to crimes of all kinds); the city authorities expect one to speak out, she said, but then leave those courageous enough to do so completely exposed to the vengeance of the perpetrators. Yet without a *denuncia*, again as in so many other situations, the police can claim to have no basis for action.

In practice the greater complicity is not that of the silent victims. It is the virtual complicity of those who have the power to intervene but who invoke the requirement that a *denuncia* be submitted first no matter what the cost to the plaintiff. A brake on the very type of intervention it is supposed to authorize, the *denuncia* thus effectively renders the authorities complicit in the persistence of threats and other symbolic forms of violence. It also, and concomitantly, absolves the police of blame for their failure to respond quickly to the committal of a crime, since the law makes the prior complaint the express responsibility of the victim except in such extreme matters as murder. The delay caused by the requirement of a formal complaint is thus arguably as much a contributory cause to the success of petty criminals as is the dangerously self-exculpatory conviction, expressed by one senior *carabiniere*, that small crimes were all committed by immigrants, or as is the weakened vigilance brought about by the shattering of local forms of sociality and especially by the departure of artisans who used to watch the street as a matter of course. By the same token, the requirement obstructs police officers who might genuinely wish to act expeditiously. The fact that it is the citizen's responsibility to lodge such complaints, which are also required for claiming both recovered stolen goods and insurance, feeds the permissive tempo of Roman life and thereby protects the criminals and perhaps also some bureaucrats.

Even—or perhaps especially—when the authors of an illegal act cannot be identified, a *denuncia* is required for any further official action to occur. In those circumstances it is simply called "a complaint against unknown persons" (*denuncia contro ignoti*). The term *denuncia* could perhaps be translated simply as "report"—except that the initial police report of an illegal activity carries a different name (*verbale*) and one that does not necessarily require further action. Any discovery of archaeological remains requires a *denuncia*; failure to provide such a document implies that the householder is probably guilty of concealing a find that might spell delays in some project of renovation. When we arrived to take up residence in our apartment in 1999, our landlord informed us that he had to make a *denuncia* of our presence to the police to satisfy the current antiterrorism laws that required the tracking of all temporary foreign residents.

The term represents a departure from the old local order. One did not, for example, make a *denuncia* about stolen property, such as a bicycle, if it was possible instead to recover it through mediation. It is *stranieri*—literally, "foreigners," but in fact simply non-local new residents—who are responsible for a string of official complaints about illegal construction that does not obviously affect them but offends their sense of legality. "Some people," remarked a butcher who spoke of three newcomers who reported on the illegal construction work on a balcony opposite their apartment, "are turds!" (*Certa gente è stronzo!*). According to him, all the offender had done was to beautify an already existing structure by displaying flowers on it in a way that did not even obstruct his own view of the Capitol (which he would have considered justifiable grounds for legal action). The owner, a lawyer, was completely unruffled by the charges, presumably because he was confident of his own ability to get the case fixed in his favor or delayed to the point where it would simply run into the ground.

Another case of reporting to the authorities in the same stretch of street evoked much greater complaisance; the proprietors were first warned (which led to what one observer ironically described as "an exchange of compliments"), they were causing a nuisance to the neighbors, they were a firm rather than private individuals, and—above all—they were not local. One woman was quite explicit about her attitude: if a well-behaved local parked a car outside her shop she would explain—albeit wearily—that this was a shop entrance, and that would be the end of the matter as far as she was concerned (especially as the police would only impose a fine without actually removing the offending vehicle); but if it was a stranger from outside the district, she would simply report the offense to the authorities and let justice take its course.

The irruption of strangers into the sometimes pleasurably guilty, often conflicted, and predominantly working-class intimacy of Monti society threatens to reinforce bureaucratic interference. Three decades before my fieldwork, an architect and her husband were fined by the city police for illegal parking because hostile locals had reported their offense; but the same hostility led others in the neighborhood to slash their car tires. Once they were incorporated into the local social round, both kinds of harassment ceased; they were now part of the solidary world of a district that deeply distrusted any kind of official interference. Even today, reporting others' offenses is clearly still generally considered uncivil. A self-professed traditionalist argued that this kind of solidarity in the face of authority was the result of a long history of municipal self-reliance throughout Italy—a perhaps disingenuous argument in a city whose inhabitants also invoke the long centuries of papal rule as an explanation of their flexible accommodations to power—and that it "is part of our culture" (*fa parte della nostra cultura*), derived in generation after generation from the school habits of children who denounce a sneak by chanting, "Spy, spy, great big spy!" (*Spia, spia, spione!*) Interestingly, he declared that ratting on a neighbor was "pretty uncivil" (*nettamente incivile*)—a phrase that bears out the persistent sense of opposition between the civil and the civic.

All this gives substance to the hostility that still greets newcomers who make a habit of reporting infractions to the police. It is worth noting that the insulting epithet *stronzo* (turd), applied to the neighbor who reported the obstructing flowerbox, then provoked a pun on the similar-sounding *strozzino* (loan shark, usurer; literally, strangler), the ultimate incarnation of antisocial behavior. The new arrivals, with their legalistic actions and sometimes snobbish refusal of engagement with established social practices, stretch ordinary relations beyond the generally accepted limits of tolerance. When an irate resident reported that a tenant in his building was placing flowerpots on a beam that was far too slight to bear their weight, the city police told him to call the fire brigade instead—and the latter informed him that they would not act unless the beam began to crack. Their combined indifference seems as much of a rebuke as any leveled by a neighbor. Both the city police and the fire brigade are, after all, intensely local.

Before the arrival of wealthy strangers made formal complaints more frequent, the entire historic center was a palimpsest of collective minor wickedness. Living cheek-by-jowl (*la convivenza stretta*) means, as I was told, closing one's eyes to neighbors' infractions; there is a sense of almost gleeful complicity—a local cultural intimacy, without which the social life of the city would die and the city administration itself would become totally inundated with petty complaints.

Even allowing for a degree of exaggeration in local accounts of the outsiders' impact, however, it is evident radical change is in the air. Unconstrained by the informal values of the local society, the new strangers are willing to accept the formal legal responsibility for initiating proceedings. This legalism rudely—uncivilly—interrupts the millennia-old pattern of dealing with minor offenses within the local social context. Yet the old values still persist in relations between the authorities and the rest of the citizenry, in part because police officers and other bureaucrats are themselves, if not residents of Monti, at least familiar with its ways and those of the encompassing Italian culture. As I discovered, delays in reporting any suspected illegality can be spectacular in the baroque complexity of their discouragement of substantive action. Once an attempt was made to break into our apartment; when we tried to enter, the door was jammed half-closed. When we looked more closely, we found unmistakable splintering and other marks of jimmying on the door; two coins, evidently unsuccessfully used to lever the door, lay on the floor nearby, along with little fragments of wood from the door.

We called both of the main national police forces, the *polizia* and the *carabinieri*. (Later, when I mentioned my difficulties to a *poliziotto*, he, not realizing that I had done this and expressing the unfriendly rivalry between the two services, said that I should have called the *polizia* as soon as I failed to get a response from the *carabinieri*.) I was unable to connect with either service, so I set out in search of a police station of any kind. The first *carabinieri* station I found, opposite the nearby headquarters of the Bank of Italy, only served the bank itself, but the duty policeman did agree to make a call to the appropriate colleagues and managed to get through; I later found out that he was probably able to succeed where I had failed because he had access to an internal service line.

Eventually, after several hours and a number of additional calls, a single, visibly bored corporal arrived and took down the details from me in order to make out his report. He refused to look at the coins we had found, and scoffed at the idea of taking fingerprints; he also categorically rejected our suggestion that perhaps the burglary attempt was somehow related to an earlier incident in which someone posing as an official had defrauded us of some money: "It's nothing to do with it," he snapped. To my complaints about the slow reaction, he said, "We must be practical," and went on to say that there were around four thousand thefts a day in Rome; it was not as though we had found a dead body—that, he solemnly assured me, would have elicited a rapid response!

Speaking of this incident subsequently, a cynical friend offered a very different explanation, claiming that police always waited a while, to give the thieves a chance to make a getaway; then "they meet up and some money changes hands." I have no reason to suppose that this was true of our situation, or even that it was a common occurrence, but it reveals a widespread view of the forces of law and order. Even a shopkeeper who was sympathetic to the authorities' difficulties said that often the *carabinieri* arrived with their sirens blaring so as to warn the thieves to get away quickly. That, he said, was vastly preferable to making an arrest only to have it overturned on a legal nicety—a common police complaint.

I cannot judge whether there was any justice to the suspicion that the *carabinieri* acted with deliberate slowness; nor do I know whether the plausible argument that authorities had more urgent cases on hand was the real reason for their slow response. I did now receive a further lesson in how the bureaucratic procedures of the police forces effectively encouraged criminal activity by throwing the weight of responsibility for further action on the citizen long after the moment for immediate action had passed.

To my astonishment, the young corporal proceeded to inform me that his report was simply a matter of archival procedure, and that I would have to go independently to the station to lodge my *denuncia* about the break-in. I expostulated, not understanding the fine distinction he was making between his report and my complaint; I thought he had already written the case up. Unmoved by my perplexity, he stolidly explained that it was my duty as a citizen to report the matter. To my responding that I was not a citizen of the Italian state, he simply said that this was irrelevant, since the law required me to do this in any case—although he was prepared to leave the decision up to me (a revealing ambiguity in itself!). His parting shot was to remark that this street was not a primary focus of police interest, which is why there were no regular patrols—a point about which residents in fact sometimes complained. The street was not important in his eyes, or, apparently, in those of his superiors; the case was crushingly insignificant; and that was that.

I mulled over his stern order over for a day or two, unsure that it was really worth the trouble (and so no doubt putting even more distance between the presumed criminals and the authorities) but decided in the end that the procedure might offer an interesting ethnographic experience. (There had been a break-in in a hardware store near our house; the proprietor had decided it would not be worth his while to make a *denuncia* but thought that I, as a foreigner, might find it interesting!) And so I went looking for the appropriate office.

What followed seemed to confirm the comic image that many Italians still hold of the *carabinieri*, the army-based police corps. (Entire books are devoted to *carabinieri* jokes; these volumes are available at newsstands throughout the city, and mostly emphasize the legendary stupidity of the force.[1]) Not knowing exactly where their station was, I asked a couple of resplendently uniformed officers I encountered on the street, who solemnly

assured me that they did not know as they were from the Piazza Venezia
station (about ten minutes' walk away). We were in fact virtually opposite
the station, which was merely on the other side of the road. But, as a young
woman friend remarked when I expressed astonishment that they could not
answer, "For heaven's sake—[that's] too much work!"

The officer who functioned downstairs as a receptionist was dubious
about the need for a *denuncia*, given that nothing had been stolen. This
was by no means a unique reaction; a Monti shopkeeper told me that when
she reported an unsuccessful break-in, a senior officer commented, "What's
she gone to do that for?" (*Che c'er' annat'a fá?*)—although the heavy dialect
usage probably owed more to the shopkeeper's sarcasm than to the officer's
own speech. In my case, I had the solemn instructions of the investigating
officer himself on my side, so, tongue in cheek (and feeling slightly irritated
by the inconsistency I was meeting), I told the receiving officer that I was
simply doing as I had been told. He called upstairs, and was evidently reassured that we had a legitimate reason for proceeding. When we finally began
the process of lodging the complaint, it transpired that the easiest approach
would be to use the officer's original report, the new copy of which I would
then be asked to sign as though it had been written specially for this purpose,
thereby transforming the text of the *verbale* into a genuine *denuncia* after
all. This, then, was the important exercise in citizen responsibility that I
had been asked to perform.

A paper copy was found, obviously printed from a computer—but apparently no file now existed on the computer itself, even though the incident
had occurred only a few days earlier. So the officer painstakingly retyped the
whole thing, word for word, and then asked me to sign it. In short, the original report and the famous *denuncia* were the same text, the only difference
being that the second rendition was produced at my explicit request. The
officer was then most annoyed when I asked him for a copy after he had
printed out what he needed for his own purposes, as it seemed that he had
not realized that he could easily print out another copy from the same file
and had thought he might have to do the work yet one more time.[2]

Such incidents—my telling of this tale would thereafter always evoke
knowing looks and a complete lack of surprise on the part of Italian friends—
show how bureaucratic rhythms effectively create collusion between criminals and the perhaps unwitting representatives of the law. These police
officers were possibly being less stupid than wary of risks to their own standing; but they were certainly engaged in a process of sanctioned prevarication,
putting ever more time between themselves and the unknown criminals.
Even the special services created to protect the victims of usury do not act

until a formal *denuncia* has been lodged with them, presumably for fear of being accused of prejudicial intervention. Thus, the law and the authorities' ostensibly reasonable desire to avoid wasting time on unproductive arrests combine to favor the crooks, which makes local residents more sympathetic to right-wing politics—a result that would certainly not displease some officers.

Performances of Policing

There are also situations in which, even after a persistent set of complaints, the police prefer not to bring charges at all, but engage in an elaborate charade of compliance with local demands for intervention against the most threatening category of outsiders—the immigrants from outside the European Union (*extracomunitari*). Both the *poliziotti* and the military *carabinieri* would frequently appear in the main square when there were heavy concentrations of these people—especially on Thursdays and Sundays, when the Ukrainians would gather in front of their cardinal's church and be joined by many Romanians, Albanians, and others—and harass them in unsubtle ways, pulling a few of them in and demanding to see their papers, or just watching them intently, but rarely doing much more than that. The local consensus was that most of these foreigners were in fact illegal immigrants.

I once noticed such a confrontation; when the policeman, who was operating from inside his car parked on a completely pedestrian area, had finished haranguing two Albanians, I approached them and asked them what had happened.[3] They said that they had been asked for their papers, of which they only had photocopies; they were allowed to leave, but were told they could not walk across the square but would have to leave by one of the side exits. I assured them that this was an illegal order and invited them for coffee in the bar of a man known to be sympathetic to the immigrants and angry at the discrimination they faced. They accepted; we ordered and then drank our coffee; and, as we were chatting, the policeman entered and glared at us. Having few options, he soon retreated. When the two Albanians had left, I went up to the officer's car and asked to speak with him. He immediately demanded to see *my* papers. When I asked him why, he replied, not unreasonably, that I had spoken to a representative of the forces of law and order and that he, in turn, had a right to see my documents. My unexpectedly British passport perhaps embarrassed him; he denied that he had issued such illegal orders to the Albanians, but claimed that their papers had not been in order. He seemed worried about my inquisitive questioning, perhaps fearing possible fallout. Officials may use fear, but, in a hierarchy of command, they can also experience it. In fact, a relatively charitable interpretation of the officer's actions suggested by one resident was that he was simply trying to save these Albanians—who indeed may not have been carrying the requisite documentation—from irascible locals, who would have demanded that the officer arrest them right away.

Forbidding these immigrants to enter the square would have no basis in legality; but it does reflect a convergence of local ideas about spatiality with the larger ideological mapping of national territory by local rightists. In this, it recalls a much earlier topography of local prejudice, especially during the sixteenth and seventeenth centuries: the convergence between carnivalesque humiliation of the Jews and their explicit debarment from approaching the area in which their erstwhile coreligionists and now newly converted Christians were housed. While the ostensible reason for this prohibition was to prevent the neophyte Christians (*neofiti*) from reverting to their old religion, the church's policy of surrounding them with a particularly hostile and notoriously violent population—especially when read in the still larger topography that opposed the reclusion of the Ghetto to the new confinement in "enemy" territory, as the historian Marina Caffiero has argued—was also a way of incorporating the Rione Monti in the larger topography of papal authority.[4] Such assertions of territorial exclusivity persist to this day, although the actors and categories are different.

To be fair, police officers are subject to severe legal constraints on action, and often question the legitimacy of a system that so severely ties their hands. When I asked one waiter why the police did nothing more, he cynically replied, "They don't want to!" (*Nun vojono!*) Whenever a police car arrived on the square, all those immigrants with irregular papers would retreat slowly and in very orderly fashion, with quick backward glances but only occasional indications of real haste, to gather nearby in solemn, slightly nervous little groups in the side streets, from which they scanned the square with worried eyes. Occasionally the officers would question or arrest one or two people, but in general they ignored the mildly panicky crowds, which then drifted back into the square as soon as the police car began to drive away. I had the distinct impression that the panic, such as it was, was also a performance—a satisfactory show of terror that was also an act of complicity, allowing the officers to look as though they were doing their job without actually arresting too many people. The police prefer to avoid individual confrontations with people who might in fact be able to argue for their rights. Such confrontations, as a local academic remarked, would reduce their authority (*autorità*); hence, presumably, the policeman's considerable discomfiture over my intervention with the two Albanians.

Once the police showed up because the local club wanted the immigrants cleared out so that they could begin setting up for their October festivities. When the police appeared the large crowd moved away rapidly and, with a derisive hoot, one of the most overtly anti-immigrant club members began leading his followers in setting up rows of chairs, filling much of the available space as quickly as possible. One of the others, a frequent critic of the immigrants' presence despite himself being married to one (of very different geographical origins) and the employer of several illegal immigrants from eastern Europe in his construction business, started placing chairs in front of the main door of the Ukrainian door and only desisted when another, less virulently anti-immigrant member remonstrated with him that local people should show respect if they wished the immigrants to do the same.

While some officers perhaps wished to take more drastic action, they were constrained by laws that also gave them a moral alibi for confining themselves to generic intimidation and maintaining their preferred pose of lofty importance. It also allowed them to accuse the government, sometimes quite explicitly, of failure to do its duty by passing more effective legislation. As a cynical restaurateur of left-wing views tartly observed: "The police has every interest in making the maladministration visible." If seriously irritated, officers can sometimes briefly demand that even someone who intervenes on the immigrants' behalf must accompany them to their station for further interrogation; but such tactics tend to backfire, being unproductive of anything more than further counter-harassment from legally astute local leftists who resent the officers' high-handedness. And there is a further, paradoxical dimension. Police and immigrants alike prefer the latter to remain undocumented. As an astute young political observer remarked: "Staying illegal [actually] confers impunity!" (*Non mettersi in regola dà l'impunità!*) Once registered with the appropriate authorities, an immigrant is subject to far more numerous and ramified forms of bureaucratic control, all of which—Italians would certainly agree—are best avoided. And immigrants briefly apprehended without documents can easily give the authorities the slip, since they are not usually taken into immediate custody. Under existing laws, when an immigrant caught red-handed in the act of committing a theft did not have the proper papers, the police could not hold the offender for more than two or three days. On release, the immigrant would sign a declaration of identity and domicile and would be ordered to leave the country within fifteen days; when, at the end of that period, they went to check on the immigrant's departure, it would usually transpire that the address had been a false one. The police expected as much; as with the *denuncia*, the whole charade allowed the police to avoid any kind of punitive action at all. Indeed, the deportation order is often served in English, apparently on the basis of the argument that foreigners should not be addressed in Italian, but this again provides both sides with an excuse for its complete ineffectiveness. Remarked my source for this illuminating detail, "Excuses are a fine thing!"

Locals were divided in their attitudes to the immigrants. A surprising number of known leftists were hostile, arguing that the immigrants had crowded out the locals in a pedestrianized social space—the main square— that they had worked hard to reclaim from its casual use as a parking area. When children used the Ukrainian church door as a soccer goal, their parents not only allowed them to do so but seemed at times to encourage them. This was disingenuously hostile, inasmuch as some years earlier, when it was only local lads who played soccer in the square, they were often chased away by those who had their business operations there. A few locals defended the immigrants' right to use the square in their own way, although even among these voices for tolerance some expressed concern that the immigrants were insensitive to local cultural values; and almost all were worried about the visible drunkenness of the morose men who hung around the square for hours at a time. Many Monti residents claimed that the immigrants included a high proportion of prostitutes, pimps, and drug dealers.

The reaction to the Ukrainian presence is more complex than might at first appear. The fear they engender is often expressed in terms of their failure to adapt to local customs or to respect the local sense of the square as a place for families and children. Yet it seems that they were damned as much by similarity as by difference; the old Fascist bogey of genetic contamination may have been a concern, although it was never openly voiced as such in my hearing, but it is also clear that what the immigrants were doing reproduced older patterns of interaction that locals could reconceptualize all too easily in their own terms. The drug dealers, for example, were pursuing activities that had been rampant among Roman operators in the area for a long time, and it seems likely, as a few locals admitted, that the pimps and pushers who hung around in the square, cell phones at the ready to transmit instructions to their minions, were in fact still Italian. One of the immigrants' most virulent critics actually acknowledged this and even identified two of the men as Italian pimps—although, he added, they were connected to foreigners, presumably traffickers of women from eastern Europe.

Thus, there is at least some recognition that certain kinds of crime may sometimes be committed, or at least directed, by Italians. A neighbor who had himself been a policeman told me that serious professionals—by which he meant "real Italians"—planned burglaries carefully and would have used their brains if they had been responsible for the attempt on our apartment. A neighbor who had some connections with the Roman underworld explained to me that successful burglars used local agents to case the joint before outsiders actually conducted the break-in. The immigrants thus provide a convenient scapegoat; but it is not clear that they should be held responsible for the increase in unsolved petty crime in Monti in recent years.

An observant non-Roman academic who had taken up residence in the area a few years earlier recalled a conversation between two elderly Monti ladies, who were commenting on what they saw as the inappropriate behavior of immigrant women sitting on the edge of the Renaissance fountain in the middle of the square. As he noted, they managed to hint that these women were prostitutes without ever actually saying so—until one of them remarked, "Yes, but let's let that fact go" (*Sì, ma lasciamo stare questo fatto*), and went on to say that the real culprits were Italian men, meaning the pimps and their customers alike.

Sympathetic recognition that it was not only the foreigners who were lowering the tone of the square was relatively common among left-wingers. Not coincidentally, the national leftist leadership of the time was praising the influx of immigrants as a way of redressing the declining birthrate—a major political issue, and one that the neofascists, as the inheritors of old ideas about miscegenation and criminality, was instead exploiting to create fears of the disappearance of genuine Italians.[5] Leftists, in short, made a clear distinction between genetic and cultural inheritance, and regarded the immigrants as a source of national salvation; rightists, by contrast, represented them as a threat to national survival.

As in so much else, however, and despite a few fairly violent clashes between individuals, the Roman propensity for staying away from real trouble prevailed. The whole country, moreover, was learning the rhetorical art of embracing cultural diversity. In the years following the Jubilee, with the arrival of a new parish priest and the opening of a dialogue between the parish church and the Ukrainians' religious leaders, as well as the active engagement of the newly constituted Monti Social Network, the gatherings of immigrants diminished in intensity and the tension ebbed away; in 2005 the two churches celebrated the feast of the Virgin, patron saint of the parish, together in a dramatically public show of communion shared by two groups with different symbols and differently attired clerics (the Ukrainian priests, although Catholics, use vestments and icons very similar to those of the Orthodox church from which they had seceded). Formerly tense scenes of confrontation had morphed into a celebration of amiable diversity.

In one sense the police intervention had protected the immigrants during the period of maximum tension, since the very fact of surveillance answered the call of less tolerant citizens for some sort of intervention without actually leading to significant numbers of arrests but also without permitting any escalation of anti-immigrant violence. The demonstrative hassling of a few immigrants by an uniformed officer, the occasional appearance of a plainclothes officer clearly following the immigrants' movements while sending out comments on a walkie-talkie, and then the cautious return of the immigrants to their positions in front of the church or to seats at the one bar that really welcomed them—this choreography of intimidation was not a scene of existential terror. Immigrants and police officers alike knew that they were playing out a mutually convenient drama.

Since it was the locals who called the police, they were forced to accept these compromises. They had filed complaints; the authorities had acted, which is all the law required them to do. The whole process turned out to be a perfect illustration of the practical logic of the *denuncia* to the extent to which it accommodated the various parties (including the police) and eventually quite literally exhausted their energy for further confrontation. Since the immigrants were usually on their best behavior as soon as the police appeared, and since the police would not ordinarily attempt to surprise them in some form of public disturbance without the prior submission of a *denuncia*, the mechanisms of citizen-state engagement worked to maintain the existing situation, until, with the arrival of a more proactive leadership in both churches, it could be managed in a more productive way.

That some police officers felt frustrated and helpless seems beyond question. In practice, however, their actions reproduced the usual pattern of compromise through performance: a display of authority, a technical act of cooperation with the complaining citizens, an occasional arrest where some specific and identifiable offense merited it. All the players, officers and immigrants alike, fully understand what to do; the officers put on a show of fierce surveillance, the immigrants of cowering timidity and respectful distance. Both sides demonstrated mastery of the timing and gestures appropriate to their complementary roles. In this sense the immigrants had in fact learned to play their own part in a distinctively (if not exclusively) Italian or at least Roman drama.

It is not only the national police who assert rather than impose their authority. A neighbor on our street pointed out that two one-way systems on that street started out from the same place but in opposite directions—a virtual invitation to drivers to break the law. Most of the time one never saw any policing of the spot. One day, however, a pair of city policemen unexpectedly appeared and proceeded to upbraid every motorist they managed to catch red-handed. But in fact they did not impose a single fine. As my neighbor suggested, "they needed to look as though they were in charge" but they also did not want to "look [socially] bad." Rather, one of the policemen—clearly, said my neighbor, an active neofascist—went on at great length about the current lack of discipline and, once again, blamed the miscreants' impunity on the stupidity of the (left-wing) government.

For many Romans, moreover, such negotiating space is not only humane; it also opens up possibilities for the play of humor and familiarity. Two workmen tried to climb up on Bernini's statue of Neptune in Piazza Navona; one of them succeeded in doing so, only to break the deity's scepter as he fell to the ground, and, when he was arrested, announced that he would sue the *comune* of Rome because it should not have been possible for him to gain access to such a dangerous place to begin with! In the gleeful report of the incident in *Corriere della Sera*, a thoroughly respectable Milan-based newspaper, we can read his words faithfully reproduced in flawless Romanesco.[6] To a dour northerner, his behavior might be an example of Roman uncouthness; to some Romans, by contrast, it was a familiar exercise in the humor that, in their view, protected their self-respect through the long years of papal oppression.

Such saucy insouciance is a Roman's best protection against the systemic indifference represented by the foot-dragging tactics of the police bureaucracy. When the authorities do choose to act, the popular presumption is not that they are performing their civic duty, but that they are either violating the norms of social civility—a tacit agreement not to interfere—or retaliating against an uncivil response to their own rhythms of action and conventional hints about what it would take to buy them off. Just as a local boss might make an example of someone who repeatedly offended against his authority, so people assume, police officers—especially the city *vigili*— must occasionally make an example of those who do not understand the system of mutual accommodation that permits the continuing exchange of favors.

There are, to be sure, important exceptions to this pattern of complaisance. Many Italians take pride, for example, in the sometimes spectacular successes of the special section of the *carabinieri* responsible for the recovery of stolen art; in a country where the official line is that it possesses "seventy percent" of the world's great masterpieces,[7] such activities are both sacrosanct and entirely admirable defenses against foreign rapacity and internal treachery. But in general recourse to the law is considered neither socially acceptable nor pragmatically effective; the *denuncia* is valued more as an instrument of social management than as an effect prompt for official action. Moreover, the representatives of the law, being no less subject to the logic of original sin than are ordinary mortals, can be and are expected to engage in the ordinary reciprocities of Roman life to an extent sometimes actually facilitated by the cover that their uniforms and official titles afford them.

Police foot-dragging takes place in a larger context of accommodation between official practices and the established habits of local people. Illegality is rife and is not considered abnormal. One of the most respected trades, for examples, is that of the jewelers and goldsmiths; yet many of them, possibly more than half of those operating in all of Rome, work without permits. Like all merchants and artisans, they must shape two entirely different budgets. One is the official response to state accounting requirements (*la contabilità*). The other is a social accounting, and it is significantly different. It should include bribes (*mazzette*) to be paid to a wide variety of officials, from tax inspectors to city policemen and even service workers; ironically, for many artisans and merchants it also includes expected fines, which for many locals are really thinly disguised bribes anyway—one greengrocer calculated that his annual budget for fines was around 1,000,000 *lire* and that this was an acceptable amount. An itinerant vendor got a ticket for driving a damaged vehicle (his windshield had been smashed in an accident); through the parking attendant (*posteggiatore*) at one of the markets where he sells his wares, he claims to have transmitted a bribe of 150,000 *lire* (of which the attendant raked off 30000 for his services as mediator) that saved him a fine of 600,000 *lire* instead. Here again precise calculation is possible: "It's an established price list!" (*È tariffa ormai!*)

Fractured Authority: The Multiplicity of Policing

The police forces display a breathtaking variety. There are the *carabinieri*, the city police, the uniformed tax officials, and the *polizia*. It is pointless to request the services of one group if the particular issue falls under the jurisdiction of any of the other three. Time, too, often dribbles slowly but steadily away through the cracks in the overall pattern of police authority. The differences are not only procedural but social, springing from different levels of engagement with the population.

Thus, if the contribution of the *carabinieri* to processes of collusion is procedural rather than mischievous, its stately pace thus serving as one of the props of a reputation for relative incorruptibility, the city police represent a very different image. Locals expect them to be corrupt, a reputation that would presumably favor their ability to exert pressure for small bribes on weak shopkeepers and artisans. One greengrocer, furious because the *vigili* had fined him 420,000 *lire* merely because a box of tangerines lacked a price label, described them as an "authorized system of theft...an authorized mafia," decrying their use of plainclothes agents as an unfair stratagem. But he had also learned to live with their rhythms. Having on one occasion been fined for placing crates of produce on the sidewalk all day long, he compromised by putting the crates out only for two or three hours a day, while also surreptitiously keeping his shop open during afternoon hours when he was supposed to have closed; these more discrete infractions were apparently tolerated, without any demand for bribes and also without any further interference. In this case, the merchant had managed to gain a small advantage simply by discretely scaling down his infraction. Had the officers been bent on extortion, he had reduced the possible gain to them beyond anything worth the risk; if their intention was instead to enforce an approximate legality, he had helped them reach an administratively, socially, and culturally appropriate compromise.

There have been accusations of partiality aplenty. Under the city force's former management, which was sympathetic to the left wing of Italian politics, plans had been drawn up for a systematic investigation of all illegal uses of public space. With reform, however, came an unexpected and dramatic shift to the Right. The new officers were allegedly more sympathetic to a restaurateur considered to be the worst offender. Instead of pursuing every possible violator of the laws regarding the uses of public space, I was told, they created a list of the ten worst cases, then informed this restaurateur that he was number eleven! Nothing further happened.

The opportunities open to city police for pursuing petty kickbacks and favors are certainly both legion and legendary, although we should beware of an element of exaggeration in what citizens who have been caught out in such deals have to say about the matter; it is also sometimes hard to distinguish between complaints about bureaucratic precision and cases of actual extortion. Some citizens, moreover, interpret the pressure tactics as a way of getting what these underpaid officials have a moral right to expect. Others, while acknowledging that entirely human response, nevertheless accuse officials of quite unnecessary rudeness and malevolence, describing how they point their fingers, increasing their hints with the number of real or imaginary violations they claim to have spotted. If the merchant is humble in response, this is interpreted as a sign of weakness, leading to ever more outrageous demands. In some cases, the city police have managed to close down entire establishments for a while; when the doors reopen, locals assume that some more substantial bribe has now been rendered.

Such tactics are necessarily indirect but, locals claim, unmistakable; "they like collecting fear with their eyes." When they are not dropping crude hints about infractions deserving huge but avoidable fines, police officers may also drop in on merchants during the festive Christmas season with expressions of goodwill—but "it is always in a form of extortion." Sometimes, too, they will use a jocose form of Romanesco to cushion their hints: "Can't we even joke at all?" (*Nun se pó manco scherzá?*) a pair of city policemen pathetically demanded of a restorer (in another district), when, having failed completely to intimidate him or find fault with his arrangements, they were forced to leave empty-handed. (Although he figured out that they were pretending to be on duty when in fact their beat was elsewhere, this innocent character—who later opened a shop in Monti—did not realize until afterward that they may have been trying to extract a bribe!) When dealing with women, in particular, the city police "feel truly powerful"—this, from a woman who had run her own artisanal business in the area for several years.

Some of the most feared city police officers are themselves women; they are feared because they are exigent, both in their bureaucratic pedantry and in their presumed capacity to extort bribes, and it is not always easy to distinguish between these two aspects of their operating style. Unlike most of the *carabinieri*, the city officers, both men and women, are tough, sardonic Roman citizens, so deeply implicated in local reciprocities that for a time the civil authorities required that their patrols always be monitored by a pair of *carabinieri*.

This surveillance followed a locally familiar idiom. A powerful sense of shared responsibility for keeping an eye on the streets, a stance that even in Monti is now thought to be fraying beyond repair, was still such that, for example, one man reported that the greengrocer near his house kept an eye on the nanny to whom he entrusted his little child. Trust exists because of, not in spite of, the collective surveillance of and by the community; it does not spring from a presumption of innate personal reliability but from the certain knowledge that social pressure is the only force that can ensure an honest performance. Thus, the government chooses to impose a system of mutual checking on the various police forces because mutual suspicion is the only possible basis for creating the conditions for mutual trust—a social guarantee rather than an interpersonal pact. On this basis, too, I was told that if one wished to make a complaint against, say, the *carabinieri*, one could only report to the *polizia*. In practice, most people would just let the matter pass; but the possibility itself follows a social logic that everyone understands.

No love is lost among the various forces. This may be a good thing; some believe that it was this tension, for example, that prevented the *carabinieri* from joining elements in the national civilian police in an attempted coup in 1974; this, said a neighbor, "saved democracy in Italy." Because they have technically different jurisdictions and functions, mutual harassment is far from rare, and officers of each force are reluctant to pass up opportunities for scoring points. In one incident, some city police slapped fines on a group of *carabinieri* for a minor offense. The latter immediately sought revenge. Dressed in civilian clothes, they followed the city officers into a bar and overheard them attempting to extract bribes from the owner; and then they pounced. A local councilor remarked, "Those guys were compromised, and so [the *carabinieri*] denounced them!"

The *carabinieri* are supposedly held to a military code of honor; nonetheless, I encountered two former *carabinieri* as well as a former member of the *polizia*, all of whom quit their respective forces because, allegedly, they were disgusted by the depths of corruption they had encountered.[8] As one of the former *carabinieri* remarked, "If you don't help others 'eat,' you can't make out yourself either" (*se non fai mangiare, non mangi*)—a remark that may also indirectly suggest that those who quit are disgusted less by the rampant corruption than by their personal failure to profit from it.

The miasma of corruption is indeed so pervasive, and so expected, that no group or individual escapes the suspicion, at least, of taking bribes and breaking petty laws; the reality of their corruption is immaterial when everyone assumes it. A clerk in the city administration whose task was to find homes for those who had suffered eviction told me not to reveal the nature of her employment to anyone in the neighborhood as they would automatically assume that she did this for profit—in other words, by taking bribes, as indeed some of her colleagues apparently did. Ironically, she herself suffered a form of eviction when the proprietor of her apartment in Monti jacked the rent up by an astronomical amount; people in such positions are so routinely assumed to be raking off illegal profits from their connections that few would believe that she and her husband could not afford the increase.

Suspicion, moreover, is built into the administrative framework, itself the product of social knowledge and a distinctly realistic understanding of how bureaucracy works in practice. Thus, the surveillance of one police force over another—now the *polizia* in turn also monitors the *carabinieri*—cannot depend on the greater probity of any one group, but is motivated by the all too public hostility and mutual jealousy that frequently erupt among these various forces. There is a hierarchy; when a pedestrians' rights activist asked a *vigile* to challenge a *carabiniere* who was illegally parked, his response made that clear: "What am I supposed to do about the *carabinieri*?" And one former policeman told me, in a moment of apparently drunken candor, that if he ever caught his daughter, a member of the city force, extorting bribes for fabricated infractions, he would let the *carabinieri* cart her off to her just deserts. Trust and mutual respect evidently do not flourish among the various forces.

Extorting Coffee and Campari

More generally, the play of intimidation among the various branches of public administration in Rome both sets an example of aggressive social management to the locals (who also recognize their own habits in it) and plays such havoc with the orderly timing of bureaucratic process that citizens feel free to impose their own rhythms as best they can. A Monticiano opened a large and clearly lucrative bar and café in an imposing square abutting Monti. Thieves broke in; and, not content with stealing whole hams and salamis, they poured all the soap they could find over the marble floor and burned the chairs and tables—a deliberate affront (*spregio*), although the motive for it apparently remained unclear. To clean up the mess, the proprietor had to lift all the marble flooring, but this was prohibited under existing conservation laws; his attempts to get permission produced no results, his establishment remained closed as a result, and so he decided to act. Together with two or three workmen he lifted the slabs and began washing them down with a powerful and abrasive detergent. At this moment an inspector from the sanitary department showed up and told him that he could not do this and that the inspector was going to write him a ticket for using potentially dangerous chemicals in a public place. His protests proving futile, he called the *carabinieri*, with some of whom he was on excellent terms, and they told the inspector not to bother. When the inspector protested, the proprietor told his friends to "let it go" (*lasciamo perdere*) because he actually wanted to pay the fine: "If they're right, why should I not pay?" His irony produced the desired effect; the *carabinieri* told the inspector, "This case is to be let go!" (*si lasci perdere!*) So the bar proprietor graciously allowed himself to be persuaded, and the humiliated sanitary inspector took himself off, knowing that his authority came to naught before that of the uniformed military force.

   This story is interesting for a number of reasons. First, the bureaucracy's slow response to his request for permission to undertake a drastic cleaning operation seemed to him to justify going ahead on his own. Second, the element of chance adds to the sense of risk but also to that of unfairness; he feared the conservation authorities, yet it was the sanitary inspector who created the problem. Most significant, perhaps, is the play of fear between the various services, and especially his own ability to manipulate it to his considerable advantage; his gently ironic willingness to back off was in fact a very effective and aggressive move in defense of his own interests and showed his mastery of locally appreciated forms of wit, politeness, and consideration. The play of fear also has a moral basis; in describing these events to me the proprietor quoted a Roman proverb—*paura non fare, paura non avere* (if you don't create fear, you won't suffer fear); the inspector, he implied, simply got his just deserts. Last, but certainly not least, the proprietor's friendship with the *carabinieri* evidently weighed more heavily on the outcome, as did the masculine authority of the policemen, than the specific requirements of the law the inspector tried to apply.

What the *carabinieri* got out of it, beyond the satisfaction of winning a fight, is unclear. One can only imagine that they were treated to a great deal of coffee in the ensuing months (and Romans would assume as a matter of course that "coffee" here was a metonym for more considerable favors). Coffee is a social drink; it is particularly the medium of reconciliation when, for example, two merchants start to quarrel and then decide that they would gain more advantages from settling their differences and sealing their accord over a companionable slurp of intense, boiling espresso while standing at the bar counter under the barman's knowing eye.

Coffee thus has many meanings. It can sometimes be a simple sign of hospitality and friendship. But there is no really reliable way for an observer to know what the offer of coffee really means at any given moment. The issue of bribery is especially sensitive and difficult to document. Its very essence consists in hints and nudges—invitations to coffee are ideal for the purpose—and is cloaked in elaborate courtesies; indeed, some locals, of the old school, consider petty rake-offs to policemen, for example, to arise from "a sense of courtesy" (*un senso di cortesia*), making them very hard to distinguish, if distinguish them we must, from the friendly gesture of an invitation to drink a quick coffee together. Remarking on his reduction of prices for police on the beat, a newspaper vendor remarked simply, "It's a small act of politeness [*correttezza*] that I perform." In short, these are ordinary social reciprocities.

The newsagent's assessment hardly corresponds to what a civic moralist would understand by "correctness," also called *correttezza*. Not at all coincidentally, coffee adjusted to a more amusing taste by the addition of a little liquor is called *caffè corretto*, literally meaning "corrected coffee"; local ideas of correction are more about adjusting to a social aesthetic than following some abstract code such as that implied by the ironic tone in which most Romans mention being politically correct (*politicamente corretto*). Accepted standards of social civility take precedence over civic formality. Sometimes it is hard to draw a line between keeping friendly relations with the local representatives of law and order and gracefully yielding to an extortion considered to be normal and even socially justifiable.

To make matters still more complicated, those whose official job it is to dig up the evidence of bribery are often thought to be deeply implicated in it themselves. Drawing lines of clear definition between the morally corrupt and the socially imperative is a fool's errand. Petty bribery is commonly linked with the stereotype of southern culture and an absence of the social culture (*cultura sociale*) or civilization (*civiltà*) of the more orderly north. That formula suggestively inverts the locals' usual understanding of what it means to be civil, which is all about politeness (*cortesia, correttezza*) and friendship (*amicizia*)—the very essence of which is the reciprocity of favors and gifts. The policeman comments on the amount of goods the vendor has piled outside his kiosk and the vendor replies, "I'll take care of it" (*ci penso io*), a genial but irreproachable indication that he has understood the nature of the transaction even as he makes a big show of tidying up; the fact of the matter is that he cannot avoid spreading his goods on the sidewalk if he is going to be able to make a living. The policeman realizes that the tidiness is temporary, but he is satisfied both by the show of slightly ironic deference and by the reduced prices that he will now get from this vendor. Locals view such amiable but agonistic reciprocity as a deeply ingrained part of their lives: "one hand washes the other" (*una mano lava l'antra*), as the vendor remarked, citing an old Roman saw. Such is the sense of cohabitation or symbiosis (*convivenza*) that so much local engagement with the bureaucracy evokes. As the vendor concluded: *Annamo!*[9]

One observer suggested that this moral configuration was an outcome of the huge and more or less continual migration of southerners into the city; with their rural connections still active, they have cheeses and hams to provide—as bribes, he hinted; another man told me of a policeman who was caught, not in Rome, because he had accumulated an enormous number of hams in his home. Those who are on the take are called gluttons (*magnaccia*)—a peculiarly apt term in this case.[10] Clientelist relations in the countryside, even in the northern areas, were once secured by the ritualistic offering of such goods to the local notables in exchange for their protection, and it is not hard to see how a poorly paid civic authority might comfortably have eased its way into the social template created by this precedent.[11] Indeed, the idea of a gift given with particular courtesy to a superior is conveyed in the term *omaggio* (homage),[12] sometimes used for the small bribe used to keep rapacious city police at bay.

The introduction of new efficiencies is steadily undermining these symbiotic arrangements. A respected left-wing intellectual, an idealist advocate of respect for the centralized state, expressed enormous annoyance about the new system of electronic surveillance that would automatically fine those who brought cars illegally into the area during certain periods of the day. His irritation was not about the violation of *la privacy*, now a hot-button issue, but at the fact that he could no longer explain to the policeman who came to write a ticket that, for example, he had brought his girlfriend home in his own car since he could hardly have offered to pay for the taxi she would now have had to take in order to enter the zone at all. He did not specifically mention the possibility of a small bribe or gift, but some such consideration would not usually be misconstrued.

Human engagement is the positive side of these informal arrangements. For some residents, however, the sheer extortion that sometimes plagues even the simplest aspects of daily living justifies any measures the authorities can take against these practices. The city police, responsible for enforcing local and municipal regulations, have the easiest opportunities. They fine those who are illegally parked, check on the hygiene and accounting of local shops, and report infractions of building and historic conservation rules. They seem to have a seasonal rhythm; one woman claimed that in the summer they were on vacation but started "sprouting like mushrooms" once September arrived, ready to pounce at the first sign of an illegally parked car—although a pizza baker remarked that they disappeared with the rain, adding, sourly, "That's the Italians for you!" One could read this last remark literally, as a comment on the difficulty of getting people to take law enforcement seriously; or perhaps one could see in it a recognition, ironic as it may be, of the convenience of having police officers who were only intermittently attentive to their duties.

Their alleged venality, of which I heard many accounts, is couched in an idiom of informal friendliness that closely resembles that of the underworld. Because at a literal level the law provides severe penalties for corruption (and has applied them with growing regularity since the state-sanctioned anticorruption operations of the early 1990s), *vigili* cannot demand bribes outright. So they turn, instead and predictably, to the threats that only an amiable courtesy can convey, especially when couched in the local vernacular. They know how to gesture to a bartender so that he understands that they expect to get their coffee free of charge. Or, as the retired journalist described it, the policeman goes into a bar and, after ordering two Camparis, "pretends to pay." The bar proprietor makes a dismissive gesture and says that it is of no importance—nothing at all. "'How come it's nothing?' recites the cop, just like an actor." Both know their respective parts well; both play them to perfection.

Others observe this interaction; they, too, understand. There are models aplenty to fuel their interpretations. A restaurateur gives his customers his visiting card so they can display it on their illegally parked cars; the police-man on the beat sees whose customers they are and looks the other way—no doubt, according to locals, in exchange for free meals. An elegant woman of militantly left-wing persuasion, and active in the Rome pedestrians' rights movement, complained to a second restaurant owner that he, too, was al-lowing cars to park illegally in front of his establishment; he had previously put up a sign offering to pay two hours' worth of parking on meters that had temporarily been placed there, but, after these were taken away, he made other arrangements. This was what the activist now discovered; as if by way of answer to her complaint, and seizing what must have seemed like a heaven-sent opportunity, the owner looked out beyond her and hailed a passing city policeman, "Come in and have a coffee!" The implications were clear and needed no further explanation. Coffee, at such moments, is not just coffee; and the kindly invitation to his dear friend also carried an un-ambiguous boast—and perhaps a threat—for the benefit of the interfering activist as well.

Acting out a role in this sense is not a performance merely in the sense of staged roles; it is performative—it has practical effects on the immediate relationship, sending a clear message to bystanders and reinforcing a well-established set of social rules and understandings. But there is a price to pay for such power. The bar proprietor, for example, is confident of being protected from parking fines when he leaves his car outside the door of his establishment. The price he pays is one of fear. He is not only afraid of the police, with their power to ruin him economically. He also fears what would happen if their extortion increased to the point where he would feel he had no choice but to file a complaint; the social damage that reporting their extortion would generate might well be greater than the security he would temporarily gain from further harassment. Going to the legal authorities with a complaint about police bullying is itself "a sign of weakness," some-thing no active local merchant can really afford—but the failure to lodge a complaint is also attributable to fear. The butcher mentioned earlier for his pleasant and polite manner is furious with the *vigili* because, he says, they always take his best cuts; it is clear that he feels unable to complain. So the advantage remains largely with what may be only a crooked minority among the officers, even though the available sanctions are now somewhat more effective than before the Clean Hands movement of the early 1990s.

Moreover, the coffee or the pair of Camparis becomes a metonym for the more substantial levels of extortion to which victims feel their tormentors may graduate. The only time I ever directly encountered this use of "coffee" occurred when a young woman delivering telephone directories told me, as I turned away from her with my directory in hand, that I should make a "contribution" (*contributo*) for, as she said, "a coffee." I gave her 5,000 *lire* and she seemed satisfied; a neighbor then told me that I should not have given her anything as she was already paid by the phone company—but this was a common pattern, whereby employees of official bodies would try anything to intimidate people. This very minor example was little more than a request for a tip (*mancia*)—indeed, that is what others called it. By contrast, and on a much grander scale, I once heard the term *caffè* used of a bribe of 3,000,000 *lire*, the sum allegedly demanded by a police officer for permitting a hotel owner to remodel a room; she could only halt the extortion because she knew the officer's captain personally.[13]

Those who know their rights can protect themselves; officials who take bribes prey on an older generation more accustomed to accepting as normal a situation that the new civic morality emphatically rejects. Today, moreover, the simplification of licensing procedures has greatly reduced the potential for extortion.[14] As a result, bent officers must now seek out those few who still fear consequences that in reality the authorities can no longer impose.

Among merchants and artisans are many who regret the new civic order and the disappearance of a system they have learned to work to their own advantage. That skill, however, still stands them in good stead; they know how to wield the rhetoric of friendship in order to represent increasingly indirect deals in terms that are still—just—acceptable under the tighter ethical scrutiny now in force. A bar proprietor, for example, made a point of always being scrupulously accurate in giving what at the time were the obligatory machine receipts for even the smallest purchase, so that, when the *vigili* came checking, their report (*verbale*)—they are required to issue one even when they find no illegalities—was entirely favorable. But the *vigili*, presumably as a way of exerting a little discreet pressure, hinted that his wife never charged them for their coffee (when a couple runs such a business it is common for the wife to take charge of the cash register); so he ran three of them a tab for two coffees—for reasons, he said, of politeness (*cortesia*). Another storekeeper, who had told me that he simply keeps smiling when the police come checking on his establishment, hailed a passing policeman with polite irony, "Hail, Caesar!" (*Ave, Cesare!*) Merchants tread a fine line between self-assertiveness and deference and hope that this ironic balance will deflect any lingering attempt at extortion.

In this sense, the bar proprietor's combination of absolute punctilious-ness and a rather pointedly reduced form of generosity sets clear limits to the extent to which he feels he must play along with the pressure to bribe. Another example of such a mixed strategy, when taken in its broader context, is even more obviously strategic in its implications. A shopkeeper who was locally famous for his archaizing Romanesco cleverly exploited the liberalized licensing laws to diversify his business. He also found ways to maintain his earlier arrangements with local police and other officials, with an appropriately refurbished rhetorical wrapping that flaunted his claim to represent traditional culture but did so in the language of the new ethics. Thus, he remarked that the city police no longer expected bribes from him but did expect a discount on the produce they bought; he viewed this as a form of friendship—"which is part of our culture, now gradually disappear-ing." His neighbors, who often furiously accused him of violating zoning and environmental laws with complete impunity, would hardly have taken this portrayal of friendship as innocent of bribery; but they would also have been forced to acknowledge that he had mastered the new rhetoric to good effect—and their attempts to get the police to intervene in his infractions, *denuncia* after *denuncia*, came to naught.

He himself ignores the neighbors' threats and denunciations and attrib-utes the occasional unwelcome attention of the police to suspicion of his leftist political activities—a heroic pose, historically justifiable given the right-wing politics of most police units in Italy, through which he deflects the entire question of possibly illicit activities and their violation, according to his neighbors, of his own political principles. (The irony is that those who are most outraged by his behavior are fellow leftists, some of whom condemn his actions precisely because they flout their shared principles.) He also claims that when the police do harass him he simply pays up, preferring not to contest the fines even though he could call on powerful friends to intervene. Is this a civic acceptance of police authority or a civil response to what would otherwise, in his words, become "a dispute that never ends"? Or is it, once again, an act of pragmatic compromise, one that fuses the civic and the civil in a strategy that is maximally convenient for him and allows him to ignore the outraged objections of other, more austerely principled leftists? Or, still more practically, are the fines in effect a way of paying for the authorities' studied disregard of his more serious wrongdoings?

Whatever the answer, he does—it is only fair to note—wryly acknowledge a certain incongruity between his cultural and ideological background
and his pragmatic acceptance of the corruption of those with official power.
With a delicately historical sense of how such coercive complicities arise,
he attributes them to the fact that for a century and a half Romans had
been forced to "think with the mind of the county squire" (*pensare colla
testa del signorotto della contrada*) who operated in the murky stretches
of power between a cowed peasantry and an autocratic state. Here, as is so
often the case, culture provides a useful social etiology not unlike, and perhaps derived from, the casuistic invocation of original sin.

Despite the persistence of relations of reciprocity and collusion patterned in an older civility, the new civic order does make it much harder
for police officers to extract substantial favors from merchants and artisans.
A city police officer, a regular customer at a certain bar, professed himself
satisfied that there were no violations; but then one of his colleagues came
by and wrote out a citation (*verbale*) because, said this worthy, the owners
did not have a license to serve cooked vegetables (*verdura cotta*). One of the
waiters, a sophisticated young man who was studying anthropology (and had
actually done fieldwork on family systems in Austria!), told the first policeman about this, and the upshot was that the second policeman—who was
clearly trying to extort a bribe on the basis of a nonexistent violation (since
cooked vegetables are part of the contents of the sandwiches [*tramezzini*]
that these bars often serve)—was suspended from the force.

Traditionalists actually object to the changes in civic administration
that have made bribery so much harder. An architect whose studio had originally been a stable for a carriage and horses, and then a garage, had to pay
50,000,000 *lire* for permission to change the functions of the property. A
few years earlier, he complained, he could have had that amount—which he
regarded as truly excessive—halved simply by paying out about 3,000,000
lire in bribes. But today, he sadly mourned, people are more afraid of accepting bribes, especially as some city police officers have been caught and
punished. Whenever "they unearth someone in city hall who's 'eating,'"
remarked a restaurateur more sympathetic to the political left wing, there
is a huge row.

Some indeed still manage to resist the new civic order to their own considerable advantage. One powerful local operator manages, year in and year
out, to place his restaurant tables on the street in a way that creates a serious traffic hazard and is in clear and even demonstrative violation of zoning
ordinances. No one touches him because, said an irate right-wing former
district councilor, he is "protected." The councilor could, he claimed, have

even this well-ensconced malefactor punished. But to do so he would have
to make a complaint (the famous *denuncia* again) to four different sources
of authority: the mayor, the *vigili*, the *questura* (police station), and the
prosecutor's office (*la procura della Repubblica*). Then the city authorities
would be able—perhaps even forced—to act. Their best strategy, the councilor thought, would be to ignite the well-known dislike of the *carabinieri*
for the *vigili*; the *carabinieri* would happily seize such an excellent chance
to embarrass and punish the city police, while the mayor's office could bask
in the reflected glory of civic order upheld. At the same time the mayor, who
was acquiring quite a reputation for his ability to avoid dirtying his hands,
could avoid responsibility for the failure of the *vigili* to keep their side of
an illicit bargain—and would perhaps therefore also be able to avoid some
embarrassing act of revenge on the part of the infuriated restaurateur.

As a rightist who would himself have benefited from the more relaxed
procedures of the past, the former councilor was not willing to put himself
out to achieve this goal; he disliked the nominally leftist mayor and his
policies, longed for the older modalities of power and complicity, and saw
the ordinances themselves as a case of over-regulation and as an attack
on the local custom of dining in the open air in warm weather. But he
had the honesty to offer this view of the violator's relative immunity from
punishment: "He profits because there's general ignorance." "Ignorance" in
this sense means not only a lack of formal knowledge but also the generic
absence of respect for correct procedure.

Younger people generally have that knowledge and are therefore better
equipped to fight the harassment of bribe-seeking officials. They know their
rights, and they can insist on them while also allowing the latter to conde-
scend to their youth (but also themselves acting the role of children who
rebel against stern parents). This is what a young woman did when she realized what the city police officers' frequent visitations to her health food
store must mean. She was able to talk back in an impressively legal language, although her educated speech may have backfired in the sense that
it induced a correspondingly intense legalism on the part of the officers.

She also displayed all the self-confident casuistry that (as she pointed
out) marks the rebellious phase of a child's adolescent school career. As she
saw it, the officers' response was precisely that of parents who see that their
child has not yet reached full maturity—and that her stance worked to get
her what she wanted as a result. She also accused the police of interfering
with the development of new forms of commerce. There was some validity
to this charge; when the Bersani rules were introduced, simplifying the
criteria for obtaining shop licenses and thereby undercutting the malicious

pedantry of venal officials, those who knew just how much the regulations had changed could quickly turn the tables on their erstwhile tormentors.

The engagement of police officers in local social relations also provides channels through which extortion can be resisted. Having a friend in the service is, however, a back channel that recalls the older styles of civility. A well-established framer who kept insisting that there was no bribery in the area—and that such matters were in any case not for artisans but for merchants, given that the two groups have "different ways of reasoning"— was once pressured for a bribe by a city policeman through the usual tactic of writing a citation for some supposed traffic violation. He managed to get the matter settled by going to another policeman, who happened to be a friend of his. No bribery was involved, insisted the framer; he just made one or two picture frames for the second policeman.

My sense is that he did not want to admit to an outsider that such disgraceful acts marred the fine self-presentation of Monti. He almost certainly did not view his actions as complicit, however, since, as an older man, he was accustomed to thinking of tokens of appreciation as the normal means of keeping social relations intact. Similarly, a merchant of the old school, rather than invoking civic values, called on his friendship with some *carabinieri* to keep the *vigili* at bay; relying on the growing hostility between the two forces, he was able to maintain his reputation as a man of local social *savoir faire*—and no one asked what favors his friends in the national force might have expected in exchange. In each of these two cases, as also in the case of the shopkeeper who was continually being cited for zoning and environmental offenses, these skilled actors strategically exploited the institutional roles and structures of officialdom by drawing on local values and practices rather than on the explicit rules and norms of civic conduct.

By contrast, the young waiter–anthropology student showed how one could resist such pressures by instead insisting on basic civic rights; clearly it is much riskier than in earlier decades to seek or accept bribes, and the tide of fear can be reversed by anyone who understands the new dispensation well enough. The son of the owner of the same bar simply tells any *vigili* who come nosing around with suggestive frowns and winks, "Write me a fine! I'll simply contest it!"—the last thing they would want to make happen. These city police officers must always weigh the risks and benefits against each other. I once saw an officer hail a young couple speeding by on a motorbike with an ironic (and unimpeachably Roman) cry of "*Ahoo!*" There was a brief colloquy; then the motorbike turned around and sped on its way. I saw no money change hands; sometimes, apparently, the satisfaction of a civic duty properly performed, but couched in this friendly dialect idiom and carrying no mean intentions, is sufficient. Not all city police are corrupt; and none can afford to be on the take all the time.

Another person who preferred the more modernist response to pressure, an electrician, knew well that crooked policemen's tactics depended on the skilled cultivation of fear. He maintained that they tended to prey on older merchants schooled in an age when bribery was so normal that no one would have dared to refuse. He himself refused to play along, preferring to turn the tables on the importunate officers by making them nervous instead. Once, when a policeman told him to "give these lads a coffee," he mock-pretended—this was a double bluff—to understand the request quite literally but, instead of treating them to a real coffee, handed the officer a 50,000-*lire* note and told him, "I don't have time... [but] I'm treating you to a coffee!" This pointed response, a play on everyone's shared understanding of what "a coffee" really meant, was the perfect defense against future harassment.

One can also simply refuse to give corrupt officials an opening. Another bar proprietor pointed out that whereas one of his neighbors had an illegal collection of flowerpots out on a balcony and was frequently embroiled in threats and arguments as a result, but never got fined by the police, he himself preferred not to engage in such obvious challenges to a venal authority and so, for example, he avoided putting out tables on the sidewalk in what is a common act of defiance against public ordinances. At this point in our conversation, he cast his eye around seeking examples of trivial infractions—some dirt on the floor, his waitress daughter's uncovered hair: these would not get him into trouble because his otherwise detached comportment gave the officials no purchase and the fines could not be large enough to prompt him to become more cooperative.

But the request for "a coffee" is a different matter. The implications of an actual cup of coffee can also be metonymic in a more than verbal sense; they may be the prelude to larger forms of extortion, lampooned with ironic precision in the electrician's contemptuous gesture. He called the crooked cops' bluff; but others are not so canny, usually because they do not know their rights and dread the consequences of a protracted tussle with the bureaucracy. The miscreants initially act with what can only be described as decidedly civil manners, showing both consideration for the proprietor's situation and a pedantic legalism—both fearful weapons of polite, indirect, but unmistakable extortion.

In a classic operation, for example, the officers, having extracted that first cup of coffee or glass of Campari, may then musingly point out a series of real—or at least plausible—petty infractions. The officers then casually remark that they are busy at that moment but plan to return to do a proper accounting the following day. This gives the storekeeper enough time both to adjust the offending display and show an appropriate appreciation of the gesture—the play of temporality being the pivot on which the mutual understanding hangs. An act of pressure is presented as friendly generosity, with enough time for that realization to establish itself firmly in the storekeeper's mind. Extortion is framed as a voluntary and amiable reciprocity.

Not all such visits are so courteous. An elderly greengrocer, who calculated that he also spent between 7,000 and 10,000 *lire* a week on beggars who regularly dropped into his shop, would have to put up with the depredations of an officer of the city force who took between 30,000 and 50,000 *lire*'s worth of fruit and vegetables each week without even pretending to offer payment. The greengrocer did not dare to object; had he done so, he claims, the policeman would have sent colleagues from a different section of town, and the newcomers would have been sure to find any number of minor but punishable infractions: a missing price label, a can past the expiry date, a box that was not quite properly sealed. And for each of three or four such infractions there would have been a fine of roughly four or five times the entire value of the original policeman's weekly plunder from the store.

If a storekeeper or bar proprietor fails to get the point, harassment will continue until there is no more room for doubt. Even when the time granted is no more than the moments between the police officers' opening gambit and capitulation, a similar process of persuasion obtains: a ruminative stare gives way to the observation that there are infractions here aplenty, then the officers carefully stage a suggestive pause, to be succeeded by repeated expressions of consternation as more small illegalities emerge under their investigative eye. If even this has no effect, punitive fines are not far behind. Some say that those in the various food trades and goldsmith-jewelers are especially subject to this kind of pressure.

But bribery? What bribery? The *vigili* were simply, they would shrug, following through on the evidence they had found in the first place. Matters turned out to be even worse than they had expected, so they imposed the full weight of punishment provided by the law. But if the storekeeper shows respect and understanding, it becomes clear that there never was any infraction; everything has been arranged, between friends: the transaction is warmly civil rather than coldly civic. The tempi of citizen and bureaucrat sometimes coalesce in such seductively matched rhythms of common interest, dramatized in the common spectacle of police of various kinds ordering coffee in a local bar and having their patently insincere offers of payment waved away with the careful insouciance that bespeaks intelligent risk management. It is perhaps not coincidental that in music, and perhaps most notably in opera, the stylish delaying of tempo is itself described as a form of theft (*rubato*).

Some officers are themselves poor players. When the right-wingers in the Piazzetta club appealed to the *carabinieri* to arrest an immigrant who had struck a child playing ball in front of the church, and to take more generic action against the entire group of immigrants filling the square, they were dubious about getting results. This was not for any lack of political sympathy; the local *carabinieri* are visibly hostile to the immigrants and convinced that they, along with wandering Gypsies, are responsible for virtually all the petty crime in the area. But in a previous year, during one of the October festivals, a senior officer had supposedly helped himself to twenty sandwiches and then sent his daughter to get more; the club officials told him that he was welcome to eat but that he could not remove the sandwiches by the sackful. Since then, said one of the club's leaders, "when he sees us he greets us" (*quanno ce vede ce saluta*), but does not look them straight in the eye— and is unlikely now to do them any favors since his attempt to gain a special rake-off was so unceremoniously thwarted.

Polite forms of dissimulation are indeed essential in all such complex social transactions; that they are instantly recognizable for what they are only makes them more effective, since no one would wish to challenge a system of conventions that protects all concerned. An itinerant vendor explained how, at the various markets he frequents, some officers leave their car parked with its doors open; preceded by an implicitly menacing demand to inspect his documents, this suggestive move is implicitly interpreted as an invitation to deposit some new underwear and socks (but never money) on the seat. The system is a convenience in that all know the rules, explained the vendor: "Look, it's all done, and we're off and running!" In his view the tax police, though also respectful of the unspoken rules, are more demanding and their stratagems correspondingly more elaborate. When pressuring the vendor to pay him a heavy bribe, for example, one officer insisted that it be wrapped in a particular newspaper. He yielded to the pressure, he complained, "out of fear that they'd find [my unreported income], because they do find [such things]"; few citizens are in a legal position to resist. On the other hand, people generally assume that officials prefer to ignore petty illegality because, by putting more people out of work, they would simply magnify existing problems. The alleged kickback of 12,000 *lire* for each undocumented foreign worker, for example, not only protects the immigrant and saves the authorities from the embarrassments of having an arrest legally overturned, but also allows the local employer to stave off bankruptcy for a relatively small consideration.

Many merchants prefer to pay bribes than go to all the trouble involved in hiring a tax accountant (*commercialista*) and finding their way through the maze of complex legislation and bureaucratic procedure. In the same way, even the street cleaners on one of the large commercial avenues bordering the district expect a bribe of 10,000 *lire* per week simply to do their job; the probable consequences of a huge pile of garbage blocking the entranceway are too horrific for any business proprietor to hesitate for long. This does not happen on the residential streets because the balance between immediate necessity and the possibility of registering a complaint is quite different there.

Official rules, it is understood, are intended to be broken, or are used to benefit the citizen in practical ways from which complicit officials can also benefit. Strict legality may be irrelevant; a man who had arranged for the decoration of his newly acquired apartment, with all necessary permits duly acquired, suddenly found himself entertaining a visit from two *vigili* who would clearly be able to find some minor problem allowing them to halt the entire redecoration if he did not pay them off. What matters is less whether the citizen has broken any laws than that the officers almost always have greater authority to describe the situation in terms that will result in punitive fines.

But citizens are often as wily as the bureaucrats who harass them. City laws require bars to keep their toilets available for all passers-by regardless of whether they are customers; bar owners circumvent this by hanging a notice saying "Out of order" (*Guasto*) on the door, safe in the knowledge that regulars will understand the stratagem while strangers will indeed be discouraged from trying to use the facilities. During the summer months, when shops are supposed to maintain a rotation system so that one of each kind stays open in each section, a bar owner who simply wanted to take a vacation put up a notice announcing that he was ill. Locals understood this stratagem too. The *vigili* are the most local of police, and they and the citizens under their care understand each other perfectly. Mutual understanding is what social life is all about.

CHAPTER NINE

Tearing the Social Fabric

Major changes came to Monti and its residents in the 1980s and especially after the "liberalization" of real estate laws in 1998. The
sudden infusion of big money in the local real estate market opened up new
fields of action for the techniques of intimidation that had hitherto protected local people from true outsiders. Now it was the outsiders who had
mastered these techniques, and even improved on them. With the intimidation came a rhetoric of urban renewal and conservation; the response from
the remnants of the traditional left was predictably supine. Moreover, the
principal moral authority of the Right—the church—was soon deeply implicated, along with the developers and the city administration, in the same
processes of reorganizing the historic center as a source of profit. Few residents owned their homes; now, often after generations of residence, even
fewer could remain in them.

Renters and Owners

Rents had long remained low in Monti because old houses were not considered desirable habitations; the fashion for living in a historic district only
really emerged in the 1980s. In some parts of Italy, people living in the same
building had paid wildly disparate rents; the introduction of rent control produced the effect of raising the lowest rents by considerable amounts, bene-
fiting landlords rather than tenants. One of its goals had been to discourage
the practice of keeping apartments vacant and thereby aggravating the growing postwar housing shortage. In Monti, however, where the idea of living
in old houses had only just begun to seem attractive to a few highly educated individuals, the new uniformity of rent levels did not entail massive
change; it simply stabilized existing arrangements. Since a high proportion

of Monticiani had low incomes, moreover, the new dispensation, which made an artificial and arbitrary distinction between those with incomes of above and below 8,000,000 *lire* per annum, protected the financially weakest sector from eviction for a few more years. Most Monti tenants, already accustomed to viewing their low rents as an inalienable right, did not see the looming danger.

Unfortunately, one effect of this artificial depression of rents was to prompt some smaller proprietors to sell off their properties; they could not make enough money from them to pay for building maintenance and extract a living for themselves at the same time. Some landlords also decided to leave apartments vacant, arguing that they were not able to demand adequate rents (and could not compete with the black market); the money was simply not worth the effort. Some of these landlords decided to wait out the remaining tenants, speculating that the overall value of a palazzo would far exceed the sum total to be gained by renting or selling the apartments one by one. A few locals did buy out their own residential quarters, and these prescient individuals now live in relative security and prosperity as a result. Much of the real estate that changed hands at that time, however, was acquired by corporate speculators who could afford to wait.[1]

Because most shops and other work spaces were exempt from the *equo canone*, the requirement of the earlier law that in each building all rents be on a similar scale, some speculators were also able to raise the rents on these spaces by dramatic leaps in all the historic centers, including that of Rome; it is at this point that gentrification really begins with a proliferation, initially slow but then accelerating, of boutiques and artists' studios. While domestic quarters could not easily be converted into such spaces under existing zoning restrictions, the inflated rents that were demanded for existing shops and ateliers began to favor activities that required specialized skills, displacing the ordinary artisans who had hitherto provided basic services and goods for local customers who themselves could not afford high prices. In a few cases, moreover, proprietors could now demand a suspension of existing rental contracts on the grounds that they needed to retake control of an apartment for their own kin (not necessarily members of the nuclear household), whether as a primary domicile or for the purposes of economic activity.

Even a leftist councilor, however, argued that the poverty of these families was to a significant degree artificial. Current legislation gave proprietors the right to use their properties as they wished within fairly generous constraints, he argued, and many of those living in buildings that had been sold off by government or religious bodies had originally been able to acquire their apartments through connections with powerful patrons. In his view the older system of rent control had allowed—indeed, encouraged—entire families to depend on a single breadwinner, since a depressed collective income entitled them to the lower rent for which the new legislation provided. But this legislation was vague, excessively arcane, and penally toothless and encouraged back-channel deals against which it offered no effective sanctions—again exemplifying the way in which laws were created to benefit legislators as much as their electorate. It did allow some artisans to continue working close to their homes. The councilor, however, argued that there was something dangerously anachronistic in a situation that permitted a television repairman to continue to occupy a space for which an artist would be willing to pay much more money.

Thus it came about that a dedicated Communist found himself recognizing the logic of the market—not, he reasonably insisted, as an acceptable ideological stance, which perhaps for him it was not, but as an "ineluctable" reality—against a group of people he regarded, in part inaccurately, as right-wing freeloaders and therefore undeserving of his support. As a left-winger he could not very well attack welfarism (assistenzialismo) outright; instead, he decried the old rent regime as "paternalist" and linked the neofascists' exploitation of the tenants' current resentment to their lack of respect for the rule of law as evidenced in their support for those guilty of illegal building in the suburbs. Only ideologically committed right-wingers were comfortable about criticizing welfarism as such; and they, unlike the leftist councilor, showed no compunction about doing so, straightforwardly and relentlessly. But they chose not to see the protection of their constituents' residential rights as welfarist at all, representing it instead as a question of social justice and the patrimonialist preservation of authentic populations.

The councilor's position shows how massively the traditional Left had embraced a view of property ownership it had once categorically rejected. In practice, too, older forms of intimidation could now harness new legal knowledge and access to big money. An elderly lady fretted to her lawyer about the difficulty of understanding and paying off the utility bills, which can be a bureaucratic nightmare almost anywhere in Italy. He reassured her—"I'll take care of it" (ci penso io), said the sly fellow—and then proceeded to get her signature on what she thought were payment slips but that in fact were deeds transferring her apartment, room by room, into his unscrupulous hands. Despite the best efforts of a kindly priest to help her, she had signed her home away, and the law gave her no recourse.

The disclaimers of mafia-like activity or of evil intentions and the professions of friendship are excellent illustrations of how politeness can convey a sense—and often also the substance—of danger. Sometimes the threat is playful, or at least familial, as when a passionately committed Communist used to tell his family members, "Vote as you wish, but.... " But sometimes the politeness amplifies true menace. Just as racist sentiments are often prefaced by the very widespread affirmation, "I'm not a racist" followed the same demurral (però, "but . . . "), so the implicit threat of violence is all the more effective in conveying deep hostility in that it rarely results in serious action.[2] The disclaimers respond to a politically correct civility (as well as to a more diffuse desire to avoid direct confrontation), while the neatly framed racism—enacted through the very denial of its presence—plays to a particularly vicious form of localism: "Look how they are doing away with romanità," declaimed a self-professed rightist, exploding with anger at the connivance of the church in this process and denying that he had been a racist until "now, because I'm fed up with seeing these things."[3]

The anger is real, and potentially dangerous; but it still rarely entails serious violence. Indeed, even when an immigrant attacked a child in the main square, the collective response was to call in the authorities, and to declaim at length about the iniquities of drunken immigrants spreading garbage around a place the locals had worked hard to pedestrianize and reclaim for their own social needs, or to accuse the newcomers of dealing in drugs and promoting prostitution. Direct violence is far closer to the surface in the less salubrious suburbs, where official brutality—in the form of the cracked heads and sudden fires that accompany forced evictions—sets a dangerous example; there, too, it sometimes takes the form of exemplary punishments administered by the henchmen of disgruntled loan sharks. But in Monti, where the distant echo of such interventions is usually enough to keep people more or less in line, and where on the other hand the visibility that comes with a central location does act as a brake on the most direct forms of violence, it is easy to imagine that it could never occur.

The fear is no less real for being largely generated by hints and indirect threats, sometimes in vaguely worded nocturnal telephone calls. When local residents complain that they have been offered assistance in moving or subject to less subtle pressure by mysterious people with Sicilian or Neapolitan accents, or when unidentified people without visiting cards and glaring expressions profess only to be interested in coming to a friendly agreement with residents, conspiracy theories invoking southern underworlds easily come to the fore. This is fertile ground for the stereotypes that constitute the basis of internal prejudice in Italy. Some residents insist that they know these people are underworld thugs. They claim, for example, that the arrival of aggressive women loudly describing what they plan to do with the apartments when they move in is a classic mafia tactic. Others, more mildly, remark that strange men who sport expensive and gaudy cars and clothes and hint at powerful backers are probably mafiosi, but that it would never be possible to prove as much. Others again insist that such claims are nonsense, that they have never heard of serious threats or people with suspicious accents, and that in any case none of the major real estate firms would dare soil their reputations in so obvious a fashion. Was this an accurate representation, wishful thinking, or the defense of local cultural pride? There appears to be no clear answer, and the very idea has little more substance than a smoker's worried puff into which one might perhaps read the form of a question mark.

Lawyers and Illegalities

It is this besetting vagueness itself that creates unsettling fears of revealing too much. An elderly lady whose lawyer, she said, was working on getting her lease extended refused to tell me her current rent, which was presumably very low: "these are secret matters," she remarked, as she now faced eviction to some undesirable suburb. The need to introduce lawyers into the equation suggests a delicate operation in which tenants try to get the best deal they can; secrecy is important since proprietors presumably do not want any concessions they might make to specific tenants to become a precedent for further retreats from their capital accumulation.

Nor are the lawyers always quite what they seem. Two young women with little money who were far from home were living in a Monti apartment when the owner, who was paying no taxes and was violating their right of first refusal (as required by law), informed them that she was raising the rent and that they would therefore have to leave. Since they had no contract—the proprietress had preferred to remain officially in residence there, which also meant that they had been forced to retain their official domicile as their place of origin—they had only the weakest of cases. They could, said sympathetic friends, have filed an official complaint, either because the lease was made without a contract (and therefore constituted a form of tax evasion) or because they had in fact been threatened with violence. But the lawyer told them, "You are poor, for which reason you have no rights." The inference was clear: only through some further illegality such as bribery could the situation be resolved in their favor. Meanwhile, the friend thought, it seemed as though the lawyer was actually working in partnership with the proprietress. And socially, as the friend's partner observed, to make an official complaint would have been disastrous; with a single gesture or a glance

among their neighbors, he added, they would have been completely isolated, marked as people who did not understand the tacit local interdiction
against appealing to the authorities. Between the lawyer's cynicism about
their poverty and the local avoidance of legal action, they were caught in a
web of complicity that lends reality and urgency to the fears of many others
who are similarly facing eviction.

The threats may also come in quite an official guise. One resident received a letter ordering him to remove his goods and his person from the
apartment where he had lived for decades. The language was peremptory,
cold, and final. He was initially keen to show me the letter. When I asked if
I might copy the text, however, he was suddenly anxious, asking me not to
use any identifying data that might betray his identity as the source—not,
he assured me, because he was actually afraid of reprisals, but because, during his court appeal against eviction, he simply did not want to risk appearing to have gratuitously acted in any way the proprietors could use to
win sympathy for their own actions. The letter itself appeared to cause him
more indignation than fear. But the fact that he worried about what was
ultimately a question of impression management shows that fear hovers
around those areas in which people are uncertain about their rights.

This man was not afraid to serve, as I did, on a Monti Social Network
committee whose task was to draw up a full list of eviction cases in the
district and to explore both the possibilities for collective action and connections with activist groups working elsewhere in the city. In a context in
which those tenants who consent to sign termination agreements often
accept a gag order, however, he was clearly uneasy about the risks involved in
speaking too specifically about his own case. Silence breeds further silence,
enhancing proprietors' freedom to act with impunity; the committee was
forced to recognize that its lists would always be incomplete because some
residents, beset by fears as corrosive as they were inchoate, did not want to
lend their names to any initiative at all. While their fear was certainly lesser
than that of the victims of usury, its collective effect was somewhat similar:
it sapped the will to collective, civic action, already weakened by those who
had quickly accepted exit sweeteners (*buonuscite*)—arrangements with no
legal status or contractual basis, which could therefore remain untaxed as
long as the recipients were prepared to maintain their silence.

One resident who was prepared to hold out as long as necessary in order
to get the best possible price herself worked for a real estate firm and probably knew how much traffic the system would bear. She eagerly provoked
the representative of the company that now owned her building and was trying to evict her, mockingly challenging his claims about the huge sums he

purportedly had paid others to leave. To his hectoring boasts—"Here people have exited with money who had an eviction date of at most one year, and came out of here with hundreds of millions. Is that clear?"—she countered with reports of especially stingy deals. "But who?" retorted the increasingly exasperated real estate agent; and she was ready with detailed answers, flinging them at him in full view of the street. Battle was truly joined; this was but one rather public moment in a long, submerged negotiation.

Some residents actively connived in the scams that further breached the walls of civic solidarity. We once went with friends to look at an apartment that was for sale. The edgy young real estate agents' representative who received us, dressed in a formal suit and a loose necktie too broad for his thin frame, assured us that the present occupant would be happy to negotiate with my friends. It was here that I encountered the young woman who adopted the Madonna-like pose; she was clearly part of the action.[4] Her posture contrived to convey both the wide-eyed innocence of the victim who was begging not to be evicted as a result of the sale and the knowing connivance of someone participating in an obvious scam. Had she been alone, she might have made an entirely convincing play for our sympathy, but the young real estate agent's evident anxiety to make a quick killing introduced the poison of incongruity into the scene, throwing the harsh light of suspicion on the tableau. As the real estate agent eagerly suggested a possible exit sweetener for the waiflike young mother, my friends looked at each other with growing disgust, wondering what her percentage of the overall profit would be; whether victim or, more probably, conniving participant in the deal, she had allowed herself to be co-opted by the neoliberal invasion of old Rome that they, very progressive and decent folks who were simply seeking to live once again in their old neighborhood, profoundly detested.

Honest real estate agents have a hard time finding work; one novice moved from office to office for a whole year, utterly disgusted by prospective colleagues' glee at the scams they had successfully perpetrated against poor, bereaved, and ill-informed clients. Such honest agents can only work at the economic margins of their profession; but they do exist. Charges of mafia or camorra involvement may be little more than an attempt to explain the high incidence of fraud in a profession already locally perceived as responsible for traumatic change. On the other hand, the very frequency of these charges paradoxically disguises them by reducing them to a routine sensation. No one really knows how to identify real crimes amid the tabloid discourse of everyday conspiracy theories.

Uncertainty is a potent weapon. When we look at the ways in which proprietors and their legal counsel manipulate the formal apparatus of the bureaucracy to put pressure on tenants to move out of their apartments, we shall see that timing is often calculatedly unpredictable. Such cat-and-mouse tactics are all the more effective against a backdrop of uncertainty about the real identity of the new speculators. Fear feeds on an absence of clear and uncontested information.

Behind the fear of earthly pain lies a far greater fear, that of eternal damnation—or, perhaps more effectively, that of a protracted stay in Purgatory. The church has not always been above threatening the intestate elderly with precisely such eschatological consequences of failing to leave their real estate to the church. When this happens, the earthly consequences for the tenants can be correspondingly dire. A dilapidated property in another section of the historic center apparently passed into the hands of a local church in this way. The residents did not immediately see the danger they faced; to the contrary, a high-ranking prelate came in person to assure them that they should go ahead with whatever improvements they were able to make to the property in order to make their lives pleasanter. On the face of it, this seemed at least a politer approach than the usual tactic of proprietors who try to drive out poorer tenants who refuse to leave their homes by refusing to carry out necessary repairs. But the courteous interest of the church's agent turned out to be no more benign in practice; after some time had passed, the prelate reappeared, declared himself deeply impressed by the wonderful work the residents had done in refurbishing the building—and announced that as a result the rents would, naturally, have to be vastly increased. The tenants were in no condition to pay the new prices, and so the church proceeded to serve eviction notices.

This unedifying tale offers yet another illustration of how the practical experience of dealing with the bureaucracy of institutionalized religion provides a model for secular action. The original owner buys an accelerated path through Purgatory with the bequest (*lascito*); the new owners profess the kindliest and friendliest of intentions, only to reveal, with appropriate expressions of regret, their intention of taking full advantage of the tenants' predicament as well as the fruits of their labors. Fear is produced at two levels: first the fear of eternal damnation; then the fear of encroaching debt and a death far from anything resembling home.

I do not wish to challenge the piety of those who decide to leave their property to the church. Nor do I wish to argue that there is a centralized church authority that relentlessly pursues every attractive piece of real estate in the historic center. On the contrary, the principle of subsidiarity means that such actions and the morality of the way in which they are carried out are entirely the responsibility of a particular priest, prelate, or con-fraternity. But whereas subsidiarity actually serves the financial interests of the encompassing organization, which thereby acquires property of consid-erable and increasing value, the temporal fragmentation of local interests and identities places rent-paying residents at a great disadvantage. They have few and inconstant allies; their support often comes at the price of alienating other groups of potential supporters; and their legal position is terrifyingly weak, especially at a time when their erstwhile supporters in the traditional Left have themselves been seduced by the attractions of the market. Moreover, church representatives who are deeply convinced of the rightness of their cause come equipped with the keys of Paradise and a com-placent acceptance that poverty and suffering on this earth is one of the most hallowed means of access to eternal bliss.

One of the tenants in this building has been facing eviction during the current papacy. She moved in some twelve years earlier under conditions that were described in a press release as "very uncomfortable," and for which she agreed to undertake the necessary repairs and construction. She had accepted this arrangement after receiving assurances that she would never be evicted from the building. In commenting on the church's perfidy in changing its mind, the author of the press release offers one sentence that is especially revealing: "It is clear [that] times are changing and the market for rental rooms in a quarter like that of the historic center attracts the desire even of those who with so much zeal spread [the doctrine of] Christian charity." The bitterness is clear; the claims of supporting the charitable work of the church rings hollow because the new pope, as the release points out, had just published an article affirming the right to housing, and because the term "charity" reminds the victims of eviction that it is above all a church-based charity, Caritas, that supports the sometimes indigent immigrants in spaces that used to be inhabited by Romans of long standing. In this painfully imperfect world, charity itself is not unmixed with sin.

Tenants are adept at turning the theological rhetoric of the church against its official bearers. Believers and atheists can unite behind a chal-lenge to the church's right to interpret a scriptural image of Christ that its own actions betray. The residents of another nearby palazzo, also owned by a church institution, found themselves faced with near-collective evic-tion with the arrival of the 1998 law. The ecclesiastical proprietors served eviction notices on all the tenants except for a relatively wealthy hotelier who had recently arrived (one suspects that he may be been viewed as the advance guard of a new wave of residents) and a group of nuns responsible for the maintenance of a nearby church. Three families held out; one of the other tenants left after experiencing tremendous pressure despite being of a family that had resided in the building since the nineteenth century and the district since the seventeenth. In a bitter letter addressed to the new pope, Benedict XVI, one of the remaining tenants remarked, "I have read the Bible and at no point in it have I read that Christ told His disciples to go and enrich themselves. A hospice is not a hotel for wealthy people." The writer then entreats the pope to prevail on his priests not to put the remaining tenants out on the street.

But it is precisely in disputes over rights to living space that assumptions about cultural quality become significant. It is surely significant that the only tenants allowed to remain in this building were a handful of religious functionaries, who probably had little choice in the matter, and a single wealthy entrepreneur of precisely the kind that the new urban politics seems designed to accommodate. In this sense, the historic center has become a metonym of the larger disdain in which Romans are viewed elsewhere in Italy. Recall that those Lega Nord activists on Lampedusa with their hotel facility made it abundantly clear that no southerners need apply for accommodation there; they were not only expelling southerners from geographically southern territory, but were also refusing to take in even the people of the capital—an especially despised group in cultural terms.

Now the same thing is happening in Rome itself. The poor, with their local dialect and their rough intimacies, are being quite literally put out on the street, replaced by hoteliers and other entrepreneurs with cosmopolitan pretensions and a cultivated sense of national identity. The Church of Rome has become complicit in the expulsion of the Romans; in a real estate equivalent of structural adjustment, the economic as well as the cultural values of the Roman working classes apparently render them unfit to remain in the newly "restructured" historic center. In the next case to be considered, a case that acquired a certain degree of fame during a decade and a half of struggle, we shall see the same institutionalized disdain for a group of people who, like the church tenants just described, invested a great deal of personal effort in maintaining the fabric the proprietor chose to neglect. Their humble efforts, so redolent of their low social status, only made them more of an embarrassment; spatial cleansing was the only solution to the problem they posed to the new urban vision. In the gentrified urban paradise now under construction, working-class Romans who are expelled with their burden of accumulated cultural and economic weaknesses truly need not apply. Unless they radically change their status on both the economic and the cultural fronts, they will not be allowed back in.

Eviction and Evasion: The High Stakes of Time and Place

Throughout this book, occasional shocking hints of eviction have disrupted a surface calm of good humor, a breathtakingly beautifully built environment, and the city's claims to holiness and hospitality. The violence they entail is structural rather than physical. In Monti, a particularly desirable residential district and service area for government and tourism, the violent mass evictions that frequently lead to charges of police abuse in the suburbs are not a viable option. Instead, as elsewhere in the historic center, lengthy legal battles usually end either with the technical vindication of the landlords or with tearful surrender to sheer exhaustion in the face of threats and harassment.

Some of these evictions happen in an orderly and submissive fashion; these fail to attract much attention, but their frequency undermines the resistance of those who do not wish to go quietly. That is the most unobtrusive kind of violence—the violence of the creeping corrosion of solidarity. Other pressures are similarly muted. Intimidation can be both discreet and unrelenting; at some point residents simply give up. One favored device is a constant stream of rings on the doorbell at night—a technique of slow attrition that is especially effective because, given its small increments of minor nuisance, the police usually refuse to take it seriously even though it is illegal. A few cases of harassment by proprietors become more dramatic and obvious, usually because their central victims are elderly and infirm and thus satisfy the "folkloric" aesthetic that journalists–unhelpfully from the perspective of most of the rest of those evicted—find compelling as copy.

One or two cases acquire real drama from the determination of a few stalwarts to defy the new owners. Such is the story of the ten families left in the palazzo at 23, Via degli Ibernesi. Their protracted battle against eviction illustrates the dangers of initial success; as the affably accessible Green Party senator, Athos De Luca, told me in an interview, once a case achieves a certain visibility, this can actually work against the tenants' interests; the property value actually increases because of the reflected fame of the case, and astute proprietors are not averse to taking advantage of this, while at the same time blaming their tenants for having brought the increase on themselves through the fuss they have created. Moreover, corporate proprietors can afford to wait for far longer than can most private individuals; time is on their side.

On the other hand, I was told by a source inside the city administration, cases in the historic center of Rome involve so many special interests that tenants would in fact need some fairly spectacular publicity before the city government could be induced to intervene. So tenants in places like Monti are often caught both ways: they need the publicity, but in some cases that publicity can add value to the property and increase a proprietor's determination to sell or rent at a huge profit.

Eviction is the most brutally tangible evidence of the emergent new order. The stakes are enormously high: for the older residents, a way of life based on neighborhood and kinship is unraveling faster than they can grasp the magnitude of the threat; for the new entrepreneurs there are enormous profits to be made. The churches have their own reasons for carrying out evictions, and the city administration—clearly strapped for available spaces in which to house the growing population of homeless and indigent citizens—is unsympathetic to those who might make claims on its property. Such a person was the laundryman in the lane leading directly to the Colosseum. His family had been summarily dispossessed of their apartment during the Fascist years, when the grandiose excavations of the ancient city took priority over the lives of ordinary people and the beauties of Renaissance and baroque domestic architecture, but they were allowed to remain as tenants on a temporary basis. Then World War II supervened and the house was spared demolition; the postwar city government, however, then invited the Fine Arts Inspectorate to assume responsibility for the restoration of the entire stretch of street and adamantly refused to consider the possibility that the apartments belonged, ethically speaking, to the residents. The laundryman described this response as "an abuse that they're carrying on" (*un abuso che stanno facendo*), using the language by which the state ordinarily prosecutes citizens found to be in violation of zoning and conservation laws. But his rhetorical turning of the tables was of no avail in the practical sphere of gaining possession of his apartment.

The city government does at least try to house those who have already suffered eviction and have no other resources. Its failure to achieve adequate redistribution, however, coupled with the clear evidence of cooperation between the *comune* and certain big construction firms, can only create doubts about its real intentions. The church, too, which often sells off properties that it has inherited as bequests from childless or extremely wealthy owners, can make a legally plausible case that the proceeds will support charitable works; again, however, local residents are skeptical, to say the least. One bar proprietor conceded that the church was in the "front line" of charitable activity, but added that whenever its own economic interests were at stake it succumbed to its own self-interest.[5] Whatever the motives behind these sales, those who stand to profit the most are the large real estate firms that can afford to buy up entire buildings and take on the expense of restructuring the interiors as modern, luxurious residential units. They are also the architects, in more senses than one, of a major restructuring of social life in Monti, a process in which prices and real estate values rise rapidly and in which, in consequence, the original owners are clearly willing to collude.

These entrepreneurs know full well that the current residents will not surrender easily. They must expect delaying tactics, legal battles, barricades, and the involvement of a wide range of political forces. The officials who have the legal responsibility for enforcing legally confirmed eviction orders are often on good terms with those on whom they must now serve the eviction papers, partly because they have already supplied information that could be used to stave off the inevitable. Politicians on different sides of the ideological spectrum—people who would not be caught dead talking to each other in Parliament—find such complex events a useful venue for exchanging information and ideas; the lawyers for the owners and the tenants must treat each other with respectful familiarity, since failure to do so will damage both their reputations and their social standing.

Resistance to eviction is certainly not new. Most Monti residents have lived in rented properties at least until the 1970s. This is perceived to be a matter of culture (cultura); the rents had been static for so long that many residents were unprepared for the sudden and drastic increases of the 1990s. Hitherto, when a proprietor threw tenants out, they simply moved somewhere nearby. A few Monticiani have owned their homes for several generations; others, evicted in the earlier stages of the processes described here, have bought their way back into the neighborhood (although rarely if ever back to their original homes). But such cases are comparatively rare.

When struggles between landlords and tenants were purely local, the tenants could count on a certain degree of solidarity; neighbors would join forces with them, blocking the entrances so that the tenants could not leave even had they wished to do so. While such memories doubtless smack of the usual nostalgia for times of greater social cohesion, they also suggest that the landlords were more vulnerable to social pressures than today. In a neighborhood famous for its mixing of people of diverse classes and occupations, and before the exponential rent increases set in, the church was virtually the only proprietor capable of enforcing eviction without incurring severe social penalties.

For its part, the church had little interest in forcing the issue, since—aside from housing the large numbers of priests who came to Rome for extended periods of training and study—it could not derive from its real estate any substantial benefit beyond the more or less nominal rents it charged to its impecunious tenants. The old houses of Monti held little commercial value at a time when most upwardly mobile Italians sought space and light in relatively distant suburbs, and when the cost of reconstructing a small house in the historic center far outweighed that of building from scratch a substantial, airy home far beyond the Aurelian Walls. During two decades of massive post–World War II expansion (1951–1971), while the overall population of Rome increased by more than half, that of Monti dropped by a comparable amount.[6] The center was largely considered unsuitable for those aspiring to new wealth and power, and so there was little either to interest the ecclesiastical and bourgeois landlords or to attract the interest of entrepreneurs with larger ambitions.

The hope of maintaining a decent—if modest—lifestyle had seemed secure to the working-class majority of Monti until the last two decades of the twentieth century. Other segments of the historic center attracted tourism, fashionable shops, and upper-echelon bureaucrats, while Trastevere eventually became something of an American colony. But Monti remained relatively untouched by these changes. Its proximity to major archaeological monuments clearly was more of a liability than an advantage, given the power of the Fine Arts authorities to interfere with any building or reconstruction at the first hint of potential archaeological interest. This held the value of real estate down for much longer than elsewhere in the ancient core of the city. Few residents saw the writing on the wall, and, with the postwar building boom under way in the outlying suburbs, rents in the urban core at first rose slowly. But the illusion of security soon faded and died. Salaried civil servants and established intellectuals as well as artisans and shopkeepers, many of them financially unable to buy the properties in which they lived or move nearby, were caught by the sudden upturn in rents that began in the 1980s and soon reached astronomical proportions. Rent gouging is often described as usury (*strozzinaccio*) by rural migrants to Rome, since the landlords knew how desperate they were to remain in the big city. At that point, faced with a choice between eviction and exorbitant rents, many fled.

Gentrification and the Last Frontier

Twenty-three, Via degli Ibernesi, is an eighteenth-century palazzo housing ten small units; another fourteen had been deserted and secured under lock and key many years earlier. Its vicissitudes came to symbolize the civil cruelty of the gentrification of Monti: eviction of the oldest and weakest inhabitants, the capitalists' preference for leaving usable apartments empty over accepting lower rents, the inexorable power of the market to define the course of events. The case mirrors many of the features of Roman social and political dynamics: claims to having lived forever (*da sempre*) in the area; the leftists' failure to protect poorer citizens in the face of the neoliberal onslaught and the opportunism of the self-styled social Right in exploiting the leftists' discomfiture; the powerful symbolism of the Jubilee year as a vehicle for expressing and exacerbating hatred of the Vatican and of its role in the city; the play of compromise and the subtle management of time; the strategic invocation of historic memories and associations ranging from the ancient glories to the Jewish presence; the short attention span of journalists, especially those whose local roots made too deep an interest potentially dangerous to them; and the mediating role of municipal and other officials in both offering solace to the besieged tenants and easing them out of their homes.

It thus seems fitting to climax this account with the story of the Via degli Ibernesi conflict. Other struggles, notably that over the Angelo Mai school, which was occupied by squatters who put on theatrical and musical performances in order to raise funds to ensure their survival, were of more obvious significance to the district as a whole. A working group of the Monti Social Network, led by two planner-architects from one of the local university departments, put together a plan that would allow the school to revert to its former functions while also including space for local civic activities. Even on this important issue, however, there were dissenting voices; when the occupiers' activities began to disturb the peace and quiet of the leftist intellectuals who had come to live in Monti, it was they who were at the forefront of an outraged civic sensibility that demanded the squatters' immediate ouster.

One good friend of mine, an older woman of considerable local knowledge and political sensibility who had consistently lamented the passing of the true Left, was morally outraged when many of her fellow leftists refused to help the Via degli Ibernesi group on the grounds that these tenants had accepted too much help from neofascists. She had no time for such petty party loyalties. But even she ended up storming out of a Network meeting about the Angelo Mai situation in almost apoplectic rage at the group's unwillingness to countenance firm action against the squatters' unconscionable abuses (as she now saw them) of Monti hospitality; she lived near the school and claimed that the noise of their numerous musical and theatrical activities made it impossible for her to sleep at night. When, in 2006, the police did succeed in removing the squatters, it was in fact some far-right Alleanza nazionale Party activists who felt free to trumpet their own gleeful triumph, arguing that it was they who had achieved the removal of a public nuisance.

The occupation of the Angelo Mai school was of wide local concern. The building is considered one of the landmarks of the neighborhood, a place where many residents were educated, and its impressive approach through a high stone stairway offered one of the best views across to the Capitol. The ability of the Network to mobilize technical expertise as well as political activism around the project of reclaiming it for local, communal use was impressive. The project engaged local attention around a specific place of monumental significance for local people.

By contrast, the more diffuse and protracted complexities of dealing with eviction across the entire area, and indeed throughout Rome, do not so easily sustain collective attention, especially as the media have successfully cultivated an atmosphere in which sensational cases rather than overarching issues and principles take center stage. In this regard, it was precisely the eventual failure of the Via degli Ibernesi group to mobilize a consistent opposition to their forcible removal from a home of several generations' standing that is especially telling. Their story suggests both the power and the limits of the strategic uses of the past, just as it shows how processes of compromise both allow for peaceful resolutions but also ultimately are more likely to serve the interests of the powerful.

It is a story that must therefore be read in the context of larger events taking place throughout Italy. First, the legislation enacted, ironically, by a national government of the center-left coalition in 1998 to protect the rights of proprietors against squatters increased the pressures on local authorities to act against any tenants considered to be outstaying their contractual welcome. Previously, tenants could force proprietors to demonstrate pressing need (*su richiesta di necessità del proprietario*), and the proprietors would still be responsible for condominium fees, maintenance charges, and taxes, and this led numerous proprietors to offer their tenants the option of buying the apartments at reasonable prices. Some did take advantage of this, although it went against established habit. The new legislation changed this pattern forever, since now proprietors had legal means to evict without having to demonstrate that they actually needed the property for their professional or personal survival. For those proprietors whose tenants were still paying artificially low rents, this change certainly brought timely relief; it is also true that not all tenants were genuinely poor or lacking in alternative housing. But in general it was the collective survival of tenant families that now came into question.

Second, this situation, and the failure of successive governments to provide adequate cheap housing for workers throughout the country, produced an emergency that reached a crescendo in the Jubilee year and by 2005 was to threaten the homes of an estimated sixteen thousand Roman families annually.[7] And third, while the various housing rights organizations were appropriately focused on the massive evictions taking place in the remoter suburbs of the large cities, the eviction of families of the lower middle class from city centers attracted much less sympathy since most observers assumed that the tenants could afford to seek new housing without further support.

Via degli Ibernesi, a tiny, steep street interrupted by stone steps, affords a fine view across to the Capitol and over Piazza Venezia. This invests it today with huge real-estate potential and correspondingly high sale prices; in earlier times, however, it meant only that its youth could effectively decide who could escape from Monti through the windows in the lower facades of their palazzi and who would be condemned to turn and try to fight off their tormentors from some other rival street. A place of relatively poor artisans and skilled workers, it marked a social boundary separating the red-light area from the city center, much as the ancient Subura had been walled off by Augustus to prevent contamination of the better parts of Rome by the denizens of this ill-reputed, dark, sunken zone.

Perhaps we should not be surprised, then, that the evicted residents of Via degli Ibernesi saw themselves as a "reservation" of "Indians" or "natives" (*indigeni* or *nativi*) on "the last frontier" (*l'ultima frontiera*).[8] That such comparisons might be made of the northerners claiming a unique kind of indigeneity is certainly not surprising at all, given the popularity of such exoticizing metaphors in Italy more generally—but it is surely astonishing to meet it in the heart of a capital city.[9] In this sense Monti, and Via degli Ibernesi more than most of the area, exemplify the paradoxical mixture of marginality and grandeur that is the enduring condition of Rome.

Although none of the families remaining in the building were living in the direst poverty, it is also true that none owned any part of it. It belonged, in the Jubilee year, to the Bank of Rome—a powerful institution that had invested heavily in major municipal projects, including the most recent restoration of the Colosseum, and was also responsible for the management of the municipal coffers. Because of the bank's deep involvement in the city's financial affairs, the city authorities were reluctant to fight it directly, especially as the bank had solid legal grounds for its action under the new legal dispensation. This miniature community, with an identity forged in battle, thus acquired a significance out of all proportion to its minute size. Left-wing friends often seemed perplexed that I would be concerned with such a tiny unit within a larger crisis that, by 2004, had attracted the attention of the United Nations and led to the signing of a joint memorandum of understanding between a UN delegation of housing rights experts and the city hall.[10] They were particularly perplexed because the leaders of the group, Paolo and Loredana, had been more successful at getting the attention of what Paolo called *la Destra cittadina* (the citizens' Right) than of the leftist politicians who had traditionally been more concerned with such issues.

This dynamic explains much of what happened to the Via degli Ibernesi group, including its ultimate failure. The Left, once it gained power, lost a great deal of its erstwhile interest in such matters; the head of the tenants' association was an active member of the Democratic Left, the majority in the ruling parliamentary coalition, and it became clear around the time that I came on the scene that he would not back the residents' desire to remain *in situ* if the authorities managed to persuade the bank to offer the tenants adequate alternative housing. Although he continued to lend the tenants support, his position became increasingly untenable, as he had to represent a weak and complaisant governing party even as he was supposed to be representing the concerns of the residents to those in power.

Because Paolo was the scion of a well-regarded local family of committed Communists and his wife Loredana was the pro–Alleanza nazionale daughter of a relatively prosperous Sardinian artisan-artist, they had access to a surprising range of political support; but, by 1999, it had become clear that the more they dallied with the neofascists, the more the Left wrinkled its collective nose at their cause. The union lawyer and a prominent leftist city councilor continued to deal with the residents, although sometimes with apparent reluctance. Paolo himself became very irate with the leftists, accusing them of being "parlor pinks" (*radical-chic*). One impassioned leftist activist who sympathized with Paolo told me that in her view the left wing was losing touch with reality; its attitude of ideological purity was not going to solve any social problems, and clearly surrendered much of the initiative to the more scrappy young local politicians of the Far Right.

The case rapidly—if in very uneven fashion—gained the attention of various political actors as well as journalists and, eventually, anthropologists. At the height of the conflict I became actively involved in organizing a press conference held jointly with a group of politicians, and on this occasion, at least, they represented virtually the entire range of significant Italian political parties. Because I also knew Carla Rocchi, an anthropologist, senator, Green Party stalwart, and then junior minister in the center-left coalition government of the time and was able to persuade her, as a neighbor and colleague, to join in this activity, the press conference restored some degree of political balance. But the residents found it hard to shake off their suspicion of the Greens, since it was another prominent party member—and neighbor who lived on the opposite side of the street—who had managed to get the bank to react quickly when the entire facade of the building began to collapse. When he told the residents that their home was uninhabitable, they leaped to the conclusion that he was helping to add to the pressure on them to depart.

Green Party members were nevertheless interested in the case as it represented a human dimension of historic conservation, one of their public concerns. The families still left in the building were in some degree representative of the Roman vernacular culture, in language, food habits, and orientation to authority; and this gave them a degree of cohesion, despite the occasional internal rupture. As one of them said, "We are the last bulwark of a Rome that is no more. Of a people that no longer exists." The evocation of a locally grounded nostalgia exercised a powerful appeal to those who recalled Monti as a village, with all the social texture that this image implies; but there was also a more generic attempt to link the people of the palazzo with the ancient past. One former resident, confronting the lawyer of the bank that was then trying to evict them, bitterly suggested that the tenants were the last of the ancient Romans but that any tourists who came now would find none of them left.

Journalists certainly helped to publicize the case, but they were more interested in the picturesque and the sensational than in pursuing issues of social justice.[11] When the stand-off with the bank became particularly intense and the newspapers suddenly seemed to lose interest, residents also wondered whether some journalists, being under the control of a powerful local magnate who was also a shareholder in the bank, were afraid to write up the case, or had been specifically told not to do so. When I visited another Monti palazzo from which several people were being evicted, the journalists assembled for the occasion were only interested in one or two dramatic cases that would catch their viewers' and readers' immediate interest; their sensationalism was again a source of deep irritation to local activists.

Not that the Via degli Ibernesi residents refused to play the sensationalist game as well; indeed, they had little choice. Among the factors that attracted the attention of so many outsiders to their case was the plight of a woman in her nineties, one Vincenza Mari Cesari; in her youth she had been a remarkable beauty, and her bust still adorned the Palace of Justice. Now the residents recycled a couple of articles about her plight, published when she was already in her nineties, in which she showed herself to be full of enthusiastic recollections and high good humor. These articles, by now five years old, were faxed to Mayor Francesco Rutelli with a note pointing out that the old lady was still alive, still living in the palazzo, and still hoping for a reprieve from eviction.[12]

The long confrontation in Via degli Ibernesi began in 1986, when the Bank of Rome sent the remaining residents a letter announcing the termination of their lease (*finita locazione*). The bank never revealed its motives; residents suspected that some influential personality wanted to buy it in order to create a luxury hotel or some other lucrative venture. Indeed, Paolo at one point said that, had they wished to use it as a school or even as a new bank branch, he would respect their motives; but that if instead they were simply using it as an instrument of financial profit, "for me that's an [act of] infamy." The bank may have been nervous about zoning requirements that would have necessitated a special request to change the use of the building. It also became apparent that one of the bank's preferred methods for dealing with its recalcitrant tenants was to ignore their communications for as long as possible.

And so—silence; each side waited the other out. Then suddenly, in 1990, the bank requested "executive evictions" (*sfratti esecutivi*), according to a regulation that required them only to wait for three years after giving notice before proceeding to the actual expulsion of tenants. Three years, in the grand scheme of things, was not very long from the bank's perspective, but it gave the residents the time to organize their response and resistance and to come to an agreement—largely maintained thereafter—to work together for their right to remain in the building. The notices of eviction were served separately, doubtless in the hope that the individual families could be persuaded to negotiate independently, or that the differing dates of the projected evictions would make it hard to organize a unified response of any kind.

For a long time the bank had refused to renovate the building. At some point in the mid-1990s an employee of Cornice, the bank's real estate arm, told one of the residents, an elderly lady who had dared to complain about the appalling state of the building, "Would you kindly understand that you will have to go away?" The old lady, recalled her son, who also said that they would not have dared to speak thus to a male, "was not one to let herself be intimidated like that," and replied, "As long as I am here, it is my home, okay?" Taken aback by her stormy defiance, the employee backed off hastily and, in a more conciliatory mode, recalled that he, too, had lived in that building and that it was the scene of "my most beautiful memories." And indeed, a couple of years later, the bank began some repairs. These, however, proved both highly irritating and of little value to the residents; indeed, they were a continuation of the bank's pressure tactics. The builders left the interior wall plaster collapsing and ignored the apartments altogether; they had been forced by the tenants' complaints to deal with the mess in the central courtyard, a large space overlooked by the apartment balconies and by now home to a dangerous population of enormous rats; but, in so doing, they retaliated with the nuisance of a great deal of noise and mess while doing nothing to improve the internal living quarters.

Such actions only increased the tenants' resolve to hang tough. In 1994, the bank tried to open negotiations, offering homes in other areas as compensation, along with a cash sweetener. But the residents still refused to cooperate. For them, the scattering of their miniature community to far-flung suburbs would have meant social disintegration. The offer of "a miserable forty million," as one of them described it, seemed insulting. They turned the bank's offer down flat. Paolo recalled that the employee with whom they dealt, after first acting with complete arrogance, calmed down, and, like his colleague, admitted that he had lived in the historic center himself and understood the value of sentimental attachment. But this sympathetic comment could not reverse new changes resulting from legislation just enacted in parliament, as a result of which their troubles picked up speed and intensity.

Under the new legislation the bank made a judicial request for an intervention by public force (*forza pubblica*)—a request that would, in other words, have allowed the police to be brought in, using force if necessary to evict the tenants. The request was rejected. Then, on 4 March 1995, the bank appealed for police intervention, and the residents were officially notified. "This was when our drama began" (*In quel momento noi entrammo nel dramma*). Their lawyer warned them that they could now be forcibly evicted but that there was still an opportunity to leave with some measure of financial compensation and perhaps new housing. They refused: "we are not 'redskins' (*pellirossi*) to be moved around at will, they declared, nor are we 'postal packages' (*pacchi postali*) for distribution!"

To English-speaking readers, the "redskins" metaphor may suggest the influence of the tenants' neofascist patrons, but this kind of language is still quite common even in relatively enlightened circles in Italy and did not necessarily carry political implications of that kind. In fact, the rhetoric seems to have been effective; the *pretore* rejected the request for a forcible removal and the residents felt that "for practical purposes we had won." For the moment they were still able to rely on the older legislation; the bank had failed to produce evidence that it needed the building for some urgent purpose, whereas the tenants could argue that they found it necessary to remain together as a group.

But the bank kept up the pressure. It could afford to be patient, since evidently whatever profit it hoped to make from the eviction and subsequent reuse or sale of the building would far outweigh the minor financial loss caused by the delay. Its managers had numerous contacts within the police and refused to yield to what had seemed a final and authoritative statement from the police chief. Again, it had failed to reckon with the residents' determination.

Matters began to take a turn for the worse, however, when the police chief was replaced and his successor paid closer attention to the laws on squatting that had just been enacted in the national parliament. Here, too, we see the real beginnings of the residents' sense of having been betrayed by the left-wing establishment to which some of them had hitherto been loyal. The Alleanza nazionale was not slow to seize the opportunity.

From this point on matters became ever more tense. The tenants would receive notice of an impending eviction; the bailiff (*ufficiale giudiziario*) and the bank's lawyer would arrive, the former jocose and sympathetic, the latter studiously correct; the politicians—usually those of the Alleanza nazionale, occasionally a local *consigliere comunale* of the reigning center-left coalition with special responsibilities for housing issues—would gather; phone calls would be made; the prefect of police would announce that he did not have enough officers at his disposal that day; and the crowd would disperse, the tension gradually ebbing away, and the residents returned to their apartments and to a continuing but ever more tenuous hold on their residential rights. After a couple of near-misses, the bailiff even allowed as how he would never agree to serve an eviction notice on the old lady in her nineties. But he kept the tone light as well; when he heard that the police had demanded to speak with Paolo and Loredana "in private" (*in privato*), he remarked that one only did that with one's wife! His constant good cheer and friendliness did a great deal to keep the tension from boiling over; the tenants saw him as a friend whose unfortunate task it was to oversee their eviction but who would at least try to warn them in advance of any underhand moves by the bank, while from the authorities' point of view his puckish humor defused potentially explosive confrontations on more than one occasion.

The bailiff's role was both conventional and inventive. He was from the Marche, and in this he followed a well-established tradition; at least from the very early days of the Italian state, allegedly in order to escape the pressures and even possible reprisals that locally born officials might have had to face in a position that was described to me as "a socially objectionable job," bailiffs had almost always hailed from that region—so much so that a local proverb claims, "Better a corpse in the house than a Marchigiano waiting outside the door." Joking allusions to this proverb and the bailiff's distinctive Marche speech aside, his long engagement with the local community was a resource for both sides. This particular bailiff had been a friend and customer of Loredana's father, so that there was already a social relationship in place. From time to time, said Paolo, they met socially: "I go there [to my parents-in-law] for lunch and we chat, he [the bailiff] explains things to us." While this occasionally allowed them to anticipate trouble, the bailiff had no real power. Rather, his usefulness to both sides lay in the fact that by giving the residents time to organize their political support he helped to deflect situations in which the police might have used physical force. It became clear over time that no one really wanted such a development—least of all the bank, which probably feared that it might alienate local investors.

The bailiff's moral sympathies seemed to lie largely with the residents. Although his powers of obstruction were limited, he could sometimes be quite effective simply by refusing to make himself available. Since evictions could not be executed without his presence and signature, his conveniently busy schedule saved the day for the residents on at least one occasion in 1996. In the same way, whenever the bank's lawyer requested the intervention of *forza pubblica*, the police commissioner could always claim—as happened several times—that he did not have sufficient men at his disposal to enforce the eviction. He, too, contributed to the delays, usually under the logic of avoiding a violent scene that might have embarrassing consequences and perhaps become the basis of legal action against the bank.

Although the bank occasionally threatened to sue the authorities for their failure to act, the caution displayed by the various officials was both legally and politically wise. To evict an entire popular building (*palazzo popolare*)—a living metonym for a whole social segment of the Roman population—would have provoked serious unrest and perhaps unleashed more violence in other parts of the city. The more famous the case became, the more difficult was the task of those charged with carrying out the eventual clearing (*sgombero*) of the inhabitants and their possessions. And they were also under political pressure; Senator De Luca, for example, never one to let the grass grow under his feet and by now palpably concerned about the growing threat to the residents, had apparently warned the authorities against precipitate action. A parliamentary inquiry was the last thing they wanted, and the local publicity was by now intense; the two newspapers that had extensive coverage of the first major stand-off, in late January of the Jubilee year, sold out rapidly at the newsstand in Monti's main square.

The legal requirement that notice be given in advance also contributed to the long duration of the struggle. On each occasion, it gave the residents enough time to organize their defense, both legal and political. In anticipation of one attempt to evict the tenants, one of them told me—this was on 14

October 1999—that the first eviction was scheduled for exactly two weeks later, with his own to take place considerably later. Technically these dates were computed on the basis of the legal documents pertaining to each lease, but the suspicion prevailed that in reality the authorities were attempting a divide-and-conquer strategy. Yet at this stage the tenants still had one ace up their collective sleeve: the Jubilee, which figured prominently in their public pronouncements, was also very much a part of the public discourse about the housing emergency. As a result, appeals had a relatively good chance of succeeding during this period. The representative of the tenants' association planned to appeal the eviction order on a legal nicety: the fact that the first evictee had been paying rent to the bank continuously for the previous eleven months and that the bank had accepted this payment without demur. His strategy was really nothing more than a delaying tactic; as the union was allied to the governing leftist coalition in the national parliament, it seems that it would never take more aggressive action of a kind that might be taken as critical of the government.

But at least the move achieved its more modest goal; nothing happened on any of the tenants' respective deadlines. The woman who faced the first potential eviction, for example, was given until January. Others were again given variable dates. The couple who had expected to leave on 8 November received no extension, but hoped that the bailiff would still give them an extra two weeks in light of the arrangement made with the other tenants; that very brief extension would have forced them out a mere two weeks later. While the tenants expected that these extensions, too, would be stretched further because of the Jubilee, they all knew that even an extended respite could still only be temporary.

Yet their range of options was limited. They continued to apply similar tactics all through the following four years. They were convinced that it was not only the bank with which they had to deal. They also saw in their plight the long shadow of Vatican power. Proof was not to be found—a circumstance that itself constituted a presumptive proof in the residents' eyes; the fact that the Bank of Rome had originally been part of another bank, the Cassa di Risparmio, that had in turn been created by the Vatican's Bank of the Holy Spirit, created fertile ground for such speculations. It was easy to see the Bank of Rome's real estate company, known as Cornice, as a "fictitious company" that stood in for the Vatican, and to assume that it was either the church or some wealthy personage for whose benefit the property was now destined. The leaders of the tenants had worked hard to uncover evidence that would trace the banks' ownership back to a bequest to the church. Such a discovery would have strengthened their cause since Italian law does not permit such bequests to be used for purely financial gain. But their efforts were not successful. Cadastral documents provided no insight; there are still debates about exactly how much of the real estate in Rome the Vatican owns outside its own perimeter. A family named Chiassi, Roman subjects of the Papal State who became Italian citizens after Unification, owned and eventually, after 1870, sold the building—possibly in redemption of a debt—to the Cassa di Risparmio. But conclusive proof of direct church involvement was not to be found.

In their desperation, the tenants appealed directly to the church for support, thinking that if they could enlist the sympathies of the highest ecclesiastical authorities they might be able to break the will of the bank. They made no mention of their suspicions about the Vatican's historical involvement in the bank's ownership of the property, but tried instead to appeal to the ecclesiastical leadership's moral authority and to its special mandate in the Jubilee year.[13] When Loredana called the Vatican, she was told to go to her parish priest. This, her husband bitterly observed, was pure buck-passing (scaricopallone). When she explained that she wished to draw the pope's attention to the fact that the bank was about to put ten families out on the street, the response was cold: "The Holy Father does not deal—okay?—with such matters." Finally, again invoking the Jubilee (with all its implications of generosity and forgiveness), the tenants tried to make a written appeal to the pope himself. They received an unhelpful response from an auxiliary bishop in the offices of the vicariate of Rome to the effect that the church—ever faithful to the rules of subsidiarity—could not intervene, but that the Holy Father would pray for them.[14] Outraged, one of the tenants put up a bitterly sarcastic notice that read, "Property of the Bank of Rome—Thanks be to God, now we can rest easy; the Holy Father writes to us that he will praying for us evictees—so much the better."[15]

They continued to put pressure on the secular authorities as well. They accosted Mayor Rutelli on a visit he made to the district, his wife's birthplace and an area in which he had himself spent part of his childhood; ironically, however, while Rutelli appeared responsive at the time, the association with Monti of this bourgeois leftist from Parioli might actually have led him to view gentrification as an ideal development, and such a perspective certainly would have been consistent with his overall policies. A housing rights activist described the larger housing emergency in stark terms: that, while the city authorities were not building low-income housing, they were providing financial help for construction on public land "to build houses that would then be sold at high prices, forcing families capable of buying them to pay for mortgages of twenty or thirty years' duration."

And so, he pointed out, "the policy of the city government is thus all in the direction of the construction magnates." Such, then, was the policy pursued with increasing visibility by a city administration that had won power on a moderately left-wing platform.[16] But this was a pattern of involvement in the construction industry, he said, that went back many years, regardless of whether a particular mayor was of left- or right-wing persuasion or somewhere in between; and he also identified as particular partners in the ownership and profiteering management of the city's "heritage of real estate" (patrimonio immobiliare) both the Vatican and the very bank that was trying to evict its tenants from the palazzo in Via degli Ibernesi.

Undeterred by such ironies, however, the residents subsequently sent Rutelli and his housing chief (assessore alla casa), Stefano Tozzi, a series of reminders of their plight. An Alleanza nazionale city councilor cornered the mayor on the tenants' behalf and demanded action, to which Rutelli replied, "But what can I do? I've written them a letter. And they don't answer." The bank's silence, which was no doubt legally judicious, also gave the beleaguered mayor—whose left-wing credentials were beginning to wear distinctly thin in the media—a partial alibi for his own failure to intervene or to challenge the bank's position in a more proactive way, and an effective cover for his own possible embarrassment at being asked to do something so much at odds with his neoliberal vision for the city. A plan to have the city buy the building from the bank and then provide subventions for those who could not pay the rent, while agreeing on a reasonable rent for the others, did not last long; the bank's asking price was evidently far too high.

Another Green Party senator had by now entered the fray. Athos De Luca described the Ibernesi group as "emblematic," a term then adopted more broadly in recognition of the group's internal social diversity. When I first spoke to him about the case he knew few of the details. Initially worried that the inhabitants might turn out to be a group of relatively well-to-do professionals, he was nevertheless soon reassured that they were indeed "this settlement that is such a cross-section [of local society]." Although his response invoked the usual nostalgia for a lost class symbiosis, he also more concretely recognized that inner-city populations, no matter how unruly, were an under-appreciated social resource.

Against the ineluctable depopulation of the historic center of Rome, De Luca cited the dramatically contrasting case of Naples, with a historic core still heavily populated by working-class families who would rise up in revolt at any attempt at mass eviction. Acknowledging the serious crime problem in Naples,[17] he nevertheless described this complex of people and architecture as a "great heritage" (un grande patrimonio).

Rome, he suggested, provokes concern for two reasons: first, because such radical demographic change "creates a cultural but also a social rupture"; and second, because the 1960s building boom that led to the creation of huge new suburbs on the outskirts of Rome created "the death of a [social] style (*stilicidio*), which got worse again during the last few years and which . . . has struck the residential quarters but also the commercial activities and especially the artisanal trades, which are the weakest link. And the historic center has become more of a shop-window for big firms, like the banks, which have all these outlets, to hoard big real estate properties and so on, the very point of which is ultimately not understandable. [It's] more of a shop-window for them. A symbol of power. . . . No one ever goes there; these are dead offices."

The new speculators rebut such nostalgic visions, claiming instead that they are improving neighborhoods rather than destroying their social fabric. Their argument, however, ignores the class-driven nature of gentrification, the beneficiaries of which have succeeded less in abolishing crime than in getting rid of its ruder or more obvious manifestations. More charitably, it is about replacing an extremely localized working-class culture with a wealthy cosmopolitan lifestyle. The palazzo in Via degli Ibernesi was emblematic, not only (as De Luca argued) of class cohabitation, but also of a decidedly ordinary lifestyle that was far from the picturesque imaginings of either the new inhabitants or the media. De Luca elegantly called the erasure of this everyday idiom stylocide (*stilicidio*); it is the erasure of a decidedly ordinary civil order by a market logic dressed in the guise of a universalizing, globalizing civic ethic.

De Luca tried to get a parliamentary motion tabled, in the hope that this would at least create some media attention. He also proposed investigating whether some of the funds earmarked for the purchase of homes for the destitute might be used to purchase this palazzo. While the residents were certainly not among the truly poor, he argued that they preserved a social fabric of considerable diversity. Paolo frequently played on this theme, recalling, for example, a marchioness who had bought a palazzo in the district in 1969 because she wanted to live among the common people—although, he conceded, she was rather aloof and did not mix with the locals despite a courteous interaction with Paolo himself: "The difference is that she belongs to a social class very different from mine. . . . There's a family crest, d' you see?"

This lofty lady had in fact, as Paolo acknowledged, contributed to the gentrification now under way, involuntarily though it may have been. There was a "good relationship"—but . . . (*però* . . .)! That familiar old disclaimer says it all; the working-class neighbors were quite put out when, after a

Fig. 6. Putting up the barricades: rightists as social activists. (Photo by Cornelia Mayer Herzfeld.)

burglary at the marchioness's house, it turned out that she had given her keys to a newly arrived American rather than to one of the local neighbors whose terrace gave a good view of the place. These real-life experiences did shed a harsh light on the historical thinness of the nostalgic gloss of class cohabitation.

De Luca's and others' appeals to that ideal image, moreover, made no more dents in the bank's silence than did the formal protests emanating from the mayor's office. The residents had meanwhile also appealed to the President of the Republic. His staff placed their documentation in files marked "social solidarity"—and that is where it stayed.

I accompanied representatives of the tenants to two meetings in the Capitol, where, amidst the imposing ruins of the ancient council chambers and the echoing heraldry of the city's grandly reconstituted history, they tried to find a way through the bureaucratic machinations of the modern state and city. Municipal housing chief Tozzi and city councilor Nicola Galloro, who had special responsibilities for eviction cases, also graciously consented to discuss the issues with me; their comments provided considerable insight into the city government's inability to reach a resolution that would have allowed the tenants to remain close to their beloved streets,

monuments, and friends. In particular, they had to work within a legislative framework that had emerged with parliamentary consensus but that
could now easily be represented by rightists as, ironically, evidence for the
parliamentary leftists' complicity with the interests of big capital.

On 2 February, 2000, the Alleanza nazionale supporters of the tenants,
along with several of the women from the palazzo, staged a noisy symbolic eviction of the bank itself at its nearby branch on Via Cavour. It was
a propaganda coup for the party; one of its local activists, Federico Mollicone, who was later to play an active role in organizing barricades in front
of the palazzo,[18] again and again harangued the crowds over a loudhailer,
denouncing the bank's social irresponsibility.

Fig. 7. "No to Deportation." (Photo by Cornelia Mayer Herzfeld.)

Among those present, Mauro Peloso, a local councilor and relatively moderate Alleanza nazionale party loyalist, argued that it was the banks who were the "legalized usurers" (*strozzini legalizzati*). Meanwhile a woman activist who was handing out flyers at the demonstration, evidently a little disconcerted by the obvious embarrassment of some of the passers-by, said to one man that he should "let it go" (*lasci stare*)—that is, not be upset that this was a Alleanza nazionale event, but take the flyer anyway. She also told me that she was not a party member but a "republican," that Italians had a "social conscience," that the Italian state "needed a complete makeover" (*è tutto da rifare*), and that one of the local Alleanza nazionale leaders, Fabio Rampelli, who was also deeply implicated in his party's activism on this case, had "a truly local knowledge of the territory"—all elements that, taken together and in conjunction with Peloso's remarks, revealed the split-level orientation of the party: defense of the poor against the banks and the church locally, reactionary conservatism nationally.

It is a pragmatism—or opportunism—that disgusts those, at both ends of the political spectrum, who claim to prefer complete ideological transparency. The extreme visibility of the protest, which highlighted the contradictions of the neofascists' approach, thus created problems of image credibility for the tenants. While Paolo, for example, thought that the Alleanza nazionale had helped to increase public knowledge of the bank's perfidy, others were decidedly disconcerted by the party's unabashedly self-serving exploitation of the situation. The embarrassment of so many passers-by dramatized the difficulty of promoting a neofascist entity in a "red" district, a task made no easier by the fact that Loredana's father was just then launching a campaign to restrict immigrants' alleged degradation of a favorite park area. On the other hand, the expected police contingent (*forza pubblica*) once again failed to materialize the next day, when the next eviction attempt had been scheduled, which suggested that the strong party showing might have achieved some impact.

Mollicone's remarks had a distinctly party-political flavor: "The Bank of Rome, as an institution of the banks that manage the finances of Rome's city administration, is evicting the residents of the Rione Monti. It's the umpteenth demonstration of the Rutelli administration," which he said was indifferent to its responsibilities toward the citizens in its care and to the importance of historical memory but was evicting long-term and elderly residents for the mere purpose of "the umpteenth building speculation" and of creating a "huge open museum" with banks and shops for tourists. The party, said Mollicone, stood instead for the importance of "continuing a system, an integral memory" (*un sistema, una memoria integra*), perhaps not so unintentionally evoking the language of far-right "integralism," with its appeal to a populist localism that excluded immigrants and critical intellectuals.[19]

This position looked distinctly disingenuous from the other end of the political spectrum, given that the 1998 law had been introduced precisely because the right-wing parties had, so Tozzi noted, regarded the previous legal arrangement as "too protective of the tenants and not sufficiently protective of the landlords." Even though both sides had voted for the newer law, however, it was on the left wing's watch that it was enacted, so that the Alleanza nazionale politicians on the street were able to blame the Left for its social consequences.

There was certainly no reticence about the party's identity either in the banners or in Mollicone's speech, and this rightist politician's evocation of social conscience was clearly intended to embarrass the left-leaning city leadership: "The Alleanza nazionale denounces the Rutelli administration's complicity and invites all citizens to boycott the local branch of the Bank of Rome. It is unacceptable that for reasons of speculation and profit elderly people living who have lived for decades on condominial terms [that is, with the special guarantees that condominium residents enjoy] in the Monti district should [now] be sent packing and deported, perhaps to end up in some municipal residence or in one of the outlying suburbs." And once again came the attack on the freezing of the historic center in historical time: "We do not wish for it to be deformed into an open museum." (In a nice irony, an opulent-looking "museum shop," a private enterprise labeled thus in English, formed part of the backdrop to his soapbox oratory.) Mollicone took care to attack, not the bank as a whole, but its local branch; a cynic might wonder whether this was a clever ploy to reduce the pressure on the bank while appearing to sustain it. If so, it was doubly devious; for, by focusing his rhetoric on the social aspects of the confrontation, he claimed the moral high ground for his party, then in opposition both locally and nationally. The left-leaning national government had, in De Luca's words, "few means even of an instrumental kind to take action." Leftist politicians and their supporters, thus outflanked on their habitual turf of championing social causes, found themselves with few options other than to show up only when eviction seemed imminent—which at least allowed those with municipal or district constituencies to look actively sympathetic to the elderly and disabled.

Local public opinion was oddly fragmented. The leftist alliance, its increasing inconsistency rather ignominiously exposed, was understandably disturbed by the rightist politicians' visibility, although a few purists, feeling that the leftist parties had foolishly betrayed traditional principles, were prepared to express some cautious sympathy for the tenants' plight. On the other hand, the tenants also discovered that neofascists' support for their cause had some suspicious flaws; one of their erstwhile supporters from the party turned out to be an employee of the very bank that was trying to evict them, while the right-wing coalition's victory in the regional elections of 2000 meant that the new regional administration, too, now had to work closely with the bank, which managed the finances of region and city alike. On the whole, however, leftists saw the struggle as an Alleanza nazionale cause from which they should keep their distance.

The tenants thus did not enjoy complete local support. Critics thought that they had operated "on the basis of a welfarist culture" for far too long; they had paid ridiculously low rents and now expected the bank to let them stay on without a reasonable increase. The tenants, on the other hand, argued that the bank was simply speculating at their expense on an expected rise in property values, and saw the low rents as "an inverse speculation" in which the bank intentionally kept their current rents artificially low because, to justify the eviction, "they want to make it look as though we pay very little."

While a few local leftists were openly sympathetic, most, following the more usual Roman habit, declined to become involved. Not all were upset by the tenants' increasingly monochromatic political affiliation. One neighbor criticized those young and upwardly mobile tenants who had moved away, leaving their elders—the majority of the current residents—to face the decline of their old homes. This artisan-merchant pointed out that he, while paying a high rent in a relatively nearby and affluent suburb, had continued to receive an absurdly low rent—about one-ninth of what he was paying for his suburban home—from his tenants. He did this because they were Monticiani; he felt it was better that locals should live there, even if he stood to lose a great deal of money (and of course he was under much less pressure to spend money on improvements as a result, since the tenants would have been afraid to rock the boat). He was even willing to contemplate selling the house to his tenants, but they declined the offer and ended up living far outside the city—a common pattern. Because he had been entrepreneurial himself, he found it hard to sympathize completely with people like his tenants, or indeed those of Via degli Ibernesi, all of whom had in his view buried their heads in the sand and were now facing a disaster they could have avoided had they sought alternative housing in time. He had acquired his own house in Monti, where he had previously lived on a rental basis, when the previous owner, under the previous laws, decided to sell off the property and offered it to him at an affordable price—a good deal for both sides.

But the Via degli Ibernesi tenants had never been offered such an option. Their proprietor was an institution, not an individual; indeed, many voices were heard during this period complaining that, while they could understand an individual's desire to use a *patrimonio* to house relatives, they opposed the idea that a bank or similar institution, with no real investment in local social life, could claim the same protections as a private owner. In the one meeting at which representatives of the bank consented to meet with the tenants and various officials and politicians, they had simply asserted that the bank was a private entity and therefore had no obligation to participate in social management. To the tenants' protest that the bank also had social responsibilities toward the city whose finances it managed, the bank's representatives responded with silence. Their tactic was to refuse all accountability beyond that specifically laid down in law.

The day after the protest, an eviction was scheduled, although no one seemed to know which family it would affect. Even though Paolo was able to find out that no action was likely, he prepared for a siege, and was ready to call on "three hundred armed people" to come to the tenants' support. Given that a major television station was also suddenly taking an interest, the visual aspects became important as well, so he decided to "dust off" (*ripolverare*) an old banner with its defiant slogan: "NO TO DEPORTATION." And he turned again to his supporters in the political world; while De Luca was already hard at work drumming up interest in the national parliament and arguing for the case for a further stay of eviction at the headquarters of the police administration, the Alleanza nazionale activists—from the local councilors to the vice president of the national party, Senator Giulio Maceratini[20] —started showing up in force the next morning. It would have been a foolhardy bank indeed to challenge such an impressive array of political weight.

The bank's representatives were nowhere to be seen. At around 10:30 a.m., after a rather visible series of calls between the local politicians and the police authorities (cell phones figure prominently in such public dramas), Paolo suddenly reported that he had managed to find out that there would, after all, be one eviction that day. He still did not know whose apartment was involved. The young Alleanza nazionale activists immediately hauled barricades into place around the front door, and the shutters of the ground-floor apartments were firmly closed. One of the residents, an older woman, now produced a jug of steaming, sweetened coffee for all those who had come to support the tenants.

After a period of considerable tension the threatened official force appeared—in the shape of a somewhat sheepish single policeman in street clothes, who soon discovered that this eviction, too, was to be postponed. The bailiff appeared and, playing the drama to the hilt, presided over the signing of documents attesting to the postponement. All of us who were present (except the diplomat husband of another anthropologist who happened to live nearby and had also come to watch) were asked to sign as witnesses to this document. Once this was done (and after the son of one of the residents remarked that we should place the videotape I had made of the scene in a time capsule), the tension and the crowd quickly ebbed away. It was by now 12:30 p.m. and people returned to their daily lunchtime routines. Another crisis weathered, the residents resignedly prepared themselves for the next round. As Peloso remarked, one should never relax one's guard, because the bank could easily take advantage of a moment of relative quiet to force the tenants' hand.

A photojournalist who had come to record the scene remarked to me that the entire sequence of negotiated steps was "one of those typically Italian things"—by which he evidently meant the pattern of temporizing and compromise. "It's a way of moving things along under the table, right?" he observed, adding that it "was a way of resolving matters bit by bit." In this he was entirely prescient; the tenants' optimism was to prove short-lived. But he also noted that if a police officer had actually used violence, the only way to file a complaint would be through the testimony of an officer of equivalent rank—which would be all but impossible to obtain. As he rightly implied, the long-term prospects were much grimmer than might have appeared to be the case on that crisp February day.

There were other reasons for concern as well. De Luca may have inadvertently complicated matters with his proposal that the city authorities buy the palazzo and then rent the apartments to the tenants at affordable prices. There was already another proposal on the table: that the authorities simply move the tenants to another of the buildings it owned in the city. Faced with a choice, said one observer whose wife worked for the city's housing bureau, the politicians would probably do nothing at all. Endless discussion of alternatives can be a useful tactic in itself. Moreover, if either proposal ended up being adopted, this would be a precedent—and perhaps a dangerous one from the authorities' perspective, since other evictees would demand comparable treatment.

The other danger lay in a legal variant of the fallacy of misplaced concreteness. Documents have a long history of symbolic force in Italy, as in so many other countries that have suffered dictatorship; even after the fall of Fascism, the Christian Democrats, in power for two and a half decades after the end of World War II, were notorious for keeping all suspected leftists *schedati* (filed away). Such experiences invest formal documents with a materiality that may be deceptive; and so it proved in this case. The many signatures to the document signed that day may have carried a measure of moral authority, and Paolo confidently asserted that the politicians had "committed themselves concretely to the resolution of this problem." But this confidence was certainly misplaced, because the document also allowed the politicians to say that they had done their best but also to claim that they could do nothing further in the face of bad faith, existing laws, the logic of the market, or several other varieties of convenient moral alibi. In the end, the document made very little difference to the outcome. Unfortunately for the tenants, the photojournalist who saw the whole process as a creeping resolution of the stand-off, and one that would not favor the tenants, had been far more realistic.

Paolo, too, recognized the element of prevarication, although he obviously hoped that this would work in the tenants' favor as matters had once again not escalated out of control. An uncle of his had become deeply impassioned in the confrontation, at one point threatening the bank's lawyer and yelling about the bank's evil responsibility for the expulsion of the last true Romans; Paolo had intervened to stave off a fistfight. His uncle, he said, was "a torrent of words" and talked "according to the Roman character." The lawyer protested that he was simply doing his job and was in fact not part of the bank staff. Had he been one of the bank directors, Paolo claims that he would have grabbed him by the neck himself; but the lawyer was "a good person" (*una brava persona*), and antagonizing him would in any case have been counterproductive in that he might have become far more rigid in his demands. As for the authorities, the prefect had found it necessary to send an official police representative because otherwise the bank would have found grounds for legal action against the authorities themselves. His goal, Paolo thought, had been to give both sides some basis for temporary satisfaction and thereby to defuse the immediate tension.

While Paolo evidently hoped that the new deferral would also give the tenants a better chance to build their case collectively—once a single family had been evicted, the others' individual cases would collapse on the basis of precedent—he was also realistic enough to understand that the bank, too, would be able to marshal new forces for the next round. But time gained by the bank was also time gained for the tenants. When the bailiff asked the bank's lawyer to suggest a date for the next deadline—"How much should we make it, counsel—five months?"—the lawyer, while demurring at so unusually lengthy an extension, nevertheless "was quite indulgent with regard to the deadlines" and replied, "You do it"—in part because, as Paolo explained, in this respect the lawyer was partly obliged to yield to the bailiff's authority. The lawyer respectfully addressed the bailiff with the polite form of address, which recognized his situational authority while denying him collegial equality; the bailiff's power to extend the reprieve was pragmatically limited in that too generous a stay of eviction might well have provoked legal objections from the bank.

The bailiff's role followed certain identifiable social procedures. He could not act with complete freedom; the law had to be respected, as the tenants explicitly recognized. But when Loredana, under extreme tension, suddenly began to cry, he jocosely demanded of her husband, "So what's she doing all this crying for, then?"—indicating, in that moment, that he had actually managed to improve their chances. In fact he had good reason to be encouraging at that point; it was evident that the bank's lawyer had tacitly recognized that the bailiff's choice of date (11 April) would almost automatically mean a further extension until June because local elections were already scheduled for 16 April, but chose not to fight the suggestion. A prominent politician, a Monti resident and junior government minister who had taken an active interest in the case, commented, "Well, of course. . . . In Italy everything is amortized!" Hence, presumably, Paolo's visible anxiety not to let his uncle antagonize the lawyer, who showed himself to be quite sympathetic to the tenants' situation and willing to go along with the bailiff's delaying maneuver. And in fact on the next occasion the deadline was extended to 28 June.

While the bailiff had to respect certain norms—he could not attend the press conference that the residents were preparing for 15 May, for example—he could continue to comment informally on their strategies for raising public awareness, and he remained firmly opposed to evicting anyone who was old or ill. The bank's lawyer's position was less clear. It is not clear whether his apparent complaisance should be attributed to simple personal kindliness or to his desire to protect the bank's reputation from a major public embarrassment; the day before there had been a hearing for the nonagenarian, which resulted in an extension of her right to remain in her apartment, but the tension that this sensationalist aspect generated had not entirely abated. Indeed, the lawyer's stance may have been motivated by both concern for the bank's good name and some degree of humanitarian decency; like the prefect, he had every interest in trying to keep all parties reasonably calm, if not exactly content. Unseemly haste would have gained the bank nothing at all. The government usually announces general extensions of eviction deadlines at Christmas and Easter as well as during elections. The bank's best prospect was therefore simply to acquiesce in a whole series of delays in the hope that eventually a window of real opportunity would appear.

The polite exchange between the bailiff and the bank's lawyer was a jousting match between two contestants whose goals nevertheless partly overlapped. Paolo's description of the negotiations that preceded the final decision is succinct and revealing; its highly generic character shows that here again there is a set piece in which all concerned knew how to play their respective parts. For every time an eviction was due, Paolo explained, the bailiff presented himself at the prefect's office along with a doctor (whose presence is required by law) and an ironworker who would bar the door once the tenants had been evicted. This group assembled in the prefect's office; the bailiff then asked the police commander if he "had officers available to carry out the eviction," and the prefect replied that he did not. "See you next time!" came the by now ritualized response, there was a formal leave-taking, and then the bailiff signaled from the window—apparently with no attempt at secrecy—waving his arms crossways but in opposite directions to indicate that nothing would happen.

Paolo who, as the tenants' representative, was waiting downstairs on the street, now called the other tenants on his cell phone to reassure them that they could relax; then he greeted the officials as they come out of the building and invited them all to coffee—a clear declaration of social accommodation—after which he took off for the palazzo on his motorbike. There the bailiff and the police officer assembled with the tenants for the formal signing of the extension of the deadline—the scene that I have just described. That, at least, was the pattern until the final, dread moment of actual eviction arrived. In Via degli Ibernesi, that moment was still in the future. But there was one ominous new sign this time around: it was the first occasion on which a policeman, albeit as sole representative of the force, accompanied the bailiff back to the palazzo.

The bank could afford to wait. Existing alliances were already distinctly frayed. Not only did residents of more left-wing orientation view the growing involvement of the Alleanza nazionale in the Via degli Ibernesi case with deep misgivings, but the residents in the palazzo were equally diffident in their dealings with the growing tide of leftist-organized protests over the housing emergency. The representatives of the tenants' association also differed with the residents over whether to compromise if suitable housing could be found elsewhere; the residents wanted to remain in Monti and together.

Internally, too, there were moments of tension over basic questions of tactics and goals. But the major difficulty remained that of getting all the political parties involved. While Paolo claimed that he was not the pawn of any political faction and that one of the Alleanza nazionale leaders had advised him to line up whatever political support he could muster, the fact that he took his line from the local party representatives undermined his claims—and, arguably, the substance—of independence.

On 23 February the newspapers announced a generic extension of the deadlines on evictions. But this brought the leaders of the Via degli Ibernesi group no relief, since it applied only to those who had very specific needs (such as having five or more children or being over 65 years old). Loredana had just recently been evicted from the shoe shop she had previously managed in a building owned by the Ukrainian church; unfortunately the apartment was in Paolo's name, for otherwise she could have claimed that she was now out of work and thus was covered by one of the categories entitling tenants to the new extension of deadline. Paolo nevertheless thought, especially after consulting with the leftist city councilor, Nicola Galloro, that there might be some "ways of smoothing things over" (*smussature*) in the law, now that it was officially promulgated; it also appeared that after sixty days from the official promulgation of the new law the central government would cede control of its implementation and interpretation to the local authorities, which again would give the tenants a chance. Meanwhile, with a national referendum coming up on the last day of May, the tenants expected to get another extension to avoid clashing with the electoral process yet again. But Paolo and Loredana had a particular problem: as the only family not entitled to an extension under the new law, they feared that the bank would seize this opportunity to put a definitive end to their rebellious presence.

Meanwhile, exhaustion was beginning to take its toll. Nerves frayed; quarrels flared, briefly, like irritable flames, although they were quickly extinguished again; residents stopped greeting each other, then began again although with a sometimes icy correctness. The tactic of making different arrangements and different deadlines was beginning to divide some of the residents away from those determined to resist. And even they showed occasional moments of willingness to compromise. Loredana, exhausted and dispirited, said that a decent offer of alternative housing might just be acceptable to her personally, although she did not know if her husband would ever accept the idea. At one point, perhaps to bring other residents back into line, she threatened to treat independently with the bank even though she was not certain that she could ever bring herself to do such a thing either. But she was increasingly tired of the petty bickering that broke out among the tenants in the later stages of the struggle and annoyed by the refusal of some to share the expense and effort involved.

The other tenants also had a temporary advantage thanks to the bank's anxiety to get these two troublemakers out of the building as fast as possible; with every likelihood of being able to stay in the building at least until the following September, they were relatively free of immediate anxiety for the moment. With the new extension to late June came the news that various politicians were talking—De Luca had apparently met with the city's current housing chief, while Gianfranco Fini, the leader of the Alleanza nazionale, unexpectedly stayed for half an hour on what was supposed to have been a ten-minute visit to the site and promised that he would try to speak with the head of the bank (although it is not clear whether he ever did).

There were still residual ambiguities about the exact extent of the law's ability to intervene. Loredana thought that the police would never use force because of the public relations disaster it would mean; but she also acknowledged that, after three attempts by the bailiff to serve the eviction notices, the prefect was required by law to send in a police detachment. The continuing involvement of prominent politicians was certainly a deterrent; and, given the presumed right-wing sympathies of the police, it seems likely that the involvement of the Alleanza nazionale in particular must have given them pause.

On 15 May, after considerable preparation, a press conference took place in the courtyard of the palazzo. A buzz of excitement heralded the event, at which the residents had, at our suggestion, mounted a photographic exhibition documenting the bank's neglect of the building. A long table was set up along one side, and chairs for guests were arranged in several rows facing the table, where a microphone was also provided. As the resident anthropologist, I found myself seated with city councilors from the Democratici di sinistra and the Alleanza nazionale, the Green Party senator and anthropologist Carla Rocchi, a senior official of the tenants' organization, the parliamentary vice-president of the Alleanza nazionale, and a representative standing in for Tozzi, who had himself been unable to come because of a cabinet reshuffle.[21]

The event was not well attended by journalists despite the residents' hope, which Tozzi had raised as a rationale for holding the press conference, that the event would put pressure on the bank to "come out into the open" (*uscire allo scoperto*). The fact that Tozzi himself was absent, and that his representative seemed to have only a very vague knowledge of what was at stake, confirmed earlier suspicions that he would offer support of a very nominal kind, although his representative—who only came when the residents called Tozzi's office to inquire why he had not shown up—did vaguely promise that "[matters] will not end here."

For the politicians, especially those of opposed factions, the event seemed as much an opportunity for informal communication about other matters as a gesture of support for the residents. At one point the two senators, mortal enemies in Parliament, were strolling around chatting comfortably in front of the palazzo; the councilors for the two ends of the political spectrum seemed similarly at ease together. Observers were also bemused by the way that the right-wing representatives end up sounding like old-style Communists. On the surface, there was indeed a striking consensus across the entire ideological spectrum. But old political antipathies remained so strong that one housing rights activist initially refused to enter when he saw the Alleanza nazionale delegation, although he eventually agreed to attend at least part of the event.

The event achieved little. The poor press attendance was reflected in the rather meager publicity it garnered: a little television coverage, and articles in *Ultime Notizie*, *Il Tempo*, and *Secolo d'Italia*—the last two being right-wing and far-right publications, respectively. There was not a word in the centrist or left-wing newspapers. Meanwhile, the bank reversed its earlier decision to allow the old lady to remain in the building to the end of her natural life, a move that the residents welcomed only as a serious public relations error that would now place the bank's credibility in serious doubt.

And so the struggle continued. On 11 June, the head of the regional housing office wrote to the director of the bank, appealing for respect for the diverse social fabric, regardless of the legal technicalities, at least long enough to avoid embarrassing confrontations that would leave a stain on the Jubilee—a concern that Loredana, in particular, had accurately predicted. Still, however, there was apparently no reply. A meeting was held at the assessor's office with the residents and their political allies. Again the bank remained silent. Then, on 27 June, the residents held a second press conference, this time in the Flag Room of the Capitol, an imposing site that gave a sense of solemnity to the group of journalists, residents, and others who sat around its long central table. Tozzi introduced the formal discussion by reminding his audience that this was not the first time the city government had confronted the particular case, which it regarded as an especially serious (*grave*) one, and that the entire administration including the mayor was involved in an attempt to reach a negotiated solution. He further reminded his hearers of the presence in the palazzo of the aged matriarch of the Palace of

Justice, by now 98 years old, whose son—as he acknowledged—was sitting at the table.

Much of his presentation appeared to be both an acknowledgment of the social injustice involved in the proposed eviction and an indirect but unmistakable attempt to throw the moral responsibility at the bank. Recognizing that the population of the historic center was changing, he remarked, "It is unthinkable that even a—how should I put this?—a landlord's mentality should be brought to the point of throwing out of her own home a person who has advanced to the hundredth year of her age." Thus, he suggested, the first goal was to appeal to the Bank of Rome to annul the eviction at least of the nonagenarian, as "an act that is even more of a symbolic than of a political nature." He then called on the bank to sit down with the city administration to resolve the problem; he was careful to recognize the legitimate interests of the bank as well and emphasized the long history of cooperation between the city and the bank. The difficulty, however, lay in the bank's intransigent refusal to discuss the matter with anyone. He declared, as a matter of general principle, "In any case the city administration has a duty, which it is carrying out, to make available all the available means for shoring up and rescuing the situation as far as possible." He then spoke about the various competitions for municipal housing, and about the creation of incentives through city tax (Ici) reductions for proprietors who offered low rents to needy families.

Then he invited Loredana to speak as the spokesperson of the residents; after she made a brief statement, Councilor Galloro spoke about the lack of response from the bank and more generally about the difficulty of getting any reasonable reaction where the now valuable properties in the historic center were concerned. Then the residents began to complain of the bank's cynical neglect of their building and its failure to respond to the tenants' concerns.

One of these concerns was especially revealing of the social solidarity the bank either ignored or hoped to smash: "We would like to mention that our building is also a closed building, and there are no speakerphones [connecting the main entrance with the apartments], which [means] that if some elderly person is ill we don't know what has happened." The speaker also pointed out that the bank's perfunctory repair work of some three years earlier could have included the installation of speakerphones, but that it did not. I then spoke of the bank's responsibility, not only to its investors but also to the society at large, of the need to get the bank to explain its actions; and of its cynicism in offering unsuitable housing in compensation and in trying to evict the nonagenarian woman despite having announced that they would not do so. Tozzi then, with an ironic but kindly smile, took the opportunity to say of my intervention, "He is the only person from the Anglo-Saxon community I know who has not espoused free-market notions; and for that, I thank him!" The Alleanza nazionale ensured its ideologically very different presence in the person of Councilor Marco Marsilio, who spoke about the historic center as a whole. And then, with the formal press conference concluded, the journalists rushed to interview the various key actors. One of them, the old lady's son, reiterated familiar themes: "In practical terms it [the building] is the last historic nucleus of residents of the Monti district, because virtually everyone else has left." And he pointed out that if his mother were kicked out along with the daughter who looks after her, another family who depends on this daughter would also suffer—another example of the residents' communal concerns.

These declarations again had little effect. The city administration was clearly caught in an impossible situation, its left-wing credentials threatened by its necessary determination not to end up confronting the bank too directly. It did eventually manage to engage the bank in some highly secret negotiations, however, and finally reached an agreement to fix a comprehensive deadline for 4 October. The bank had every interest in accepting; the government had meanwhile announced that by the end of September no more evictions could be deferred. But the residents had other ideas, and were already talking heatedly about "civil war." When September arrived and there was still no sign that either side would yield, Tozzi, who was sometimes prepared to be more outspoken about his social beliefs than were others in the city administration, declared in a television interview that he would chain himself to the front door if the eviction went ahead. Meanwhile, Mayor Rutelli had decided to run for national office, and the entire city government was in uproar; the former minister of culture, Walter Veltroni, successfully stood as the candidate of the Left.

On the day scheduled for the eviction virtually all the local politicians, including Tozzi, showed up in force; Tozzi was heard speaking on his cell phone to the minister of social services—and the bailiff announced that the eviction had been postponed to 21 November, the date—as it turned out—already set for one of the tenants. The bank's lawyer had himself proposed this date, which ostensibly made the tenants' resistance easier because it finally brought them all into line and allowed them to operate as a single group. The suspicion began to dawn, however, that perhaps this was a ruse—that they were all being lulled into a feeling of security because after so many cries of "Wolf!" (as one of the tenants wryly put it) they were in fact still living in the palazzo. And indeed, after another unsuccessful attempt by the bank to get the tenants out of the building en masse (on 13 February), the eviction deferrals began to spread out again, with the first group (including the ringleaders) due to go on 20 June and the others in the following month (11 July).

With the Jubilee now well and truly over, the bank must have hoped for a speedy resolution at last, and continued its cat-and-mouse game with the tenants. Rumor began to spread again of a forced eviction, and one resident murmured, "[It's] already pretty strange that they'd leave it to the bailiff to decide [the date]." The seeming complaisance of the perpetually polite lawyer for the bank might just, it seemed, have itself been a ruse. Yet eventually, at the last minute, the eviction was again put off until 3 September. At that point, surmised someone who was facing eventual eviction from another house, there was going to be a tidal wave of evictions, already deferred many times because of the Jubilee and the administration's failure to find alternative housing. He thought that the bank, unnoticed amid the general uproar, would then immediately seize the opportunity to pounce.

By the summer of 2001, the leftist coalition, now in charge of the entire historic center (a *municipio*, or subunit of the city administration, following Mayor Rutelli's rearrangement of the entire administrative structure of the *comune*), seemed more willing to contemplate lending the Via degli Ibernesi group its support, although a junior politician affiliated to the coalition warned me not to raise the residents' hopes too far. The issue had by now acquired far greater public significance; the number of evictees in the historic center was growing, and the skill of the Via degli Ibernesi group in mobilizing public sympathy, however sporadic and compromised by the right-wing nature of their most public support, had made their cause more useful to others. The topic of eviction was now high on the new and more locally focused administration's list of key concerns, and Giuseppe Lobefaro, first president of the first *municipio* of Rome, actively sought to address the issue at the local level.

When I returned for a further spell of fieldwork in the summer of 2004, the situation had again changed dramatically. After a further series of attempts to evict the residents—each ending, as had its predecessors, with a further postponement—the bank evidently decided that there was no profit to be gained by clinging to the building and that it would be wiser to sell it. The real estate department of the internationally famous Pirelli tire company, acquired the property. At this point, the city administration stepped in and negotiated an arrangement whereby the residents would have the option of remaining in the building on the basis of gradated and gradually increasing rental payments, the terms to be fixed by mutual consent. It seemed that the residents had finally won by sheer persistence, forcing the bank to transfer ownership to an enterprise that was more open to direct negotiation.

Endgame

Sadly, however, their victory proved to be entirely Pyrrhic. The new owners unobtrusively resold the property to another company, which quickly— indeed, on the same day—sold it to a third, at a vastly higher price. This kind of insider trading is not in itself illegal, although the (entirely unsubstantiated) suspicion remained that the second and third companies actually belonged to a single entity. Such practices are fairly common. One set of three properties in the historic center (one actually in Monti), for example, was sold at auction, but all the companies bidding were subunits of the same business group—"like Chinese boxes," remarked a man who nearly lost his right to live in one of the palazzi as a result of the sale. He was especially incensed because the building in which he lived had been inalienable under the terms of a bequest made to a confraternity some two hundred years earlier; an administrator in the regional government, however, had ruled in favor of the sale, and the ghost companies that were ostensibly competing to buy it quickly took advantage of the new disposition to arrange the sale at an impressive price that would also justify heavily increased rents. We should recall that apparently something of the kind, albeit in more complex fashion, had occurred over many decades in the case of the palazzo in Via degli Ibernesi.

The firm that had now acquired the Via degli Ibernesi property was directed by two members of Rome's Jewish community. They claimed ignorance of the previous agreement with Pirelli, which they had not the slightest intention of respecting. Various alarmed bodies—including the leadership of the Jewish community—tried to intervene. The new owners were adamant; they confirmed, and perhaps traded on, their reputation as ruthless entrepreneurs who had turned their backs on their own community. The elder of the two family heads who ran the business allegedly even snarled at the widely respected community head, "Mind your own business!" (*fat[t]e gli affari tuoi!*)—in fact, said one resident, he used a far ruder version of this expression, adding that the businessman had behaved arrogantly even to the mayor. The two businessmen then challenged the city administration to make a counteroffer for the property, but their asking price was far higher than the administration was prepared even to challenge. It became clear that nothing further could be done; this company soon thereafter sold the property to yet another firm, one that was developing extensive interests in the neighborhood, and the struggle finally came to an end.

The roots of this collapse were, in the final analysis, legal rather than political. To one of the women's impassioned demand that the city authorities intervene and demand a solution and an end to all the pressure tactics, Galloro pointed out that the city actually had quite limited powers. Over the long years of their struggle, which he had followed in person, "what used to be the relationship one had with, with one's house, has changed... From a social right it has moved into the realm of economic goods." As a result, under the national constitution, it was now the owner's rights that were protected. His own frustration was palpable. A set of laws, promulgated at the national level by the coalition to which he belonged at the city level, and reinforced by already existing constitutional guarantees for the rights of property owners, had now effectively undercut any serious prospect of resolving the dispute as an issue of the social right to a home.

Effective timing sealed this endgame. The company that so brusquely rejected the interventions of city and community was, said Paolo, remarkably swift in its demands. After the almost surreptitious acquisition of the property they did nothing for several months; but, when time came to deal with the residents, they gave them virtually no time at all to muster their forces or organize financing. The company had acquired a set of 27 buildings in a single sale from Pirelli; for these, the company had 18 months to pay back a Milanese bank for loans that had made this massive sale possible, while the Bank of Rome—the original owner—still retained some shares in the deal, with 38 percent apparently also remaining in the hands of subgroups of the Pirelli Company. The residents thus first thought that they could fight the takeover on the grounds that the Bank of Rome was still a part owner and that the new owners were therefore still obliged to respect the deal signed with Pirelli.

But it was not to be. Within a year, the residents were again facing the prospect of a forced eviction; the final owner had acquired the building.[22] While the Alleanza nazionale activists remained involved at the local level, the electoral victory of the so-called center-right coalition led by Silvio Berlusconi had hardly increased their appetite for a fight that would have pitted their party against the representatives of big business and the banks. The legal grounds for an appeal were weak, since the agreement signed with Pirelli was in no sense binding on any subsequent proprietor under Italian law. The new owners were well connected; and they were in a hurry. After a last, desperate meeting with the city authorities at the Capitol on

11 February 2005, on 18 March the first five residents signed documents ceding the property to the new owners. The battle was over.

I was present at the signing of the final surrender. The tenants' lawyer had to explain to them, with some difficulty, that all legal avenues had been exhausted and that the judge's final word must now be respected. The evident anguish of tenants who had lived for decades in the same house contrasted with the businesslike manner of the lawyers, although the tenants' lawyer—a cousin of Paolo's—was visibly agitated. It is hard to do justice to the sense of futility that residents experience in the face of the neoliberal juggernaut and its program of remorseless gentrification.

Marsilio, the Alleanza nazionale councilor, organized a press conference together with one of his party colleagues; the ostensible goal was to pressure the city administration to take responsibility for protecting the few tenants who were not leaving that day, since the departure dates were staggered. Chatting beforehand in a solemn voice, he acknowledged that in a standoff to see who is stronger, wealthy proprietors "win this arm-wrestling" and pointed out that there was little choice but to yield "after fifteen years, aside from the stress, [there's] also the reason of having the public force come every month, of living with this monthly appointment—terrible!" The first five tenants signed the documents (one had already left), in which they agreed to move out within a few weeks, relocating to new homes they had found for themselves and, Marsilio claimed, without any official assistance from the authorities.

At the press conference that followed the signing, Marsilio announced that he and his colleagues from the Alleanza nazionale would remain vigilant on behalf of the four remaining families; he accused the city authorities of having been too willing to engage in idle chatter (*due chiacchiere*, literally, "two chats"), taking generic refuge behind the enormity of the housing emergency all over Rome: "Citing the big numbers, [they said] there had been no capability to provide these families with a concrete solution." So, as long as the other four families remain, he declared, "we are continuing to guarantee our political and human support, to prevent these four from remaining abandoned on the inside of this building." They would, he promised, be "a physical sign" of that commitment; "in January of last year we physically prevented the police from carrying out the eviction."

A meeting was held at the Capitol on 21 March, with the lawyers of both sides present; Galloro represented the city authorities. Nothing happened; the elections precluded any forward motion. The next access was scheduled for 4 May. The lawyer thought that the city authorities might have forgotten or become too absorbed in preparing for the elections. He was awaiting a formal proposal from the city authorities to the new owners; legally, the city can enforce a certain degree of protection for people who are disadvantaged economically or otherwise. It is probably true that the city no longer had at its disposal a sufficient supply of houses to rent; the collapse of the old welfare system is nowhere more apparent than in the sale of municipal property previously used to provide affordable housing. The less indigent tenants, those whose signing of the agreements I had witnessed, were already on their way to new homes, victims of what the lawyer, who was also the lawyer for the club evicted from the Piazzetta, admitted was "an inflamed (*esasperato*) free-market ideology."

An agreement was eventually reached and the other tenants also left. The new owner's advertising began to appear on the building—so hastily, in fact, that a reused banner incorrectly announced the sale of shops as well as apartments. Soon the company's agent's booming voice could be heard, full of genial bluster, with potential clients, his temporary office in the building filled with a seductive display of apartment designs and plans. His was a modern, prospering business; there was no time to lose.

Although the evicted tenants all eventually found decent homes, their ability to maintain a sense of community and a collective identity was now in serious doubt. Paolo and Loredana at least had the good fortune to find a residence only a few meters from the Monti border; others had to live further out. Paolo, devout if anticlerical in the past, now became actively involved in parish affairs, his annual participation as a confraternity member in the procession marking the parish festival of the Madonna dei Monti a powerful symbolic link with the place that has never ceased to be the locus of his affections. His attachment now converged with that of the parish priest, for whom, we should recall, attachment to place was an act of deeply sensual devotion. Paolo continues to visit the shrinking community of his friends; but they no longer meet on the main square, from which their club was evicted a few years earlier. His children still go to school nearby, and many of their friends still live in the neighborhood, but it is clear that the old reticulated engagements are weakening and dying even as I write.

Who has come in their place? Certainly there are some powerful affections that still animate life in Monti. A colleague, a political scientist with strong interests in Africa, remarked that he had only been vaguely aware of the social networks that predated his arrival as a resident in the neighborhood a few years earlier. He had thought that my interest in the idea of a Monti community life was "a form of unrequited complaisance" (*un compiacimento gratuito*). But when his first child was born, he discovered these links in all their specificity—in the public gardens at the presidential palace of the Quirinale, in the kindergarten, and so on—as a response, not so much to a shared sense of *romanità*, but as "a kind of compensation for the inadequacies of the municipal administration." And the resulting sense of belonging was not the product of older social ties; indeed, he said, it took place in "a context relatively disengaged from social life." He came to realize that many others, globe-trotters and intellectuals like himself (their number included several journalists), had been drawn into a social network by the needs of their children, and that as they walked around the area they all came to understand that involvement as a central part of their lives. It was a new social aggregation, one that had little to do with the older forms of social life in Monti except for those few who participated in the Monti Social Network and found themselves involved in the dying agonies of the old order as much as in the ambitions of the new.

The relatively happy conditions of life that financially secure newcomers enjoy, however, come at a heavy price for others. In particular, the evictions that have wrought the most fundamental demographic and structural changes relied on an atmosphere of intensifying fear, and contributed to it; the fewer of the old residents are left, the greater the terror they face. Fear of one's neighbors and even of a local boss was a manageable part of life under the old order. Even the fear of the Vatican, powerful though it was, dealt with a familiar presence in everyday life; it offered negotiable terms of redemption through the confessional and the indulgence. The new fear, by contrast, comes from forces that refuse to negotiate—forces that are extraneous to the local society, economically overwhelming, and institutionally beyond the control of the local municipal authorities or the pressure of conscience from familiarly Roman allies (such as the Jewish community leaders, city politicians, or even the officials charged with executing the order of eviction). This is fear of a very different order.

The Future of Eternity

How should we react in the face of such new dispositions? Should we shrug our shoulders along with the left-wing district counselor, whose ironic awareness of his acceptance of market logic was not enough to commit him to a fight he felt no one could win? Should we accept the instrumental morality of entrepreneurs who argue that their active role in gentrification is a form of urban renewal (*riqualificazione*) and a rejection of degradation (*degrado*) rather than gentrification that has destroyed the solidary base of a once well-established working-class population? Should we be persuaded that these are inevitable changes that have at least left some middle-class people basking in the sunlight of a new Roman spring, their children cavorting happily in newly pedestrianized spaces and enjoying the security of a zone practically closed off to unwanted immigrants and homeless paupers? Should we accept the argument that those who were living in the historic center were not the rightful beneficiaries of a concern better invested in the far more marginal populations suffering in the suburbs?

While my rhetorical framing of these questions should make my own political attitudes clear, I want to emphasize the complexity of the situation. I recognize that the intense attachment to place that aroused my sympathies can also be the source of some no less intensely forms of cultural fundamentalism and racism.[1] Just as the Monticiani turned their hearts against Ukrainians and other eastern European immigrants who flooded into the square, for example, I have seen Thai localists who were fighting against eviction and for the right to remain in their home community assert those rights on the grounds that "we are Thai people"—thereby implicitly if perhaps inadvertently endorsing a national policy of denying Thai citizenship to certain groups of "hill tribes" and refugees. I am aware that in many corners of Europe, Fascism has begun to feed on discontent with the nation-state's failure to recognize local forms of autonomy. The Roman situation is in this sense far from unique.

But it is also easy to oversimplify; and the media will encourage that tendency if given the chance. In particular, we cannot assume that attempts to co-opt discontent over massive economic change will automatically feed the forces of reaction and prejudice. In the Thai community, where this tendency to adopt "officializing strategies" and the cooptation of nationalist and royalist rhetoric is strong,[2] the community leaders spoke out strongly on the importance of lending a helping hand to foreigners and the Muslim minority in the country's southern regions in the aftermath of the 2004 tsunami that devastated entire communities; they argued that, as victims of a targeted eviction, they were particularly well placed to understand suffering, and so—although destitute—they held an auction of old clothes and used the proceeds to send two volunteers and some much-needed supplies to one of the stricken areas. One of the leaders argued that compassion was a particularly Thai virtue—but he deployed this to champion tolerance, empathy, and inclusion.[3]

In the same way, one of the leaders of the Via degli Ibernesi group who had been particularly willing to accept help from the Alleanza nazionale was also vociferous in his condemnation of the Vatican's intolerance of gays and of the general tide of racism that was infecting the entire country's attitudes toward immigrants. Others, be it said, were less generous. But I want to emphasize that there is no *necessary* connection between localism and racism or other forms of intolerance, and in fact what has impressed me throughout both field projects—one in Italy, the other in Thailand—has been the firmness with which some reject the seductions of intolerance in the midst of their own sufferings, even as they recognize the bitterness that drives others in far less attractive directions.

None of this will make much sense except in the further context of a consideration of the history of nationalism, both in Italy and elsewhere. I have already attempted a brief comparison of the respective situations in Greece and Italy, showing how the very different relations between the state and its constituent regions in each of these two countries is reflected in the production of scholarly discourse about national and local traditions.[4] Some of that comparison is also present in earlier sections of the present book, inasmuch as I have indicated that the passionate defense of culturally intimate secrets, which in Greece primarily concerns the defense of the national level of cultural identity, in Italy more commonly concerns a local region or city. The fragmentation of Italian identity contrasts powerfully with the homogeneous face presented by officialdom of the Greek people and their state.

And yet there are also points of similarity. Not least among these is the deep awareness of cultural and moral flaws in the body politic—flaws that are accounted as such under the censorious gaze of more powerful countries that have appointed themselves the arbiters of international political ethics and cultural values. In Greece, the entire structure of justification invokes past events—the Fall of Adam and Eve as an explanation of common personal weaknesses and failures, the fall of Constantinople in 1453 as the source of that "oriental" taint that other European states use to marginalize Greece in the context of pan-European development. In Italy, while the occupation of the land by numerous foreign powers is often invoked to explain its extreme fragmentation, the same idiom of justification is particularly apposite to the forms of everyday legal practice. In the very shadow of the Vatican, its historical domination of the city never a moment out of mind, the specter of original sin looms large: it informs the laws, explains deeply ensconced social habits, and provides an ethical alibi that is increasingly important in a country now painfully aware of the difficulties of maintaining a reputation for such ideals as democracy, transparency, and efficiency.

These values form part of an ethical framework by which the outside world judges a country's performance. The resulting hierarchies are also reproduced internally, as in the north's contemptuous evaluation of the south—the very attitude that both feeds the separatism of the north and yet at the same time leads to serious doubts about the very possibility of national identity when these same northern separatists participate as coalition partners in a national government they seem more intent on undermining than perpetuating, march into Rome to a chorus of local sympathy, and colonize an island in the country's southernmost regions from which they ban holidaymakers from the capital. In the end, it seems rather clear that the northern separatists' moral claims on greater rationality and efficiency do not live up to their own oft-proclaimed standards.

These curious dynamics are also the political and cultural backdrop to the demographic, historical, and cultural changes now occurring in Rome. The widespread view that Rome is culturally southern and that it is little more than an agglomeration of villages (*paesi*) leaves it vulnerable to economic colonization, while its unquestionable historical importance—and the equal primacy of Monti among the districts of Rome—also make it a tempting target for the acquisitive tastes of "gluttonous" (*golosi*) consumers. Arguably the most conservative forces affecting the city's fate, the Vatican, can invoke ancient religious claims and principles in support of its own profitable engagement with the neoliberal economy and ideology at the very moment when its leadership inveighs against materialism.

In the same way, while the faded remnants of the old underworld protest that their only role was to protect the defenseless and arrange the restitution of stolen property, the larger moral universe within which they operated—a universe of compromise, prevarication, and bribery and menace packaged as friendship and experienced as a kind of solidarity among the local working-class population—paved the way, through the structure of fear and complaisance that it nurtured, for the intentionally divisive and intimidating tactics of the new property entrepreneurs. At a local level, intimidation had mostly served to keep would-be molesters of women and indiscriminate petty thieves in line and to ensure that the word of the local bosses was always respected; the complicity that fed on people's certain knowledge of each other's petty infractions and minor sins encouraged an ad hoc ethics that rejected the very possibility of human perfection.

There was fear, to be sure, and some used it malevolently; but overall it was the fear of social ostracism that really mattered. When the stakes were suddenly raised, that fear became instantly more potent and dangerous. Serious bids for the control of central Roman real estate by state, church, and underworld threatened and soon largely obliterated the forms of the old social polity, replacing them with the massive conformity appropriate to a newly essentialized national heritage. Yet many of the idioms of symbolic violence that these forces employed were the familiar idioms of the older order.

Local people, with their unusually detailed and passionate engagement with history, know about such continuities, and invoke them—sometimes stereotypically, sometimes with quite fine-grained analysis—to explain their present predicaments, and to resist the forces that have produced them. They also know about the long-term processes whereby the entrepreneurs have built a secular property empire on the spaces created by bequests to the church. It is probably no coincidence, for example, that one of the leaders of the Via degli Ibernesi group should have been a bibliophile taxi driver—a man, in other words, whose knowledge of the intricate geography of Monti and rich understanding of the city's long history rivaled, albeit in a different key, that of the parish priest. We shall probably never know whether the property in Via degli Ibernesi had really begun its modern career as a bequest to the church; one effect of the repeated transactions over its ownership has been to bury its past. But the generic links are still visible, a source of brooding suspicion that the eventual eviction of the tenants has yet to expunge from neighborhood consciousness.

That process of oblivion nonetheless continues inexorably. Even the new activists of the Monti Social Network, with its concerns to create a new and viable social environment for the remaining population (including the more engaged of its recently arrived members), inadvertently contribute to this process of dememorialization. While its operational style resists the banal formality of the new state order, its helpless documentation of the process of eviction may actually reinforce the power of the property dealers by demonstrating their inexorable invincibility yet again. Its negotiations with the city administration did not recapture the Monti district market for its erstwhile social role but confirmed the greater economic power of the small but dense supermarkets that now monopolize the grocery trade, while its successful campaign to recapture the Angelo Mai school for the neighborhood—now challenged anew by the city authorities—has also created new rifts among its members and raised questions about whose collective ends are at stake.

Gentrification is unquestionably a global phenomenon, sharing with the worldwide celebration of "heritage" the curious irony that local distinctiveness has now become a generic good. At the same time, it is too easy to follow the conventional view of globalization that would represent all instances of a global product as essentially the same. That view is mistaken, if only because local conditions produce a grid of attitudes and expectations that refracts—to use again the metaphor I borrowed from Evans-Pritchard to talk about the localization of forms of worship—the global templates in locally unique and sometimes unexpected realizations.[5]

In Italy, local identities are intensely and complexly fractured. The dynamics of their mutual engagement nonetheless permits recomposition in occasional effusions of solidarity. Similarly, the very idea of heritage, like the highly localized art restoration schools that vie with each other over the most appropriate forms of historic reconstruction and conservation, glitters in a thousand different glints and hues, with an intensity that belies the universalist claims of the economic ideology driving the entire gentrification process.

That same variety, however, is a source of political weakness. It is virtually impossible, in a land of shifting coalitions and uncertain loyalties, to maintain a solidary front against the invasive force of neoliberal ideology. The Monti Social Network, with its flexible adaptation of local modalities of social interaction and its tough intellectual leadership, is perhaps better equipped than most such enterprises to combat the rapid homogenization of the city. But even this laudable effort is compromised. It cannot confidently claim the support of traditional leftists, who have adopted many of the neoliberals' stances and are further compromised by a widespread perception that their own wealth has undermined their commitment to workers' concerns. Even some devout Catholics increasingly question a church that contributes to the gentrification process. Many residents, too, reject the opportunistic social engagement of the political far Right, seeing it as bound, at the national level, by its dependence for power on a political party—Berlusconi's Forza Italia—that exemplifies, to most Italians, both the entrepreneurial ruthlessness of neoliberalism and the corruption that runs counter to any attempt to install participatory civic values as the ultimate political ideal.

In that situation, with weak and distrusted national political leadership and a city administration that has largely endorsed the anodyne banality of neoliberal management, the more determined agents of the new order— whether honest business people, church prelates, or underworld crooks— meet only disorganized and disjointed resistance. That resistance can be fierce and protracted, as in the case of the palazzo in Via degli Ibernesi. It can be well-coordinated over a period of time, deploying the specialized technical knowledge of the professional and academic segments of the membership. It can even achieve lasting impact on the physical fabric of the district, as the slowly spreading pedestrianization of certain streets suggests. But it can win only those battles that also serve the interests of the new power brokers and economic managers; in this case, for example, concerns over the impact of heavy traffic are shared by many of the newcomers, who imagine themselves living in an idyllically quiet and calm place and are infuriated to discover the level of everyday noise and disruption. Improvements are possible only when larger economic interests are thereby well served—as also when church authorities encourage their tenants to refurbish dilapidated quarters only to take cynical advantage of their pious labor by raising the rents.

Against such forces the small subunits of Roman society, which once protected their intensely local interests through an ethic of minding one's own business, now have few defenses; their history of instrumental compromise, segmentary social organization, and flexible but often evanescent alliances has not nurtured habits of durable solidarity. This is what the Via degli Ibernesi case so depressingly illustrates. The eventual failure of that particular effort illustrates with particular clarity how difficult it is for small and disunited groups to win a war of attrition. The various local societies, most of which were formed to represent the interests of a single street or professional group, prove too evanescent to be genuinely effective; they lose their impetus early in the disgust of the majority at the chatter (*chiacchiere*) of the loquacious few and in the frustration that conflicting interests quickly produce.

It is here that the Monti Social Network, with its recognition that real social life entails conflict and that loyalty is not obtained through lofty ideals but through a pragmatic assessment of socially embedded attitudes and needs, has succeeded in outlasting most other such associations; but even in the Network there are those who claim to have no time to waste in idle conversation and others who feel slighted by the priorities that emerge through the overall consensus. And time is rarely on the Network's side. Creating a register of threatened evictions might have been an effective strategy, for example, but, by the time it was put into effect, and despite the creation of links with such national organizations for housing rights as Action, it had little effect beyond, once again, the creation of a surge of hope that was soon crushed by the market juggernaut. The future of the Network is itself increasingly uncertain.

The segmentary structure of Monti, and of Rome, partly explains the remarkable survival of an economically weak artisanal class in the core of this famous capital city until the early 1980s and, diminishingly, beyond. Gentrification occurred earlier in other large cities around the world, in some cases by many decades. Rome remained a socially fragmented city without a major industrial base, its commitment to "tradition" and to its monuments undoubtedly serving as its strongest source of economic survival, and with ad hoc economic institutions left forever vulnerable by their technical illegality and by their dependence on the honesty or otherwise of their leaders.

The postwar emergence of an expanded bourgeoisie brought with it a desire for large, airy suburban homes far from the urban core. For two decades or more, the artisanal class was largely left to its own devices, its rents more or less stable and astonishingly low. Those arrangements persisted in part because they afforded owners a steady income in rents, in part because regulation of the architectural *patrimonio* already meant that visible changes to the physical fabric were controlled and restricted and because these constraints also discouraged further private investment in restoration and renovation. For the city, the maintenance of this remarkable complex of historic domestic architecture was a priority because it supported the growth of the tourist trade; but what might have become one of the highest-yield areas of the city in terms of real estate prices remained economically depressed and unproductive.

During this period, social change was slow; the center of the capital city remained a marginal place where one heard the despised local dialect more often than the cultivated standard Italian of intellectuals and the emerging new elite. The population was considered uncouth and uncooperative even though the attention of a few filmmakers had already begun to lend it a somewhat romantic cast. In this sense Monti was indeed a *paese*—not a rural village, but a civil community with its own solidarities and its own conflicts, a persistent incarnation of the *civiltà* that urban living had once meant throughout much of the Italian peninsula. Its life was neither the civic order of the idealized nation-state nor the artificial consensus that so often masquerades as democracy in the new economic order, but a theater of manners and menaces in which a culturally conservative population sustained a strong sense of local belonging if not of collective political interest.

Far from the new civic order associated with the modernities of both Left and Right, the inhabitants instead shared a *civil* order—an order where rough but polite manners masked constantly shifting interests and alliances. Civil life encapsulates memories of deep injustice and mutual hurt, not as purely moral issues, but as things that happened, and happened repeatedly, not least because the nominal removal of Vatican power did not prevent the church's continuing interference in everyday existence. Not for nothing do Romans say that the Vatican's deity is "not triune but a *quatrino*"; the casuistic justifications for usury, the cynical paternalism that subjected the Jewish population to isolation and forced conversion while exploiting its status as a way of controlling the forbidden practice of usury and deploying it in the service of the ecclesiastical coffers,[6] and the role of churches and confraternities in the accelerating pace of eviction all serve to confirm Romans' conviction that the church represents the corruption of the collective soul more dramatically and more substantively than do any of its flock.

Corruption itself is a process—a process of decay, starting out from the original condition of sinfulness. That model of original sin seems to provide a conceptual explanation for many of the paradoxes that this city instantiates, especially inasmuch as it has long provided the theological justification for economic practices that appeared to disobey divine law. The irony of this all-too-human Eternal City is precisely that nothing is eternal; all is provisional, fixable, negotiable. Indeed, ironically, it is Rome's very claim to eternal and inimitable status that in every era demands anew "a reinsertion of antiquity into a declaredly contemporary system of values."[7] In such culturally fertile terrain, all can be condoned; here, in thinking of the secular *condono*, etymology does not betray us as it so often does in the treacherous straits between Italian and English, and we can see that a literally indulgent legal and theological arrangement sustains the contingency and the provisionality of many of the actions necessary to a viable social life. The imperfection of the human condition is such that arrangements must always entail the calculation and manipulation of time. Such, too, is the historicity of social life, of its embedding in experienced realities. Rome instantiates and exaggerates the expulsion from eternal bliss. Its pleasures and its agonies are real and present, and both the flawed morality of the church's agents and the equally common agonies of those of its priests who take their calling seriously are ever-present reminders of that unavoidable imperfection and historicity—as are the temporizing of the rotating credit manager who seeks ways of deferring his trial; as are the calculations of the architect who wants to build illegally and wonders how much he will need to pay when the inevitable collective *condono* comes around and when that will be necessary; and as are the triumphs and failures of the barman and the cook as they commit their earthly bodies to the delicately timed production of tantalizing tastes and smells amid an argumentative, salacious, gossip-laden stream of eloquent chatter.

Until the real estate market started to accelerate, the fragmentation of local society held few substantive consequences for the economic life of the district. Incomes were low and sometimes precarious although usually also adequate for daily living, and trades were humble and practical, suited to a small-scale and face-to-face modality of social interaction. By the same token, however, once the onslaught began, often with its own distinctively heavy-handed strategies for breaking or exploiting laws that residents had merely subverted in a tactical sense,[8] there was no organized basis for class solidarity or resistance except the political parties—and, especially after the redistribution of the parties in the early 1990s, no one party seemed to stand effectively for the defense of working-class interests. Increasingly wealthy, the traditional leftists became a part of the problem as they moved into houses from which workers and artisans had been evicted. The "social Fascists" remained unpalatable to many, their presence a powerful disincentive to concerted political action in defense of local society; the case of the Via degli Ibernesi evictions illustrates the degree to which their involvement could deter others from joining an emblematic cause against the destructive powers of the new economy.

Nor did old patterns of patronage by the few local aristocrats afford a viable basis for collective action. The very idea of class symbiosis, so frequently invoked as a mark of the old Roman ways, began to seem more laughable than laudable; the new entrepreneurial class had little interest in romantic images of an aristocracy now deemed outmoded and irrelevant, as was the lordly condescension that had been the basis of its mutualist coexistence with the artisanal class. This mutualism was no more of use in the new struggle than the segmentary patterns of street alliances. What had once been a source of flexibility under the Vatican's repressive rule now became sources of weakness in the face of organized economic expropriation—expropriation of space, expropriation of identity, expropriation of the past.

Now more than ever before, the measure of power was money—and here the Vatican, with its proverbial devotion to self-enrichment, was especially well-prepared to adapt to the new conditions. But there were many other contenders as well. While the local *malavitosi* looked on helplessly as they were evicted from house after house, the new representatives of a far more ramified underworld, nattily suited and rushing hither and thither in their elegant sports cars, poured enormous sums of money into the purchase of entire palazzi and into their restructuring as blocks of tiny but fabulously expensive apartments. The stuttering helplessness of artisans silenced because their working noises disturbed the new residents, the outrageous prices charged by some of the new and even noisier pubs that shattered the night with their raucous music, the banners that first proclaimed "No to Deportation" only to be replaced by others declaring "Apartments for Sale"—these were the marks of a collapsing social world and its rapid erasure from the freshly laundered image of the past.

This, then, is the irony of heritage: too often it entails the destruction of a local society in the name of preservation. The fencing of monumental structures and the eviction of inconvenient residents are both ways of creating taxonomic facts in the very fabric of the city; they are materializations of an ideology that has little tolerance for poverty, eccentricity, or creativity. Nationalism, with its encompassing mythologies and its passion for homogenization and clearly defined categories, paved the way; but in Italy, where nationalism is as often an exercise in collective self-castigation as it is a celebration of common virtue,[9] it was not a sufficiently strong force in its own right to bring about such regimentation until it could be combined with the global economics of heritage management and gentrification. Ironically, it may be at the moment of yielding political sovereignty to the European Union and cultural expertise to the United Nations that Italy has finally been able to assert a collective identity that possesses greater legitimacy than vague and often self-deprecatory ramblings about national character. But it does so, not as an independent entity, but as a module in a set.

Consider the claim that Italy owns 70 percent of the world's great art. That claim itself admits to the subjection of the nation to an encompassing aesthetic hierarchy. Audit culture replaces taste as the arbiter of a country's position within that hierarchy; and this is a development that suits both the nationalists who want some specific basis for their boasting and the neoliberals who find such devices to be an effective means of managerial control.

The picturesque streets of Monti could undoubtedly be included in a similar quantification of cultural capital. The demographic changes now under way and the increasingly sophisticated mapping of the historical fabric would certainly favor such a development. The physical body politic, that inhabited place with which the parish priest has developed such an intense and intimate rapport, that living past in which taxi drivers debate the relative merits of editions of old books, that palimpsest of acknowledged sins against the divine order and infractions of the human—the entire pulsing, complex presence would be displaced by the abstractions of official historiography, commoditized heritage, and real estate values manipulated by absentee landlords and faceless firms. The symbolic and structural violence that erases community life will have achieved the banal finality that was surely never the imagined telos of the Eternal City. But it was the original, fatal infection of civic discord, the divisive germ of fear and menace, that underlay the theatricality of urbane courtesy and working-class irony alike; it eventually breached the body politic's powers of resistance and left it at the mercy of external forces it could not control. The activists may succeed in rolling back these processes to some extent, but there is probably now no nostalgic act of historical reconstruction that can bring the rough, affectionate intimacies of a disappearing social life back from the brink of extinction.

Yet their memory will continue to infuse the actions of those—and they are many—who refuse the bland vision offered by the current civic leadership and by the operators of the new real estate market. In many ways the parabolic career of Silvio Berlusconi, with its remarkably close parallel in the career of his Thai counterpart Thaksin Shinawatra,[10] offers a suggestive intimation of both the powers and the limits of the neoliberal machine. Both have faced a critical response from economists and other local critics unpersuaded by the allure of massive globalization, and both were forced out of office without being able to dismantle previously existing structures altogether.

This was perhaps to be expected. I have argued here that globalization, for all the surface similarities that it brings, may not create cultural uniformity in terms of how people locally intercept and interpret these new developments. The failure of the European Union to impose fiscal or legal discipline on the Italian state may at some level be a source of embarrassment; but it also suggests a robust resistance to forms of political life and to civic values that are seen as intrusive and unmanageable in the Italian context. The extraordinary degree of cultural fragmentation that characterizes not only Italy but its capital suggests that attempts to impose a uniform civic code will always be refracted through very different visions of social life, even if these have supplanted the earlier modalities described in this book. That is a message to which political scientists and economists should pay greater heed. One does not have to be a cultural determinist to see that local reworkings of supposedly universal themes—civil recastings of civic values—are powerful forces precisely because their capillary form and their emergence from a lived social experience invest them with greater reality than the most coherent formal models.

Roma è Roma (Rome is Rome)—I often heard this phrase, usually not with any sense of resignation, but with the pride of specificity that recognizes Rome's place in world history but also recognizes the tenacity of its people's adherence to their own way of doing things. In associations like the Monti Social Network, the echoes of the old rotating credit associations still occasionally reverberate—ghostly reminders of the conflicts, the distrust, and the underhand dealings without which social life would perhaps have very little meaning. Those who hear the echoes value the conflict. They will be the bearers of memory, but also of social practices deeply sedimented in the play of gesture and indirect hint; of jokes and quarrels; of dizzying alternations between fierce resistance and humble self-abasement; of menaces in the night and promises during the day; of jealous precision in the conservation of old buildings and crafty cunning in the pursuit of new construction; of images and even human performances of the Madonna's role given meaning only by the sins of their authors.

Roma è Roma, and Monti is its "first rione," even if for some it has also proved to be the "last frontier." Here, eternally, eternity continues to fracture and to coalesce, repeatedly and without rest; for such, paradoxically, is the eternity of the Eternal City. It seems still that no bureaucratic hand can yet stay the corruption, at once and forever corrosive and creative, of time. When and if it succeeds, Rome will no longer be Rome.

NOTES

OVERTURE

1. I use the term *tempo* in Bourdieu's sense of a distinctive and manipulable rhythm (1977, 6–7).

2. See Herzfeld 2008. This rendition of a heritage held in trust by the state perhaps also implies the equally gendered sense of paternalism.

3. On the French term *patrimoine* and the link with concepts of property, see Handler 1985, 1988; Herzfeld 2002. On the term *patrimonio* in Spanish (Mexico), see Ferry 2005, 82–88, 215–16. On the Italian sense of *patrimonio*, see especially Palumbo 2003, 17–34.

4. Smith (2006) offers an excellent account of how global economic forces penetrate local urban practices, and especially of ostensibly left-wing and liberal governments' preference for "regeneration" over the invasive and class-directed implications of "gentrification."

5. On this, see especially Lozada's remarks on Catholicism in China (2001, 198–99).

CHAPTER ONE

1. The original was in Latin: *Quod non fecerunt Barbari, fecerunt Barberini.* It was during the papacy of Urban VIII (1623–1644) that Galileo was tried for heresy. Stendhal (n.d. a, 27) notes a version of the comment.

2. About thirty years earlier, the youthful Rutelli swept the steps of the Church of Sant'Agnese in Piazza Navona in a symbolic gesture of cleansing them of clerical corruption.

3. Pasquino is an ancient statue (originally female) on which people deposited satirical poems commenting on current affairs. See Giovannini 1997. A Monti taxi driver with strong historical interests commented that Mayor Francesco Rutelli should have feared his colleagues' opposition to the mayor's policies because "when the people murmur . . . when Pasquino speaks," there is "some point of truth."

4. Pope Benedict XVI's recent admonition that the corrupt should not expect to enter Paradise (see "'Chi prende tangenti non sale a Dio': Il Papa contro i corrotti," *La Repubblica*, 2 April 2007, p. 15) is only new in its specific emphasis on *tangenti* (kickbacks); Romans, forever practical, are used to taking such reminders of the dangers of eternal

damnation—the reality of which has also been a theme in this pope's theology—in their stride.

5. Giuseppe Gioacchino Belli, famed dialect poet of Rome, satirizes the church's willingness to use the brothels in a sonnet (no. 326, 11 December 1834, "Er Bordello Scuperto," also cited in Rizzo and Stella 2007, 25).

6. Bordellos were known as houses of tolerance (*case di tolleranza*) because the state, from Independence to the fall of Fascism, generally accepted prostitution as a necessity; the Fascist state updated the relevant legislation in the Unified Text on Public Security of 1931, restricting prostitutes' rights and effectively placing them under the control of their landlords and local police. The brothels were also called *case chiuse* (closed houses) because of an 1888 law that required them to keep their shutters permanently closed and also forbade the selling of food and drink at these establishments. In 1958, under the so-called Merlin law (law no. 75/58, named for the Socialist senator Lina Merlin, on the "abolition of the regulation of prostitution and struggle against the exploitation of the prostitution of other [persons]"), state control was lifted, but with it went a great deal of protection previously provided for the prostitutes' health and well-being, and this has hit foreign prostitutes especially hard (see Cole and Booth 2007, 111).

7. Reported in "Una settantanove anni, l'altra ottantatré: sfruttavano le prostitute nelle case squillo," *Il Messaggero*, Rome section, 1 May 2005, p. 40.

8. For an extensive parallel case, see Palumbo 2003.

9. See, for a well documented historical example, Bocquet 2007, 293–304.

10. The urbanist Carlo Cellamare (2007, 53–54) uses this aspect of Monti's physical relation to the modern city to give a sense of its rooted intimacy, while the mystery novelist Mario Quattrucci (n.d., 8) uses the sunken gloom of Monti's streets at dusk in a very evocative fashion.

11. Thus, for example, Quattrucci (n.d.; see also Ravaro 1994, 632, s.v. "Subbura"). But the more usual, "philologically correct" (Palumbo 2003, 305) explanation is that is somehow related to the nearby "Sucusa" of an even earlier date, located on the present-day Celio Hill (Lewis and Short 1900, 1785, s.v. "Subura," the ancient spelling).

12. See his discussion of the relationship among time, place, and identity (D'Aquino 1995, 18–21).

13. On this, see D'Aquino 1995, 81.

14. Sabetti 2000, esp. ix.

15. On this, see also Bocquet 2007, 304, 341.

16. Note the slight hyper-correction (*per* for *pe'*), perhaps suggestive of the slight embarrassment this particular individual always showed when exposing the more disreputable aspects of Monti life or when criticizing the Vatican.

17. Contrast, for example, mainland Greek village architecture (see Friedl 1962, 12–14).

18. Inasmuch as it can mean both "country" and "local community," it strongly resembles both the Greek *patridha* (Herzfeld 2005, 79) and the Thai *moeang* (e.g., Tambiah 1976, 112–14).

19. I was struck by a resident's comparable comments on my own ethnographic film (Herzfeld 2007a); Monticiani retain a great deal of the spoken and gestural mannerisms to be found in neorealist films set in Rome.

20. On the articulation of sin, disgrace, and perhaps also poverty in Christian identity, see also Heatherington 2006.

21. The position of *caporione* appears historically as an elected office under the authority of the papal state; in the seventeenth century, the *caporione* of Monti, who was elected for a three-month term, had at his disposal thirty men, recruited from the artisanal and shopkeeper segments of the population, for keeping public order (Paita 1998, 57–58). The control of this office gradually passed to the noble families, and, in the eighteenth century, directly to the pope (at which point the *caporione* of Monti alone was considered to be a member of the magistracy and thus of the ruling class, an indication of Monti's status as "the first *rione* of Rome"); by the end of papal rule, the office had been replaced by a presidency (also appointed by the pope). The term *caporione* remained in popular usage, linked to the local underworld until the middle of the twentieth century (see *Virtual Roma* at www.geocities.com/mp_pollett/rioni.htm). This series of transitions reveals an interesting continuity between papal authority and local forms of social management.

22. This is especially clear in the history of Spain, where Catholic mutualism was a key component of collusion between church and state. See Maddox 1993, 125–26; for Italy, see Holmes 1989, 109, 192–95.

23. The term clearly alludes to the sudden post-Unification expansion of Rome in the second half of the nineteenth century. See Insolera 1993, 38–51.

24. Law 432/98, article 3*d*, permits a proprietor to refuse to renew a rental contract "when the property is part of a seriously damaged building."

25. See also Berdini 2000, 50–64. Berdini particularly taxes the Left with having abandoned a "culture" that had long emphasized both concerted planning and the importance of everyday social life instead of the extraordinary (*straordinarietà*); there is perhaps a direct parallel here with the Left's espousal of market forces from which many leftist intellectuals benefited at the expense of poorer Romans.

26. On this, see especially Smith's scathing critique of the term "urban renewal" (2006).

27. This almost exaggeratedly laconic use of dialect is always ironic. When I said to a plumber that I expected to see him on my return the following year, he retorted, "*E, 'ndo vado?*"—meaning, evidently, that he had no such choices: "Well, where do you suppose *I* would be going?"

28. See Doumanis 2001 for a useful account of the successes and failures of the national project. For a critical account of the possibilities for Italian national sentiment, see Rosati 2000. Both authors find evidence for the increased importance of national identity at the end of the twentieth century.

29. For an intriguing analysis of the Northern League's "ludic" mockery of Italy's formal state institutions, conventions of courtesy and masculinity, and subversion of normative political discourse and imagination, see Dematteo 2007. Significantly, she notes that many of the marginalized and resentful northerners whose support had propelled the party into eventual power left in disgust when, jettisoning its largely unattainable secessionist and other antiestablishment goals, leader Umberto Bossi took the party into coalition with Berlusconi's Forza Italia and Gianfranco Fini's Alleanza nazionale (National Alliance; 226). After the coalition's defeat at the polls in 2006, Bossi reverted to some of his old secessionist rhetoric. Rumiz's analysis of the Lega Nord (1997), generally more

sympathetic to the sources of its disaffection from the Italian nation-state, focuses on its deployment of symbolism in resisting official power structures.

30. See, for example, "Le nuove Leghe autonomiste che irrompono nel duello tra i Poli,"*Venerdì di Repubblica*, 27 May 2005 (no. 897), p. 13.

31. See also Pardo's discussion of the role of narrow self-interest in the stereotyping of working-class Neapolitan identity (1996, 13). On the *arte d'arrangiarsi*, see especially Pardo's careful resistance to automatically including informal economic arrangements under this rubric (11). On "muddling through" as a basis for managing bureaucratic irruptions into daily life, see de Certeau 1984, xix; Reed-Danahay 1996, 212–13; and Scott 1998, 328–33.

32. It can also be a menacing mode, as when a middle-aged man, disturbed during the night by some wealthy Spanish youths living above him, threatened to chase them away. As he reported the encounter, "'You'll have to leave,' I told them in Roman dialect (*'Dovet' annávene', ho detto in romanaccio*)." The fact that he emphasizes the Roman morphology (*annávene* instead of *andarvene*) suggests that for him it was a way of getting rough with these irritating young foreigners.

33. Such expressions are widespread and can be found far beyond the Italian borders. See Herzfeld 2007b. On the more self-congratulatory views of an alleged absence of racism from Italy, see Cole 1997, 9.

34. The politically correct term in Italian is *Gitani*. *Rom*, a form of *Roma*, is also used in a relatively respectful sense; since other traveler communities are covered by the term, however, I prefer here to employ the admittedly suspect term "Gypsies," although in a value-neutral and highly generic sense, to indicate a category that is the object of active discrimination at many levels of Italian society.

35. Cole (1997, 131–32) argues that middle-class residents of the Sicilian city of Palermo generally do not express openly racist views against non-European immigrants, whom they employ as markers of their own class position, while their working-class fellow citizens display some empathy toward immigrants from the perspective of their own resentment of Rome and the wealthy north (see also Cole 1997, 112). He rightly argues that describing either group as racist or otherwise is simplistic and misleading. In Rome, the ability to employ the cultural capital (see Bourdieu 1984) of educated speech and urbane civility—in a city largely despised by the rest of the country—disguises an analogous ambiguity, further complicated by distrust of immigrants from the countries of the former Eastern European bloc. The neofascist Alleanza nazionale profits from working-class anger over potential threats to an already precarious economic viability, but former Communists among the working-class population may be relatively unwilling to vote for neofascists. Civil manners do not necessary guarantee civic values; disclaimers of racist intent may be especially useful for disguising it.

36. At the opposite end of the social scale, a working-class friend who had grown up in Puglia (Apulia) was once walking through Piazza di Spagna with a Roman coeval; when they overheard some people speaking the dialect of the area around Bari and Foggia, the Roman was astonished to learn that it was a form of Italian!

37. See Jane Hill's analysis of nostalgia as an expression of power (1992). The "noble savage" view of working-class Romans suffuses nationalist discourse in its treatment

of local traditions. Educated residents praised few older speakers of Romanesco for their adherence to traditional speech and values while deploring as "folkloric" those who were more aggressive or disrespectful in manner.

38. Although more self-consciously expressed, as perhaps befits an intellectual and linguist, this observation comes remarkably close to the experiences of peasants from Locorotondo, in Puglia (see Galt 1991, 205).

39. Even passionately left-wing localists sometimes seem embarrassed by their habit of using Romanesco. A good friend who has evidently committed himself to a political career corrected himself twice in a short stretch of conversation (*mó* to *adesso* for "now" and *annavo* to *andavo* for "I was going"). When I gently remonstrated with him, he replied, "I'm trying to force myself to speak Italian" (*Sto cercando di sforzarmi di parlare italiano*)—a particularly revealing remark in that, despite his efforts to speak the official language, he implicitly attributes equivalent status to Romanesco and Italian. In Greece, by contrast, people contrast "our dialect" with "correct" or "official" Greek, indicating a very different history of nation building.

40. One of my wife's local Italian teachers initially expressed puzzlement at my interest in a Roman dialect that, for her, did not exist; she conceded the point after discovering in a supermarket that she could not follow the conversation of two obviously very local women!

41. These comments are culled from relatively recent attempts to compile dictionaries of Romanesco: Malizia 1999, 7; Ravaro 1994, 17.

42. Their tendency to argue that Romanesco is incomprehensible to the outsider confirms the impression that in Italy probably, and in Rome certainly, cultural intimacy is more usually defended at the local than at the national level. In Greece, by contrast, it is the national language that people hold to be impenetrable by outsiders, and the dialect of the capital died out within a few decades of Athens's elevation to that status (see Newton 1972, 14–15).

43. Some of these usages also rest on a bedrock of amused recollection; an artisan told me that once a baby had been abandoned at a church in front of a wheel device specially designed for that purpose (see Kertzer 1993) with a note saying "*figlio di m. ignota*" (for *figlio di madre ignota*, son of an unknown mother) and that this had been read as *figlio di mignotta*! The pun is suggestive of both the dishonored origins of the child's mother and the intimacy of a world in which such unfortunate incidents occur and are resolved.

44. For example, *Er Cipolla*, "The Onion." Mayor Rutelli was sarcastically known as *Er Cicoria*, "The Chicory." A lightly ironic title for the toughest of bosses was *Er Mejo*, "The Best."

45. For comparative examples, see Kapferer 1988, 155–61; Papataxiarchis 1991. Kapferer's recognition of the links between Australian (masculine) egalitarianism and racism (1988, 192–200) is suggestive.

46. Detienne (2007, 2) has recently reminded us that "anthropologists" were, for Aristotle, "chatterboxes" as well, as they had been "scandal-mongers" for Aristophanes a few decades earlier—the latter genealogy offering an identity that the profession has seemed as happy as my Roman friends to claim in celebratory terms (Gluckman 1963).

CHAPTER TWO

1. One especially indignant right-wing entrepreneur, implacable in his opposition to the left-wing city administration and national government of the time, saw this as yet another example of the way the authorities were destroying the glorious Italian tradition of small-scale entrepreneurship (on which see Piore and Sabel 1984; Yanagisako 2002) in order, he claimed, to create larger units more amenable to control by the central authorities under the guise of adjusting to European Union regulations.

2. Parisi (2002, 155), writing of a town in Basilicata, shows that artisans there nostalgically employ the categories of *artisti* and *scienziati* to recall the higher prestige they claim to have enjoyed in the past.

3. This appears in Article 45, which nevertheless places artisanship in the context of a general concern with promoting social development over economic gain and therefore, ironically, sidesteps the practical economic concerns of artisans struggling to survive. The article begins, "The Republic recognizes the social function of cooperation in the form of reciprocity and without goals of private speculation. The law promotes and favors its increase by the most suitable means and assures, given appropriate controls, its character and purposes." Only then, in a separate paragraph, does it continue, "The law provides for the stewardship and development of artisanship."

4. On Italy, see Angioni 1989; Lai 2004, 20–21; and Maher 1987. For discussions of equivalent expressions in other cultures, see also Herzfeld 2004, 107–8, 115; and Singleton 1989, 26–27. See also Lanoue 1991. Grasseni's work (2003, 180–85; 2007) suggests that closer attention to the links between epistemology and the social uses of vision might usefully challenge the conceptual distance between educated observers and skilled workers.

5. Some young immigrants have been happy to work as apprentices and assistants, often illegally, as they could thus at least acquire skills that allowed them to escape the lowest levels of the labor market. Their goals are usually explicitly economic, the newly acquired skills a basic instrument of survival.

6. Jacqueline Leavitt, a member of the United Nations commission that investigated the situation in Rome in 2005, notes that the effects of such displacements fall disproportionately on women; as wives and mothers, they must care for the children while often being unable to find work of their own. Her observations were incorporated into the final report of the commission (AGFE 2005, 115–27); see also "Onu: 'Roma libera dagli sfratti: Missione internazionale per capire l'emergenza abitativa," *La Repubblica*, Rome section, 17 February 2005, p. II. The report also discussed Pom Mahakan, the Bangkok community where I have been working on related issues (AGFE 2005, 11–12; see also Herzfeld 2006).

7. Tolerance of noise is strikingly selective. A woman who came out of her home at 3 a.m. to protest the loud noise emanating from a bar was beaten up by the owner, who was never prosecuted for either the attack or the public nuisance, whereas another woman whose birthday party went on until 1 a.m. was fined half a million *lire*. Such discriminations raise the unverifiable but locally plausible suspicion that the new intruders are protected politically.

8. Pardo (1996, 114–15) reports that the Neapolitan poor see banks as more bureaucratic if slightly cheaper sources of loans than the more reasonable usurers. My Roman

informants rarely credited banks with the slightest accessibility, and felt that even those artisans who might have persuaded a bank manager to lend them money faced a joyless choice between the avarice of illegal moneylenders on the one side and the banks' legalized usury—for so they perceived it—on the other. Obviously some did succeed in obtaining bank loans. The overall perception of banks, however, was almost uniformly unforgiving.

9. The allusion to Africa is inspired by Ferguson 1990.

10. Others include the urbanist Enzo Scandurra, two architects engaged in the Angelo Mai project, another who has been surveying all the historic buildings of the center of Rome, and even another foreign anthropologist—a Uruguayan student (Adriana Goñi Mazzitelli), an activist with the Network. I talked with at least three resident architects, one linguist, two economic historians, and an archaeologist, none of whom are regulars at the Network's meetings. Two waiters turned out to be, or to have been, students of anthropology. The lines between local and academic knowledge are truly blurred today. See also the discussion by Palumbo (2003, 11–13), who himself once lived in Monti. Cellamare (2008) offers an innovative analysis of planning and activism in Monti.

CHAPTER THREE

1. On the formal gifts that marked this arrangement, see Holmes (1989, 98). In Italy such obedience meant devout Catholics long followed the dictates of the church in casting their votes exclusively for the Christian Democrats in post–World War II elections (and for thirty years after Unification did not vote at all) (Putnam 1993, 107). Obedience and "acceptance of one's station in life" (Putnam 1993, 107) reproduce the dictates of religious doctrine as class structure. As Sabetti (2000, 231–34) points out, however, this does not mean that civic institutions can never flourish where the church is strong.

2. See the interesting—if too generic—discussion of this development by Putnam (1993, 107–9).

3. The tradition extends from Banfield (1958) to Putnam (1993); some foreign commentators have been significantly resistant to, or ignorant of, the trenchant critiques of such ethnocentric judgmentalism (see, e.g., Faeta 2004; Lai 2002; Minicuci 2003).

4. Campbell 1964; see also du Boulay 1974, Herzfeld 2004. See Herzfeld 1992 for an exploration of the extension of this idea to the secular realm of Greek culture. For a parallel from a Catholic culture (Portugal), see de Pina-Cabral 1986.

5. Pardo 1996, 113–19. The harsh Neapolitan judgment reported by Pardo excludes truly evil humans—especially the more merciless usurers—from any hope of redemption. Like Pardo's Neapolitan informants, however, Romans sometimes recognize in the less relentless usurers the redeeming quality of a useful social role—in Rome, bringing hope to those whom the banks have callously abandoned to their fate.

6. For a comparable account of popular refractions of doctrine in Hindu morality and manners, see Prasad 2007.

7. Lukken 1973, 167.

8. Mueller (2001) shows how medieval preachers, by using the language of credit and debt to explain theological matters and especially those pertaining to original sin, could not free their cosmology from the logic of the usury they sought to condemn.

9. "This primitive accumulation plays approximately the same role in political economy as original sin does in theology" (Marx 1976, 873). The idea has been revived by economists in recent years for countries that seem to experience difficulty in borrowing abroad in terms of their own currencies; see Bordo 2006; Bordo, Meissner, and Redish 2003; Eichengreen and Hausmann 2004; Eichengreen, Hausmann, and Panizza 2003. Debt is thus not only financial; it also concerns time and relationships, both of which are morally charged in an imperfect world acknowledged as imperfect. Cultural and ethical assumptions about reciprocity and dependence thus affect social and economic relations while also becoming in some sense their product.

10. For an important study of contingency and the management of tempo in the social life of gamblers, see Malaby 2003.

11. Aho 2005, 45; Haney 1922, 94. On Vatican anti-Semitism, see Kertzer 1997, 2001.

12. See Caffiero 2004 for the period from medieval times to Unification and Kertzer 2001 for the nineteenth and twentieth centuries.

13. The phrase *cittadini romani di religione ebraica* appears on the monument in Via Portico d'Ottavia, at the entrance to what used to be the Ghetto and next to the Church of St. Gregory where Jews were once forced to listen to Christian sermons threatening them with eternal perdition (and using Old Testament texts to do so). On the shared elements of the discourse of original sin, see Lifschitz 1993.

14. The relationship between Fascism and the Jewish community is complex. The Fascists were reluctant to aid the Nazis in their policies of extermination, and a Jewish Monti resident defended one active Fascist in a postwar trial on the grounds that this man had saved his life by hiding him from the German troops. It is also true that some Jewish merchants supported Mussolini before German pressure to persecute the Italian Jews overwhelmed his professed—if perhaps strategic—rejection of Nazi racial theories. But to absolve Mussolini of racism seems dangerously ingenuous at best. For an overview of racial concepts in Italy, see Burgio 1999.

15. Some of the betrayals may have had more to do with economic resentment than hatred of the Jews as such. For several accounts of the Jews' wartime experiences, see Impagliazzo 1997.

16. Mussolini's racism was highly instrumental (see Sarfatti 1999, 332); the introduction of explicit legislation against the Jewish population nevertheless probably had nothing to do with German pressure—as he himself angrily insisted (see Gillette 2002, 94).

17. Aho 2005, 47; Haney 1922, 95.

18. See Todeschini 1989, 168–72.

19. Ago 1998, 118.

20. See Kaye 2001; Todeschini 1994; Vismara 2004, 37–85.

21. Pardo (1996, 202n16) found some evidence that this was still happening in Naples during his fieldwork.

22. In one of the many ironies of the church's accommodation with materiality, the Cassa di Risparmio—direct predecessor of the Banca di Roma, central player in the major eviction case to be discussed later—was created as a bulwark against usury through the provision of an alternative, regulated source of loans to small merchants and artisans. (http://www.istess.it/Cassadirisparmio.htm. Accessed 11 July 2007.) On the increasing "invisibility" of the Jews in the years between the baroque era and Unification, see Caffiero (2004, 16).

23. Much of this discussion draws on the illuminating account by historian Sylvain Piron (2001, 74–76).

24. See Piron's discussion of this in terms of theories of reciprocity (2001, 84).

25. See especially Calabrò 1991; Cornwell 1984; Guarino 1998, and Ledl 1997.

26. On this, see Putnam 1993, 109; see also Kertzer 1980, 208–9.

27. According to Haney (1922, 94), the scholastics argued that to pay for money is to pay for time. Hence the offense against divine law; time belongs to all and therefore ultimately to God. See also Piron 2001, 78.

28. See the remarks of Tano Grasso, national anti-racketeering commissioner, reported in "Per Tano Grasso, il pericolo della capitale: 'Roma è la città dell'usura,'" La Repubblica, Rome section, 18 July 2001, p. VIII.

29. This is the central argument of Aho 2005. See also the related argument of Todeschini 1994, 147.

30. Piron 2001, 99–100.

31. See, for example, Pocino 2000.

32. For events associated with the Jubilee, church authorities provided sidewalk booths for the confessional, focusing on individual pardons rather than the relief of collective sin; on one occasion, in a celebration held on the site of the ancient Circus Maximus, two thousand priests took turns to hear confession at 312 special booths. The church hierarchy also reaffirmed and promoted the centrality of indulgences. See Vigli 1999, 152–54.

33. Left-wing critics of Vatican intolerance toward the gay organizations invoked the importance of the state's independence of what is, legally, another state enclosed entirely within its borders. Leftist politician Nicola Zingaretti, in a passionate speech at a rally in front of the Pantheon, attacked the interference in Italian affairs of a state, the Vatican, that was extracommunitario—now a derogatory label for migrants, especially illegal ones, into the European Union.

34. On the complaints about the offense to the pope, see "Crociata contro il raduno gay," La Repubblica, 29 January 2000, p. 23.

35. A brief summary of these events is to be found in Schneider and Schneider 2006, 77.

36. This term also reflects the confessional, since pentito technically means "penitent." On the emergence of the pentiti and their subsequent appearance in trials of prominent camorristi and mafiosi, see Arlacchi 1994 and Jacquemet 1996.

37. Accountability has been a key emphasis at least since Evans-Pritchard's analysis of Zande witchcraft (1937). See also Douglas 1970. On audit culture, see Strathern 2000.

38. See especially Handler 1986.

39. This has certainly been a target in some other countries. See, for example, Askew 1996 and Herzfeld 2006 on the pursuit of this goal in Thailand.

40. Under Mussolini, this road was called Via del Impero (Empire Street), clearly a name to obliterate in the post-Fascist era through the clever substitution of "Street of the Imperial Forums"—which displaced its meaning back to the ancient era that Mussolini had tried to appropriate for the glorification of his own rule.

41. See, for example, the negative reporting in Enzo Siciliano, "E da Termini comincia la caccia al taxi," La Repubblica, Rome section, 20 July 2001, p. I.

NOTES TO PAGES 69–72

42. Enrico Fermi, who worked with colleagues in a laboratory located on Via Panisperna in Monti, was friendly with my mother, who held a doctorate in chemistry from a German university. When she visited Rome for the last time, at age 92, I was in midfieldwork, and a visit to the house—which we could not enter—was a moment of high emotion for both of us, linking her past and my memories of her recollected youth with the present excitement of doing fieldwork in and around the street now powerfully linked with his name. Fermi, whose wife was Jewish, had dissuaded my mother from fleeing to Italy rather than to England when the Nazis came to power.

43. Mirri (1996, 47) notes that Italian cities are characterized by this kind of stratigraphy but also by the reuse of old materials and a contrast between spatial closeness and temporal distance between buildings. She suggests that such a pattern, which produces a particular understanding of the relationship between past and present in those who dwell in such places, is not unique to Rome. Rome nevertheless, I suggest, displays the time-space torsion with particular intensity. De Cesaris (2002, 54–59) points out that—archaeological excavations notwithstanding—the subterranean stratigraphy of Rome has, by contrast with its visible counterpart, largely been ignored as a key factor in determining the urban landscape since ancient times.

44. In early 2007, Mayor Walter Veltroni announced his decision to replace the *sampietrini* along the Via Nazionale, which links Piazza della Repubblica with the descent to Piazza Venezia. See "Via Nazionale diventa sicura: in estate sampietrini addio," *Il Messaggero*, Rome section, 28 March 2007, p. 38; "Via Nazionale, addio ai sampietrini," *La Repubblica*, Rome section, 28 March 2007, pp. II-III; "Non toccate i sampietrini ma nessuno li sa riparare,"29 March 2007, p. VII; and "La soprintendenza: in via Nazionale resti la 'memoria' dei sampietrini," 30 March 2007, p. XI. On an earlier phase of this gradual asphalting of many of Rome's central roads, for which one of the city administration's arguments was that these cobblestones no longer had much to with Rome since they were made in Hong Kong, see "Via i sampietrini da Piazza Venezia," *La Repubblica*, Rome section, 13 July 2005, p. I. For an earlier discussion, see "I maquillage dei lungotevere," *La Repubblica*, Rome section, 1 March 2005, p. I.

45. The *casa e bottega* arrangement (see p. 45) persisted until after World War II. For a more detailed account of the relationship between the *insulae* and their medieval successors, see Mirri (1996, 25).

46. Aside from tactical code-switching, individual speakers exhibit idiosyncratic usages; a few retain supposedly archaic forms and at least one, a Jewish itinerant vendor, occasionally uses Hebrew-derived words characteristic of the older Jewish dialect of Rome (*giudio-romanesco*).

47. See Sanfilippo n.d., esp. 94–97.

48. See the reports in *City* (Rome), "False guide e centurioni abusive, 28 denunciati," 15 April 2005, p. 22; "Centurioni abusive al Colosseo erano assoldati dalla malavita," *Repubblica*, 15 April 2005, p. 31 (the source of the quotation); "Colosseo, il racket dei centurioni," *Il Messaggero*, 15 April 2005, p. 34.

49. The chorus is one of the highlights of Verdi's third opera, *Nabucco*; there have been suggestions that it should be made the official national anthem. The Northern League views it as an allegory of their own liberation from the Italian state and as a work of northern genius despite the fact that Verdi himself was a committed if somewhat unorthodox

Italian nationalist. For obvious reasons, it has had resonance in Israel and even in Greece. It was probably the inspiration of the words that he set to this piece that kept Verdi inspired to work on the composition of opera at the most critical juncture in his life despite the loss of his first wife and both his children (Toye 1931, 21–25).

50. Bellicini is the technical director of Centro Ricerche Economiche Sociali di Mercato per l'Edilizia e il Territorio (CRESME), which makes the current state of his and his associates' research available through regular publication and Web postings.

CHAPTER FOUR

1. Antonello Ricci 1999, 38.

2. See the lengthy and quite analytical discussion of the "geography of prostitution"—showing linkages between specific national groups or countries of origin with particular districts of Rome—in "Prostituzione, linea dura con i clienti," *La Repubblica*, Rome section, 5 March 2000, p. III. On links between prostitution, immigration, and national identity in Sicily, see Cole and Booth 2007, 109–17.

3. See, for example, the urban planner Lidia Decandia's proposal that new ideas and forms might emerge from sites marginalized by their association with conflict (2000, 262). For a less sanguine view of conflict in determining the city's trajectory, see Bocquet 2007.

4. See especially Palumbo 2001, 33; 2003, 12–15, 47–48. To say that "conflict" marks social relations is merely to restate a local perception and to invest it with the aura of a theoretical construct. By focusing instead on the specifically conflict-laden *quality* of particular social relations as conveyed by the abstract Italian noun ("conflictuality"), we can more easily avoid the assumption, common in older anthropological writings and popular with Italian civic moralists, that conflict is necessarily evil.

5. He is especially acerbic about the ways in which the bureaucratic culture of the municipal authorities tends to recast "participation" as a routine activity, and emphasizes the importance of resisting that tendency (see Scandurra 2003, 18; 2006).

6. Scandurra 2006, 10. See also Cellamare 2008, 84.

7. See especially Sabetti 2000, 212–38.

8. See Putnam 1993, 88); on officializing strategies, see Bourdieu 1977, 37–40. Sabetti's critique (2000) is especially pertinent here. Petrusewicz (1998) documents the historical process whereby southern Italian intellectuals partially came to absorb the negative stereotype of their region, while Moe (2002) offers a critique of simplistic accounts of north-south dualism; on the reproduction of these stereotypes in journalism within as well as outside Italy, see Schneider 1998, 7.

9. See Herzfeld 1985, 92–122.

10. On the metaphor of sedimentation, see especially Connerton 1989.

11. Elias 2000; Ferguson 1990.

12. See Faeta 2004; Minicuci 2003; Petrusewicz 1998; Schneider 1998; Teti 1993. Faubion's discussion of historical constuctivism in Greece is useful (1993), and has been appreciated by Italian scholars, for its sensitivity to the possibility of multiple modernities. Faeta's commentary is particularly helpful in disaggregating the various discourses—including visual ones—about "oriental" and "African" elements in "southern" culture.

13. Putnam 1993, 23.

14. Buchowski (1996, 79–85) offers a very different, but persuasive, distinction between the civil as that larger zone of social interaction that incorporates all aspects of communal activity (here productively expanding a political term much as Geertz [1973, 193–96] had done with 'ideology"), and "civic society" as the assemblage of institutions that operated against the oppressive control of the state (and thus the area largely understood hitherto by the term "civil society"). While his schema works well to describe political life under a largely totalitarian system of government, I prefer to reserve the idea of the civic for the values and practices found in associational activity of all kinds *including* that sanctioned by the state at all its component levels; I retain the Italian sense of *civile* as describing the ability to get along with others—sometimes an oppressive quality.

15. Lai 2002, 302–5. See also Maria Minicuci's important discussion of the role of the south in the respective imaginations of Italian and foreign anthropologists (2003).

16. The assumption that southerners engage in a much greater degree of domestic violence, for example, serves the pragmatic interests of male northerners as well as the promotion of northerners' collective self-respect, as Plesset (2006, 199) demonstrates for the prosperous northern city of Parma; her evidence is especially suggestive in conjunction with the observation by Cole and Booth (2007, 110) that northern men apparently frequent prostitutes more than do Sicilians.

17. On the legitimacy of the illicit (*la liceità dell'illecito*) as an expression of the dilemmas faced by well-meaning clergy who conducted baptisms even when the evidence suggested that the children in question were not voluntarily surrendered to the church, see Caffiero 2004, 81–87. This kind of casuistry has deep roots in Roman society, being linked to pragmatic ideals of "accommodation," as in the remark (p. 129) about the permanence of the provisional.

18. For the parallel case of Greece, see Stewart 1989.

19. See below, pp. 131–33.

20. Minicuci (2003, 144) makes this observation specifically, and acutely, in contrast with the opposite trend she discerns in foreign anthropologists' research strategies. See also the critiques by Schneider (1998, 6–8) (and, for a comparable discussion of Spain, see Fernandez 1983). On the deployment of stereotypes, see Herzfeld 2005, 156–64.

21. See also Arlacchi 1983; Galt 1991, 2.

22. Palumbo 2003, 145.

23. Putnam (1993, 167–71) is especially careful to point out that the effectiveness of such associations does not require absolute mutual trust or altruism among all members. It is nevertheless surprising that, in a book about Italy, Putnam does not address the seeming paradox of the flourishing of these institutions in a city that regards itself as stereotypically "southern." In one significant respect my argument accords with Putnam's, inasmuch as I present the Roman rotating credit associations as precursors of other forms of political association and civic self-management.

24. In truth nothing much appears to have changed, if Italian chroniclers are not exaggerating. Among recent critiques, see especially Caporale 2007; Rizzo and Stella 2007.

25. A famous, stereotypical account of "the Italians" is provided by Barzini (1964); for a more recent attempt to generalize about the country, but more from the perspective of its laboring classes, see Bravo 2001.

26. Loizos (1996, 56–58) points out that Margaret Thatcher's ostensible attempts to reduce the role of government in everyday life may in fact have been quite the opposite; and the parallel with Italy is striking in this respect.

27. This dismissive phrase recalls a similar expression used to express contempt for a discussion carried out by a few unimportant people, described as four cats (*quattro gatti*).

28. On one of the Web sites devoted to the Romanesco dialect, the Roma club flag serves as the equivalent of the national flag for the two columns comparing Romanesco with standard Italian.

29. Frosinone is a hinterland town in Lazio.

30. His choice of the term *quartiere* (quarter), however, shows that he did not grow up here. Technically, but importantly in Monti eyes, the districts within the Aurelian walls are classified as *rioni*, while only those outside the walls are *quartieri*.

31. See especially the description in Cellamare 2007, 69–71

32. The passage, which my friend read to me from an Italian translation, is as follows: "Cette nuit il y a eu deux assassinats. Un boucher, presque enfant, a poignardé son rival, jeune homme de vingt-quatre ans, et fort beau, ajoute le fils de mon voisin, qui me fait ce récit. *Mais ils étaient tous deux*, ajoute-t-il, *du quartier dei Monti* (des Monts), *ce sont des gens terribles*. Notez que ce quartier est à deux pas de nous, du côté de Sainte-Marie-Majeure; à Rome, la largeur d'une place change les murs" (Stendhal n.d. b, 23, diary entry of 27 February, 1828; original emphasis). The passage also shows that in Stendhal's day the extreme fragmentation of Rome into micro-quarters was already very marked (and in fact had long been so). For an assessment of Stendhal's accuracy in reporting, see Tillett 1971, 99, 106. His information on these particular points certainly accords well, at least in a generic sense, with current memory in Rome.

33. See his engraving of a stone throwing contest between young men of the two districts, reproduced in Cascioli 1987, 219.

34. Classically, see Evans-Pritchard 1940; cf. Peters 1967.

35. See, for example, Herzfeld 1985; Papataxiarchis 2006; Salzman 1978.

36. That leader then became the king of Libya, himself eventually overthrown in a revolution that further consolidated national unity under the secular leadership of Qaddafi (Evans-Pritchard 1949; on the later developments, see Davis 1988).

37. See Niola 1995, especially 33, 79, 111. On segmentation in the context of the European nation-state, see more generally Herzfeld 2005, 95.

38. This tendency to baronial fragmentation was accentuated anew, especially in the shaping of the city plan, in the final decades of papal rule; see Lanoue, forthcoming.

39. See, on the *palio*, Handelman 1990,: 116–35; Silverman 1979. On "wars of saints," see especially Magliocco 1993; Palumbo 2003, 110–25; 2004.

40. See Niola 1995, 77–78. On the social production of scholarly purism, see especially Palumbo 2003, 250–63.

41. See Holmes 2000, 29–30; and, for an example of the ecclesiastical implications of subsidiarity in another context, that of Malta, see Ranier Fsadni, The Writings of Mgr Paul Cremona, *The Times* (Malta), 7 December 2006. Interestingly, Holmes (2000, 30), immediately after this discussion, invokes the concept of original sin (although more metaphorically than I do here?) as a means of exploring the tensions between multiculturalism and some of the underlying assumptions of leaders of European Union member states.

42. In a richly expressive appreciation of the then newly appointed Archbishop of Malta, the Maltese Catholic intellectual Ranier Fsadni notes the new primate's experience of subsidiarity as service in a variety of positions that do not add up to a career-based climb to a summit but constitute "the exercise of distributed authority, and not a centralised one"; he then implicitly links that experience with the imperfection of human existence, the source of original sin, by remarking that "in a religion with a crucified man at the centre of its attention, achievement is measured not by the rate of intended outcomes, but by how splendidly, how lovingly, one fails" (The Writings of Mgr Paul Cremona, *The Times* (Malta), 7 December 2006.) That remark could almost be a motto for the conduct of political and cultural life in Rome.

43. Or, as Malaby (2003, 21) dubs it in the Cretan context, "instrumental nonchalance."

44. Savagnone 1995, 172–73.

45. It is possible that this, rather than a deliberate complicity, prompted the slow response of the Vatican to recent multiple revelations of pedophilia and other priestly abuses around the world. We should also note, however, poet Belli's cynical view; in his lifetime, during much of which the papacy was the sovereign power in Rome, the clergy apparently extracted bribes at every level of what Belli described as a staircase that grew ever narrower until it reached the very top of the building, where "the big cheese (*er più grosso*), as we all know, naturally / wants to keep himself at a distance / so he can say he never got anything out of it" (sonnet no. 284; 26 April 1934). The allusion is clear. Today the term *pezzo grosso* (literally, "big piece") is used of any wealthy and powerful person, often in the context of property ownership.

46. See the useful discussion by Berdini 2000, 93–94.

47. See "Torna l'Ici per i beni della Chiesa," *La Repubblica*, 29 June 2006, p. 11. The church conducted a vigorous press campaign to argue that all officially recognized religions benefited from the same exemption, and that the Catholic Church authorities had always paid tax on buildings used for commercial purposes. The former statement appears to be accurate. But it is the latter proposition that, as the *La Repubblica* article suggests, might now be in contention. See also Lorenzo Salvia, "Prodi boccia i tagli all'Ici per la Chiesa: cercano voti," *Corriere della Sera*, 7 October 2005, p. 5.

48. It is worth noting that Pope Benedict XVI has reaffirmed the reality of hell (see *La Repubblica*, 30 March 2007, pp. 47–49); he also averred that those guilty of corruption would not be able to avoid eternal damnation (*Il Messaggero*, 2 April 2007, p. 9; *La Repubblica*, 2 April 2007, p. 15). His predecessor, John Paul II, was at some pains to insist that indulgences did not constitute some kind of price reduction (*sconto*) (*Il Tempo*, 30 September 1999, p. 5). This does not seem to have convinced the general public, as is clear from the press reaction to the creation of a special catechism for Jubilee indulgences ("Il manuale delle indulgenze: Giubileo, tutti i trucchi per andare in Paradiso," *Il Messaggero*, 18 September 1999, pp. 1, 11; Orazio La Rocca, "Anche una sigaretta in meno aiuta ad andare in Paradiso" (Even one cigarette less helps you get to Paradise), *La Repubblica*, 18 September 1999, p. 21). The Romans' cynicism is nothing new; in a sonnet dated 20 October 1883 (no. 231), Belli has an irrepressible fornicator demand, "So what if it is a sin? There's always at the ready / a good confession and communion / to make your peace with God on all the feast-days."

49. See Lombardi Satriani 1999b, 13; Niola 1995, 77–78.

50. In Sicily such silence is regarded as the fullest expression of male continence, and its violation is often punished violently; see Blok, 1974: 211–12.

51. Such a code itself communicates clear messages, to be understood in the context of a culture that invests great value in verbal dexterity and may take speech to be more deceptive or ambiguous than silence. This clearly affects the reading of performances that invoke a stereotypically silent idiom of masculinity. Di Bella (2008, 27 and passim) provides an important analysis of the phenomenon at the source.

52. In one of his sonnets (no. 2; 14 September 1830), Belli pays tribute to a father's wisdom (*Iggnuno penzi a li fattacci sua*, "let each think about his own business") and comments that being a Christian is all well and good as long as one also carries a knife along with the rosary.

53. See Nicotri 1993. This exposé of priestly compromises, expressed in the confidentiality of the confessional, is interesting for the ethical issues it raises. The author pretended to be a businessman in search of guidance after he had benefited financially from commitments made to a political party; he received quite a wide range of answers, many of which nevertheless shared a tone of understanding and even ethical complicity. The ethics of the confessional are supposed to protect the penitent; this is the only extensive piece of investigative journalism on the confessors' practices that I have encountered.

54. For an excellent overview of this concept, see Rodotà 2005. This author and official served as the national ombudsman for privacy (*garante della privacy*) during my fieldwork. It is interesting to note that the nearest Italian equivalent of "privacy," *riservatezza*, has not been adopted for Italian legal purposes; indeed, Rodotà, a left-wing politician, openly acknowledges the American origins of the idea, showing how far the Italian left wing has gone in accepting ideals of democratic process and the protection of that process that allegedly originated in the United States in their present form.

55. Gramsci 1975, 184, cited in Scaraffia 1990, 23.

56. Stendhal (n.d. c, 134) gives a brief sketch of the verbal exchange between the woman and the man, showing that it is usually the woman who both initiates and terminates the liaison.

57. It is also worth noting that the elegant inscription was mounted in the name of Pope Pius VI, who was reviled by the poor and satirized by Pasquino precisely because of his energetic promotion of the monumental embellishment of the city; see, for example, Anon. 1993, 72–74.

58. Much of this information comes from Cardilli 1990a, 153.

59. On the paradoxical combination of piety and ill repute associated with these images, see Antonello Ricci 1999, 38–44; Scaraffia 1990, 19; Di Nola (1990, 34) notes that in addition to the difficulty of crowd control these images encouraged forms of devotion that fully escaped the church's surveillance and control.

60. Scaraffia 1990, 22. This phrase suggests the common assumption that the "inside" must be that of domestic space, a perception belied by the remarkably inclusive intimacy of Roman street life until World War II.

61. See Cardilli 1990a: 155, citing Rufini 1853, VII. Odorisio (1990, 25) notes the scarcity of historical sources on the *Madonnelle*; the personal character of early devotion was very much a public matter, whereas it was precisely the public control of shared space

that, almost literally, paved the way for the most recent processes of privatization—now an economic rather than a devotional process, one that has substantially inhibited public devotions by private individuals and social groups alike. It is important not to confuse "personal" activities, which can be very public affairs and can involve a great deal of shared knowledge and experience, with "private" matters that are considered the business only of those who conduct them.

62. On this process, see Cardilli 1990a, esp.153–55; several authors in that volume (e.g., Scaraffia 1990, 20) speak of the images' anti-institutional character, their association with resistance to clerical power, and their capacity for dissolving the boundaries between public streets and private homes. For an exploration of similar processes of monumentalization and the occlusion of local memory in Greece, see Caftanzoglou 2000, 2001a, 2001b.

63. See Francescangeli 1990, 53, 58–59; on a parallel example of cartographic reorganization that similarly preceded and framed historic conservation in a very different context, in Greece, see Herzfeld 1999. On Mussolini's programs of civic cleansing, see especially Horn 1994. On spatial cleansing, see Herzfeld 2006.

64. See Savagnone 1995, 173.

65. On the very different way that objectification comes to be understood in Protestant contexts, see especially Keane 2007. On the hegemonic nature of the supposed separation of folk from ecclesiastic religion, see Stewart 1989.

66. This expression is especially revealing of the church's engagement with the physical—and thus sinful—world inasmuch as the *mattone* often stands as a metonym for the properties from which speculating real estate agents are trying to squeeze profit.

67. For a somewhat different priestly attempt (in Sardinia) at the in-gathering of a parish congregation and the varied reactions this provoked, see Heatherington 1999, 318. For a more critical view of Catholic proselytization, especially in relation to third world immigrants already technically within the faith, see Napolitano 2007, 83–85.

68. The image of effervescence is intentionally Durkheimian; it is invoked by Di Nola (1990, 39), but in the context of the older practices with their wild outpourings of popular ecstasy. I want to suggest that state and church alike now try to channel and, to borrow an appropriately neoliberal metaphor, to "privatize" that effervescence and so to subject it to new forms of civic discipline.

69. See, for example, Lombardi Satriani 1999b.

70. The icon was discovered when a poor woman saw the Madonna in a vision and sought the image in accordance with what she heard therein; see Corrubolo 2004, especially 133–34 and 147–51; Pifferi 2004. On miraculous visions and the discovery of icons in the Greek tradition, see Stewart 1991: 84–87. While the Roman church largely resisted the paroxysms of iconoclasm that had so disrupted the Orthodox church and that eventually fostered the Reformation as well (see Antonello Ricci 1999), the fear of idolatry was nevertheless a real one, repeatedly revived by outbursts of deep veneration for local relics and images.

71. See Kertzer 1980, 148–59; 1996; his insights are also prefigured, in the specific ethnographic context of an Umbrian town and the parish priest's role in organizing ritual and social events, by Silverman (1975, 173–74). Less surprising (except, perhaps, for its unquestioned pervasiveness) is the tendency for secular events organized by those with

church affiliations to take on religious overtones derived from ritual practices, as in the use of the "stations [*sc.* of the Cross] as a key metaphor for the phases of a Sicilian historical pageant described by Palumbo (2003, 281). For evidence of the religious organization of domestic space among self-professed atheists in Greece, see Hirschon 1989, 233.

72. Stendhal n.d. b, 26 (diary entry of 27 February 1828).

73. Here see especially Berdini 2000.

CHAPTER FIVE

1. The passage, which I have quoted elsewhere, reads in part: "Of that conceit of nations we have heard that . . . nations . . . have each had the foolish conceit of having been ahead of all the others" (Vico 1744, 174–75).

2. On Rutelli's cultivation of his image as a dashing male, see Bruto 1997. His subsequent enthusiasm for laws requiring the wearing of helmets evidently marks the transition of an ambitious politician from local to national modalities of self-presentation.

3. On this aspect of *trasformismo*, see Putnam's succinct account (1993, 19, 142). Like many Italian observers, he views it as contrary to the good governance that devolution was intended to strengthen. I have no quarrel with that assessment as long as notions of "efficiency" are not taken to be culture-free. Putnam sees the system as having given way to greater regionalism after World War II—an unquestionably accurate assertion, although the underlying logic of *trasformismo* evidently still persists in many quarters.

4. See also the very useful discussion by Pardo (1996, 141), who shows that future gains may be calculated on an impressionistic basis that nevertheless reflects experienced realities and risks.

5. For example, and in a mode characteristic of the critics, the Federazione Lavoratori della Conoscenza put out a protest in its online journal, *Sindacato Nazionale Università Ricerca*, no. 70 (14 November 2003), arguing, "In reality it [the *condono*] reinforces the conviction of impunity for those responsible for the violations and for those who continue to act in illegal ways." The device is also applied to parking offenses and similar minor illegalities. Harney (2006, 378) shows how, through rumor, immigrants from very different religious, political, and cultural backgrounds enter the tense game of speculating on *sanatorie* they hope will absolve them of their illegal status—apparently in recognition of their crucial, if necessarily inadmissible, contribution to Italy's economic health.

6. The plans date from 1882–1883, 1906, 1908, 1909, 1931, 1962, 1967, 1997 (a revision of the 1967 plan), and 2000 (a draft).

7. Berdini 2000.

8. Berdini 2000, 64, 89–90. For a detailed, micro-historical analysis of one important phase from this perspective, see Bocquet 2007. Another study attributes the rapid depopulation of the historical center and the massive growth of the suburbs, as well as the negative consequences for both, to Rome's "provincial satisfaction of calling itself a metropolis for the sole purpose of counting its inhabitants in millions" (Italia Nostra 1976, 16)—a striking instance of the capital's paradoxical image as fundamentally a provincial, marginal place. That image acquired a sense of concrete reality through the early decision, promulgated as soon as Rome became the capital of Italy, to prevent it from developing a significant industrial infrastructure (Bocquet 2007, 45).

9. For a useful preliminary account of her position on the cultural politics of the archaeology of Italy, see Andreina Ricci 1996.

10. Berdini 2000, 51.

11. Insolera 2001, 129. He also quotes an enthusiast of the Fascist regime who asked, "Who could have imagined that [the new road] could have been traced out in a straight line like a legionnaire's sword?" (129).

12. On *romanità*, see the useful discussion in Gillette 2002, 54–55. This concept had strongly racial implications in Mussolini's usage, which contributed both to its subsequent decline and to its evocation by various extreme-right groups today.

13. Berdini 2000, 38, 130.

14. Legge 9 dicembre 1998, n. 431 ("Discipline delle locazioni e del rilascio degli immobili adibiti ad uso abitativo," *Gazzetta Ufficiale* n. 292 del 15 dicembre 1998—Supplemento Ordinario n. 203/L, IV.8.1. The law also permitted a shorter-term agreement that was subject to more stringent rent controls. A proprietor could now refuse to renew a contract, even after the first four years, for a wide variety of reasons, mostly concerning proprietors' and their immediate families' economic viability.

15. See especially Giustiniani 1982, 25–33. Giustiniani was then a young journalist with *Il Messaggero*, a newspaper with a predominantly Roman constituency—but ironically also one of the newspapers Berdini charges with complaisance toward the Rutelli administration's flawed approach to planning.

16. Law 432/98, article 3e; article 3g stipulates that proprietors may refuse to renew a contract if they intend to sell the building and do not possess other properties except for their own homes.

17. This is why I prefer not to use the terms "legal culture" and "political culture" (see especially Nelken 2004 and Kavanagh 1972, respectively; but cf. Kapferer 1988); while recognizing the larger socio-cultural context of legal and political practice is important, the fact that many of the formal models originate outside their immediate national contexts (see, e.g., Pollis 1987) makes a more finely tuned set of distinctions desirable—although, to be sure, even foreign-trained legislators remain answerable to local values.

18. Mirri 1996, 34.

19. This remark recalls a Greek observation to the effect that nothing is more permanent than the provisional (Herzfeld 1991, 250).

20. During Pope Benedict's first visit to his native Cologne after assuming the papacy, indulgences were issued to anyone who attended his homily; see "Indulgenze per chi va a Colonia" and Agostino Paravicini Bagliani, "La clemenza che non piaceva a Lutero—così in Germania si scatenò la rivolta," *La Repubblica*, 9 August 2005, p. 21. The practice, which famously drew Luther's ire, retains strongly material implications. On the problems of fetishism and materiality in Christianity, see Keane 2007. On the offer of indulgences to mafiosi who sought reconciliation by financially compensating their victims' families, see "Palermo, indulgenza ai boss—'Ma se risarcite le vittime,'" *La Repubblica*, 29 January 2000, p. 23.

21. See especially Salvatore Settis, "La bellezza rubata e l'archeocondono," *La Repubblica*, 11 August 2005, p. 16. The original law, no. 947, was promulgated in 1985, and was later subsequently amended mostly to adjust the specific time frames for the procedures involved.

22. Marcelloni 2003, 38–39.

23. The parallel is widely expressed among opponents of the practice. See, for example, Santoloci 2002. (The relevant passage is also reproduced in a 2003 version at the Web site of the group Diritto all'Ambiente (http://wwf.na.agoramed.it/ambiente/dossier/Condoni&sanatorie.pdf. Accessed on 13 May 2008.

24. Lanoue (forthcoming) describes the Vatican's strategy and its political vicissitudes in this framework.

25. See Schneider and Schneider (2003, 18) for an especially well documented account of the effects of this connection; the fact that the *condono* applies to builders as well as owners shows, once again, how far the convenience of legislators and their friends influences how laws are written. In Rome, charges of collusion between city administration and construction industry are commonplace.

26. Kertzer 1980 and 1986.

27. Bourdieu 1977, 6–7.

28. The official view of time is nicely encapsulated in a booklet titled *Il Tempo È Un Diritto* (Time is a Right), in which one key contributor wrote, "I am especially pleased to think that the telephone is the instrument in which, during these years, we have invested the most effort. [This is] because not only does it inform and orientate, but above all it exalts the function of listening that, among all the forms of communication, is that to which I give the greatest affection. The punctuality of reply, the waiting time, the tone of the response, a precise content of information or details of a service: all of this, if it works well, is a sort of hospitality offered to each and every individual" (Gremaglia 2005, 6). Consistently with this recasting of a formal device as a social one ("a sort of hospitality"), she then goes on to note that a major concern of administrators is the creation of a sense "of community, of social ties" (6). While residents certainly recognize these civic virtues as ideals they share with the administrators' rhetoric, they are justifiably skeptical about both their own ability to maintain them and the administrators' sincerity in promoting them. This "hospitality" is a simulacrum, not unlike that of the "hospitality industry" rhetoric whereby hotels recast customers as "guests"; it should be considered within the same framework as the *festa dei vicini* (see p. 198).

29. See Nelken's fine discussion of delay in Italian judicial procedure (2004, 21–24).

30. Nelken (2004, 21) is in part concerned with explaining why countries like Italy are not more responsive to the external pressures of such larger systems as the European courts. While for jurists the concept of "legal culture," like that of "political culture" for political scientists, may be a useful device for liberating themselves from positivistic models, it does produce a compartmentalized vision of how social values affect formal practices. In reality, as my culinary example (see below) is intended to show, and as the discussion of usury should also indicate, such temporal manipulation probably owes at least as much to the encompassing local understanding of time as it does to any tradition internal to the legal profession alone; when Italian cases are appealed in Strasbourg, one should ask whether this move, too, might not be a means of temporizing that uses a wonderful new instrument for the purpose.

31. This is an elaboration of the point made by Nelken (2004, 20).

32. This is an important dimension of what I have called "social poetics"; see Herzfeld 2005, 21–26, 169, 171.

33. See below, pp. 199–212.

34. This is the correct rendition of the name of the coin in Romanesco. The Italianized spelling is *quattrino*. Readers may be reminded of the notorious tag about the Venetian Republic, *"prima veneziani e poi cristiani"* (First Venetians and only after that Christians). There is, however, an important difference: whereas the Venetian saying can be read as either boastfully independent or morally regretful about a deficient relationship with the dominant religion, the Roman proverb explicitly attacks the religious authority as failing to live up to its own standards.

35. Some of the power of surviving conflicts lies in their great age. Thus, notably, Palumbo (2003) has traced centuries of conflict through the shaping of historiography as well as of the landscape in a Sicilian town, where modern political life, now attached to national electoral processes, nevertheless continues to reproduce fissures dating back to interparish rivalries and the struggles of princes and their followers in the high Renaissance.

36. Rutelli, once a conspicuous critic of clerical corruption, ran as a member of the Green (environmental) party; once elected, however, he implemented some neoliberal policies and also muted his former anticlericalism. For a frontal attack on his earlier inconsistencies, see Bruto 1997. On the Jubilee, see Berdini 2000, 89–104.

37. The city authorities easily breach the walls of proprietors' resistance through a provision that requires that about 40 percent of the costs of restoration be undertaken from public monies.

38. The usual phrase is "of seven generations" (*de sette generazioni*); since her great-grandmother had already been entitled to that description, however, this restorer took great pride in being able to extend her pedigree even further back. Romans of fewer than seven generations' presence in the city are considered still to be Romans "by adoption," although this distinction appears to be quite imprecisely applied.

39. See, for example, Rosenau 1943, 228.

40. See, for example, Plesset 2006, 31–33.

CHAPTER SIX

1. In one instance, for example, he sold a necklace valued at 800,000 *lire* for 300,000.

2. *Fiducia*, which can also have the more general moral sense of "trust" in English, is disproportionately underreported in the available ethnographies of Italian society; but see Pardo 1996, 88; Suputtamongkol 2007, 203. Cf. Putnam's ideal-typical representation of "trust" in the Italian context (2003, 167–71); it is not clear that this corresponds to local understandings of *fiducia*.

3. And I found myself wondering whether the jeweler claimed this as a different event somewhere near the sea as a way of not admitting that it happened in Monti!

4. Haney (1922, 95–96) notes that such social proximity was the basis of all significant economic relations in medieval Europe and suggests that this is what made usury between close associates especially disgusting.

5. For the involvement of the Sicilian mafia, see especially the parliamentary inquiry to be found at *Verbale seduta* no. 15, pp. 537–538 (http://clarence.dada.net/contents/societa/memoria/antimafia/violante01/index.html).

I am grateful to Bernardino Palumbo for bringing this useful resource to my attention. Although the family in question figures in the inquiry, it is not specifically mentioned as being involved in racketeering in Rome—but my sources were unusually specific in this case.

6. This I obviously cannot do, but the documentation is specific and entirely persua⁻ sive.

7. This, as Augusto Ferraiuolo (2000, 48) points out in his rich analysis of historical texts, "reveals . . . the modalities of social control operated by the Church through the instrument of the confession."

8. Actually this case returned to public view, although the prosecution never succeeded in making its case. *La Repubblica* ran the following articles (the list is not exclusive): 21 October 1999, p. 18; 19 November 1999, pp. 1, 9; 6; 20 November 1999, pp. 1, 6–7; February 2000, p. 11; 18 June 200, p. 30; 3 July 2000, p. 29.

9. The most fearsome of these bosses was known as the Eel (*Anguilla*); a transitional figure, he became heavily involved in drug trafficking. Formal personal names of such characters are rarely mentioned even today for fear of reprisals. It is not clear that these minor bosses have really disappeared, although the one such character I met proclaimed his innocence and insisted that even his brother, a notorious criminal, had been a good man. But this is the public rhetoric of underworlds everywhere.

10. The mixture of Italian and Romanesco here does seem to suggest that it is the "lazy" forms (note the two infinitives) that persist even when other morphological features of the dialect disappear. But it could simply reflect the fact that someone who normally spoke an educated Italian was trying to imitate the rough speech of the bosses.

11. On the *bulli* of Rome, see especially Mariani 1983; Rossetti 1979. They are a stock character of local dialect comedy; *Gigi er Bullo*, a play by the Monti writer Ettore Petrolini, is regarded as a particularly good example of this genre, as are the cinematic adventures of the actor Alberto Sordi (made honorary mayor of Rome for a day; see *Il Messaggero*, 10 June 2000, p. 21). The commemorative plaque on Petrolini's house likens his writings to the "talking poems" of Pasquino (on which, see pp. 8, 9, 134); this is a good illustration of the domestication of Roman authenticity by local authorities. A related category is that of the *coatto*, literally "coerced" or "forced" (as in forced labor)—the man who, having been evicted from his original home (and usually expelled to the rougher suburbs), emphasized his tough-guy status by using a particularly slang-laden version of Romanesco and through forms of violence and rudeness that emphasized both his local power and his marginality to official power. While the association of the *coatto* with eviction goes back particularly to the Mussolini era and the expulsion of large numbers of Monticiani from the area cleared to make way for the Via dei Fori Imperiali, as well as with the flight to the suburbs in the 1960s, it may be gaining new resonance because of the current, catastrophic epidemic of evictions.

12. Giuseppe Scandurra, the anthropologist son of the urban planner Enzo Scandurra, has suggested, in an interesting and thoughtful response to my earliest, most schematic published account of Monti (Herzfeld 2001) that this view of matters may be somewhat romanticized and that it might more accurately be applied to outlying districts with a demonstrably greater underworld presence (Scandurra 2007, 151–52). It is a view widely expressed by local residents, however, and I have sought here to show that, even allowing

for nostalgic distortion, their idealized model appears to have some basis in social experience. Scandurra's comment nevertheless usefully underscores the risk of reading such recollections too literally or sweepingly.

13. See the recent coverage of the mafia share (roughly 7 percent) of the national economy, in *La Repubblica* (p. 11), *Corriere della Sera* (p. 18), and, in the international media, *International Herald Tribune* (p. 3), all on 23 October 2007.

14. See especially Das and Kleinman 2001, 25–26.

15. See Bianconi's account of the Magliana gang (1995), probably the most feared and vicious of all post–World War II underworld groups operating in Rome.

16. The acquisition of social capital by illegal means somewhat undercuts Putnam's idealistic portrayal of the phenomenon as a prerequisite for effective civic transparency (1993, 167–71); as I have tried to show throughout this book, the sharp categorical separation of the civic and legal from notions of civility does not correspond to local concepts.

17. The elderly grandmother was considered to be completely disabled and the daughters were aged 12 and 16, respectively. In such cases, an eviction could have been contested on legal grounds, but the family was clearly in no position to undertake the necessary costs.

18. Vismara 2004, 24–26.

19. This phrase, like the ubiquitous "*ci penso io*" (let me think about that), is redolent of mafia associations; see Boissevain 1974.

20. Male sociality can be very intense. Groups of men often take extra vacations together, leaving their wives and children at home. But the respective social spheres of men and women during the normal working day are not clearly demarcated at all, and women are often vocal participants in bar banter and political activities.

21. These secondary loans are not necessarily offered at exorbitant rates of interest, since they may simply be a way of helping a close friend and making a little extra money on the side—money that is far more likely to materialize if the interest is not too high. One proprietor of an upscale store told me he had bought his shop with a loan obtained in this way from a friend who belonged to a rotating credit association; the interest was 5 percent.

22. The media reports (see *City*, Rome section, 15 July 2005, p. 18; *Il Messaggero*, Rome section, 15 July 2005, p. 37; *La Repubblica*, Rome section, 15 July 2005, p. VI) confirm in all the key details the operational organization of such scams reported to me several years earlier by informants.

23. One official of an artisans' credit union claimed that there was no such thing as a genuinely poor artisan, and that those who applied for loans—which they did only because they were temporarily short of liquid funds—always turned out to own workshops or even seaside homes; this view, however, conflicts sharply with both the president's assessment and the testimony of the many artisans with whom I discussed their economic problems. It is noteworthy that the artisan-official in question was openly proud of his ability to make huge profits out of restoring objects obtained at very low prices and was also suspected of absconding with some of the funds of another organization to which he belonged. His unusual interpretation thus seems to reflect an implicit justification of his professional practices, especially as he argued that those artisans who failed to accumulate sufficient savings (for example, to buy a house by the sea!) only had themselves to blame. I did nevertheless hear one other local claim that artisans only declared themselves poor in order to prevent their rental costs from rising.

24. See especially the detailed argument in Tagliavini 1997.

25. Tagliavini (1997, 171) speaks of "cases in which the bank, even without having lent money at a usurious rate, has nevertheless carried out—intentionally or simply by chance—some infraction, against which the customer rebels and formulates the accusation of usury (even when it is substantially insufficient), which seems both more effective and fashionable."

26. Masciandaro and Porta 1997a.

27. Vismara 2004, 14.

28. Or, as Filotto (1997, 150) puts it: "It [the church] had maintained, on the basis of biblical and patristic tradition, the prohibition of credit and interest; all the same, a certain de facto tolerance was to be found and also the scholastics' teaching, even though it condemned usury as a mortal sin, did permit the use of certain devices that made the extension of credit feasible." He also points out that the ecclesiastical authorities had to come to terms with the reality of heavy debt incurred by certain orders and convents toward the end of the Middle Ages. Ultimately the huge wealth of the church compromised the purity of its opposition to charging interest on loans; its engagement in the temporal world meant that it could not manage without bankers and creditors—and, we might add, the temporal dimension of interest charges made usury inevitable. "So for the church, too, credit and bankers were an unavoidable evil—unavoidable and thus something to be managed, but evil nonetheless and thus also to be condemned and controlled" (Filotto 1997, 150). The ownership of real estate similarly strained, and still strains, the moral fiber of the clergy, but also provides them with a framework for the collective accumulation of wealth—ostensibly as a means of avoiding the corruption of individual souls. Presumably this is why, when the Vatican dissolves an order and takes control of its properties, no compensation goes to the disbanded friars (as Italian law would seem to require) but, in the form of the proceeds of the sale of the order's properties, reverts to the Vatican itself (Guarino 1998, 89).

CHAPTER SEVEN

1. On the economics of the Sicilian *pizzo*, see Schneider and Schneider 2006, 77–78.

2. See Silverman 1975, vii, 1–8; cf. Galt 1992, 8; and, more contrastively, Pratt 1994, 57. Silverman in fact anticipates this difference at the outset (1975, 1). We should nevertheless avoid assuming clear-cut differences between large regions of the country; on this see, among others, Sabetti 2000, 208.

3. It is tempting, but it would be inaccurate, to describe the mafia as a form of civil society, because its use of violence overshadows and informs the menace implied by its elaborate code of courtesy. Rather, as Jane and Peter Schneider (2001) have shown, the rhetoric of civil society informs the anti-mafia movement, but not always in ways that conduce to concerted or democratic action.

4. See Suputtamongkol (2007, 30, 198) on the exclusion of *i diversi* (people who are different) by those whose everyday actions, patterned in accordance with a long history of concern with good manners (208–24), marked them as respectable.

5. Requests to help the police are not always refused. Block janitors are often expected to assist the police in this way; they depend on police clearance for their employment.

But thieves may also suborn someone internal to a business they are intending to rob; such persons, known as *bassisti*, are essential to any operation organized from outside the district.

6. A Neapolitan friend living in Monti remarked that a certain storekeeper had been of the Piperno family; he then checked to make sure I knew what that meant, this kind of indirect hinting at Jewish identity being a further reflection of the discretion that is both attributed and directed to Jewish citizens of Rome.

7. See especially Jolly 1994; Keesing 1982.

8. This illustrates the central point in Verena Stolcke's discussion of "cultural fundamentalism" in Europe (1995).

9. The deep-seated right-wing and popular invocation of genetic explanations for attitudes and aptitudes (see Horn 1994) underlies much of the current rhetoric of racism against Eastern European immigrants (see Herzfeld 2007b). Note also the common Italian metaphor for the strongly entrenched views of a group of people as being "in their DNA." The nature-nurture debate has still barely touched public consciousness and everyday idioms of speech in much of Italy.

10. He did not himself have such a background and felt that this enabled him to make decisions independently because "I don't care in the least who you are" (*non mi importa niente chi sei*).

11. The use of the Romanesco form *de* is not only characteristic of his everyday speech but gives a slight emphasis to his working-class credentials in what is an intellectually engaged comment.

12. See also below, pp. 281–84. I have also heard the term *fascistone* used with pride by a former policeman speaking positively of himself.

13. Putnam 1993, 105.

14. Palumbo 2003, 371.

15. See especially Smith (2006) for a useful—if rather generalizing—perspective on the political and economic logic of gentrification.

16. Palumbo 2003, 335.

17. Putnam (1993) uses the "civic" in precisely this ideal-typical sense. Palumbo's analysis (2003, 371), however, shows that the key distinction is less between the civil and the civic than it is between two radically different meanings of the civic, the local and the universal, the first of which emphasizes civility—a culturally embedded value in Italy—while the latter assumes that ideals of good governance will have little to do with cultural peculiarities.

18. This nicely illustrates how elites manipulate cultural values to their own advantage, restricting access to the benefits subsumed under the heading of "civil society"; see Chatterjee 2004, 40–41.

19. Cellamare (2007) has particularly asked what is meant by "common goods" (*beni comuni*), a question that nicely parallels Palumbo's critique of the official model of "cultural goods" (*beni culturali*) (2003).

20. See the reports in *Il Messaggero*: RaffellaTroili, "Vicini di casa? È qui la Festa," 15 March 2005, p. 29; Maria Lombardi, "La lite abita nei condomini: una causa su due è tra vicini," 28 April 2005, p. 10; and Raffaella Troili, "È qui la Festa? Sì, ma dei vicini di

casa" and Claudia Alì, "Verdone: 'Più solidarietà e più buon senso' – Muccino: 'Io cresciuto dalla sora Fernanda,'" Rome section, 5 May 2005, p. 49; and in *La Repubblica*: Renata Mambelli, "Pic-nic e bicchierate da Corviale a Testaccio," Rome section, 7 May 2005, p. IV.

21. The Baudrillardian tone of this passage is intentional (see Baudrillard 1994). I am nevertheless not claiming that such simulacra of sociality are unreal; they constitute an alternative reality, and one that has its own logics and motivations, among which, in turn-of-the-century Rome, the interests of the neoliberal economy would seem to be paramount.

22. In this respect, Collier's discussion of duty and desire (1997) is complicated by the idea that "duty" as a an *internal* psychological *desire* is one of the ends of civic education.

23. Under the Fascist regime, any condominium with five or more residents was required to have a janitor (*portiere*) who could also act as a police spy—a classic way whereby dictatorships try to thwart any attempt at assembling significant numbers of people for any potentially political end. The current arrangement, which had already replaced the old janitorial appointment, was economically advantageous, since, along with door phones (*citofoni*), its presence replaced the employment of a regular janitor (who at that time would have cost about 40,000,000–50,000,000 *lire* a year) by a family that paid no rent to the condominium but also received no wages.

24. This is the micropolitical equivalent of *trasformismo*, the recycling of civic rhetoric for the purposes of self-interest; but here, as we shall see, the reverse process also occurs. See also, albeit in an idiom still frankly and strongly influenced by Banfield's view of the south, Signorelli 1983, 48.

25. As in Elias 2000. Pardo (1996, 13, 48, 170) rightly points out that distinctions between instrumental and affective uses of friendship simplify and distort the experiential reality of life in urban Italy; friendship may be deployed for instrumental purposes with no necessary loss of affect, although accusations of self-interest sometimes also serve to explain away a breakdown in social relations.

26. Inoue 2006, 49.

27. Hemment 2007, 100.

28. Monticiani who decried these developments claimed that they had already effectively ruined the old ambience of Trastevere, where they had already long been well advanced.

29. There were also much earlier bursts of spatial expropriation by the rich and powerful, especially in the baroque era; see Lanoue (forthcoming).

30. He also defended the restaurateur on the grounds that his enterprise generated new money for the area—a comment apparently contradicted by those who observed that some of his establishments were usually empty. On *coatti*, see p. 333, n. 11, above.

31. The ruling was reported in *Corriere della Sera* (Lorenzo Salvia, "Cassazione: Vietato dire 'tu non sei nessuno,'" p. 14, and Beppe Severginini, "Sì, lui non è nessuno. Ma è meglio non dirglielo" pp. 1, 14) and *Il Messaggero* (Raffaella Simone, "Reato dire: non sei nessuno," pp. 1, 18) on 9 July 2004, and was also reported overseas—sometimes with political glee (as in an untitled article by Charles Oliver in the libertarian journal *Reason*, October 2004 [36] (5): 14).

CHAPTER EIGHT

1. See, for example, Aquisti 1988. Two jokes I heard locally were: Why do *carabinieri* patrol in pairs? One to read and the other to write! And if you see a mounted *carabiniere*, you would do better to talk to the horse! There is also the well-known joke about the red stripe down the sides of their uniform trousers, which is there so that the officers know which way up to wear them. A Monti resident provided this example: two *carabinieri* see an accordion one decides he wants to buy, but suggests that they should show up in civilian clothes because the shopkeeper would think they were trying to get a better price if they showed up in uniform—the joke at least respects their reputation for relative honesty. When they returned and asked about the accordion, the shopkeeper asked them if they were *carabinieri*. Surprised, they asked how he knew. Because, replied the shrewd fellow, this is a water heater!

2. I used the opportunity to ask the officer in charge about the local pattern of minor crime. Without any hesitation at all, he attributed it entirely to Gypsies and immigrants. Yet this remark, along with the license that the requirement of a *denuncia* gives the citizen to determine what categories of activity and of people should be reported, seems to produce precisely the effect that Palidda (2000, 205) describes as a "short-circuit" (*corto-circuito*) in the production of crime statistics—albeit, as he also acutely observes, filtered through local cultural predilections. Palidda's observations about the "postmodern" police provide an interesting amplification on a nationwide basis of much of what I describe here for the specific case of Rome.

3. One of them had previously lived in Greece and seemed more comfortable speaking Greek than Italian; this may have helped to establish a degree of confidence between us, although he did say that the Greek police had also been quite unpleasant to him.

4. See especially Caffiero 2004, 21–24.

5. On the demographic issue, see especially Krause 2006 and Schneider and Schneider 1996 (and Halkias 2004 and Paxson 2004 for the comparable situation in Greece).

6. This was widely trumpeted in the press following the reporting of a UNESCO assessment in the eighteenth Eurispes report (*1800 Rapporto Italia 2006*, Istituto di studi politici, economici e sociali, Rome).

7. I heard about one of these individuals from a friend of his. Later, when they quarreled, the friend told me that in fact the former officer had been forced out because he was caught stealing—but, he demanded, what was he supposed to tell me when they were still friends? Despite the impossibility of knowing which version was true, in either case we see corruption in the very institution that is supposed to combat it. The one former *poliziotto* in this group initially told me that it was not true he resigned in disgust but only because he wanted to get married; this is entirely plausible, but he may also, being of right-wing persuasion, have been more concerned to protect the honor of the forces from a foreigner he suspected—as I later discovered—of being a spy. And later he did say that after all he had resigned because he could not stand the corruption.

8. This Romanesco expression, which literally means "let's go," implies that everyone is satisfied with the existing arrangement and business as usual can go ahead.

9. Note, too, the expression *ce magnano sobra* (they are eating on top of it; that is, with excessive greed). Such people are considered analogous to the pimp (*pappone*), another exploiter of human need.

10. For one version of the gifts given by client to patron, see Holmes 1989, 98.

11. The term is also used of the free extras—DVDs, special journal issues, and the like—that come with many newspapers as a promotional device.

12. She had to resort to complaining to her captain friend again when another officer, discovering that a civil servant was living in the hotel, hinted that he expected a bribe of 50,000 *lire*, presumably to accept this as the official's permanent domicile.

13. The so-called *legge Bersani* (law no. 114/1998), in which the granting of food and other shop licenses was liberalized, was enacted precisely in order to undercut the prevalence of bribery by robbing it of its most vulnerable pressure point.

CHAPTER NINE

1. The 1998 legislation did also benefit private owners, who were now able to evict tenants—with reasonable notice—if they could demonstrate a family need for the property.

2. On disclaimers in the expression of Roman racism, see Herzfeld 2007b. These disclaimers often adopt rhetorical forms that have been globalized in recent years, yet their expression in a local context both expresses and conveys tensions that might be differently articulated elsewhere.

3. It is interesting that the notion of *romanità* is associated with the speaker's emergent racism, since the concept reached an apogee of sorts when Mussolini adopted it as a counterweight—scarcely less racial in its implications—to Hitler's embrace of Aryanist theories of race. See Gillette 2002, 53–56.

4. See above, p. 141.

5. He bolstered his criticism with a reminder that the Vatican had been involved in shady deals with mafiosi and crooked bankers, especially those that culminated in the spectacular crash of the Banco Ambrosiano. On these events, see Cornwell 1984.

6. The total city (*comune*) population rose by 65 percent, from 1,695,477 to 2,799,836, while that of Monti *dropped* by 51.3 percent, from 46,630 to 22,690. The overall population of the historic center dropped by 53 percent during that period (Italia Nostra 1976, 19–20).

7. "Emergenza sfratti, appello di Veltroni: 'Intervenga il governo,'" *City* [Rome], 15 April 2005, p. 22.

8. A fellow resident, underscoring his indignation that they all faced eviction, described three women as *native doc* (genuine natives); *doc* is an abbreviation for a wine appellation (*d'origine controllata*) and is often used as a semi-humorous metaphor for authenticity or guaranteed quality (see also Galt 1991, 31).

9. Marcel Detienne (2007, 84) draws an immediate and ironic comparison of these newly autochthonous "Padanians" (inhabitants of the area for which the Northern League was claiming autonomy) with the Sioux.

10. An Italian-language report was compiled, completed, and signed in 2005; the signatories included representatives of the United Nations–Habitat–AGFE and of the *comune* (city administration) of Rome. See AGFE 2005.

11. Scandurra (2003, 118) also points out that such folkloric sensationalism characterizes the superficial uses that officialdom makes of older ways of life in the city. It is relatively easy to weep for the predicament of a single elderly evictee while also dismissing such cases as the inevitable result of "progress"; it is not only in the third world that the poor and the marginal find themselves excluded by governmental practices grounded in a colonial, essentially survivalist-evolutionist perspective (on which see especially Ferguson 1990).

12. She died about two years later. The copies of these articles, by Maria Lombardi (perhaps in *Il Messaggero*) and Riccardo Morante (in *Gente*), were unfortunately not marked with precise citation data.

13. This was a key theme in activists' rhetoric during the year; for example, flyers for a demonstration on 15 January 2000 under the banner headline "SOS Jubilee," announced, "While the pope blesses the pilgrims, the government saves merchants and evicts tenants."

14. The letter, sent by auxiliary bishop Luigi Moretti to Loredana Acca on 20 March 2000, acknowledged that the case has been "dragging on for a while" but asserted that neither the Vicariate of Rome—technically the pope's parish—nor the Vatican's Secretariat of State could become involved in a legal dispute. "Nevertheless," the letter continues, "please accept sentiments of solidarity for you and for the families that are being forced to uproot themselves from their district, and I assure you of the special proximity and prayer of the Holy Father."

15. The actual text is mostly in capital letters; I have repunctuated it here for easier readability. The formula *pregherà per noi* (will pray for us) has potentially penitential overtones (see p. 55).

16. It is the growing ubiquity of this hypocritical disjuncture between political identity and active policy in respect of housing that Smith (2006, 193, 201) has pinpointed.

17. For useful discussions of life in Naples, see Belmonte 1979; Broccolini 1999; Goddard 1996; Pardo 1996. It is hard to compare the nostalgic reconstruction of a largely vanished local Roman *malavita* with a present-day phenomenon in another city, but some features appear to be common to both.

18. He was also later to try to claim his party's and his own responsibility for securing the eviction of the squatters from the Angelo Mai school, presenting this as a victory for the people of Monti and a failure of the Veltroni administration. See the press statement that he and his fellow party member and city councilor Marco Marsilio, also deeply involved in the Via degli Ibernesi case, released on 22 May 2006. In this statement, they described those squatters as representing "the extremists and the agit-prop [people] of the [leftist-inspired] social centers" (*gli estremisti e gli agit-prop dei centri sociali*) and called on the city administration to take action to protect other spaces which, they claimed, are "the sole bulwark of real tradition in the area" (*l'unico baluardo di vera tradizione nella zona*)—a position that underscores their instrumental understanding of heritage and its social significance.

19. On "integralism," see Holmes 2000; Stolcke 1995. For a discussion of the increasing interest of exponents of local cultures in collective self-production for tourism, an

exploitation of the visitors' searching for cultural distinction that does not necessarily conflict with a simultaneous distrust or dislike of foreigners and that might also be encouraged by the subsidiarity of supranational organizations such as the European Union, see, by way of a brief but suggestive comment, Simonicca 1997, 247.

20. Maceratini represented the Far Right of his party, having been a local activist in the nearby Colle Oppio neighborhood with the old *Movimento sociale italiano*, the link between Mussolini's Fascists and the present-day Alleanza nazionale. By this time, however, he had gained considerable international respectability; he always presents himself, said a local left-wing political activist, "in jacket and tie" (*in giacca e cravatta*), but he represents the more confrontational elements in the party.

21. At my urging, two fellow anthropologists were in attendance, as were five anthropology students from the University of Rome.

22. This sale was the subject of a question in the national parliament: *Interrogazione a risposta scritta* 4–09211, presented by Vincenzo Fragalà on 4 March 2004, in session no. 433. The text can be found by going to http://legislature.camera.it/_dati/leg14/lavori/stenografici/btestiatti/ and then clicking on 4–09211.htm. (Accessed 15 May 2008.)

EPILOGUE

1. See Stolcke 1995 on "cultural fundamentalism" in this sense; see also Herzfeld 2004, 169, for an illustration.

2. On officializing strategies, see Bourdieu 1977, 38–40.

3. For accounts of this community, see AGFE 2005; Herzfeld 2006.

4. Herzfeld 2003. It was the comparison between Greek and Italian nationalism that Stanley Tambiah, to whom this book is dedicated, insisted I not abandon in order to pursue new and possibly uninformed interests in the anthropology of Thailand.

5. Anthropologists and sociologists have made substantial empirical inroads into the conventional view of globalization as necessarily entailing cultural homogenization. The most useful critiques oppose such simplistic formulations on the basis of detailed ethnographic evidence to the contrary. See especially Burawoy 2000; Fisher and Downey 2006b, 22; Watson 2005.

6. Napolitano's discussion of the continuing evangelization in Rome of Catholic immigrants from Latin America (2007) suggests a somewhat similar pattern of paternalistic subjection, while also pointing to the possibility of alternative understandings by these new recruits to the local labor force.

7. Guidoni 1990, x–xi.

8. For a useful discussion of the strategy-tactic distinction, see de Certeau 1984, 52–60.

9. See especially Patriarca's helpful historical contextualizations of this peculiar tendency (2001, 2005).

10. Both became successful businessmen by creating cell phone companies; both eventually attained political leadership of their respective countries when they realized that only a party with a nationalistic agenda (*Forza Italia*, Force Italy; *Thai Rak Thai*, Thais Love Thais) could succeed; both ran on anticorruption platforms only to be charged

with corruption themselves, in trials that, had they been convicted, would have led to their debarment from politics for an identical ten-year period; both managed to escape conviction more or less at the moment of their electoral success; both appealed to the football interests they shared with their electoral bases; both were notoriously thin-skinned in their management of the press, and both creatively manipulated public discourses about "transparency" to their advantage (Morris's article on Thaksin offers many parallels with Berlusconi [2004]); and both eventually failed to stay in power, one losing an election (although he returned to power in 2008), the other ousted in a coup.

REFERENCES

AGFE. *See* Advisory Group on Forced Evictions.

Advisory Group on Forced Evictions. 2005. *Forced Evictions: Towards Solutions? First Report of the Advisory Group on Forced Evictions to the Executive Director of UN-Habitat.* Nairobi: AGFE.

Ago, Renata. 1998. *Economia Barocca: Mercato e istituzioni nella Roma del Seicento.* Rome: Donzelli.

Aho, James. 2005. *Confession and Bookkeeping: The Religious, Moral, and Rhetorical Roots of Modern Accounting.* Albany: State University of New York Press.

Angioni, Giulio. 1989. Rubar cogli occhi: Fare, imparare e saper fare nelle tecnologie tradizionali. In *La Trasmissione del Sapere: Aspetti linguistici e antropologici,* ed. Giorgio Cardona, 7–16. Rome: Bagatto Libri.

Anon. 1993. *Le Pasquinate Celebri (1447–188 . . .).* Palermo: Reprint.

Aquisti, Danilo, ed. 1988. *Carabinieri—La superbarzelletta: Ridere e ancora ridere sulla "Benemerita."* Rome: Roberto Napoleone.

Arlacchi, Pino. 1983. *Mafia, Peasants, and Great Estates: Society in Traditional Calabria.* Cambridge: Cambridge University Press.

———. 1994. *Addio Cosa Nostra: La Vita di Tommaso Buscetta.* Milan: Rizzoli.

Askew, Marc. 1996. The Rise of *Moradok* and the Decline of the *Yarn:* Heritage and Cultural Construction in Urban Bangkok. *Sojourn* 11(2): 183–210.

Banfield, Edward C. 1958. *The Moral Basis of a Backward Society.* Glencoe, IL: Free Press.

Barzini, Luigi. 1964. *The Italians: A Full-Length Portrait featuring their Manners and Morals.* New York: Athenaeum.

Baudrillard, Jean. 1994. *Simulacra and Simulation.* Trans. Sheila Faria Glaser. Ann Arbor: University of Michigan Press.

Belmonte, Thomas. 1979. *The Broken Fountain.* New York: Columbia University Press.

Berdini, Paolo. 2000. *Il Giubileo senza Città: L'urbanistica romana negli anni del liberismo.* Rome: Riuniti.

Bianconi, Giovanni. 1995. *Ragazzi di Malavita: Fatti e misfatti della Banda della Magliana*. Milan: Baldini & Castoldi.

Blok, Anton. 1974. *The Mafia of a Sicilian Village 1860–1960: A Study of Violent Peasant Entrepreneurs*. New York: Harper & Row.

Bocquet, Denis. 2007. *Rome ville technique (1870–1925): Une modernisation conflictuelle de l'espace urbain*. Rome: École Française de Rome.

Boissevain, Jeremy. 1974. *Friends of Friends: Networks, Manipulators and Coalitions*. Oxford: Blackwell.

Bordo, Michael D. 2006. Sudden Stops, Financial Crises and Original Sin in Emerging Countries: *Déjà Vu?* Working Paper 12393, National Bureau of Economic Research, Cambridge, MA.

Bordo, Michael D., Christopher Meissner, and Angela Redish. 2003. How "Original Sin" Was Overcome: The Evolution of External Debt Denominated in Domestic Currencies in the United States and the British Dominions, 1800–2000. Working Paper 9841, National Bureau of Economic Research, Cambridge, MA.

Bourdieu, Pierre. 1977. *Outline of a Theory of Practice*. Trans. Richard Nice. Cambridge: Cambridge University Press.

———. 1984. *Distinction: A Social Critique of the Judgement of Taste*. London: Routledge & Kegan Paul.

Bravo, Gian Luigi. 2001. *Italiani: Racconto etnografico*. Rome: Meltemi.

Broccolini, Alessandra Maria Paola. 1999. Poetiche della Napoletanità: Turismo, folklore e politiche dell'identità al borgo di Santa Lucia. Doctoral thesis, Università degli Studi di Roma "La Sapienza."

Bruto, Lucio Giunio. 1997. *Cicciobello del Potere: Francesco Rutelli politicante in carriera*. Rome: Kaos.

Buchowski, Michał. 1996. The Shifting Meanings of Civil and Civic Society in Poland. In Hann and Dunn 1996, 79–98.

Burawoy, Michael, ed. 2000. *Global Ethnography: Forces, Connections, and Imaginations in a Postmodern World*. Berkeley: University of California Press.

Burgio, Alberto, ed. 1999. *Nel Nome della Razza: Il razzismo nella storia d'Italia 1870–1945*. Bologna: Il Mulino.

Caffiero, Marina. 2004. *Battesimi Forzati: Storie di ebrei, cristiani e convertiti nella Rome dei papi*. Rome: Viella.

Caftanzoglou, Roxane. 2000. The Sacred Rock and the Profane Settlement: Place, Memory and Identity under the Acropolis. *Journal of Oral History* 28:43–51.

———. 2001a. Shadow of the Sacred Rock: Contrasting Discourses of Place under the Acropolis. In *Contested Landscapes: Movement, Exile and Place*, ed. Barbara Bender and Margot Winer, 21–35. Oxford: Berg.

———. 2001b. Στη σκιά τομ Ιερού Βράχον: Τόπος και μνήμη στα Αναφιώτικα. Athens: Athens Center for Social Research/Ellinika Grammata.

Calabrò, Maria Antonietta. 1991. *Le Mani della Mafia: Vent'anni di finanza e politica attraverso la storia del Banco Ambrosiano*. Rome: Edizioni Associate.

Campbell, J. K. 1964. *Honour, Family, and Patronage: A Study of Institutions and Moral Values in a Greek Mountain Community.* Oxford: Clarendon.

Caporale, Antonello. 2007. *Impuniti: Storie di un sistema incapace, sprecone e felice.* Milan: Baldini Castoldi Dalai.

Cardilli, Luisa. 1990a. Le edicole nei documenti ottocenteschi dell'Archivio Capitolino. In Cardilli 1990b, 153–55.

———, ed. 1990b. *Edicole sacre romane: Un segno urbano da recuperare.* Rome: Fratelli Palombi.

Cascioli, Lino. 1987. *Proverbi e Detti Romaneschi.* Rome: Newton & Compton.

Cellamare, Carlo. 2007. Progett-azione e quotidianità a Monti. In *Storie di Città*, ed. G. Attili, L. Decandia, and E. Scandurra, 53–73. Rome: Edizioni Interculturali.

———. *Fare città: Pratiche urbane e Storie di luoghi.* Milan: Elèuthera.

Chatterjee, Partha. 2004. *The Politics of the Governed: Reflections on Popular Politics in Most of the World.* New York: Columbia University Press.

Cole, Jeffrey. 1997. *The New Racism in Europe: A Sicilian Ethnography.* Cambridge: Cambridge University Press.

Cole, Jeffrey E., and Sally S. Booth. 2007. *Dirty Work: Immigrants in Domestic Service, Agriculture, and Prostitution in Sicily.* Lanham, MD: Lexington.

Collier, Jane Fishburne. 1997. *From Duty to Desire: Remaking Families in a Spanish Village.* Princeton, NJ: Princeton University Press.

Connerton, Paul. 1989. *How Societies Remember.* Cambridge: Cambridge University Press.

Cornwell, Robert. 1984. *God's Banker: The Life and Death of Roberto Calvi.* London: Unwin.

Corrubolo, Federico. 2004. L'Historia dell'Origine e Miracoli della Madonna de' Monti in Roma. *Archivio italiano per la storia della pietà* 17:129–213.

Cossu, Tatiana. 2007. Immagini di patrimonio: Memoria, identità e politiche dei beni culturali. *Lares* 71:41–56.

D'Aquino, Riccardo. 1995. Il Luogo ed il Paesaggio: La lunga durata dell'immagine di Roma. Rome: Dedalo.

Das, Veena, and Arthur Kleinman. 2001. Introduction. In *Remaking a World: Violence, Social Suffering, and Memory*, ed. Veena Das, Arthur Kleinman, Margaret Lock, Mamphela Ramphele, and Pamela Reynolds, 1–30. Berkeley: University of California Press.

Davis, John. 1988. *Libyan Politics: Tribe and Revolution—An Account of the Zuwaya and their Government.* Berkeley: University of California Press.

Decandia, Lidia. 2000. *Dell'Identità. Saggio sui luoghi: per una critica della razionalità urbanistica.* Soveria Mannelli: Rubbettino.

de Certeau, Michel. 1984. *The Practice of Everyday Life.* Trans. Steven F. Rendall. Berkeley: University of California Press.

De Cesaris, Alessandra. 2002. *Lo spessore del suolo parte di città: La costruzione del suolo, condizione contemporanea dell'abitare la città.* Rome: Palombi.

Dematteo, Lynda. 2007. *L'idiotie en politique: Subversion et néo-populisme en Italie*. Paris: Éditions de la Maison des Sciences de l'Homme/CNRS Éditions.

de Pina-Cabral, João. 1986. *Sons of Adam, Daughters of Eve: The Peasant Worldview of the Alto Minho*. Oxford: Clarendon.

Detienne, Marcel. 2007. *The Greeks and Us*. Trans. Janet Lloyd. Cambridge: Polity.

Di Bella, Maria Pia. 2008. *Dire ou taire en Sicile*. Paris: Éditions du Félin.

Di Nola, Annalisa. 1990. Spazio aperto e spazio protetto: Le immagini della Vergine tra culto locale e controllo ecclesiastico (XVI–XVII secolo). In Cardilli 1990b, 31–39.

Douglas, Mary, ed. 1970. *Witchcraft Confessions and Accusations*. London: Tavistock.

Doumanis, Nicholas. 2001. *Italy: Inventing the Nation*. London: Arnold.

du Boulay, Juliet. 1974. *Portrait of a Greek Mountain Village*. Oxford: Clarendon.

Eichengreen, Barry, and Ricardo Hausmann, eds. 2004. *Debt Denomination and Financial Instability in Emerging Market Economies*. Chicago: University of Chicago Press.

Eichengreen, Barry, Ricardo Hausmann, and Ugo Panizza. 2003. Currency Mismatches, Debt Intolerance and Original Sin: Why They Are Not The Same and Why It Matters. Working Paper 10036, National Bureau of Economic Research, Cambridge, MA.

Elias, Norbert. 2000. *The Civilizing Process: Sociogenetic and Psychogenetic Investigations*. Trans. Edmund Jephcott, ed. Eric Dunning, Johan Goudsblom and Stephen Mennell. Rev. ed. Oxford: Blackwell.

Evans-Pritchard, E.E. 1937. *Witchcraft, Oracles and Magic among the Azande*. Oxford: Clarendon.

———. 1940. *The Nuer: A Description of the Modes of Livelihood and Political Institutions of a Nilotic People*. Oxford: Clarendon.

———. 1949. *The Sanusi of Cyrenaica*. Oxford: Clarendon.

Faubion, James D. 1993. *Modern Greek Lessons: A Primer in Historical Constructivism*. Princeton, NJ: Princeton University Press.

Faeta, Francesco. 2004. Rivolti verso il Mediterraneo: Immagini, questione meridionale e processi di "orientalizzazione" interna. *Lares* 69:333–67.

Ferguson, James. 1990. *The Anti-Politics Machine: "Development," Depoliticization, and Bureaucratic Power in Lesotho*. Cambridge: Cambridge University Press.

Fernandez, James W. 1983. Consciousness and Class in Southern Spain. *American Ethnologist* 10:165–73.

Ferraiuolo, Augusto. 2000. *"Pro exoneratione sua propria coscientia": Le accuse per stregoneria nella Capua del XVII–XVIII secolo*. Milan: FrancoAngeli.

Ferry, Elizabeth Emma. 2005. *Not Ours Alone: Patrimony, Value, and Collectivity in Contemporary Mexico*. New York: Columbia University Press.

Filotto, Umberto. 1997. L'Usura e il sistema finanziario italiano. In Masciandaro and Porta 1997b, 139–65.

Fisher, Melissa S., and Greg Downey, eds. 2006a. *Frontiers of Capital: Ethnographic Reflections on the New Economy*. Durham, NC: Duke University Press.

———. 2006b. Introduction: The Anthropology of Capital and the Frontiers of Ethnography. In Fisher and Downey 2006a, 1–30.

Francescangeli, Laura. 1990. Dalle guide devozionali all'inventario storico-artistico: simboli e valori. In Cardilli 1990b, 50–58.

Friedl, Ernestine. 1962. *Vasilika: A Village in Modern Greece*. New York: Holt, Rinehart & Winston.

Galt, Anthony H. 1991. *Far From the Church Bells: Settlement and Society in an Apulian Town*. Cambridge: Cambridge University Press.

———. 1992. *Town and Country in Locorotondo*. Fort Worth, TX: Holt, Rinehart & Winston.

Geertz, Clifford. 1973. *The Interpretation of Cultures*. New York: Basic Books.

Gillette, Aaron. 2002. *Racial Theories in Fascist Italy*. London: Routledge.

Giovannini, Cristina. 1997. *Pasquino e le Statue Parlanti: Le mille voci del malcontento popolare in quattro secoli di satire, beffe e invettive*. Rome: Newton & Compton.

Giustiniani, Corrado. 1982. *La Casa Promessa: Un problema che condiziona milioni di italiani*. Turin: Einaudi.

Gluckman, Max. 1963. Gossip and Scandal. *Current Anthropology* 4:307–16.

Goddard, Victoria A. 1996. *Gender, Family, and Work in Naples*. Oxford: Berg.

Gramsci, Antonio. 1975. Quaderni del carcere. Ed. Valentino Gerratana. Turin: Einaudi.

Grasseni, Cristina. 2003. *Lo Sguardo della Mano: Pratiche della località e antropologia della visione in una comunità montana lombarda*. Bergamo: Sestante (Bergamo University Press).

———. 2007. Introduction. In *Skilled Visions: Between Apprenticeship and Standards*, ed. Cristina Grasseni, 1–19. Oxford: Berghahn.

Gremaglia, Mariella. 2005. Pazienza e tenacia. *In* Anon., *Il Tempo È Un Diritto* (in *Quaderni del Dipartimento Semplificazione Amministrativa e Comunicazione*, Comune di Roma), 6. Rome: Palombi.

Guarino, Mario. 1998. *I Mercanti del Vaticano: Affari e scandali: l'industria delle anime*. [Milan]: Kaos.

Guidoni, Enrico. 1990. *L'Urbanistica di Roma tra Miti e Progetti*. Bari: Laterza.

Halkias, Alexandra. 2004. *The Empty Cradle of Democracy: Sex, Abortion, and Nationalism in Modern Greece*. Durham, NC: Duke University Press.

Handelman, Don. 1990. *Models and Mirrors: Towards an Anthropology of Public Events*. Cambridge: Cambridge University Press.

Handler, Richard. 1985. On Having a Culture: Nationalism and the Preservation of Quebec's *Patrimoine*. In *Objects and Others*, ed. George Stocking, 192–217. History of Anthropology, vol. 3. Madison: University of Wisconsin Press.

———. 1986. Authenticity. *Anthropology Today* 2(1): 2–4.

————. 1988. *Nationalism and the Politics of Culture in Quebec.* Madison: University of Wisconsin Press.

Haney, Lewis H. 1922. *History of Economic Thought: A Critical Account of the Origin and Development of the Economic Theories of the Leading Thinkers in the Leading Nations.* Rev. ed.. New York: Macmillan.

Hann, Chris, and Elizabeth Dunn, eds. 1996. *Civil Society: Challenging Western Models.* London: Routledge.

Harney, Nicholas. 2006. Rumour, Migrants, and the Informed Economies of Naples, Italy. *International Journal of Sociology and Social Policy* 26:374–84.

Heatherington, Tracey. 1999. Street Tactics: Catholic Ritual and the Senses of the Past in Sardinia. *Ethnology* 38:315–34.

————. 2006. Sins, Saints, and Sheep in Sardinia. *Identities: Global Studies in Culture and Power* 13:533–56.

Hemment, Julia. 2007. *Empowering Women in Russia: Activism, Aid, and NGOs.* Bloomington: Indiana University Press.

Herzfeld, Michael. 1985. *The Poetics of Manhood: Contest and Identity in a Cretan Mountain Village.* Princeton, NJ: Princeton University Press.

————. 1991. *A Place in History: Social and Monumental Time in a Cretan Town.* Princeton, NJ: Princeton University Press.

————. 1992. *The Social Production of Indifference: Exploring the Symbolic Roots of Western Bureaucracy.* Oxford: Berg.

————. 1999. Of Language and Land Tenure: The Transmission of Property and Information in Autonomous Crete. *Social Anthropology* 7:223–37.

————. 2001. Competing Diversities: Ethnography in the Heart of Rome. *Plurimondi* 3 (5): 147–54.

————. 2002. The European Self: Rethinking an Attitude. In *The Idea of Europe: From Antiquity to the European Union,* ed. Anthony Pagden, 139–70. Cambridge: Cambridge University Press; Washington, D.C.: Woodrow Wilson Center Press.

————. 2003. Localism and the Logic of Nationalistic Folklore: Cretan Reflections. *Comparative Studies in Society and History* 42:281–310.

————. 2004. *The Body Impolitic: Artisans and Artifice in the Global Hierarchy of Value.* Chicago: University of Chicago Press.

————. 2005. *Cultural Intimacy: Social Poetics in the Nation-State.* 2nd ed. New York: Routledge.

————. 2006. Spatial Cleansing: Monumental Vacuity and the Idea of the West. *Journal of Material Culture* 11:127–49.

————. 2007a. *Monti Moments: Men's Memories in the Heart of Rome.* Film, produced by Michael Herzfeld as an En Masse Films Associated Production. Berkeley: Berkeley Media LLC.

————. 2007b. Small-Mindedness Writ Large: On the Migrations and Manners of Prejudice. *Journal of Ethnic and Migration Studies* 33:255–74.

————. 2008. Mere Symbols. *Anthropologica* 50:141–55.

Hill, Jane H. 1992. "Today There Is No Respect": Nostalgia, "Respect," and Opposi-
tional Discourse in Mexicano (Nahuatl) Language Ideology. *Pragmatics* 2:262–
80.

Hirschon, Renée. 1989. *Heirs of the Greek Catastrophe: The Social Life of Asia Minor
Refugees in Piraeus.* Oxford: Clarendon Press.

Holmes, Douglas R. 1989. *Cultural Disenchantments: Worker Peasantries in Northeast Italy.* Princeton, NJ: Princeton University Press.

———. 2000. *Integral Europe: Fast-Capitalism, Multiculturalism, Neofascism.*
Princeton, NJ: Princeton University Press.

Horn, David. 1994. *Social Bodies: Science, Reproduction, and Italian Modernity.*
Princeton, NJ: Princeton University Press.

Impagliazzo, Marco, ed. 1997. *La Resistenza Silenziosa: Leggi razziali e occupazione
nazista nella memoria degli Ebrei di Roma.* Milan: Guerini.

Inoue, Miyako. 2006. *Vicarious Language: Gender and Linguistic Modernity in
Japan.* Berkeley: University of California Press.

Insolera, Italo. 1993. *Roma Moderna: Un secolo di storia urbanistica 1870–1970.*
Turin: Einaudi.

———. 2001. *Roma Fascista nelle Fotografie nell'Istituto Luce.* Rome: Riuniti and
Istituto Luce.

Italia Nostra. 1976. *Roma Sbagliata: Le Conseguenze sul Centro Storico.* Rome:
Bulzoni.

Jacquemet, Marco. 1996. *Credibility in Court: Communicative Practice in the
Camorra Trials.* Cambridge: Cambridge University Press.

Jolly, Margaret. 1994. *Women of the Place: Kastom, Colonialism and Gender in
Vanuatu.* Langhorne, PA: Harwood.

Kapferer, Bruce. 1988. *Legends of People, Myths of State: Violence, Intolerance, and
Political Culture in Sri Lanka and Australia.* Washington, D.C.: Smithsonian
Institution Press.

Kavanagh, Dennis. 1972. *Political Culture.* London: Macmillan.

Kaye, Joel. 2001. Changing Definitions of Money, Nature, and Equality *c.* 1140–1270,
Reflected in Thomas Aquinas' Questions on Usury. In Quaglioni, Todeschini,
and Varanini 2001, 25–55.

Keane, Webb. 2007. *Christian Moderns: Freedom and Fetish in the Mission Encounter.*
Berkeley: University of California Press.

Keesing, Roger. 1982. Kastom in Melanesia: An Overview. *Mankind* 13:297–301.

Kertzer, David I. 1980. *Comrades and Christians: Religion and Political Struggle in
Communist Italy.* Cambridge: Cambridge University Press.

———. 1993. *Sacrificed for Honor: Italian Infant Abandonment and the Politics of
Reproductive Control.* Boston: Beacon.

———. 1996. *Politics and Symbols: The Italian Communist Party and the Fall of
Communism.* New Haven, CT: Yale University Press.

———. 1997. *The Kidnapping of Edgardo Mortara.* New York: Alfred A. Knopf.

————. 2001. *The Popes against the Jews: The Vatican's Role in the Rise of Modern Anti-Semitism*. New York: Alfred A. Knopf.

Krause, Elizabeth. 2006. *A Crisis of Births: Population Politics and Family-Making in Italy*. Belmont, CA: Thomson/Wadsworth.

Lai, Franco. 2002. Imprenditori e contesto culturale: Il dibattito sull'invidia come vincolo all'attività imprenditoriale nella ricerca antropologica. In *Frammenti di Economie: Ricerche di antropologia economica in Italia*, ed. Valeria Siniscalchi, 279–312. Cosenza: Pellegrini.

————. 2004. Trasmissione e innovazione dei saperi locali. In *Fare e Saper Fare: I saperi locali in una prospettiva antropologica*, ed. Franco Lai, 17–30. Cagliari: Cooperativa Universitaria Editrice Cagliaritana.

Lanoue, Guy. 1991. Life as a *Guaglió*: Public and Private Domains in Central and Southern Italy. *Ethnologia Europaea* 21:47–58.

————. Forthcoming. Memories and the "Religious" Use of Civic Space: The Creation of the Myth of Rome. *Archives de sciences sociales des religions*.

Lewis, Charlton T., and Charles Short. 1900. *A Latin Dictionary*. Oxford: Clarendon.

Ledl, Leopold. 1997. *Per Conto del Vaticano: Rapporti con il crimine organizzato nel racconto del faccendiere dei monsignori*. Naples: Tullio Pironti.

Lifschitz, Daniel. 1993. *L'Inizio della storia: Il peccato originale*. Rome: Edizione Dehoniane.

Loizos, Peter. 1996. How Ernest Gellner Got Mugged on the Streets of London, Or: Civil Society, the Media and the Quality of Life. In Hann and Dunn 1996, 50–63.

Lombardi Satriani, Luigi M., ed. 1999a *La sacra Città: Itinerari antropologico-religiosi nella Roma di fine millennio*. Rome: Meltemi.

————. 1999b. Il santo corpo e l'anatomia dell'anima. Itinerario nelle reliquie. In Lombardi Satriani 1999a, 9–32.

Lozada, Eriberto P., Jr. 2001. *God Above Ground: Catholic Church, Postsocialist State, and Transnational Processes in a Chinese Village*. Stanford, CA: Stanford University Press.

Lukken, G. M. 1973. *Original Sin in the Roman Liturgy: Research into the Theology of Original Sin in the Roman Sacramentaria and the Early Baptismal Liturgy*. Leiden: E. J. Brill.

Maddox, Richard. 1993. *El Castillo: The Politics of Tradition in an Andalusian Town*. Urbana: University of Illinois Press.

Magliocco, Sabina. 1993. *The Two Madonnas: The Politics of Festival in a Sardonian Community*. New York: Peter Lang.

Maher, Vanessa. 1987. Sewing the Seams of Society: Dressmakers and Seamstresses in Turin between the Wars. In *Gender and Kinship: Essays toward a Unified Analysis*, ed. Jane Fishburne Collier and Sylvia Junko Yanagisako, 132–59. Stanford, CA: Stanford University Press.

Malaby, Thomas M. 2003. *Gambling Life: Dealing in Contingency in a Greek City*. Urbana: University of Illinois Press.

Malizia, Giuliano. 1999. *Piccolo Dizionario Romanesco*. Rome: Newton & Compton.

Marcelloni, Maurizio. 2003. *Pensare la Città Contemporanea: Il nuovo piano regolatore di Roma*. Bari: Laterza.

Mariani, Riccardo. 1983. *I (Veri) Bulli di Roma*. Rome: Nuova Editrice Spada.

Marx, Karl. 1976. *Capital*. Vol 1. Trans. Ben Fowkes. New York: Random House.

Masciandaro, Donato, and Angelo Porta. 1997a. Il mercato dell'usura: Analisi macroeconomica e alcune evidenze empiriche sull'Italia. In Masciandaro and Porta 1997b, 1–38.

———, eds. 1997b. *L'Usura in Italia*. Milan: Edizioni Giuridiche Economiche Aziendali dell'Università Bocconi e Giuffrè Editori.

Minicuci, Maria. 2003. Antropologi e Mezzogiorno. *Meridiana* 47–48:139–74.

Mirri, Maria Beatrice. 1996. *Beni Culturali e Centri Storici: Legislazione e problemi*. Genoa: Edizioni Culturali Internazionali.

Moe, Nelson. 2002. *The View from Vesuvius: Italian Culture and the Southern Question*. Berkeley: University of California Press.

Morris, Rosalind. 2004. Intimacy and Corruption in Thailand's Age of Transparency. In *Off Stage/On Display: Intimacy and Ethnography in the Age of Public Culture*, ed. Andrew Shryock, 225–43. Stanford, CA: Stanford University Press.

Mueller, Reinhold C. 2001. *Eva a Dyabolo Peccatum Mutuavit*: Peccato originale, prestito usurario e *redemptio* come metafore teologico-economiche. In Quaglioni, Todeschini, and Varanini 2001, 229–45.

Napolitano, Valentina. 2007. Of Migrant Revelations and Anthropological Awakenings. *Social Anthropology* 15:71–87.

Nelken, David. 2004. Using the Concept of Legal Culture. *Australian Journal of Legal Philosophy* 29:1–26.

Newton, Brian. 1972. *The Generative Interpretation of Dialect: A Study of Modern Greek Phonology*. Cambridge: Cambridge University Press.

Nicotri, Pino. 1993. *Tangenti in confessionale: Come i preti rispondono a corrotti e corrottori*. Venice: Marsilio.

Niola, M. 1995. *Sui palchi delle stelle. Napoli, il sacro, la scena*. Rome: Meltemi.

Odorisio, Maria Linda. 1990. Il ritrovamento miracoloso. In Cardilli 1990b, 25–30.

Paita, Almo. 1998. *La Vita Quotidiana a Roma ai Tempi di Gian Lorenzo Bernini*. Milan: Rizzoli.

Palidda, Salvatore. 2000. *Polizia Postmoderna: Etnografia del nuovo controllo sociale*. Milan: Feltrinelli.

Palumbo, Berardino. 2001. The Social Life of Local Museums. *Journal of Modern Italian Studies* 6:19–37.

———. 2003. *L'UNESCO e il Campanile: Antropologia, politica e beni culturali in Sicilia orientale*. Rome: Meltemi.

———. 2004. "The War of the Saints": Religion, Politics, and the Poetics of Time in a Sicilian Town. *Comparative Studies in Society and History* 43:4–33.

Papataxiarchis, Evthymios. 1991. Friends of the Heart: Male Commensal Solidarity, Gender, and Kinship in Aegean Greece. In *Contested Identities: Gender and*

Kinship in Modern Greece, ed. Peter Loizos and Evthymios Papataxiarchis, 156–79. Princeton, NJ: Princeton University Press.

———. 2006. Τα άχθη της ετερότητας: Διαστάσεις της πολιτισμικής διαφοροποίησης στην Ελλάδα τον πρώιμον 21ᵒᵛ αιώνα. In *Περιπέτειες της ετερότητας: Η παραγωγή διαφοράς στη σημερινή Ελλάδα*, ed. Evthymios Papataxiarchis, 1–85. Athens: Alexandreia.

Pardo, Italo. 1996. *Managing Existence in Naples*. Cambridge: Cambridge University Press.

Parisi, Rosa. 2002. *Il Paese dei Signori: Rappresentazioni e pratiche della distinzione*. Naples: L'Ancora del Mediterraneo.

Patriarca, Silvana. 2001. Italian Neopatriotism: Debating National Identity in the 1990s. *Modern Italy* 6:21–34.

———. 2005. Indolence and Regeneration: Tropes and Tensions of Risorgimento Patriotism. *American Historical Review* 110:380–408.

Paxson, Heather. 2004. *Making Modern Mothers: Ethics and Family Planning in Urban Greece*. Berkeley: University of California Press.

Peters, Emrys. 1967. Some Structural Aspects of the Feud among the Camel-Herding Bedouin of Cyrenaica. *Africa* 37:261–82.

Petrusewicz, Marta. 1998. *Come il Meridione divenne una Questione: Rappresentazioni del Sud prima e dopo il Quarantotto*. Soveria Mannelli: Rubbettino.

Pifferi, Francesco. 2004. *Storia dell'origine e primi miracoli della Madonna dei Monti in Roma (1583), Versione in italiano moderno a cura di don Federico Corrubolo*. Rome: Aracne.

Piore, Michael J., and Charles F. Sabel. 1984. *The Second Industrial Divide: Possibilities for Prosperity*. New York: Basic Books.

Piron, Sylvain. 2001. Le devoir de gratitude: Émergence et vogue de la notion d'*Antidora* au XIIIᵉ siècle. In Quaglioni, Todeschini, and Varanini 2001, 73–101.

Plesset, Sonja. 2006. *Sheltering Women: Negotiating Gender and Violence in Northern Italy*. Stanford, CA: Stanford University Press.

Pocino, Willy, ed. 2000. *Roma dei Giubilei*. Rome: Edilazio.

Pollis, Adamantia. 1987. The State, the Law, and Human Rights in Modern Greece. *Human Rights Quarterly* 9:587–614.

Prasad, Leela. 2007. *Poetics of Conduct: Oral Narrative and Moral Being in a South Indian Town*. New York: Columbia University Press.

Pratt, Jeff. 1994. *The Rationality of Rural Life: Economic and Cultural Change in Tuscany*. Chur: Harwood Academic.

Putnam, Robert D. 1993. *Making Democracy Work: Civic Traditions in Modern Italy*. Princeton, NJ: Princeton University Press.

Quaglioni, Diego, Giacomo Todeschini, and Gian Maria Varanini, eds. 2001. *Credito e Usura fra Teologia, Diritto e Amministrazione*. Rome: École Française de Rome.

Quattrucci, Mario. n.d. *Hai Perso, Commissario Marè*. Rome: Robin.

Ravaro, Fernando. 1994. *Dizionario Romanesco*. Rome: Newton & Compton.

Reed-Danahay, Deborah. 1996. *Education and Identity in Rural France: The Politics of Schooling*. Cambridge: Cambridge University Press.

Ricci, Andreina. 1996. *I Mali dell'Abbondanza: Considerazioni impolitiche sui beni culturali*. Rome: Lithos.

Ricci, Antonello. 1999. Gli occhi, le luci, le immagini: le madonnelle. Spazio del sacro e pratiche devozionali delle edicole religiose. In Lombardi Satriani 1999a, 33–75.

Rizzo, Sergio, and Gian Antonio Stella. 2007. *La Casta: Così i politici italiani sono diventati intoccabili*. Milan: Rizzoli.

Rodotà, Stefano. 2005. *Intervista su Privacy e Libertà*. Ed. Paolo Conti. Bari: Laterza.

Rosati, Massimo. 2000. *Il Patriotismo Italiano*. Bari: Laterza.

Rossetti, Bartolomeo. 1979. *I Bulli di Roma*. Rome: Newton & Compton.

Rosenau, Helen. 1943. The Prototype of the Virgin and Child in the Book of Kells. *The Burlington Magazine for Connoisseurs* 83 (486): 228–31.

Rufini, Alessandro. 1853. *Indicazione delle Immagini di Maria Santissima collocate sulle mura esterne di taluni edifici dell'Alma Città di Roma*. Vol. 2. Rome: Giovanni Ferretti.

Rumiz, Paolo. 1997. *La Secessione Leggera: Dove nasce la rabbia del profondo Nord*. Rome: Riuniti.

Sabetti, Filippo. 2000. *The Search for Good Government: Understanding the Paradox of Italian Democracy*. Montreal and Kingston: McGill-Queen's University Press.

Salzman, Philip C. 1978. Ideology and Change in Middle Eastern Tribal Society. *Man* (n.s.) 13: 618–37.

Sanfilippo. Mario. n.d.. *Roma: I negozi della tradizione*. Rome: Il Parnaso.

Santoloci, Maurizio. 2002. *Edilizia e Vincoli Paesaggistici: Tecnica di controllo ambientale*. Rome: Saurus Robuffo.

Sarfatti, Michele. 1999. Il razzismo fascista nella sua concretezza: La definizione di "Ebreo" e la Collocazione di Questi nella Costruenda Gerarchia Razziale. In Burgio 1999, 321–32.

Savagnone, Giuseppe. 1995. *La Chiesa di fronte alla Mafia*. Cinisello Balsamo: San Paolo.

Scandurra, Enzo. 2003. *Città morenti e città viventi*. Rome: Meltemi.

———. 2006. Presentazione. In Carlo Cellamare, ed., *RomaCentro: dal Laboratorio alla Casa della Città*, 9–11. Rome: Palombi.

Scandurra, Giuseppe. 2007. *Il Pigneto: Un'Etnografia fuori le Mura di Roma—Le storie, le voci e le rappresentazioni dei suoi abitanti*. Padua: CLEUP (Coop. Libreria Editrice Università di Padova.

Scaraffia, Lucetta. 1990. Immagini sacre e città. In Cardilli 1990b, 19–24.

Schneider, Jane. 1998. The Dynamics of Neo-Orientalism in Italy (1948–1995). In *Italy's "Southern Question": Orientalism in One Country*, ed. Jane Schneider, 1–23. Oxford: Berg.

Schneider, Jane, and Peter Schneider. 1996. *Festival of the Poor: Fertility Decline and the Ideology of Class in Sicily, 1860–1980*. Tucson: University of Arizona Press.

———. 2001. Civil Society versus Organized Crime: Local and Global Perspectives. *Critique of Anthropology* 21:427–46.

———. 2003. *Reversible Destiny: Mafia, Antimafia, and the Struggle for Palermo.* Berkeley: University of California Press.

———. 2006. Sicily: Reflections on Forty Years of Change. *Journal of Modern Italian Studies* 11:61–83.

Scott, James C. 1998. *Seeing Like a State: How Certain Schemes to Improve the Human Condition Have Failed.* New Haven, CT: Yale University Press.

Signorelli, Amalia. 1983. *Chi Può e Chi Aspetta: Giovani e clientelismo in un'area interna del Mezzogiorno.* Naples: Liguori.

Silverman, Sydel. 1975. *Three Bells of Civilization: The Life of an Italian Hill Town.* New York: Columbia University Press.

———. 1979. On the Uses of History in Anthropology: The Palio of Siena. *American Ethnologist* 6:413–36.

Simonicca, Alessandro. 1997. *Antropologia del Turismo: Strategie di ricerca e contesti etnografici.* Rome: Nuova Italia Scientifica.

Singleton, John. 1989. Japanese Folkcraft Pottery Apprenticeship: Cultural Patterns of an Educational Institution. In *Apprenticeship: From Theory to Method and Back Again,* ed. Michael W. Coy, 13–30. Albany: State University of New York Press.

Smith, Neil. 2006. Gentrification Generalized: From Local Anomaly to Urban "Regeneration" as Global Urban Strategy. In Fisher and Downey 2006a, 191–208.

Stendhal. n.d. a, b, and c. *Promenades dans Rome.* Vols. 1, 2, and 3. *Œuvres complètes.* Ed. Victor Del Litto and Ernest Abravanel. Vol. 7, new ed. Geneva: Edito-Service, for Cercle des Bibliophiles.

Stewart, Charles. 1989. Hegemony or Rationality? The Position of the Supernatural in Modern Greece. *Journal of Modern Greek Studies* 7:77–104.

———. 1991. *Demons and the Devil: Moral Imagination in Modern Greek Culture.* Princeton, NJ: Princeton University Press.

Stolcke, Verena. 1995. Talking Culture: New Boundaries, New Rhetorics of Exclusion in Europe. *Current Anthropology* 36:1–24.

Strathern, Marilyn, ed. 2000. *Audit Cultures: Anthropological Studies in Accountability, Ethics, and the Academy.* London: Routledge.

Suputtamongkol, Saipin. 2007. *Technicians of the Soul: Insanity, Psychiatric Practice, and Culture Making in Southern Italy.* PhD diss., Harvard University.

Tagliavini, Giulio. 1997. Fenomeni illegali e riflessi sul sistema bancario: l'"Usura strumentale". In Masciandaro and Porta 1997, 167–90.

Tambiah, S. J. 1976. *World Conqueror and World Renouncer: A Study of Buddhism and Polity in Thailand against a Historical Background.* Cambridge: Cambridge University Press.

Tillett, Margaret. 1971. *Stendhal: The Background to the Novels.* London: Oxford University Press.

Teti, Vito. 1993. *La razza maledetta: Origini del pregiudizio antimeridionale*. Rome: Manifestolibri.

Todeschini, Giacomo. 1989. *La Richezza degli Ebrei: Merci e denaro nella riflessione ebraica e nella definizione cristiana dell'usura alla fine del Medioevo*. Spoleto: Centro Italiano di Studi sull'Alto Medievo.

———. 1994. *Il Prezzo della Salvezza: Lessici medievali del pensiero economico*. Rome: La Nuova Italia Scientifica.

Toye, Francis. 1931. *Giuseppe Verdi: His Life and Works*. New York: Alfred A. Knopf.

Vico, Giambattista. 1744. *La Scienza Nuova*. Ed. Paolo Rossi. Milan: Rizzoli, 1977.

Vismara, Paola. 2004. *Oltre l'Usura: La Chiesa moderna e il prestito a interesse*. Soveria Mannelli: Rubbettino.

Watson, James L., ed. 2005. *Golden Arches East: McDonald's in East Asia*. 2nd ed. Stanford, CA: Stanford University Press.

Yanagisako, Sylvia Junko. 2002. *Producing Culture and Capital: Family Firms in Italy*. Princeton, NJ: Princeton University Press.

INDEX